When the Steam Railroads Electrified

NORTH AMERICAN railroad electrification
began its second century with the introduction
of Amtrak's *Acela Express* high-speed tilting trains
in the Boston-New York-Washington Northeast Corridor.
One of the 150-mph trains raced southward across
New York's Hell Gate Bridge on a pre-inaugural
test run on November 9, 2000.
Photo by Joe Greenstein.

FOREWORD BY JOHN W. BARRIGER III

INDIANA UNIVERSITY PRESS
Bloomington & Indianapolis

WHEN THE STEAM
RAILROADS ELECTRIFIED

Revised, Second Edition   *William D. Middleton*

For my sons Bill and Nick,

who learned early that there was something very special about a GG1.

This book is a publication of

Indiana University Press
601 North Morton Street
Bloomington, Indiana 47404-3797 USA

http://iupress.indiana.edu

Telephone orders 800-842-6796
Fax orders 812-855-7931
Orders by e-mail iuporder@indiana.edu

Library of Congress Cataloging-in-Publication Data

Middleton, William D., date
  When the steam railroads electrified / William D. Middleton.—Rev ., 2nd ed.
    p. cm.
  Includes bibliographical references and inde x.
  ISBN 0-253-33979-0 (cloth : alk. paper)
    1. R ailroads—Electrification. I. Title.

TF858.A4 M5 2001
625.26'3—dc21   2001024681

1 2 3 4 5 06 05 04 03 02 01

Contents

Foreword

COMMANDER MIDDLETON'S book WHEN THE STEAM RAILROADS ELECTRIFIED appears at a very timely juncture, when general interest in railway electrifications is waking up from a Rip Van Winkle slumber not of 20 years duration but of nearly 40. The awakening is owed to a convergence of technological, ecological, economic, social, and managerial forces which together have generated sufficient force to insure a breakthrough in favor of a major railroad electrification in the not very distant future, possibly within the next year. Paradoxically, instead of there being a rush to be in the lead to accomplish such a major transportation reformation, there seems to be the opposite tendency, with a number of lines poised for a race to be second but hesitant to seek first place. Probably this tendency is owed to the recognition that the first long-distance very high tension electrification will inevitably contain some imperfections, commonly referred to as "bugs," which doubtless will soon be corrected, but the inconvenience and expense thereby incurred will lead others to wish to avoid them.

At a time when the future of railway electrification spreads out before us, an interest in railway electrifications of the past inevitably is reawakened. What were the factors that led to their original installation? What were the extents of such operations? What were the successes and limitations of their performance? What reasons, if any, prevented major extensions? Except for electrification of commuter suburban services, few, if any, of these earlier projects still are in operation, and the recent de-electrification of 660 miles of Milwaukee Road main line that during its nearly 60-year lifetime was the longest railway electrification in the United States sent a shiver down the spines of railway electrification enthusiasts. These observers, however, should have realized that the Milwaukee installation had been made so obsolete by intervening electrical engineering developments that it was as out of date as a carbon filament light, and modernization was economically impossible.

Bill Middleton is recognized as the leading popular authority on the birth of electric traction in this country. In prior books he has told the story of the rise and fall of electric rapid transit, which is an integral part of the history of the electrification of steam railroads. This book happily concentrates its attention on railway electrifications of the past, treating them as a springboard to the electrifications it is hoped and believed will emerge within the next few years. Persons who are skeptical point to the fact that it was as far back as 1928 — 46 years ago — that the Pennsylvania Railroad announced its intention to electrify its main lines between New York, Washington, and Harrisburg, and 1938 — 36 years ago — that this project finally was completed, and take satisfaction in pointing out that there have been no major electrifications installed since then, although two very interesting smaller ones have been constructed in Ohio and Arizona which embody many of the interim improvements in the art. Those unfamiliar with electrical engineering are seemingly unaware of the important developments in railway electrical engineering since even the Pennsylvania Railroad electrification of 1928-1938 that offer magnificent opportunities for an advance to new peaks of railroad service, economy, and efficiency.

Let us consider some of these important developments. All prior electrifications have had to include railroad-owned and -installed transmission lines carrying high-voltage current along the right of way to their substations. At the substations the electrical pressure was reduced to the 11,000-volt standard carried in the distribution system serving the catenaries that fed the pantographs on the locomotives. In the past the railroads have had to provide their own transmission system, which was a costly addition to the other features of electrification. Today the entire country, except for desert and mountain areas of the West, is so interlaced with high tension electric transmission grids that few railway electrifications would require that railroads construct their own transmission lines.

References to 11,000-volt electrifications relate to alternating-current installations. Direct-current systems operated at various voltages from 600 to 3000. For reasons of transmission efficiency the alternating-current system has been preferred in the past. This system necessitated the use of A.C. motors. Direct-current motors, however, are much the more satisfactory. In earlier electrifications it was difficult to combine alternating-current transmission and direct-current traction motors to achieve the benefits of both. When alternating-current locomotives were used, it was necessary to have the current characteristics of 25-cycle alternation.

Today, through silicon rectifiers carried on the locomotives, A.C. transmission and D.C. traction motors can be combined and the best of both possible worlds can be obtained. Using D.C. motors, 60-cycle commercial power can be used in railway electrifications, an important advantage in the cost of construction and operation. The recent successful introduction of 25,000- to 50,000-volt electrical pressures in the distribution systems and catenaries permits wires of much reduced cross section and hence lighter weight to be used, thereby providing important construction economies. Further advantages can be secured by using standard components throughout the electrical distribution system following European and Japanese experience.

In comparison with the prevalent form of motive power, the diesel-electric locomotive, the all-electric locomotive offers important advantages, which may be summarized as follows:

● Electric locomotives can perform up to three times as much work as diesels of the same power because they have continuous access through the catenaries to all of the electric power that the traction motors can use in the higher ranges of speed. Diesel engines can only supply the power consumption necessities of the traction motors in the lower ranges of speed. For high-speed haulage, two to three times as much locomotive horsepower is required as would be sufficient if all-electric locomotives were used.

● Diesel-electric locomotives require generator capacity to meet the full requirements of the continuous rating of their motors. However, data from Pennsylvania Railroad operations during World War II indicates that electric locomotives seldom used electric power at any one time equivalent to more than 22 per cent of the total installation, and averaged only 17 per cent. It would be possible from the standpoint of necessary tractive effort and horsepower to meet the nation's requirements with 12 million horsepower of electric locomotives and less than 3 million horsepower of generating capacity.

● Since all-electric locomotives do not have high-wear components, such as the reciprocating engines of diesel-electrics, their useful life exceeds that of diesels by factors of two or three, with consequent advantages in comparative depreciation charges. Compare the lifetime performance of Pennsylvania's GG1 electric locomotives built in 1935-1938 with diesels, now in the "third generation."

● The cost of lubricants and maintenance for diesel locomotives is from three to four times as much per mile as for electric locomotives. The higher level of maintenance required by diesels reduces by at least 10 per cent their availability as compared to electric engines. Electric locomotives can be run almost continuously between stated inspection periods, and they lose no time taking on fuel.

● Electric locomotives also weigh less and have

greater adhesion than diesels, and produce less noise and air pollution.

• Although custom-built electric locomotives constructed in small numbers cost more per horsepower than do diesels, mass production would result in a first cost of one quarter to one third less than diesels of the same rated tractive capacity.

Fernand Nouvion of Paris, the former Director of Electric Traction Research of the French National Railways and generally recognized as one of the world's foremost authorities on railway electrification, said in 1971, "the electric railway almost invariably operates on a plane which is just not accessible to the diesels. It is far from certain that a diesel will ever be produced that equals today's electric locomotives, and from this point of view the modern diesel can be disregarded as obsolete before it is built. Indeed, because it is so much superior to the diesels, the performance of modern electrics is suspect in North America."

Nouvion computed, some years ago, fuel factors to measure the yearly energy requirements per railmile representing the minimum required to justify electrification. The data indicated that for a double-track line a daily consumption of 73 gallons per mile of line would provide economic justification for electrification, while an average daily burn of 46 gallons would do so for a single-track route. The heavy density lines of railroad in the United States will meet these criteria. The recent drastic increase in the cost of fuel oil would considerably reduce the quantity of diesel oil marking the economic point of transition from diesel to electric motive power.

Fuel and other considerations have led the French National Railways to electrify their main lines and to dieselize the others. This has proved highly advantageous. Indeed, the rapid electrification of rail mileage all over the world and the impressive proportions of electrified route mileage in foreign countries should raise questions in the U. S. as to why the country has lagged so far behind in this basic railroad development.

Seven billion dollars have been spent in dieselizing the American railways. Five billion dollars, or less, will pay for the electrification of the 25,000 miles of heavy density lines having the traffic necessary to justify it. A problem that has deferred electrification, in addition to ones outlined, is that dieselization could proceed in easy stages, a few locomotives at a time, on a number of railroads. Electrification must be applied to long stretches of line and the work must be completed before any of its benefits can be realized. Therefore, Federal fiscal assistance may be essential to go forward with electrification. The justification for this is that railroad electrification is an essential prerequisite to the technological breakthrough necessary to enable the railroads to keep in step with the economic progress of the last quarter of the 20th century.

Few, if any, of the present generation of railroad managers in policy-making positions will recall the earlier period of railway electrification from the Baltimore & Ohio in 1895 to the Pennsylvania Railroad in 1938 sufficiently to have gained the background of these developments from their own personal experiences and observations, and probably few have read extensively on the subject because, among other reasons, the literature has been sparse. Happily William Middleton has covered these gaps through the illuminating and exciting pages of his book. A careful reading by many persons in authority on the American railroads will accelerate railway electrification and thereby lend impetus to restoring this primary agency of transportation to its rightful place in the American economy.

John W. Barriger III

St. Louis, Mo.
1974

8

Preface to the Second Edition

THE original edition of this book was the third and final volume in a survey of electric transportation in America, the first two being *The Interurban Era* and *The Time of the Trolley*. For their constant support and encouragement throughout the eleven-year period it took to produce this "traction trilogy," I remain deeply indebted to the late Al Kalmbach, the Kalmbach Books founder and publisher, and the late David P. Morgan, the long-time editor of *Trains* magazine. I am grateful, too, to Indiana University Press for their enthusiastic support of the publication of this revised, second edition.

It is particularly appropriate that this history of American steam railroad electrification begins with a foreword by the late John W. Barriger III, the indefatigable special assistant to the Federal Railroad Administrator, and former chief executive of the Boston & Maine, Missouri-Kansas-Texas, Pittsburgh & Lake Erie, and Monon railroads. John Barriger was one of the most visionary leaders of the American railroad industry in the last half of the twentieth century and a tireless advocate of railroad electrification. For many years he, perhaps more than any other individual in the industry, kept alive the cause of electrification. It was entirely fitting that French National Railways' Fernand Nouvion, one of the foremost authorities on modern railroad electrification, once referred to John Barriger as the "high priest of U. S. A. railway electrification." I know Mr. Barriger considered it the highest sort of compliment. I remain deeply grateful to him for his foreword to this volume. More than a quarter century after it was written, it remains a current and powerful statement of the potential benefits of American railroad electrification.

The author's most sincere thanks and appreciation are extended also to the many individuals and organizations who contributed so much to both the original edition and this second edition. For a wide variety of assistance to the original edition particular thanks are owed to John Baxter, Donald Duke, Edward T. Francis, Herbert H. Harwood Jr., and the late Stephen D. Maguire, who generously made their personal collections available; to Michael R. Farrell and David J. Williams III, who provided valuable material concerning the early history of the pioneer Baltimore & Ohio electrification; to George H. Yater, who furnished data on the 1893 electrification of the Kentucky & Indiana Bridge Co.; to Harry L. Eddy, then librarian of the Association of American Rail-

roads' Economics & Finance Department, who provided immeasurable assistance from the resources of the library; to the late Norton D. Clark, who provided details of the obscure Boston & Albany "ping pong"; to Freeman Hubbard and David P. Morgan, the late editors of *Railroad* and *Trains* magazines, who kindly made available many items from the files of their magazines; to Joseph D. Thompson, who furnished information on the preservation of the historic Ponemah Mills locomotive and the original New York Central S-1; to Leo Ross of the Electric Railroaders' Association, who lent a variety of material from the files of ERA's Sprague Library and *Headlights* magazine; to Jerrold F. Hilton, who helped identify several elusive Great Northern photographs; to the late Winfield S. Boerckel, who assisted with details of the Long Island Rail Road electrification; to David L. Klepper, who provided information concerning Erie Lackawanna re-electrification plans; to John H. White Jr. of the Smithsonian Institution, who made available the extraordinary illustrative material of the Charles B. Chaney collection, as well as items from the Smithsonian's regular collections; and to Philip G. Craig of the Port Authority of New York and New Jersey, Robert S. McKernan of the Penn Central, Robert W. Downing and Frank Perrin of the Burlington Northern, J. Norman Lowe of Canadian National, Marc Green of the Milwaukee Road, H. E. Beeson of the Detroit, Toledo & Ironton, G. R. Genest of the Iron Ore Company of Canada, S. H. Binder of Kennecott Copper, and J. F. McDermott of General Electric, who so ably represented their respective corporations in providing a great variety of assistance. I am equally appreciative of the assistance to this new edition of Dan Cupper and J. W. Swanberg, who have provided both illustrations and information reflecting developments on the eastern electrifications during the intervening years, to Warren J. Kiefer, who has provided similar assistance concerning the new western coal-hauling electrifications, and to Christian Goepel, who prepared the new and revised electrification maps. I am no less grateful to the many other photographers, collectors, and organizations whose pictorial contributions are individually credited. Finally, I remain deeply indebted to June Bento and Kiyoko Yumibe for their skill and reliability in the arduous task of typing the final manuscript for the original edition.

William D. Middleton
Charlottesville, Virginia
September 2000

BALTIMORE & OHIO No. 1—the first mainline electric loco-motive in America—rumbles through the mile-and-a-half Howard Street tunnel in Baltimore with a northbound passenger train. Opened in 1895, the Baltimore electrification was another first for the pioneering B&O and a technical triumph for the young General Electric Company, the supplier of the equipment.—*Library of Congress.*

◆◆◆◆◆◆◆◆◆◆◆◆◆◆◆◆◆◆◆◆◆◆◆◆◆◆◆◆◆◆◆◆◆◆◆◆

1. Electricity challenges steam

◆◆◆◆◆◆◆◆◆◆◆◆◆◆◆◆◆◆◆◆◆◆◆◆◆◆◆◆◆◆◆◆◆◆◆◆

I SEE in the recent subjugation of the subtle and hitherto elusive force of electricity to the needs of man," said American Street Railway Association President H. H. Littell at Chicago, Ill., in 1883, "boundless possibilities for the world's three great requisites of advancement; heat, light, and motion."

When Littell spoke, electricity was little more than a curiosity. Within the preceding decade, however, great progress had been made in developing practical applications of the principles of electricity, and before the end of the 19th century the electrical industry would achieve an importance that even the prophetic Mr. Littell would have been hard pressed to imagine.

Fundamental to the ultimate successful application of electricity to transportation was the work of English physicist Michael Faraday, beginning with the discovery of electromagnetic rotation in 1821 and culminating in 1831 with a series of electromagnetic induction experiments which demonstrated that electricity could be produced from magnetic force.

Between 1829 and 1831, Prof. Joseph Henry, an instructor at the Albany (N. Y.) Academy, developed a practical electromagnet and used it to power an experimental motor that used magnetic attraction and repulsion to produce reciprocating motion.

Among the earliest attempts to apply Faraday's and Henry's discoveries to the development of a

11

JOSEPH HENRY made some of the basic discoveries in electromagnetism that led to the development of the practical electric motor. One of the most distinguished men in 19th-century American science, Henry was an instructor in mathematics at the Albany (N.Y.) Academy at the time of his discoveries. Later he became a professor of philosophy at Princeton University, and he served for 32 years as the first secretary of the Smithsonian Institution in Washington, D.C.—*Collection of William D. Middleton.*

VERMONT blacksmith and electrical inventor Thomas Davenport was fascinated with the mysterious power of electromagnetism, and in 1834 he successfully harnessed it to power one of the first rotary electric motors. The small circular electric railway powered by Davenport's motor survives today at the Smithsonian Institution in Washington, D.C., as a relic of the very beginning of electric transportation.—*Both photos, Smithsonian Institution.*

practical electric motor were those of a young Vermonter named Thomas Davenport. Davenport, a blacksmith who had little formal education, was a man of remarkable curiosity and ingenuity. He acquired an electromagnet in 1833 and conducted experiments at his Brandon (Vt.) home. In 1835 Davenport demonstrated a working model of his first motor at the Rensselaer Institute in Troy, N. Y., which subsequently acquired the model as part of the school's scientific apparatus. Davenport later developed an improved motor which he used to power a small circular railway and a printing press. Although he obtained a patent for his motor in 1837, the design was too early and too crude for practical exploitation. Davenport died a poor and disillusioned man at Salisbury, Vt., in 1851.

Only a few years after Davenport demonstrated his electric railway, Robert Davidson, an electrical inventor of Aberdeen, Scotland, made the first attempt at constructing a full-sized electric locomotive. Financed by a grant from the Scottish Society of Arts, Davidson built a 5-ton machine powered by a 40-cell zinc-iron sulphuric-acid battery and electromagnetic motors of his own design. Thus powered by what he termed "galvanic power," Davidson's machine made several successful trips on the Edinburgh & Glasgow Railway about 1838, attaining speeds as high as 4 mph. Soon afterward, the railway's enginemen reportedly destroyed the locomotive, presumably fearful for their employ-

ment. More favorably impressed with the experiment, however, was a Lieutenant Lecount of the Royal Navy, whose "A Practical Treatise on Railways," published in 1839, predicted: "We have no hesitation in saying that electromagnetism will at no distant day compete with steam as a motive power, and successfully."

In 1847 Prof. Moses G. Farmer, a notable American scientist, successfully operated an experimental locomotive, powered by a 48-cell Grove nitric-acid battery, that carried two passengers along an 18-inch-gauge track at Dover, N. H. During 1850 and 1851, Professor Farmer, aided by Thomas Hall, exhibited at the Charitable Mechanics' Fair in Boston a second small electric railway that was distinguished by its use of the running rails to transmit power to the locomotive.

A more ambitious experiment was carried out in 1851 by Dr. Charles G. Page, a Harvard-educated physician and a lifelong experimenter in electricity and magnetism. Page, then employed as a principal examiner in the United States Patent Office, built a small electric locomotive powered by a 100-cell Grove battery and a 16 h.p. electric motor, in which the reciprocating action of a system of magnets and solenoids drove a flywheel through crankshafts. Page's locomotive reached 19 mph and covered the 5 miles between Washington, D. C., and Bladensburg, Md., in only 39 minutes in a trial run on April 29, 1851. However, the rough ride almost

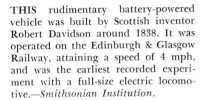

THIS rudimentary battery-powered vehicle was built by Scottish inventor Robert Davidson around 1838. It was operated on the Edinburgh & Glasgow Railway, attaining a speed of 4 mph, and was the earliest recorded experiment with a full-size electric locomotive.—*Smithsonian Institution.*

PROF. MOSES G. FARMER conducted several important experiments with electric propulsion of railways between 1847 and 1851. A prolific inventor and experimenter, Farmer later made a number of important discoveries that advanced the development of electric generators and electric illumination. —*Collection of William D. Middleton.*

THIS small electric railway, built by Professor Farmer and Thomas Hall, was exhibited at Boston in 1851. Batteries supplied power to the motor through the running rails. Note the worm-and-gear drive.—*Collection of William D. Middleton.*

entirely destroyed the fragile pottery cells of the battery. Congress, which had put up $20,000 for the experiment, lost interest, and Page was unable to continue development of his ideas.

These attempts to produce a practical means of electric transportation shared a common weakness in their dependence upon batteries for power. Further progress was to await the development of electrical generators as a more satisfactory means of power supply.

In 1860 Italian physicist Antonio Pacinotti built a continuous-current dynamo, or generator, utili-

A PHYSICIAN, a U.S. Patent Office examiner, and an indefatigable electrical experimenter, Dr. Charles G. Page invented a type of electric motor in 1837 while he was a young medical student. He later developed several important electrical devices, and in 1851 he ran his small battery-powered "electro-magnetic" locomotive from Washington, D.C., to Bladensburg, Md., a distance of 5 miles.—*Smithsonian Institution.*

DURING the 1870's Belgian-born inventor Zenobe Gramme developed the first electric generators and motors that were considered practical enough for commercial use.—*Collection of William D. Middleton.*

DR. ERNST WERNER VON SIEMENS —*Collection of William D. Middleton.*

13

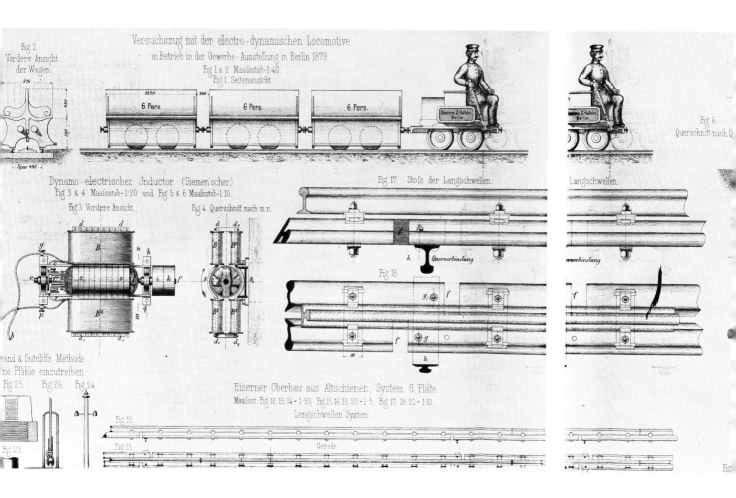

Fig. 2
Vordere Ansicht
der Wagen.

Versuchszug mit der electro-dynamischen Locomotive
in Betrieb in der Gewerbe-Ausstellung in Berlin 1879.
Fig 1 & 2 Maaßstab 1:40.
Fig. 1. Seitenansicht.

6 Pers. 6 Pers. 6 Pers.

Fig. 6.
Querschnitt nach Q

Dynamo-electrischer Inductor (Siemen'scher)
Fig 3 & 4 Maaßstab 1:20 und Fig 5 & 6 Maaßstab 1:10.

Fig 3. Vordere Ansicht.   Fig 4. Querschnitt nach m n.

Fig. 17. Stofs der Langschwellen.

Langschwellen.

Querverbindung

Fig 18.

and & Sutcliffs Methode
ne Pfähle einzutreiben.
Fig 25. Fig 26. Fig 24.

Fig 23.

Eiserner Oberbau aus Altschienen, System. G. Plate.
Maaßst: Fig 12, 13, 14 = 1:50, Fig 15, 16, 19, 20 = 1:5, Fig 17, 18, 21 = 1:10.
Langschwellen System.

Fig 12.

Fig 13. Gerade

zing a ring armature winding. About 1867 several inventors in the U. S. and Europe, including Farmer, independently formulated the principles of self-excitation of the field magnets, and in 1870 Belgian-born electrical inventor Zenobe Gramme combined these discoveries into a practical generator which came into wide commercial use. In 1873 Gramme demonstrated at the Vienna Exhibition that his generator worked equally well as a motor to reconvert electric power to mechanical energy. With the advent of practical generators and motors the development of electric railways resumed after more than two decades of inactivity.

THE first generator-powered electric railway to operate with any success was constructed by the German electrician and inventor, Dr. Ernst Werner von Siemens, for the Berlin Industrial Exhibition in the summer of 1879. A small locomotive, powered by a 5 h.p. motor and capable of speeds of 8 mph, pulled a train of three cars around a loop of half-meter-gauge track about 1000 feet in length. A steam-driven generator supplied power to the locomotive through a center third rail. Capable of hauling 18 to 20 passengers at a time, the Siemens railway transported close to 100,000 persons during the course of the exhibition.

At the same time that Siemens installed his railway at Berlin, two American inventors developed similar projects. In 1879 Stephen D. Field originated plans for an experimental electric railway utilizing a third rail placed in a slotted conduit for power supply. In the latter part of 1880 Field began building a small railway at Stockbridge, Mass.

The celebrated American inventor, Thomas A. Edison, laid 1400 feet of track at his Menlo Park (N. J.) laboratories in the spring of 1880 and experimented with a small generator-powered locomotive that pulled two small cars at speeds as high as 40 mph. Late the following year, Edison contracted with Henry Villard, president of the Northern Pacific Railway, to construct two larger locomotives and a 2½-mile test track. Villard, a German-born journalist who became interested in railway finance, was one of Edison's earliest and strongest backers and had an optimistic view of the future of the youthful electrical industry. According to press reports of late 1881, Villard contemplated electrifying at least 50 miles of NP track in Minnesota if Edison's experiments were successful. Two curious-looking locomotives, resembling small steam locomotives, were built and tested at Menlo Park in 1882. Shortly afterward, however, the Northern Pacific became insolvent because of

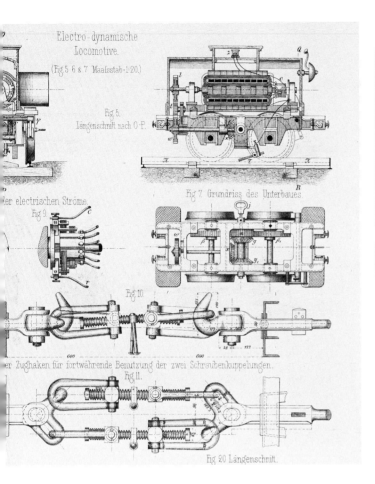

A LEADING figure in the development of the European electrical industry was Dr. Ernst Werner von Siemens, who was one of the founders of the electrical firm that still bears his name. Siemens's small passenger-carrying electric railway built for an 1879 exhibition in Berlin (left) was the first successful generator-powered electric railway. The historic Siemens locomotive (above) is now on public exhibit at a Munich (Germany) museum.—*Photos at left, Smithsonian Institution; above, Deutsches Museum, Munich.*

the high costs of its extension to Seattle, Wash. Villard was forced to resign, and no more was heard about NP electrification.

Both Edison and Field, as well as Siemens, applied for patents on their similar ideas at almost the same time. After several years of litigation, the Electric Railway Company of the United States was formed in 1883 to consolidate the interests of Edison and Field. In June 1883, the company exhibited an experimental locomotive, *The Judge*, at the Chicago Railway Exposition. During the exposition *The Judge* transported 26,000 passengers around a 1500-foot, 3-foot-gauge circular track. The locomotive drew power from a center third

ONE of the great inventors of the early years of the electrical industry, Thomas A. Edison (left) carried out some notable electric railway experiments at his Menlo Park (N. J.) laboratories between 1880 and 1882.—*Collection of William D. Middleton.*

GERMAN-BORN journalist, financier, and railroad tycoon Henry Villard (right) was one of the earliest advocates of railroad electrification. While president of the Northern Pacific Villard backed Thomas Edison's experiments of 1881-1882. Several years later, Villard organized the consolidation of the Edison and Sprague electrical companies into the Edison General Electric Company. In 1892 he initiated a project for the electrification of an NP subsidiary railroad at Chicago, Ill.—*Northern Pacific, collection of Railroad Magazine.*

EDISON'S first electric railway experiment in 1880 employed one of his early electric-lighting dynamos as a motor to power this small locomotive, which pulled two cars at speeds up to 40 mph. A belt drive connected the motor to the wheels. Electric power was supplied through the running rails from a central generator.—*Collection of William D. Middleton.*

THE truck of Edison's historic electric locomotive of 1880 is on display at the Edison National Historic Site in West Orange, N.J.—*Robert A. Le Massena.*

IN a series of experiments conducted in 1882 for Northern Pacific President Henry Villard, Edison operated two of these locomotives, the appearance of which seemed calculated to put steam railroad men at ease. NP ran into financial difficulties within the year, and the proposed electrification of NP Minnesota branch lines was never carried out.—*Collection of William D. Middleton.*

rail and had a maximum speed of 12 mph. The locomotive made an appearance at the Louisville Exposition later in the year. In 1887 Field developed a larger, more advanced locomotive, which operated experimentally on New York's 34th Street El.

Leo Daft, a New Jersey electrical manufacturer and inventor, was still another entrant in the field of electric railway experimentation. During 1881 and 1882 Daft tested several small electric locomotives on a short section of narrow-gauge track at the Greenville (N. J.) plant of his Daft Electric Company. Seeking a more practical test, Daft designed and built the 2-ton, 12 h.p. experimental locomotive *Ampere* which was operated on the Saratoga & Mt. McGregor Railroad in New York in November 1883. The little locomotive, hauling a standard steam railroad coach carrying about 75 passengers and negotiating an average grade of nearly 1.5 per cent, covered a mile in 11 minutes. Power was supplied through a center third rail and two small contact wheels mounted on the locomotive.

According to an account of the event in *Scientific American,* four horses were felled by contact with the third rail, and several persons narrowly escaped injury when the *Ampere* derailed on its return trip. Still, reported the journal, "Mr. Daft was warmly congratulated on the degree of success obtained, and most of the numerous party present were confident the trial was a proof of the practical success of the system."

Less than two years later, in August 1885, Daft completed a 2-mile electrification of a Baltimore (Md.) horsecar line. Although the line later returned to horsecar operation, the Daft electrification operated regularly for several years, and generally is regarded as the first electric road to have operated successfully in the United States.

Soon after Daft's Baltimore electrification began service, he operated the locomotive *Benjamin Franklin* for several weeks over an experimental electrification on the Ninth Avenue line of the Manhattan Elevated Railroad. The locomotive's motor was mounted on a platform and pivoted at one end, with power transmitted to the single driving axle through grooved wheels held in contact by the weight of the machine, supplemented by an adjusting screw. The *Benjamin Franklin* was rebuilt in 1888 and ran for eight months in regular tests between 14th and 50th streets on the elevated road. Speeds as high as 28 mph were obtained with heavy, four-car trains, and in one test, an eight-car train was pulled up the line's maximum grade of nearly 2 per cent at 7 mph.

Much of the electric railway experimentation of the 1880's, such as Daft's installation at Baltimore, involved street railways. In 1881 Siemens com-

BUILT by the electrical firm established by Thomas A. Edison and Stephen D. Field, *The Judge* was exhibited in 1883 at expositions in Chicago and Louisville. The 3-ton locomotive ran on 3-foot-gauge track. The motor drove one axle through an arrangement of gears and belts. Power was drawn from a center third rail by a "traveling vise."—*Smithsonian Institution.*

BRITISH-BORN electrical inventor Leo Daft built and tested a number of experimental electric locomotives during the late 1880's. In 1885 he electrified a 2-mile-long Baltimore horsecar line. It was the first electric railway in America to operate successfully in regular service for an extended period of time.—*Smithsonian Institution.*

DAFT'S experimental locomotive *Benjamin Franklin* hit a top speed of 30 mph on a test run from 14th Street to 53rd Street on New York's Ninth Avenue elevated on August 26, 1885. The cutaway drawing (below left) and the side elevation and plan view (below), all from an 1885 issue of *Scientific American,* depict the interior of the locomotive and illustrate Daft's novel motor-mounting and drive arrangement. The motor was pivoted at the left, and the screw device in the center kept the friction drive wheels on the motor shaft in contact with the grooved wheels on the axle. A wheel collector drew power from a third rail between the running rails. —*Left, collection of William D. Middleton; below left and below, Library of Congress.*

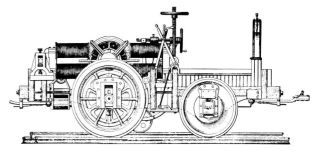

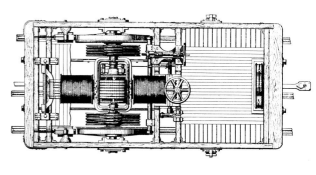

THE dynamo station that powered Leo Daft's *Benjamin Franklin* at New York City contained an impressive array of flywheels and belt drives.—*Library of Congress.*

FRANK J. SPRAGUE, shown here as a young Naval Academy midshipman, was a leading figure in the development of electric transportation. Among his most important inventions were the nose-suspended method of traction-motor mounting and the multiple-unit control system. Both inventions are still in general use today. His successful electrification of the Richmond (Va.) street railway system in 1887 and 1888 was followed by the wholesale electrification of urban transportation systems across America.—*Courtesy of Railroad Magazine.*

pleted the world's first successful commercial street railway electrification at Lichterfelde, a Berlin (Germany) suburb. An experimental Siemens electric tram car operated at the Paris Exposition in 1881 and a second commercial line electrified by Siemens opened at Portrush, Ireland, in 1883.

A number of other electrical experimenters also began to experience success at this time. Edward M. Bentley and Walter H. Knight opened a 2-mile electric street railway at Cleveland in 1884. Belgium-born Charles J. Van Depoele ran a short electric line at Toronto, Ont., in the summer of 1884, and in 1886 he installed the world's first completely electrified street railway system at Montgomery, Ala. John C. Henry, a former telegraph operator, built an electric line in 1884 at Kansas City, Mo.

A young Naval Academy graduate named Frank J. Sprague was the most important of the early electric railway experimenters. In 1885, when he conducted electrification experiments on the elevated tracks of the Manhattan Railway, Sprague devised the nose-hung or "wheelbarrow" method of motor mounting and gearing that was to become almost universal in electric railway equipment.

Despite successful experiments, Sprague was unable to interest the owners of the elevated in electrification and subsequently devoted his efforts to street railway electrification. His 1887-1888 electrification of the Richmond (Va.) Union Passenger Railway generally is regarded as the first large-scale, fully successful street railway electrification. Within a few years of its opening, electric street railways became commonplace.

Although much electric railway development

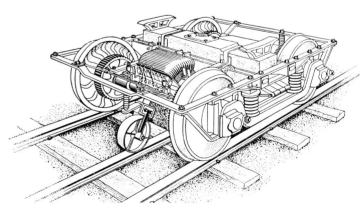

THIS drawing depicts the nose-suspended method of traction-motor mounting developed by Sprague in 1886 for experiments on the Manhattan Elevated Railroad. One side of the motor was suspended by a spring mounting from the truck frame, and the other side was supported directly by the axle. Bearings on the axle permitted the motor to rotate about the axle to maintain perfect alignment of the gears on the motor shaft and the axle, regardless of track irregularities and the motion of the axle.—*Collection of William D. Middleton.*

THIS experimental wood-bodied locomotive designed by Stephen D. Field was one of the first electric locomotives to employ a side-rod drive. The closeup view of the truck shows the manner in which a counterbalanced crank on each end of the armature shaft of the traction motor drove a side rod attached to the drive wheels. The rods and the counterbalanced, spoked driving wheels were reminiscent of steam locomotive practice. The locomotive operated experimentally on New York's 34th Street elevated in 1887 (below).—*Left and above, Industrial Photo Service; below, collection of William D. Middleton.*

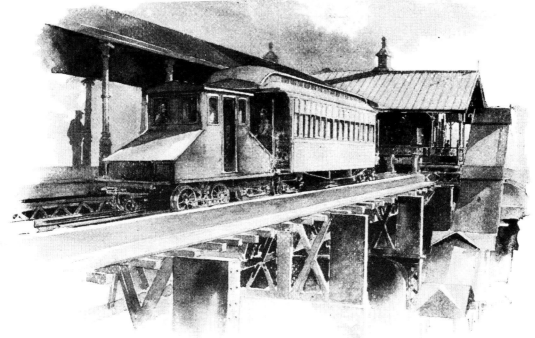

work was devoted to street railways, interest and experimentation in the electric operation of steam railroads continued. In 1887 a 7½-ton electric locomotive capable of hauling 100-ton coal trains on a 1.5 per cent grade was placed in regular service on a 3-mile line at the Lykens Valley Colliery in Pennsylvania, and similar mining and industrial electrifications were installed during the ensuing few years. Another significant advance came in December 1890, when the City & South London Railway began operating its 3.5-mile London (England) subway with electric locomotives. The four-

wheel, 10-ton locomotives could haul 40-ton trains at 25 mph. They were powered by two 50 h.p. gearless motors with armatures wound directly on the axles.

BY the beginning of the 1890's electric locomotives had succeeded in several applications where operating conditions and train tonnages at least approached those of steam railroad service. Several interesting, if unsuccessful, railroad electrification projects were advanced during this period.

Quite remarkable among these early projects

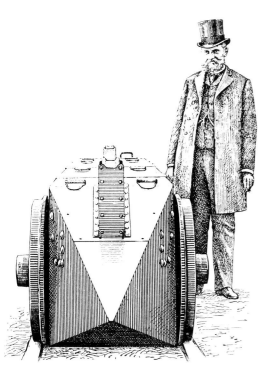

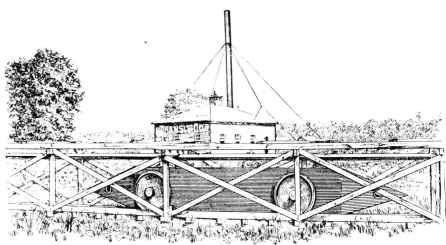

INVENTOR David G. Weems is shown with his 2-foot-gauge experimental electric locomotive in this engraving from the September 14, 1889, issue of *Engineering News*. Operated on a 2-mile test track at Laurel, Md., by Weems' Electro-Automatic Transit Company, the beak-nosed locomotive hit speeds as high as 115 mph. The side view of the locomotive shows the supporting structure that carried the line's overhead conductor.—*Both illustrations, Smithsonian Institution.*

were high-speed tests carried out by the Electro-Automatic Transit Company of Baltimore in the summer of 1889. The Electro-Automatic company, organized by inventor David G. Weems, engaged Oscar T. Crosby to conduct the test of the Weems system. Crosby, a graduate of the U. S. Military Academy at West Point, had been one of Sprague's associates in the Richmond street railway electrification.

The Weems company constructed a 2-mile circle of 28-inch-gauge track at Laurel, Md., for the initial high-speed tests. The bright red, wooden-bod-

ied locomotive was rectangular in cross section — 2½ feet high and 2 feet wide — and 21 feet in length, including a 4-foot pointed "prow" at each end. Two traction motors were installed, with the armatures mounted directly on each of the locomotive's two axles. The Weems high-speed train, including two cars, weighed about 6000 pounds. Power was supplied at 500 volts through an overhead third rail and an upward-bearing brush mounted on the locomotive. The unmanned train was controlled from the power station inside the circle of track. Locomotive brakes were applied

DESIGNED by Frank Sprague and Doctors Duncan and Hutchinson of Johns Hopkins University, this big steeple-cab locomotive was built by Baldwin in 1893 to be the prototype locomotive for a projected Chicago suburban electrification of a Northern Pacific subsidiary. NP entered bankruptcy, and the locomotive was never operated.—*Collection of H. L. Broadbelt.*

WEDGE-NOSED cars running at 100 mph were part of Dr. Wellington Adams's 1892 proposal for
a Chicago-St. Louis "air line" electric railway. For the February 1893 issue of the European
magazine *Ile,* an artist visualized the railway as a broad, straight right of way with four tracks plus
frontage roads forming the principal thoroughfare of Illinois prairie towns. The scheme never
advanced beyond the prospectus stage.—*New York Public Library.*

automatically whenever the current either was shut
off or failed for any reason.

The test track, constructed with only poorly laid
16-pound rail on grades as steep as 2 per cent, was
ill-suited for the contemplated high speeds. Nevertheless, the train attained speeds of 115 mph, and
data was obtained concerning air and train resistance at high speeds.

Based on the test results, Crosby proposed full-
sized standard-gauge electrification tests in which
150-mph speeds were contemplated. Crosby's working drawings included such advanced features as
all-steel passenger cars, magnetic brakes, regenerative braking, and streamlining. An 18-ton locomotive of about 600 h.p. was planned. As in the previous trials, traction-motor armatures would have
been carried directly on the locomotive's driving
axles. The locomotive would have had a parabolic
or wedge-shaped front end, and the train would
have had a continuous exterior surface.

A 1500-volt power system was planned, with
supply and return conductors mounted on opposite sides of the track. A special switch on the loco-

motive's "trolley arm" collector would energize
only a short section of power-supply conductor adjacent to the passing locomotive.

The Weems company was unable to raise the
necessary money for a trial of Crosby's standard-
gauge high-speed electrification, and it suspended
operations soon after the trials at Laurel were
completed.

Henry Villard, who had financed some of Edison's experiments a decade earlier, briefly re-en-
tered the field of steam railroad electrification
about this time. After losing his personal fortune
and the presidency of Northern Pacific in the financial depression of 1883-1884, Villard went back
to his native Germany for two years. He returned
to New York City in 1886 with new German financial backing and became instrumental in planning
the consolidation of Thomas Edison's various electrical enterprises, along with Frank Sprague's
Sprague Electric Railway & Motor Company, into
the Edison General Electric Company. Villard was
president of the new firm from the time of its establishment in early 1889 until he was forced out

21

by financier J. P. Morgan three years later, when Edison General Electric was merged into the Thomson-Houston Electric Company to create the present-day General Electric Company.

Shortly after his return to the U. S., Villard again became affiliated with the Northern Pacific, serving as chairman of the railway's board of directors from 1889 until 1893. Through a subsidiary Chicago terminal company, the Chicago & Northern Pacific, which was organized and leased to the Wisconsin Central in 1890, the NP had an interest in WC's growing suburban traffic. In early 1892 Villard initiated a feasibility study of a Chicago terminal electrification. Electric traction pioneer Frank Sprague, together with Doctors Louis Duncan and Cary T. Hutchinson of Johns Hopkins University, designed a locomotive for experimental operation at Chicago. Baldwin built the 60-ton eight-wheel locomotive, which was rated at 1000 h.p., in 1893. At the time it was the largest electric locomotive ever built. A large center operating cab afforded unobstructed visibility, while sloping hoods at each end housed various equipment, creating a "steeple-cab" arrangement. Four gearless traction motors and a pneumatic control system were employed. Unfortunately, financial reverses intervened again. Northern Pacific entered bankruptcy, Villard lost his post as chairman of the board, and the tests never took place.

Far more ambitious but no more successful than the Weems and Villard electrification projects was the remarkable Chicago & St. Louis Electric Railway proposed by Dr. Wellington Adams in 1892. The railway, according to its promoters, would be built in an absolutely straight "air line" between its terminal cities, cutting more than 30 miles from the shortest steam railroad mileage. Low-slung, wedge-nosed cars, capable of running at 100 mph on 6-foot driving wheels, were planned for the railway. The line initially would be built with double track, but provision would be made for an eventual two more tracks. Such advanced features as automatic block signals and telephone communication between moving trains were planned. At night, an automatic system of incandescent lamps along the right of way would illuminate the roadbed for a mile before and behind a moving car.

Editorial writers in the railway trade press were not kind to the proposal. Noting that the railway's "air line" route managed to miss every intermediate point of consequence, *Railway Age* observed, "Drawing straight lines on paper and running them through the air are easier achievements than providing the capital for the construction of a projected railway." This indeed proved to be the case, and Adams' grandiose project never went beyond the prospectus stage.

GENERAL ELECTRIC'S first locomotive designed for steam railroad service was a four-wheel, 30-ton machine built at the company's Lynn (Mass.) works in 1893. The locomotive was exhibited at the World's Columbian Exposition in Chicago and went to work on the Manufacturer's Railroad in New Haven, Conn., in 1896. The two gearless motors, which were suspended from the truck frame, are shown in the closeup view. *—Both photos, Industrial Photo Service.*

But by this time, too, the cause of railroad electrification had recorded a few successes. What may be regarded as the first successful steam railroad electrification in the United States began operation at Louisville, Ky., in 1893. The Kentucky & Indiana Bridge Company, organized to construct a steam railroad bridge across the Ohio River between Louisville and New Albany, Ind., which it completed in 1886, also ran a local passenger service between the two cities. For the first several years, the "Daisy Line," as it was popularly known, operated with steam power, but on August

DESIGNED to do the work of a steam locomotive, General Electric's second locomotive was completed by GE's Lynn works in 1894. The 35-ton "Black Maria" was sold to a Connecticut cotton mill a year later and worked 70 years in regular service. Today it is in the collection of the Connecticut Electric Railway Association at Warehouse Point, Conn.—*General Electric.*

THE Pennsylvania Railroad first explored the possibilities of electric traction with the 1895 electrification of its 7-mile Burlington & Mount Holly branch in New Jersey. Jackson & Sharp motor car No. 1 and a Pennsy coach serving as a trailer are shown on a trial run at Mount Holly on June 3, 1895.—*Collection of Edward T. Francis.*

25, 1893, electric cars displaced steam trains on the 5-mile run. Equipment was constructed to typical street railway standards except for its somewhat larger size. Double-truck motor cars pulled trains of one or two trailers. Trolley poles collected current from a street-railway-type overhead wire. Freight and through passenger trains continued to operate behind steam power. Electric cars ran across the bridge in local service until 1945.

Also in 1893, the new General Electric Company completed at its Lynn (Mass.) works a small four-wheel electric locomotive intended for passenger and light freight service. The 30-ton locomotive could develop a 12,000-pound drawbar pull and

FOUR big street-railway-type 16-bench open cars were included in the original equipment for the New Haven's 1895 electrification of its Nantasket Beach branch. Two GE motors of 100 h.p. each gave the cars a drawbar pull of 4000 pounds. No. 2510 is shown on a section of Nantasket Beach track that was electrified with a center third rail. The cars had striped side curtains to protect the passengers from summer showers.—*Industrial Photo Service.*

AS departure time drew near, the crew of one of the New Haven's Nantasket Beach branch electric trains posed with their charge in front of the many-gabled, verandaed Nantasket Beach hotel. The big deck-roofed motor car was able to seat 80 picture-hatted and bow-tied passengers and could pull three or four trailer cars.—*Collection of Stephen D. Maguire.*

SIX heavy motorized baggage cars were among the original Nantasket Beach equipment. Weighing more than 30 tons fully loaded, the 42-foot-long cars were powered by two or four 100 h.p. GE motors. They pulled express trains of open trailers on the line. Note the immense gong and the slatted pilot.—*Industrial Photo Service.*

could run up to 30 mph. Two gearless traction motors, one on each axle, powered the locomotive. In what was one of the earliest uses of a quill drive, the motor armatures were wound on hollow shafts through which the axles passed. The hollow shafts were connected to the axles through universal couplings which allowed freedom of movement in all directions. Power was supplied at 500 volts D.C. through an overhead trolley-wire system.

The little machine was exhibited at the World's Columbian Exposition in Chicago, where the builders claimed it to be "the first practically operative high speed electric locomotive in the world adapted to the requirements of the steam railroad." It was only a matter of time, opined GE, before electric locomotives "will invade the province of the trunk line steam locomotive, and the millennium of railroad travel will be within the realities of life."

A year later GE's Lynn plant turned out a second and considerably larger locomotive, designed, as *Electrical World* put it, "to perform the ordinary work of a steam locomotive of similar capacity where excessive speeds are not requisite . . ." The locomotive weighed 35 tons, was 24 feet long, and had two four-wheel trucks. Four 500-volt D.C. traction motors, one on each axle, were mounted in the nose-suspended arrangement developed by Sprague. The rated drawbar pull was 14,000 pounds. The locomotive employed the steeple-cab configuration that was to become virtually standard for light electric locomotives. It was sold to the Taftville Cotton Mill in Taftville, Conn., in 1895, and entered service on the mill's mile-long railroad spur, where it operated until retirement to a museum collection in 1964.

General Electric's principal rival in the electrical industry, the Westinghouse Electric & Manufacturing Company, began a long series of trials with an experimental electric locomotive at its East Pittsburgh (Pa.) plant in 1895. Almost another decade passed, however, before the first Westinghouse-equipped electric locomotive entered regular commercial operation.

A SMALL electrification contract landed by Westinghouse in 1895 had important implications for the future. The Pennsylvania Railroad incorporated the Burlington & Mount Holly Traction Railroad Company in late 1894 for the purposes of electrifying a 7-mile New Jersey branch line and exploring the potential of electric operation. Electrification took place in the spring of 1895 with a Westinghouse installation that was technically comparable to contemporary street and interurban railway systems.

Wood poles supported an overhead trolley wire, which was supplied with 500-volt D.C. power from a steam-driven 225-kilowatt Westinghouse generator in a power plant at Mount Holly. Three wooden motor cars, built for the line by the Jackson & Sharp Company of Wilmington, Del., were sufficiently powerful to pull a standard PRR coach as a trailer at speeds of 45 to 60 mph. Two of the combination passenger-baggage cars were powered by two 75 h.p. Westinghouse motors while the third was powered by four 50 h.p. motors. A trial trip ran over the line on June 3, 1895, and regular operation began on July 22, 1895.

TWO tandem-compound Greene engines, operating at 110 rpm and each driving a 500-kilowatt, 600-volt GE generator, powered the New Haven's electrification of its Nantasket Beach branch in Massachusetts.—*Industrial Photo Service.*

MOTOR CAR N-3326 paused with a train on the single track (formerly double) at Surfside station at Nantasket on August 10, 1929.—*Carleton Parker, collection of Norton D. Clark.*

A similar branchline electrification the same year with General Electric as the supplier was the forerunner of large-scale electrification by another steam road. As early as 1892, Charles P. Clark, president of the New York, New Haven & Hartford Railroad, had noted prophetically in the annual report to stockholders, "If electricity as a motive power becomes commercially practicable, the two interior tracks of the four now in the process of construction between New York and New Haven, with their improved grades and alignment and absolute freedom from grade crossings, will prove especially adapted to its use."

Throughout his tenure as New Haven president, Clark maintained a keen interest in electric operation, and early in 1895 he decided to electrify the New Haven's Nantasket Beach branch in Massachusetts. Like the Pennsylvania's New Jersey experiment and the 1893 Kentucky & Indiana electrification, the Nantasket Beach line employed equipment that was comparable to street and interurban railway practice.

Power was distributed to the 7-mile line through a 600-volt D.C. trolley-wire system supplied from a steam-driven power plant near the south end of the electrification. Motive power included four closed and six open motor passenger cars, each of which was capable of pulling three or four trailers.

Regular electric operation of the Nantasket Beach line between Nantasket Junction and Pemberton began on June 28, 1895. Clark, completely satisfied with the installation, declared that electricity "will be promptly adopted by the Company at other points on its lines." And indeed it was. A year later New Haven extended the Nantasket Beach electrification 3½ miles to East Weymouth, this time using a third-rail power-supply system personally developed by Clark. The line again was extended in 1898, to Braintree, and a year later, to Cohasset. At the peak of electric operations, as many as a hundred daily trains ran between Braintree and Nantasket. From 1896 to 1907 a

number of New Haven branches in Connecticut, Rhode Island, and Massachusetts were electrified at 600 volts D.C., with either overhead trolley-wire or third-rail systems.

IMPORTANT as the Pennsylvania and the New Haven's 1895 branchline electrifications were, they were overshadowed by an electrification opened in the same year at Baltimore, Md., by the Baltimore & Ohio Railroad. The B&O's installation, not quite 3 miles in length, was the world's first electrification of mainline steam railroad freight and passenger operation, and it represented a technical triumph for the General Electric Company.

The B&O's historic undertaking at Baltimore had its origin in a severe competitive disadvantage with the rival Pennsylvania Railroad. Until 1895, B&O was obliged to ferry all of its traffic between the west and points north of Baltimore ¾ of a mile across the Patapsco River between Locust Point and Canton. The railroad was handicapped further by several miles of time-consuming running through public streets in South Baltimore. The Pennsylvania, which had acquired an all-rail route through the city in the early 1880's, had much the better of the situation.

At one time B&O considered the construction of an elevated connecting railroad across town along Pratt Street from Camden Station to a connection

B&O No. 1 was actually two semi-permanently coupled units operated as a single locomotive. Appurtenances included a standard B&O 23-inch headlight at each end, a bell, a whistle, and an 8-inch brass signal gong. What appears to be a ship's wheel inside the cab is actually the hand brake. The engineer's controls and the inside of the controller are shown in the two interior views.—*Left and right, Smithsonian Institution; above, Industrial Photo Service.*

THE running gear of B&O No. 1 would look like this with the top field frame lifted off and the end of the frame cut away. The primitive pantograph held a shuttle-like brass shoe which slid through the slotted overhead power conductor. Difficulties with this power distribution system led to its replacement with a third-rail system in 1902.—*Library of Congress.*

with its Philadelphia main line near Canton. Local opposition and anticipated high costs killed the idea.

In the late 1880's the B&O came up with another proposal: a long tunnel beneath Howard Street and a 7.2-mile belt-line railroad that would connect Camden Station with the Philadelphia main line at Bay View Junction. The Baltimore Belt Railroad was chartered on December 17, 1888, and the following spring the Baltimore City Council passed an ordinance giving the Belt Line company the authority to build its planned line. A projected user of the Belt Line in addition to B&O was the narrow-gauge Maryland Central, which planned to

THE overhead conductor consisted of two Z-bars arranged to form a box-shaped structure with a slot in the bottom. At the time of this photograph, catenary construction had been completed only as far as the bridge over North Avenue and the Northern Central Railroad (Pennsylvania).—*Smithsonian Institution.*

A STEAM-DRIVEN 2000-kilowatt power plant near Camden Station furnished power for the B&O electrification. A large set of storage batteries later was installed near Mount Royal Station to provide additional capacity sufficient to haul a 1600-ton freight train through the tunnel. In 1909 the B&O began buying commercial power, and by the end of 1914 B&O had closed its own power plant and was totally dependent on purchased power.—*Smithsonian Institution.*

convert to standard gauge and extend north from York, Pa., to a connection with the Lehigh Valley. Nothing came of this scheme and B&O later assumed full ownership and control of the Belt Railroad.

Construction of the 8-million-dollar Belt Line started in September 1890. The Howard Street tunnel was by far the largest and most difficult item of work. A construction contract was awarded to the Maryland Construction Company, which had been organized for the purpose. Tunneling began in 1891. Chief engineer for the project was Samuel Rea, who later built the Pennsylvania Railroad's New York tunnels and Penn Station, and became the Pennsy's president in 1913.

The double-track Howard Street tunnel was one of the longest soft-earth tunnels driven to that time. It extended 7339 feet from Camden Street Station to the site of a new passenger station at Mount Royal Avenue. Shafts were sunk at four intermediate locations, and the tedious tunneling work was carried out without interruption to street traffic. There were no major mishaps, except for one serious cave-in which collapsed the building of the Baltimore City College. The contractors were obliged to build a replacement for the ruined building.

"THERE is no uncertainty about it now—it pulls," reported the *Baltimore Sun* after No. 1 completed a trial trip through the Howard Street tunnel on June 27, 1895. Displaying white flags beside her headlight, No. 1 posed a few days later with proud engine crews and officials a short distance outside the north portal of the Howard Street tunnel. The train behind No. 1 was the first regular freight to be hauled through the tunnel by electric power.—*Industrial Photo Service*.

ON July 1, 1895, a few days after its first run, No. 1 headed a special train on which the Baltimore & Ohio entertained civic dignitaries and the press. With 4-4-0 No. 852 and four "Royal Blue Line" cars in tow, No. 1 paused for the wet-plate camera at the south portal of the tunnel beside Camden Station.—*Baltimore & Ohio, TRAINS collection*.

ON September 1, 1896, a year after electric operation of its Baltimore belt line began, the B&O opened a handsome new station of Early Renaissance design at Mount Royal Avenue, where trains emerged into the open for a short distance between the Howard Street tunnel and a 265-foot tunnel to the north. No. 1 paused under Mount Royal Station's graceful arched trainshed with a northbound "Royal Blue Line" express soon after the station opened. After passenger service ceased, the building was used by the Maryland Institute of Art.—*Smithsonian Institution.*

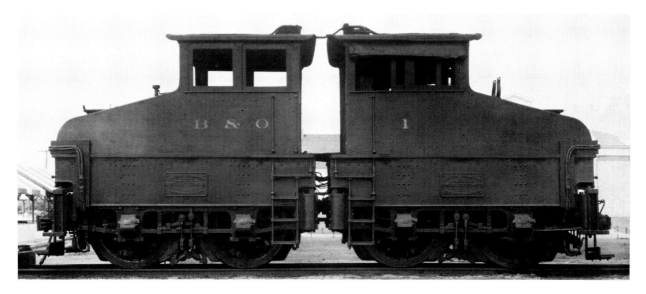

LONG AFTER the B&O's original electric locomotives were withdrawn from regular service, one of them was a featured exhibit at the railroad's Fair of the Iron Horse at Baltimore in 1927. Although it carried the number 1, the locomotive was actually No. 2, renumbered for the occasion. The locomotive was scrapped after the fair; the other two had been scrapped several years earlier. —*Baltimore & Ohio, TRAINS collection.*

When the Howard Street tunnel was started, B&O apparently was undecided on the form of motive power to be used. Since the line would have a steady 0.8 per cent grade up from Camden Street, the operation of trains with steam power would present severe smoke and gas problems. In the ordinance that permitted the tunnel's construction, the City stipulated that no ventilation holes or openings would be permitted in any streets or avenues. If ventilation was required, the railroad would have to erect "chimneys, shafts, flues, or other appliances" on its own property, and of such a height and construction to ventilate the tunnel "without annoyance to persons or property." The operation of the tunnel with a form of cable traction was considered but deemed to be impractical.

The motive-power problem was resolved in early 1892, when tunnel work already was half completed. In May B&O contracted with General Electric to electrify the Belt Line route through the tunnel. The decision to electrify was well received. "When the Belt Railroad tunnel is completed and the trains are hauled back and forth by the subtle power of electricity," said the *Maryland Journal* on May 28, 1892, "it will be one of the most wonderful events of the world. If it is a success, and there seems no doubt, it will completely revolutionize railroad power and be a great boon to all travelers."

The electrification contract was an audacious one for both firms. The railroad risked the success of an 8-million-dollar project on an unproven form of motive power. GE, which contracted to provide the electrical installation and locomotives that could handle 500-ton passenger trains at 35 mph or 1200-ton freight trains at 15 mph up the tunnel's 0.8 per cent grade, risked its reputation in the electric traction field. The experience of the new electrical firm as well as its predecessors had been limited almost exclusively to street railway equipment. Except for a few tiny mining locomotives the company never had built an electric locomotive. The little 30-ton GE machine exhibited at the World's Columbian Exposition was still a year in the future, and the largest electric locomotives operating in the world were the 10-ton motors hauling diminutive trains through London's City & South London Railway tube.

The Howard Street tunnel was completed in early 1895 and was placed in service for passenger trains on May 1. Although the powerhouse and power distribution system were almost completed, the locomotives had not yet been delivered and the tunnel initially was operated with steam power.

31

AS esthetic as shoe boxes were these freight motors built by General Electric in 1903 (Nos. 5-8) and 1906 (No. 9). The units weighed 75 tons and usually operated in pairs or threes. The four axles were mounted in a single rigid frame but could move laterally so the locomotive could negotiate curves easily. A two-unit locomotive could pull a 1500-ton train up the grade through the tunnel at 10 mph, and a three-unit consist, such as Nos. 7, 6, and 9 (far right), could exert a starting tractive effort of 120,000 pounds, more than the B&O's largest Mallets.—*Right, Smithsonian Institution; far right, Baltimore & Ohio,* TRAINS *collection.*

Within a month the first of three identical electric locomotives was shipped from GE's Schenectady (N. Y.) works.

Prototype electric locomotive No. 1 made a successful trial run through the tunnel at 11 a.m. on June 27. Pulling a steam switcher, No. 1 ran from Camden Station to the end of the electrification at North Avenue in 7 minutes, operating at 20 mph. Afterward, the big steeple-cab machine was placed on display at a siding near Mount Royal Avenue, where it drew a large and appreciative crowd. The engine's piercing air whistle seemed to create something of a sensation. Said the *Baltimore Sun* "Bellowing bullfrogs, croaking foghorns and shrieking steam-whistles would have to form a syndicate to beat the hoot from electric locomotive No. 1. It is as loud as the whistle on an Atlantic steamer."

B&O No. 1 was an impressive locomotive for its time. Weighing 96 tons, No. 1 was made up of two semi-permanently coupled single-truck units. Each of the four-wheel trucks was equipped with 62-inch driving wheels, with a 360 h.p. D.C. motor mounted on each axle. A gearless drive was employed, in which the motor armatures were carried on a sleeve or quill surrounding the axle. The armature quill, in turn, was connected to the driving wheels through rubber pads, which served to cushion impact. A small pantograph that employed a sliding brass shoe collected 600-volt D.C. power from an inverted iron trough or channel mounted above the track. In a test at GE's Schenectady plant the first four-wheel truck completed had been matched against a New York Central six-wheel switcher in a tug-of-war and had pulled the steamer up and down the track at will.

Although a few difficulties were encountered at first, General Electric engineers soon had No. 1 performing well in excess of the contract requirements. Thirty-car trains were started without taking slack, and on one test with a 36-car freight and three dead engines totaling 1600 tons, the big electric developed a drawbar pull of more than 45,000 pounds. Speeds of 35 and 40 mph were recorded with 500-ton passenger trains, and the locomotive topped 60 mph in one high-speed test.

The power plant was erected about two blocks south of Camden Station. A dozen 250 h.p. coal-fired Root water-tube boilers supplied steam to four Reynolds-Corliss horizontal tandem-compound engines. Each engine was direct-connected to a 500-kilowatt GE generator. These were the largest direct-connected generators built to that time. A separate lighting plant in the powerhouse supplied A.C. power for the incandescent lighting system installed by General Electric through the length of the tunnel.

The novel metal-trough overhead power-distribution system was supported directly from the masonry arch of the tunnel. Outside the tunnels, the conductor was carried by a catenary system of iron rods supported by transverse steel trusses on latticework columns at intervals of 150 feet. The electrification extended almost 3 miles, from just south of Camden Station to a point near Huntington Avenue.

The first public operation under electric power occurred on July 1, 1895, and within a few months, No. 1 was hauling a daily average of 12 freight trains through the tunnel. The second locomotive arrived at the end of November, and the third was completed the following May, at which time full electric operation began. Under normal operating practice, the electrics pushed northbound freight trains through the tunnel. Steam locomotives remained on the head end but did no work. After the train cleared the north portal at Mount Royal Avenue, steam power commenced working again on the steeper 1.52 per cent grade to Huntington Avenue, where the electrics cut off. Northbound pas-

FOR its third generation of electric power B&O adopted a heavy double-truck steeple-cab locomotive of a more conventional design than its previous electrics. The first two units, built by General Electric in 1909, were patterned after a half dozen units delivered by the same builder in 1908 for the Michigan Central's Detroit River Tunnel electrification. B&O received six more virtually identical units between 1912 and 1927. No. 11 (right), built in 1909, weighed 92 tons. Rated at 1100 h.p., it could develop a starting tractive effort of more than 46,000 pounds. Class O-E-4 unit No. 18 (lower right), the last of the series, weighed 120 tons. The closeup view (below) shows the adjustable third-rail shoes that swung on booms to reach the third rail while the locomotive was running on the gantlet track that was installed in the tunnel in 1937 to permit the movement of high and wide loads. In 1942 the eight steeple-cabs, Nos. 11-18, were renumbered 151-158, and in 1949 they received their old numbers back. About the same time they traded their black livery for royal blue.—*Right, Smithsonian Institution; below and below right, Baltimore & Ohio,* TRAINS *collection.*

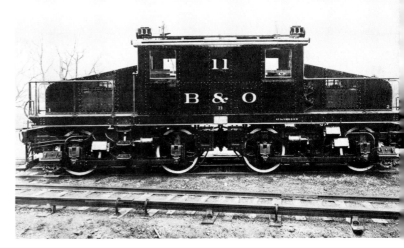

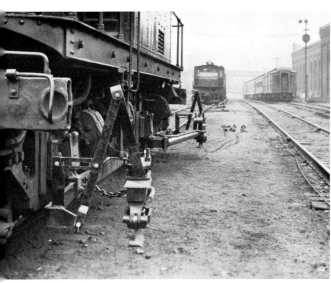

senger trains were pulled only as far as the end of the tunnel at Mount Royal Avenue. Southbound trains, both freight and passenger, simply coasted downgrade through the tunnel, while the electrics returned to Camden Station light.

B&O's pioneer electrification was an unqualified success from the beginning. The three original GE steeple-cabs worked until 1912, when they were replaced by heavier locomotives. The novel overhead distribution system was the only part of the installation that gave much trouble. Corrosive gases from steam locomotives and water seepage caused continuing problems of improper electrical contact in the tunnel sections, and a conventional third-rail system replaced the overhead in 1902. Two generations of successively more powerful locomotives followed the original three units, and the world's first mainline electrification continued to operate until 1952, when B&O dieselization eliminated the need for tunnel electrification.

At Baltimore, the practicality of mainline steam railroad electrification was established, and its proponents waited confidently for the bright future of electric traction.

BELOW: On May 21, 1938, steeple-cab motors 13 and 14 drift downgrade across the bridge over the Pennsylvania's electrified line, on their way to pick up another northbound train. Beyond them a Pacific heads the Chicago-bound *Capitol Limited* toward Mount Royal Station.—*A. D. Hooks.*

ABOVE: Delivering a total of 2200 h.p. and 100,000 pounds of tractive effort, a pair of steeple-cab motors—No. 13 in the lead —drag a 2-8-2 and its freight train northward up the grade near North Avenue in 1912. Wood sheathing made the third rail less dangerous.—*Baltimore & Ohio*, TRAINS *collection.*

BELOW CENTER: Ready to pull a northbound passenger train up the 0.8 per cent grade of the Howard Street tunnel, motors 17 and 18 have locked couplers with a Pacific beside the wooden platform in the shadowy depths of Camden Station's lower level.—*Baltimore & Ohio,* TRAINS *collection.*

BELOW: On a sunny day in August 1946, only a few years before dieselization would end the historic electrification, electrics 151 and 152 assisted a 1000 h.p. Baldwin diesel switcher with a heavy northbound transfer drag near the north terminus of the electrification.—*Alfred F. Tyrrill.*

SCIENTIFIC AMERICAN
SUPPLEMENT. № 1544

Entered at the Post Office of New York, N. Y., as Second Class Matter. Copyright, 1905, by Munn & Co.

Scientific American. established 1845.
Scientific American Supplement. Vol. LX., No. 1544.

NEW YORK, AUGUST 5, 1905.

Scientific American Supplement. $5 a year.
Scientific American and Supplement. $7 a year.

THE NEW AND THE OLD: A RACE BETWEEN THE ELECTRIC AND STEAM LOCOMOTIVES OF THE NEW YORK CENTRAL AND HUDSON RIVER RAILROAD, BOTH THE LATEST TYPES.

ELECTRICITY challenged steam in tests near Schenectady, N.Y., in the spring of 1905. Motor No. 6000 was matched against the New York Central's newest Class K Pacific. Although the steam engine made a faster start, the electric soon overtook it in nearly every test.—*Library of Congress.*

❖❖

2. Electrics into Grand Central

❖❖

THE Baltimore & Ohio's success in its 1895 electrification venture at Baltimore might have been expected to encourage similar projects on other North American steam railroads. But for nearly a decade after B&O No. 1 made its initial run through the Howard Street tunnel, there were no subsequent electrifications of even equal importance. In New England, the New Haven followed its Nantasket Beach electrification of 1895 with a series of branchline electrifications in Connecticut. In 1897 General Electric built a 540 h.p. steeple-cab locomotive for the Hoboken Shore Railroad in New Jersey, which had electrified its 2-mile line between Weehawken and the docks at Hoboken. In 1898 the Buffalo & Lockport Railway in New York acquired a pair of 36-ton GE locomotives and electrified an 18-mile line leased from the Erie Railroad. None of these installations, however, involved more than switching service or relatively light branchline traffic.

Even though little was happening in the field of mainline electrification, there were nevertheless a number of developments in electric traction that later would be important to steam railroad electrification.

The boom in street railway electrification that followed Frank Sprague's successful installation at Richmond during 1887 and 1888 was to continue unabated through the 1890's and well into the current century. The rapid growth of the electric railway industry was paralleled by an equally rapid improvement in the capacity and efficiency of generators, transmission lines, controls, current-collection systems, traction motors, and other electrical equipment. Electrification over long distances was made practical by the development in 1896 of distribution systems which used high-voltage alternating-current transmission lines together with transformers and motor-generator sets in substations to convert the A.C. power to the low-voltage D.C. required by contemporary traction equipment. From the late 1890's onward, the development of light intercity "interurban" electric railways paralleled the growth of street railways.

Most important to the electrification of steam railroads, however, was the rapid development after 1895 of the heavy electrical equipment required for electrification of rapid-transit systems in the nation's principal cities. New York City acquired its first elevated railways during the 1870's, and at the beginning of the 1890's El systems were in operation in both Manhattan and Brooklyn. Chicago's first elevated opened in 1891. All of them used steam motive power.

Although Daft, Sprague, and Field successfully conducted several electric-power trials on the New York elevated system between 1885 and 1888, none of the tests led to electrification of the elevateds. Even the electrification of the City & South London subway in 1890 failed to stimulate comparable projects in North America. Steam locomotives continued to power the New York and Chicago elevateds.

Following the successful operation of the electrically powered Intramural Railway on the grounds of the 1893 World's Columbian Exposition at Chicago, the Metropolitan West Side Elevated Railway adopted electric power for its line under construction on Chicago's West Side. Opened in 1895, the West Side elevated was operated entirely with 600-volt D.C. electric power drawn from a third-rail power-supply system. Heavy locomotive cars pulled trains of trailers. A second Chicago line, the Lake Street Elevated Railroad, converted to an identical power system the following year.

An electrification project for still another Chicago "L" line, the South Side Elevated Railroad, became the proving ground for an important advance in electric railway technology.

After the sale of his electrical firm to the new General Electric Company, traction pioneer Frank Sprague took up the development of electric elevators. For an elevator installation in New York's Postal Telegraph Building in 1893 and 1894, Sprague designed a control system which enabled a number of elevators to be controlled from a single master switch. The same approach, Sprague believed, could be applied to the control of electric trains. Details for the "multiple-unit system," as Sprague called it, were rapidly worked out. Utilizing a train line, a master controller on one car could simultaneously work any number of controllers on other cars in the same train, permitting an entire train of electric cars to be operated as a unit.

For several years, Sprague was unable to interest anyone in even a demonstration of the system, but in 1897 he was retained as a consulting engineer for the electrification of Chicago's South Side line. He convinced the company that his multiple-unit system would be superior to the previously planned locomotive cars, and he contracted to install the necessary equipment. With but two months to prepare the cars for testing, Sprague successfully operated a six-car test train at GE's Schenectady (N.Y.) test track late in July of 1897. By November, a five-car test train was operating on the South Side "L," and by the following April, 20 cars were in service. By the end of July 1898, all 120 cars for which Sprague was to provide electrical equipment were in service, and steam operation of the South Side elevated was discontinued.

Similar installations elsewhere followed the successful demonstration of Sprague's multiple-unit control on the South Side elevated. By 1900 the entire Chicago elevated railway system had adopted multiple-unit control, and between 1898 and 1903 the New York El system was converted from steam power to electric operation — all of it with mul-

tiple-unit control. One of the most important advances in electrical equipment for railway operation, the Sprague M.U. system was to have almost universal application in both rapid-transit and suburban railroad electrification.

By the end of the 19th century, then, a successful mainline electrification had been in regular operation for five years, and all of the basic electrical equipment required for heavy electric traction installations — at least for direct-current systems — had been developed and was considered thoroughly practical.

AT LEAST one major railroad — the New York Central & Hudson River — was seriously looking at mainline electrification. At its New York City terminal, the Central was confronted with an exceptional traffic density. The railroad's Grand Central Station accommodated the extensive long-haul services of both the Central and the New York, New Haven & Hartford, as well as the heavy and rapidly growing suburban traffic of both railroads. The terminal itself required replacement with a structure of substantially greater capacity, a requirement that was complicated by the prohibitive cost of land in midtown Manhattan. The approaches to the terminal presented a problem of equal severity. Smoke and cinders from the locomotives of 700 daily trains were an intolerable nuisance for Manhattan residents along the Central's tracks. More critical was a problem associated with the 2-mile Park Avenue tunnel that carried trains into Grand Central. Actually a partially covered cut, the tunnel frequently was so heavily choked with smoke and steam that signals were impossible to read, a condition that contributed to several serious collisions.

Although the New York Central had begun to study New York terminal electrification as early as 1899, a severe accident in the Park Avenue tunnel helped force a decision. On the morning of January 8, 1902, an inbound New York Central train ran past a red signal in the smoke-filled tunnel and crashed into the rear of a halted New Haven commuter train at 54th Street. The rear car of the New Haven train was completely crushed, and 15 commuters lost their lives. Public outcry was intense, and the following year the New York Legislature passed an act prohibiting the use of steam locomotives south of the Harlem River after July 1, 1908.

Compelled to act on its New York terminal electrification study, the Central moved boldly. A special Electric Traction Commission, formed to plan the general features of the electrification, included an impressive array of engineering talent. Chairman of the commission was New York Central

NEW JERSEY'S Hoboken Shore Railroad, a short switching road operating between Hoboken and Weehawken, was an early convert to electric traction. General Electric built this 540 h.p. steeple-cab motor (above left) for the line in 1897. The controller and the air-brake stand were located in the middle of the cab (above right).—*Industrial Photo Service.*

TWO General Electric steeple-cab locomotives, each powered by four 160 h.p. motors, went to work on the Buffalo & Lockport Railway in 1898. They weighed 36 tons and could haul a 340-ton train at 15 mph. The 18-mile line, an Erie branch near Buffalo, N. Y., leased and electrified by the B&L, was perhaps the first steam railroad electrification to be carried out purely for reasons of operational economy.—*Collection of William D. Middleton.*

THE smoke and congestion that prevailed at New York's Grand Central Station before electrification and construction of the new terminal are evident in this November 19, 1906, view of the approach to the station and the adjoining yards. Although third rail already was in place on much of the terminal trackage, regular electric operation had not yet begun and steam still was the dominant form of motive power.—*New York Central.*

THE distinctive shape of the hoods of the New York Central's S-class motors is evident in these views of prototype unit No. 6000. The locomotive was the first of a fleet of S motors that numbered 47 units by 1909. The remarkable simplicity of the axle-mounted armature of the bipolar motor design is shown in the view (left) of one of the driving axles. The field magnets and the pole pieces were carried directly on the locomotive frame. The operating cab (above) of the S motors was remarkably roomy. The large piece of equipment in the center is the electrically driven air compressor. The two-wheel guiding trucks soon were replaced with four-wheel trucks.—*All photos, collection of Herbert H. Harwood Jr.*

Vice-President and Chief Engineer William J. Wilgus, a civil engineer of remarkable ability and accomplishment. Members included Frank J. Sprague, whose many contributions to the advancement of electric transportation already have been noted, and Bion J. Arnold and George Gibbs, both distinguished electrical engineers who were responsible for a number of important advances in electric railway power systems and equipment. Arthur M. Waitt, one of the original members, later was succeeded by John F. Deems. Edwin B. Katte, the Central's chief engineer of electric traction, acted as secretary of the commission and was in charge of the actual electrification work.

The installation recommended by the commission exceeded the immediate requirements of terminal improvement. In addition to electrification of the trackage in the new Grand Central Terminal and its supporting yards and approaches, the commission proposed that the electrification be extended the length of the Central's two principal suburban routes. The four-track Hudson River main line was to be electrified to Croton, 34 miles from Grand Central, and the double-track Harlem Division was to be electrified as far north as White Plains, 24 miles from Grand Central. It would be, as *Scientific American* termed it, the application of electric traction "on a vast and sweeping scale."

By this time the Westinghouse Electric & Manufacturing Company had introduced its A.C. electrification system, although the system had not yet been proven in any installation of importance. In any case, legal obstacles to the use of high-voltage overhead trolley lines within New York City and restrictive overhead clearances in the Park Avenue tunnel precluded the adoption of an A.C. system.

Instead New York Central selected the low-voltage D.C. third-rail system that had worked well in the pioneer B&O electrification and in elevated railway installations at New York, Chicago, and Boston. The Central system, unlike previous third-rail systems, utilized an underrunning shoe. This system, jointly developed by Wilgus and Sprague, offered the advantages of greater safety to personnel and protection of the contact surface from snow and sleet accumulations.

CONTRACTS for electrical equipment and motive power were awarded to the General Electric Company by the fall of 1903. Power was to be supplied to the electrification from two new railroad-owned power plants, one at Yonkers, on the Hudson Division, and the other at Port Morris, on the Harlem Division. Each of the coal-fired plants was designed for an ultimate capacity of 30,000 kilowatts. Sixteen 625 h.p. Babcock & Wilcox water-

THE rugged and simple design of the Central's S-class locomotives was the work of General Electric's Asa F. Batchelder, who held four patents for various features of the design. The merits of Batchelder's design are evidenced by the fact that nearly seven decades after the locomotives were built, a few of them were still faithfully switching cars in the depths of the Grand Central Terminal that they made possible.— *Courtesy of Railroad Magazine.*

NO. 6000 was put through a 50,000-mile test program on a 6-mile stretch of the New York Central main line west of Schenectady on which third rail had been installed. Shown here are the substation and the enginehouse which were erected at Wyatt's Crossing, N.Y. The short section of overhead power rail, which was contacted by miniature roof-mounted pantographs, maintained the continuity of the power supply at the road crossing. Similar installations over complicated trackwork were a feature of the Grand Central Terminal electrification. The third rail at the test track was of the customary overrunning type.—*Industrial Photo Service.*

41

NO. 6000 is shown with a five-car test train. In one test, the locomotive was able to accelerate to 80 mph with an 11-car train in only 2 minutes.—*Collection of Herbert H. Harwood Jr.*

WITH dynamometer car X2501 and 10 coaches in tow, No. 6000 was ready for an eastbound run on the Wyatt's Crossing test track. On one occasion the motor reached a maximum speed of 85 mph while running without cars.—*Collection of Herbert H. Harwood Jr.*

WITH each locomotive pulling a six-car train, electric motor No. 6000 has gained better than a two-car-length lead over Pacific No. 2799 in a speed test on April 29, 1905. Such scenes were repeated many times during the testing program.—*Collection of Herbert H. Harwood Jr.*

PACED by a 4-2-4 inspection locomotive on the adjacent track, No. 6000 hustles westward along the test track with nine heavy cars.—*Collection of Herbert H. Harwood Jr.*

tube boilers were installed in each plant; room was provided for eight additional boilers. Each plant was equipped with four 5000-kilowatt Curtis turbogenerators, which produced three-phase alternating current at 25,000 volts. The generator output was transmitted to eight substations, where transformers and rotary converters converted the power to 660-volt direct current for the third rail.

The substations accommodated what was claimed to be the largest railway storage-battery installation in the world. With a combined capacity of more than 22,000 ampere-hours, eight huge storage batteries provided ample extra power to handle load fluctuations and were capable of operating the entire railroad for as long as an hour in the event of generating plant failure.

For suburban service, the railroad purchased a fleet of 180 multiple-unit cars from American Car & Foundry and St. Louis Car during 1906 and 1907. Originally, 125 cars were equipped with motors and 55 were trailers, but the trailers later were equipped with motor equipment. The steel cars were 62 feet 2 inches long and seated 64 passengers. Fully equipped, each motor car weighed just over 51 tons. Two 200 h.p. GE traction motors on each car provided an acceleration rate of 1.25 mph per second and permitted a maximum speed of 52 mph. The entire suburban-car fleet used the multiple-unit control system developed by Sprague in 1897.

The Central's M.U. cars were technically similar to cars then being delivered to such other electrifications as those of the New York subway system and the Long Island Rail Road, but the locomotives built for the railroad by the American Locomotive Company and General Electric departed radically from previous electric locomotive designs. The locomotive design was largely the work of GE's Asa F. Batchelder, who obtained four patents for various features of the design. The locomotives employed a 1-D-1 wheel arrangement, weighed 95 tons, and measured 37 feet over buffer platforms. The principal feature of Batchelder's design was the use of bipolar gearless motors. The armatures of the four traction motors were mounted directly on the driving axles, while the field magnets and pole pieces were carried on the locomotive frame. The arrangement eliminated the need for either gearing or the usual motor mountings.

Hourly rating of the locomotive was 2200 h.p.; maximum short-time rating was 3000 h.p. Maximum starting tractive effort was 32,000 pounds. The locomotive was capable of an acceleration rate of 1 mph per second with trains of up to 800 tons and could maintain a speed of 60 mph with a 500-ton train. Sprague multiple-unit control — the first installation of its kind on a locomotive — permitted the running of two locomotives under the control of one engineer to pull exceptionally heavy trains.

A large center cab was arranged for bidirectional operation. Equipment was housed in a low rectangular hood at each end. A raised center section in the hoods, which provided space for a covered passage the length of the locomotive, gave the design an unusual appearance. The locomotives were equipped with third-rail shoes plus miniature pantographs for current collection from overhead third rail installed where the ground-level third rail was interrupted by complicated switchwork.

A prototype locomotive, No. 6000, was completed in late 1904 and began an exhaustive series of trials on a 6-mile electrification installed for test purposes on one of the Central's four mainline tracks west of Schenectady. Power was furnished to the test track by a 2000-kilowatt Curtis turbogenerator installed at General Electric's Schenectady plant. A high-voltage transmission line delivered power to a rotary-converter substation near the midpoint of the test track.

Several months of testing was culminated on April 29, 1905, when No. 6000 was pitted against the latest New York Central Pacific-type locomotive in a remarkable series of comparative tests. The steam locomotive, one of the railroad's first 4-6-2's, was one of five Class K locomotives built by Alco's Schenectady works the previous December. Weighing 171 tons with tender, the 75-inch-drivered Pacific delivered a starting tractive effort of 28,000 pounds.

Test runs were made with six- and eight-car trains. In almost every case, the steam locomotive initially accelerated faster than the electric, but within 2 miles No. 6000 overtook the Pacific and was well ahead by the end of the run. Pulling an eight-car train, with a total train weight of 513 tons, the electric was able to reach 60 mph, while the 4-6-2 could do only 54 mph over the same run with an identical train. In one test with six-car trains, held near the substation to avoid the effects of a severe voltage drop at the ends of the test track, No. 6000 accelerated faster than the Pacific from the first turn of the wheels and gained a full train length on the steamer in only 1500 feet. The electric reached 50 mph in only 2 minutes 7 seconds, less than two-thirds the time the Pacific required to attain the same speed.

In speed tests conducted on the same day as the test runs, the electric motor attained a speed in excess of 80 mph running light, and two days later hit a record maximum speed of 86 mph. In still another test, on September 7, 1905, No. 6000 accelerated a 434-ton, 11-car train to 80 mph in only 2 minutes.

SEPTEMBER 30, 1906, was a great day for electric traction. S motor No. 3405 and seven cars pulled away from the platform at 3:19 p.m., the first electric train out of Grand Central. Shortly afterward the train paused at High Bridge for a photograph (below). In the front row under the "T" of "Central" is Frank J. Sprague.—*Both photos, collection of Herbert H. Harwood Jr.*

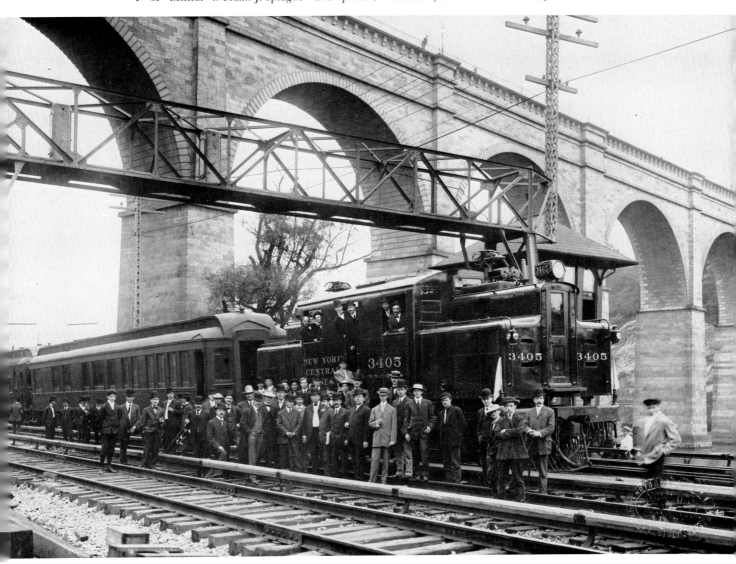

THE inner workings of Grand Central were revealed in a cutaway drawing by F. Cresson Schell, which appeared in the February 4, 1905, issue of *Harper's Weekly*, soon after plans for the terminal were made public. Among the features of the original design were (A) ticket lobby, (B) upper-level concourse, (C) waiting room, (D) suburban concourse, (E) restaurant, (F) suburban loop, and (G) track connection to the New York subway system. Despite several major architectural and engineering changes subsequently made in the design of the terminal, most of the features shown here survived in somewhat modified form. One feature that did not was the contemplated track connection to the subway.—*Collection of William D. Middleton.*

Following the extraordinary success of No. 6000, the prototype of the T class, the Central purchased 34 more T-class locomotives in 1906.

Electrification also solved the Central's second major problem at its New York terminal. Because Grand Central Station was surrounded by some of the world's costliest real estate, the railroad could ill afford to add the track space that was needed to accommodate the station's growing volume of traffic. Thus by eliminating the first problem of locomotive smoke, electrification also reduced the space required for ventilation, and Central could add trackage by double-decking the terminal.

IF IT WAS simple in concept, the New York Central's new Grand Central was breathtaking in execution. Developed by Vice-President and Chief Engineer Wilgus, the terminal plan called for 31 tracks on an upper level intended for long-distance trains and 17 tracks on a lower level for suburban trains. Loops at the south end of both levels would allow inbound trains to turn rapidly and leave the terminal after discharging passengers.

Costing 65 million dollars, the new Grand Central Terminal was begun in June 1903, and the magnificent structure was finally opened to the public on February 3, 1913. By far the most difficult part of the work was excavation — largely out of solid granite — of a deep gallery to accommodate the two tiers of terminal tracks. The gallery was 40 feet deep, 770 feet wide, and a half mile long. Excavation went on almost continuously for nearly a decade. Two million cubic yards of gran-

THESE three drawings by Vernon Howe Bailey from the January 12, 1907, issue of *Harper's Weekly*, the first drawings to be "officially sanctioned by the architects," depict the appearance of the completed Grand Central Terminal and its surroundings. Although Park Avenue did indeed become a grand avenue flanked by impressive buildings, the buildings had nowhere near the degree of uniformity contemplated by the artist (below, far left). Park Avenue also is illustrated without the expected building development (below left) to show the manner in which the new streets would span Grand Central's two levels of tracks. Bailey's version of the completed terminal (below), obviously based on architect Warren Wetmore's redesign of the original concept by Charles Reed, resembles only in its facade the structure that eventually was built. The railroad returned to an enlarged version of Reed's original design.—*Collection of William D. Middleton.*

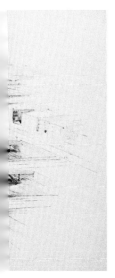

CONSIDERABLE progress already had been made in excavating the great hole required for the new terminal when artist Edwin B. Child completed a drawing for the October 27, 1906, issue of *Harper's Weekly*. The drawing depicts the view south toward the existing terminal yards and station from 50th Street between Park and Lexington avenues. Visible on the skyline are the two towers of the Manhattan and Belmont hotels on 42nd Street.—*Collection of William D. Middleton.*

A MONUMENTAL undertaking to begin with, construction of Grand Central Terminal was made infinitely more complex by the need to simultaneously dig the deep gallery for the two levels of tracks, install the new tracks, demolish the old station, and erect the new building in its place, all the while maintaining regular service in and out of the terminal without any interruption. The northward-facing 1908 view (upper photo) shows that some of the new platforms have been placed in service on the right, while to the left a section of the original ground-level track still is in use. In the view toward the south (lower photo) the 200-foot wrought-iron arches of Commodore Vanderbilt's Grand Central Station of 1869-1871 are being removed and replaced by temporary umbrella sheds. In the center background, the headhouse of the annex added to the station during the 1870's still stands, although its tracks and platforms have vanished to make way for the excavation. In the left foreground is the new post office that was one of the first structures to be built above the tracks of the new terminal. On the right is a line of New Haven electric locomotives.—*Both photos, Library of Congress.*

SUNLIGHT dramatically illuminated Grand Central's majestic concourse through the high south windows. For six decades "I'll meet you under the clock" has been a common expression, referring to the golden clock atop the information booth at the center of the concourse, a favorite rendezvous for New Yorkers.—TRAINS *collection*.

THIS mid-1930's view of Grand Central from the Murray Hill Hotel provides a good view of the circumferential plaza conceived by architect Charles Reed to carry Park Avenue traffic around the exterior of the building. On the south facade surrounding the clock is the statuary group "Transportation." A statue of Commodore Vanderbilt stands on a pedestal facing Park Avenue. Visible above and beyond the terminal is the tower of the New York Central Building, constructed above the tracks. The Third Avenue Railway streetcars on 42nd Street drew current from a conduit between the rails. —*New York Central*, TRAINS *collection*.

ite and another million cubic yards of earth were dug and blasted from the site, and an average of 400 carloads of excavated material was hauled out of the site every day for several years. Meanwhile, regular service in and out of the terminal was maintained.

By depressing the tracks below street level, the terminal design allowed the crosstown streets north of the terminal to be built across the terminal tracks on bridges. Because electrification eliminated the smoke problem, the eventual construction of buildings on "air rights" over the Central's tracks was made possible. Indeed, potential earnings from this source of income were a part of Wilgus's economic justification for the entire terminal project.

The architects for the terminal building, chosen after a widely publicized design competition, were the St. Paul (Minn.) firm of Reed & Stem, later associated in the project with the New York firm of Warren & Wetmore. The design concept, largely the work of Charles Reed, incorporated an imaginative system of ramps between the various levels within the terminal, visualized Park Avenue wrapped around the building's exterior on a "circumferential plaza," and conceived a lofty, splendid main concourse 272 feet long, 120 feet wide, and 125 feet high.

By late summer of 1906, work was well along on the installation of the power distribution system north from Grand Central, and the first train to run behind an electric locomotive left High Bridge for Grand Central on September 30, 1906. Regular M.U.-car electric operation between Grand Central and High Bridge, 7 miles away, began in December, and electric commuter service started on the Harlem Division the following month, with M.U. cars initially running as far as Wakefield, 13 miles north of Grand Central. Electric locomotives began handling through trains out of Grand Central in February 1907, and all operations out of the terminal were electrified by July.

The beginning of electric service on the Central was marred by a disastrous accident on February 16, 1907, only three days after the electric locomotives had entered regular service. A White Plains and Brewster express train, made up of five wooden cars and a pair of the T-class motors running M.U., derailed on a curve near 205th Street in the Bronx. Four cars overturned, and 23 passengers lost their lives.

Although investigation and testing failed to reveal the exact cause of the accident, the 35 T-class locomotives subsequently were modified by the installation of four-wheel guiding trucks in place of the original two-wheel pony trucks in order to improve the riding qualities of the locomotives. They

were redesignated S class with the change in wheel arrangement.

The distinctive profile of the Central's first electrics helped make them one of the best known of all American locomotives. Ives, Lionel, and American Flyer all used the design as a prototype for thousands of tinplate toy trains that circled the living room floors of several generations of Americans.

Appropriately, the success of the tinplate replicas ably reflected the acclaim accorded their real-life S-class prototypes: "They are of unprecedented power," reported *Scientific American.* "[They] have shown satisfaction as regards maintenance and durability." No one in 1907 had the slightest idea just how much satisfaction these exceptional locomotives would give in the latter categories.

In late 1907, after the installation of the electrics in regular service, the New York Central conducted a series of tests to compare the costs of steam and electric power in both switching and road service. The tests showed net savings in maintenance and operating costs for the electric locomotives of anywhere from 12 per cent in transfer service between Grand Central and Mott Haven to 27 per cent in road service. Because of their greater availability, the electric locomotives produced an average of 25 per cent more ton-miles than steam power.

"The working, side by side, of both kinds of motive power has given unsurpassed opportunity for the observation of their comparative capacities and efficiency," reported New York Central Chief Engineer Wilgus of the tests to a meeting of the American Institute of Electrical Engineers. "The results are even more gratifying than were expected, and substantiate many of the claims of the superior capacity of electric equipment."

Aside from the 1907 change to a 2-D-2 wheel arrangement and a few modifications during the 1920's for switching and "storage train" service, few mechanical or electrical alterations were ever made to the S-class locomotives during their extraordinarily long lives. After 35 years fewer than half of them had even required rewinding of their original armatures. The entire fleet survived through a half-century of service, and the prototype itself, No. 6000, finally was retired to a museum collection in 1965 after 61 years of service. Seven S-class engines — the oldest motive power in Class 1 service in North America — still serve today on Penn Central, and there are no plans to retire them.

NEW YORK CENTRAL electric operation did not reach its full extent for several years. Third rail reached its northernmost Harlem Division point at White Plains North in 1910 and was extended to

EMPLOYEES of the American Car & Foundry Company's Berwick (Pa.) steel passenger car department posed proudly with an example of their handiwork, one of the New York Central's new multiple-unit suburban coaches—almost completely obscuring it—in 1906. Although the cars were of all-steel construction, they retained one feature unchanged from the era of wooden cars—ornate leaded cathedral glass in the arched upper sash of the windows.—*Library of Congress.*

MADE UP of M.U. rolling stock of two vintages, a 12-car northbound Hudson Division suburban train approaches Marble Hill station in the Bronx, on the north bank of the Harlem River. The lead car is one of the Central's original M.U.'s, as are three other cars of the train. The original arched windows were plated over during a rebuilding.—TRAINS *collection.*

Croton-on-Hudson on the Hudson Division in 1913. An additional electric route was added to the system in 1926, when third rail was installed on the Getty Square branch of the Putnam Division into its Yonkers terminal. The freight-only Port Morris branch, which connected with the New Haven, was electrified the same year. New York Central electrification reached its peak in 1931, when the railroad's West Side freight line along the Hudson was electrified south from Spuyten Duyvil to 30th Street.

An additional dozen S-class locomotives, slightly larger and heavier than the original design, were ordered in 1908. Following the advent of heavy steel passenger equipment, which required motive power of considerably greater capacity, the railroad acquired 36 T-class motors between 1913 and 1926 (reusing the class letter vacated by the S class). Ranging in weight from 115 tons, for the first order, to 139 tons, the T-class locomotives could exert a starting tractive effort of as much as 69,000 pounds and were capable of a maximum safe speed of 75 mph. Although a B-B+B-B wheel arrangement was adopted, the newer locomotives em-

THE New York Central's main line from Spuyten Duyvil to Albany is exposed to the harshest of weather from the broad expanse of the Hudson River, and the railroad has mounted some memorable battles with the elements. Titled "A Railroad's Battle With Winter," this Howard V. Brown drawing for the cover of the February 3, 1917, *Scientific American* depicts a Central trackman thawing out switches along the river. In the background can be seen part of the wooden barricade installed along many miles of riverside trackage to keep snow and wind-driven river ice from piling up on the rails. Seemingly indifferent to the harshness of the weather, a T motor hums south toward Grand Central.—*Collection of Donald O'Hanley.*

ployed eight GE traction motors of the same basic gearless design so successful on the original S-class units. Fifty-three locomotives with B-B and C-C wheel arrangements were added to the roster between 1926 and 1931 for freight service on the West Side line. In more recent years, the railroad's huge 2635 h.p., 2-C+C-2 Cleveland Union Terminal locomotives were transferred east after the discontinuance of electric operations at Cleveland in 1953.

The Central's original 180-car M.U. fleet was supplemented by 31 cars built by St. Louis Car and Pressed Steel Car in 1910 and 1913. Standard Steel Car delivered another 145 cars in a series of orders between 1917 and 1929. During the two decades following World War II, a new generation of 85-foot, 130-passenger M.U. cars — 100 from St. Louis in 1950 and 87 from Pullman-Standard between 1962 and 1965 — began replacing the original electric-car fleet. In 1972 New York's Metropolitan Transportation Authority, which had assumed responsibility for commuter services, completed the renovation of the fleet with 128 M-1 Metropolitan high-performance M.U.'s almost identical to new cars also provided by MTA for the Long Island.

All told, the New York Central's grand design for a solution to its New York terminal problems — the electrification and Grand Central Terminal — represented an investment of approximately 100 million turn-of-the-century dollars. Looking back at the efforts of Wilgus, Sprague, Arnold, Gibbs, Deems, and Katte over the span of almost seven decades, the project seems a work of remarkable and enduring achievement.

Its transportation capacity was enormous. In the late 1920's, when the long-haul passenger train was at its zenith and the *Twentieth Century Limited* often ran in three to six sections, New York Central and New Haven traffic in and out of the terminal averaged almost 500 daily trains and 134,000 passengers. On one record day 800 trains, aggregating over 6000 cars and carrying more than 166,000 passengers, arrived or left Grand Central.

During World War II, even greater traffic levels were recorded. By the end of the war, daily traffic averaged 600 trains and 180,000 passengers, and on a record-breaking Thanksgiving eve in 1945, more than 240,000 passengers passed through Grand Central's vast spaces.

Today, Grand Central still endures as one of the great landmarks of New York City. Little-changed from the installation devised in the infancy of heavy electric traction, the Central's electrification continues to support an intense daily traffic.

If mainline electrification began on the Baltimore & Ohio in 1895, it came of age on the New York Central in 1907.

THE 36 T-class locomotives were the workhorses of the Central's electrified passenger service from the time they were built until the advent of rebuilt Cleveland Union Terminal motors during the 1950's. B-B+B-B unit 1162 was a T-2a locomotive built by Alco-GE in 1914. Powered by eight 330 h.p. gearless motors, the 125-ton T-2a's could develop a maximum tractive effort of more than 65,000 pounds. Maximum safe speed was 75 mph. The view of the No. 2 end of T motor 1174 (right) shows the miniature pantograph that contacted the overhead conductor at third-rail gaps and the exhaust stack for the train-heating boiler.—*Above, General Electric; right, General Electric, from Penn Central.*

MOTOR 1166, a T-2b, sweeps around the curve near Marble Hill with the westbound *Twentieth Century Limited,* the flagship of the New York Central's Great Steel Fleet.—*General Electric.*

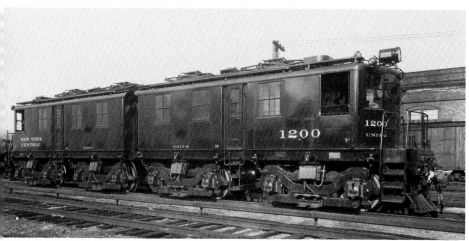

ANTICIPATING the electrification of its West Side freight line, the Central ordered its first electric freight locomotives for the New York electrification from Alco-GE in 1925. Seven Class Q double-truck steeple-cab locomotives (above left) were delivered for switching service in early 1926. They weighed 100 tons and were rated at 1330 h.p. Two Class R road freight locomotives (left) received later the same year each consisted of two box-cab units semi-permanently coupled together. Total weight of each R-class locomotive was 175 tons; maximum speed was 60 mph. The Q and R classes employed identical running gear, electrical equipment, and motors. Unlike the earlier locomotives built for NYC's New York electrification, which had gearless motors, the Q's and R's had conventional geared, axle-hung motors.—*Above left, General Electric; left, General Electric, collection of Edward T. Francis.*

ON its way from White Plains to the Port Morris freight yards in 1948, Class Q switcher No. 155 has just passed under the concrete arch bridge that carries 238th Street over the tracks and the Bronx River. The Q-class motors were renumbered from their original 1200 series in 1936.—*Stephen L. Meyers.*

IN 1928 the New York Central acquired a tri-power switching locomotive which could operate as a conventional electric drawing power from the third rail, as a diesel-electric powered by a 300 h.p. Ingersoll-Rand engine, and as an electric powered by a 218-cell battery. The running gear, traction motors, and control equipment were identical to those of the Q-class switchers. No. 1525 became the prototype of a series of tri-power units delivered by Alco-GE in 1930. No. 1525, shown at the 60th Street Yard on the West Side freight line in 1930, was converted to a hump trailer in 1945.—*General Electric*, TRAINS *collection*.

AFTER an extended period of testing and evaluation of tri-power locomotive No. 1525, the Central placed an order for 35 similar units. The new tri-power units also were built by Alco, GE, and Ingersoll-Rand, and they included a number of improvements in the design, the most obvious of which was the change to a more conventional box-cab configuration. No. 552 is shown at Harmon with a northbound switch run, drawing power from the third rail. No. 552 was retired in July 1955, only two months after this picture was taken, and the entire tri-power fleet was gone by 1957.—*Herbert H. Harwood Jr.*

GUIDED by its experience with the pair of two-unit Alco-GE locomotives delivered in 1928, the Central ordered 42 Class R-2 units from the same builders. The 133-ton box-cabs were delivered in 1930 and 1931. They employed a C+C wheel arrangement and were rated at 3000 h.p. No. 1202, pictured at GE's plant, was among the first units delivered in late 1930.—*General Electric*.

HEADING up the Hudson on the West Side freight line with a mail and express train in May 1954, a pair of R-2's has crossed Spuyten Duyvil

TRAINS leaving Grand Central first encountered daylight at 96th Street and Park Avenue when this photo was taken before World War II. Later the tunnel roof was extended north one block to 97th Street.—*New York Central.*

reek and is about to join the Hudson Division main line. In the distance is the George Washington Bridge.—*Herbert H. Harwood Jr.*

ALL of the Central's seemingly indestructible S motors lasted more than half a century in regular service. In 1955 49-year-old No. 113 rolled northward (above left) at 102nd Street and Park Avenue with a train of equipment bound for Mott Haven Yard. On a similar mission (above right) No. 131 met the inbound *Twentieth Century Limited* just south of the Harlem River drawbridge in 1961.— *Above left, Herbert H. Harwood Jr.; above right, David Plowden.*

NORTH of the Park Avenue tunnel the New York Central's electrics climbed to a broad viaduct above the teeming streets of Harlem. (Above) Class T motor No. 271 approaches NK Tower at 106th Street on its way into Grand Central with commuter express No. 192 from Poughkeepsie early in the morning on November 9, 1951. (Left) A westbound through train slides into the 125th Street station behind a former Cleveland Union Terminal 2-C+C-2 in the mid-1950's. It's late afternoon, and the tracks on either side of the express are occupied by commuter trains.— *Above, E. B. Dawson Jr.; left, Henry T. Raudenbush, collection of Electric Railroaders' Association.*

RUNNING on the leftmost track to avoid the dense commuter traffic, former Cleveland Union Terminal Class P locomotive No. 227 swings into the curve at 138th Street, just north of the Harlem River drawbridge, with the Chicago-bound *Twentieth Century Limited.—J. C. Smith Jr.*

HEADING north in the afternoon with a commuter express, a T motor has cleared the big lift bridge over the Harlem River and approaches Mott Haven Junction, where the Harlem and Hudson divisions part company.—*Henry T. Raudenbush, collection of Electric Railroaders' Association.*

CLASS T motors meet at Marble Hill station in the early 1920's. The time is midafternoon, and the baggage-club car and all-Pullman consist hint that the approaching train might be the *Twentieth Century Limited.—Fred Eidenbenz.*

CLASS T-2b motor No. 263 leans into the curve at Mott Haven Junction with train 167, the New York-Utica *Upstate Special*, in May 1955. The train is on the Hudson Division; beyond are the tracks of the Harlem Division.—*Herbert H. Harwood Jr.*

IN the spring of 1955 the New York Central was still dispatching passenger trains of impressive dimensions. Train 41, the St. Louis-bound *Knickerbocker*, was 17 cars strong as it rolled through a curve on the north bank of the Harlem River near Marble Hill. On the point was ex-Cleveland Union Terminal P motor No. 226, rebuilt for New York terminal service and decked out in a paint scheme inspired by the Central's passenger diesels.—*Herbert H. Harwood Jr.*

ON a splendid July morning in 1964 the *Twentieth Century Limited* rolls south along the Hudson at Greystone with Class T motor No. 278 on the point (right). In the distance an M.U. train heads for Harmon on the local track.—*John E. Pickett.*

THE morning shadows are still long on July 31, 1966, as an ex-Cleveland Union Terminal motor (right) skims along the Hudson, westbound by the timetable and northbound by the compass. On its drawbar are the cars of the *Empire State Express*, destined for Buffalo, Cleveland, Detroit, and Montreal.—*John E. Pickett.*

TRAIN 15, the westbound *Ohio State Limited* (above left) rolls under the Henry Hudson Parkway bridge and past Spuyten Duyvil station behind T-1b motor No. 253. The *Ohio State*'s opposite number, train 16 (left), is nearly at the end of its journey as it swings away from the Hudson River at Spuyten Duyvil. The year is 1964, and the ex-Cleveland Union Terminal motor has coaches and sleepers from Cincinnati, Cleveland, Toronto, and St. Louis in tow. In the years between the two photos the weeds have crept toward the tracks and the paint on the signal has yielded to the weather.—*Above left, Jim Shaughnessy; left, John E. Pickett.*

(LEFT) The conductor and the engineer of train 134 converse on a spring evening in 1957. In a few moments ex-CUT locomotive No. 233 will slip away from the platform at Harmon, heading for Grand Central.—*Jim Shaughnessy.*

(BELOW LEFT) Ex-CUT motor No. 236 heads for the ready track at Harmon after being serviced and inspected.—*Jim Shaughnessy.*

(RIGHT) Engineer John White is ready to notch back the controller of his ex-Cleveland Union Terminal P motor to accelerate the train away from 125th Street station in New York.—*Jim Shaughnessy.*

(BELOW RIGHT) No. 255, one of the last surviving T-class motors, was fitted with footboards and served as a switcher at Harmon. After the Penn Central merger it was transferred to Sunnyside Yard to replace an even older DD1 on a wire train.—*J. C. Smith Jr.*

(BELOW) Harmon, 33 miles from Grand Central, is the northern end of electric operation on the Hudson Division. Class T motor No. 259 slowed to a stop at the platform on a rainy day in May 1940 with a westbound coach train. In a moment the electric would run ahead into the clear and steam power would back down onto the train to continue the run north.—*Charles B. Chaney, collection of the Smithsonian Institution.*

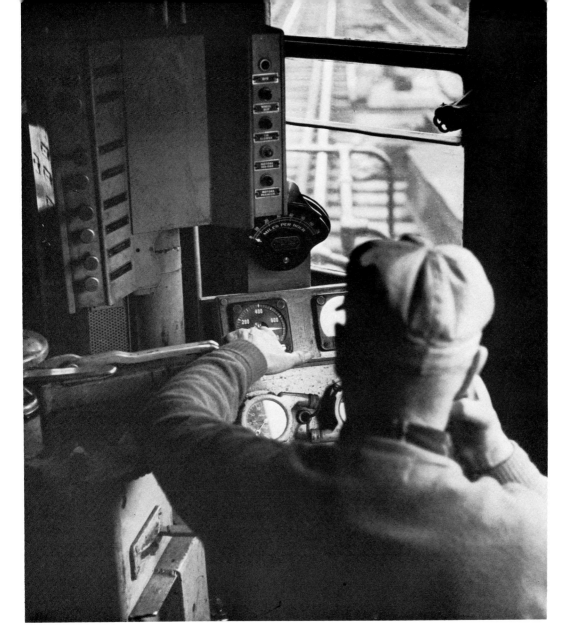

(LEFT) Framed by the arch of the 238th Street bridge, Penn Central train 9014, a Harlem Division Brewster-to-Grand Central express, hurries through Woodlawn in May 1970 behind a P motor. The overpass in the background carries southbound trains from the former New Haven line over the Harlem Division; the two lines join at Woodlawn Junction a short distance behind the camera. New Haven catenary ends just east of the abutment of the overpass.—*Fred W. Schneider III.*

(RIGHT) The M.U. cars of an inbound Hudson Division local are reflected in the placid waters of the Harlem River in a 1948 winter scene. NYC's M.U. cars had one motor truck and one trailer truck, and the accumulation of snow shows which is which.—*Stephen L. Meyers.*

(RIGHT) The Hudson Division leaves the bank of the Harlem River and slices through the granite backbone of the Bronx east of Spuyten Duyvil. A train of monitor-roofed M.U.'s coils through the cut in this 1954 scene.—*Herbert H. Harwood Jr.*

(LEFT) The exhaust from its train-heating boiler mingles with kicked-up snow as Class T-2b motor No. 266 races through Scarsdale on its way to Grand Central with a commuter train in 1959. —*Don Ball.*

NEW YORK CENTRAL commuters got their first new equipment of recent times during 1949 and 1950, when St. Louis Car Company delivered 100 air-conditioned M.U. coaches. The 85-foot-long, 75-ton cars offered 3-and-2 seating for 130 passengers and were finished in Pullman green trimmed with yellow.—*St. Louis Car Company.*

(RIGHT) Three postwar M.U. cars roll south near Hastings-on-Hudson in May 1970. By this time the Penn Central logo and a new shade of green had replaced the familiar New York Central livery.—*Fred W. Schneider III.*

(ABOVE LEFT) The scene is repeated every morning, Monday through Friday, in suburbs across the country as commuters wait for city-bound trains. Here on a summer morning in the late 1940's commuters wait at Bronxville on the Harlem Division.—*Courtesy of Railroad Magazine.*

(CENTER LEFT) The Getty Square branch of the Putnam Division in Yonkers was one of the last NYC suburban lines to be electrified, and it was the first to lose electric operation. In two scenes recorded in 1943 shortly before electric operation ceased, three-car trains wait at the Getty Square terminal of the line (the 10-story building belongs to the First National Bank, not NYC) and pause at the Caryl Avenue station.—*Both photos, Herman Rinke.*

(LEFT) An M.U. baggage car leads a northbound train past JD Tower at Woodlawn on the Harlem Division on a July afternoon in 1954.—*Herbert H. Harwood Jr.*

(RIGHT) The older heavyweight M.U. cars also received Penn Central colors and in some cases Penn Central lettering on NYC colors, as on the last and next-to-last cars of train 552, shown leaving 138th Street station on its way to Crestwood on the Harlem Division, July 21, 1970.—*Fred W. Schneider III.*

HEADING for Grand Central, a three-car train of postwar M.U.'s accelerates away from Marble Hill station in the Bronx in October 1969.—*Fred W. Schneider III.*

SCARSDALE commuters scurry to board the green M.U. cars of Harlem Division train 9518, a North White Plains-Grand Central local, on an overcast May morning in 1970.—*Fred W. Schneider III.*

A MID-MORNING local from North White Plains to Grand Central ducks under the former New Haven inbound main lines and the 238th Street concrete arch bridge at Woodlawn in May 1970.—*Fred W. Schneider III.*

IN 1972 commuter service on the Harlem and Hudson divisions was upgraded with 128 M-1 Metropolitan cars owned by the Metropolitan Transportation Authority. The high-performance M.U.'s are almost identical to those on the Long Island Rail Road.—*J. C. Smith Jr.*

THREE of America's oldest locomotives still in trunk-line service rest in the depths of Grand Central Terminal between switching chores in March 1972. GE built the electrics in 1906 as the original motive power for the NYC electrification.—*J. W. Swanberg.*

MORE than 60 years after its successful demonstration opened the way for electrification into Grand Central, New York Central & Hudson River 6000 went to an honored retirement in 1964 as a museum piece. The locomotive bore five different numbers during its career and retired as NYC 100.—*Jim Shaughnessy.*

COMMUTING by train is an institution that changes little with the years. Superficial elements, such as rolling stock and hats, may vary, but these New York Central scenes are universal: the passage through the gate on the lower level of Grand Central; the ubiquitous newspaper, folded to half-page width; and the ticket collector working his way through the car.— *All photos, David Plowden.*

TWO New Haven Class EP-1 box-cab motors, No. 029 in the lead, pose with a long westbound train on the four-track main line shortly after the opening of the first 21 miles of electrification between Woodlawn, N.Y., and Stamford, Conn. The novel triangular catenary of this original section was not completely successful and later was modified. Subsequent extensions of the New Haven electrification used a more conventional form of overhead catenary.—*Smithsonian Institution.*

3. New Haven's bold venture

THE New York, New Haven & Hartford Railroad, in common with the New York Central, was obliged to comply with the 1903 act of the New York Legislature that prohibited the use of steam into Manhattan after July 1, 1908.

By 1903 the New Haven had acquired almost a decade of electric traction experience on several branch lines in Massachusetts, Rhode Island, and Connecticut. The railroad's electrification of its Nantasket Beach branch in 1895 was among the earliest railroad electrification projects. Between 1896 and 1898 a third-rail system was installed on several branches in the vicinity of Hartford and

New Britain, Conn. In 1901 the Stamford-New Canaan branch in Connecticut and the Providence, Warren & Bristol branch in Rhode Island and Massachusetts were electrified using an overhead trolley system. Although both third-rail and overhead-trolley current-collection systems were used on these electrification experiments, all of them used a 600-volt D.C. power supply.

Because of this experience with low-voltage D.C. power, as well as the requirement that its trains be able to operate over 12 miles of New York Central trackage between Woodlawn and Grand Central, the New Haven would have seemed likely to adopt the same 660-volt D.C. third-rail system being in-

AMONG the New Haven's several branchline electrification experiments of the 1890's was a line between Berlin and New Britain, Conn., which was electrified with a 600-volt D.C. third-rail system. The line's big open cars, one of which is shown at Berlin pulling a closed trailer, seated 96 passengers. A suit brought jointly by the State of Connecticut and the City of New Britain, citing the hazard of the exposed third rail, compelled the New Haven to remove its third-rail installation in 1906.—*Industrial Photo Service.*

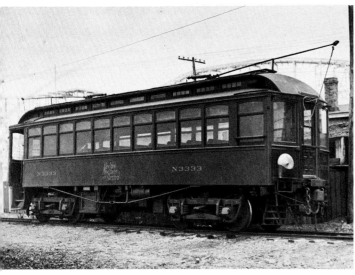

stalled by the Central for its New York terminal electrification. Imagine, then, the surprise in electrification circles when the New Haven announced a contract with the Westinghouse Electric & Manufacturing Company for the installation of an 11,000-volt, 25-cycle, single-phase electrification of its main line from Woodlawn, N. Y., to Stamford, Conn.

The New Haven contract marked the first major victory for A.C. in the celebrated "battle of the currents" that had raged between Westinghouse and General Electric — and with the Edison companies even before GE was formed — since the 1880's, and which was to continue for several decades into the 20th century.

During the formative years of the electric lighting and traction industries, direct-current systems and equipment were developed much more rapidly, and D.C. electrification established a clear advantage over A.C. During the 1880's, however, important advances in A.C. equipment and technology began to make A.C. electrification a more practical and efficient rival of direct-current systems.

In 1881 and 1882 two European inventors, Lucien Gaulard of France and John D. Gibbs of England, obtained patents for a jointly developed system of alternating-current distribution. George Westinghouse, the inventor of the automatic air brake and a system of railroad signals, entered the electrical field about this time, and in 1885 acquired rights to the Gaulard and Gibbs patents. Only a year later the Westinghouse firm built the first commercially successful A.C. generating station, based on these patents, at Buffalo, N. Y.

One of the most important devices in the Gaulard and Gibbs system was a transformer that could step A.C. voltage up or down. In 1887 Westinghouse developed and patented an improved transformer based on the Gaulard-Gibbs design. Assembling an impressive group of electrical engineers that included William Stanley, Oliver B. Shallenberger, Guido Panteleoni, and — a few years later — Benjamin G. Lamme and Yugoslavian electrical genius Nikola Tesla, the Westinghouse firm rapidly

THE most important of the New Haven's early experiments with D.C. electrification was on its 24-mile Providence, Warren & Bristol line, which was electrified with a 600-volt overhead trolley system in 1901. At its peak, more than a hundred daily trains were scheduled over the line, which operated electrically for almost 40 years. A two-car train (above left) of electrified steam road coaches bound from Fall River, Mass., to Providence, R.I., clatters through the switches of the junction with the Bristol line at Warren, R.I. One of the line's Brill-built motor cars (left) stands at Crescent Park, near Riverside, between Providence and Warren.—*Both photos, collection of LeRoy O. King.*

advanced the development of A.C. electrification and soon became a formidable rival of the Edison and the Thomson-Houston firms.

Because Edison himself was opposed to A.C. electrification, his firm was slow to enter the field even after Westinghouse demonstrated its superiority for both generation and distribution. Eventually, however, the Edison company, and the General Electric firm that succeeded it after the merger with Thomson-Houston in 1892, developed a full range of A.C. equipment. In 1896 Westinghouse and GE licensed each other to manufacture under the other's patents, and the two firms became competitive in marketing almost every type of electrical equipment.

Although by this time the superiority of A.C. for large-scale electric-power generation and transmission was almost universally recognized, strong differences of opinion remained among electrical engineers concerning the relative merits of A.C. or D.C. power for heavy railroad traction.

The D.C.-series motor was extremely efficient and offered good control characteristics for railroad purposes. A.C. motors, on the other hand, were more cumbersome, and locomotives required heavy

RAILWAY and electrical inventor and industrialist George Westinghouse (1846-1914) pioneered the development of alternating-current electrical systems. His Westinghouse Electric & Manufacturing Company furnished the equipment for the New Haven's 11,000-volt, single-phase installation of 1907, the first major A.C. electrification of an American steam railroad. —*Westinghouse Electric Corporation.*

THE New Haven's 8-mile Stamford-New Canaan (Conn.) branch, originally electrified in 1901 with a 600-volt D.C. trolley system, was converted in 1908 to the 11,000-volt A.C. catenary system employed for the railroad's new mainline electrification. Shortly after the conversion to A.C. a two-car local waited at the New Canaan station.—*Library of Congress.*

75

and bulky transformers and control equipment. Because of the relatively low voltages used, D.C. systems required large amounts of current. To avoid excessive transmission losses, expensive substations were required at frequent intervals, and — until high-voltage D.C. systems were perfected — third-rail current collection was necessary to meet the heavy current demands of mainline railroad electrification. Because of the ease with which voltage could be stepped up or down by transformers, A.C. electrification permitted more efficient and economical distribution systems, particularly where long distances were involved.

Although the two firms manufactured both A.C. and D.C. equipment for railroad electrification, Westinghouse engineers clearly favored the A.C. equipment that had been the basis for their firm's original success, while GE men just as clearly preferred D.C. electrification.

General Electric had established an early lead in the railroad electrification field with its successful D.C. locomotive experiments of the early 1890's, the 1895 B&O electrification, and its several branchline, shortline, and rapid-transit electrifications of the late 1890's. In 1903 GE landed the contract for the New York Central's unprecedented New York terminal electrification without serious consideration having been given to the proposals of the rival Westinghouse firm.

Westinghouse had entered the steam railroad electrification field in 1895. Joining forces with the Baldwin Locomotive Works, which built the mechanical components, the Westinghouse firm's East Pittsburgh (Pa.) works produced a small experimental passenger-freight locomotive that was the first of a long line of electric locomotives to carry the joint builders' plate of the two firms. The 32-foot-long box-cab locomotive was mounted on two four-wheel trucks and weighed 46 tons. For more than a decade, it was operated in a variety of trials with both A.C. and D.C. equipment at East Pittsburgh.

Soon after the turn of the century, Westinghouse developed and marketed a high-voltage, single-phase A.C. system for railroad electrification. The first road to use the system was an Indiana interurban, the Indianapolis & Cincinnati Traction Company, which in 1905 opened a 41-mile line between Indianapolis and Rushville electrified with 3300-volt, single-phase A.C.

The New Haven, confronted with the need to electrify its operations into New York, developed a project on an even grander scale than that of the New York Central. Like the Central, the New Haven saw that a change from steam to electric motive power at any point in its suburban zone would be difficult, particularly during peak traffic periods when trains operated at close intervals. Equally important, an uneconomic duplication of motive-power fleets and engine crews would be required. Consequently, the New Haven decided to electrify to the limit of its suburban territory at Stamford, 33 miles from Grand Central.

Because the New Haven's four-track main line carried what was perhaps the heaviest mainline traffic of any American railroad, the railroad also considered electrification as a way of increasing the capacity of its main line without laying additional tracks. If the initial electrification was successful, a later extension to New Haven, Conn., was almost certain, and ultimate electrification of the entire New York-Boston main line seemed highly probable.

With this long-distance electrification in mind, the advantages of an A.C. system were more important to the New Haven than they had been to the New York Central, which apparently had given little thought to a future extension of its electric zone. Both General Electric and Westinghouse submitted electrification proposals to the New Haven in 1905. Although both submitted a variety of A.C. and D.C. systems, GE favored some form of D.C. electrification, while Westinghouse recommended an 11,000-volt, 25-cycle, single-phase A.C. system. Despite the lack of any successful example other than the modest Indiana interurban, the New Haven boldly adopted single-phase A.C. for the longest mainline railroad electrification project yet undertaken.

The New Haven had to construct its own generating plant at Cos Cob, Conn., a short distance west of Stamford, because commercial power-generating capacity sufficient for the new railroad load was not available. Fourteen coal-fired, water-tube boilers supplied steam at 180 pounds pressure to a bank of three multiple-expansion, parallel-flow Westinghouse-Parsons steam turbines which were connected to 3000-kilowatt Westinghouse generators. A fourth 3330-kilowatt generator was added shortly after the first three generators were installed. Power was generated at the contact-wire voltage of 11,000 volts and supplied directly to the overhead system. An observer almost literally could say that one Cos Cob generator terminal was wired directly to the overhead trolley wire, while the other was wired to the running-rail return circuit.

The railroad adopted a novel type of triangular cross-section catenary for the overhead system on the 21-mile electrified section between Woodlawn and Stamford. By using two side-by-side catenary cables and triangular trolley hangers, the contact wire not only was held in a horizontal position, but was restrained from lateral movement. Steel bridges, spaced at 300-foot intervals and spanning

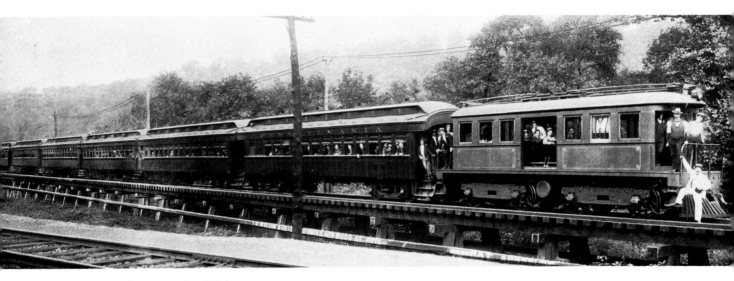

IN 1895 Baldwin Locomotive Works and Westinghouse jointly built a box-cab locomotive (above) which was used for more than a decade of A.C. and D.C. experimentation at the Westinghouse East Pittsburgh (Pa.) works. Equipped as a 600 h.p., 500-volt D.C. locomotive, it was sold in 1906 to the Lackawanna & Wyoming Valley Railroad in northeastern Pennsylvania, on which it operated until 1953.—*Collection of Stephen D. Maguire.*

BALDWIN-WESTINGHOUSE locomotive No. 9 (right), completed in 1904, was the first single-phase locomotive built in America. It was designed for operation on 6600-volt power, and it was driven by six 225 h.p. traction motors. The motor armatures were on quills surrounding the axles, and the motor frames were spring-suspended from the locomotive body, an arrangement similar to that subsequently used on the first Baldwin-Westinghouse electrics for the New Haven. The 126-ton locomotive was made up of two six-wheel units, each capable of independent operation. In tests at the East Pittsburgh Westinghouse plant, No. 9 exerted a drawbar pull of 97,000 pounds.—*Industrial Photo Service.*

from 4 to 12 tracks, supported the overhead catenary system.

The Westinghouse engineers faced some difficult problems in the design of an initial 35 New Haven electric locomotives. Not only did they have to overcome the problems of the virtually untried high-voltage A.C. system, but the equipment had to be capable of operation over 660-volt D.C. third rail on the 12 miles of New York Central track between Woodlawn and Grand Central.

A prototype Class EP-1 double-truck locomotive,

No. 01, was completed by Baldwin-Westinghouse in late 1905, and the remainder of the order was delivered over a two-year period. The locomotives, which weighed 102 tons and were 37 feet 6½ inches long, employed a box-cab configuration with operating cabs at both ends. A gearless drive similar to that of the B&O's pioneer 1895 electrics was used. The motor armatures were carried on hollow quills that drove 62-inch-diameter driving wheels through flexible spring connections. The main frames of the motors were split on the center line,

PROTOTYPE unit No. 01, constructed by Baldwin-Westinghouse in 1905, was the first of the 41 A.C./D.C., 102-ton, box-cab passenger locomotives that powered the New Haven's initial electrification. Remarkably successful, some of the Class EP-1 locomotives, including No. 01, remained in service for more than 40 years.—*Collection of H. L. Broadbelt.*

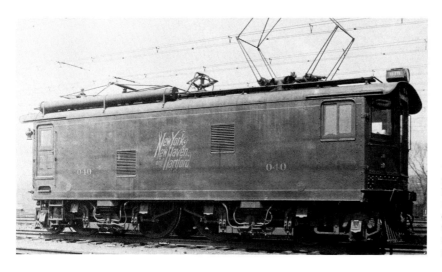

ONE of the second order for six EP-1's delivered in 1908, No. 040 reflects the several design changes that were made in the units shortly after delivery. The most apparent change is the addition of a guiding axle at each end of the locomotive, which corrected the tendency of the four-wheel drive trucks to nose at high speed.—*Collection of H. L. Broadbelt.*

and were supported through springs from a cradle resting on the main journal boxes. This method of motor mounting allowed the axle to rise and fall in accordance with track inequalities, independently of the armature. Unlike GE's bipolar gearless design for New York Central, which carried the armature directly on the driving axle, the Baldwin-Westinghouse gearless quill drive bore the entire motor weight on the truck frame. This greatly reduced the unsprung weight on each driving axle — an important consideration in reducing rail impact forces in high-speed operation.

The requirement for dual A.C./D.C. capability was met by using motors of the series commutator type, which performed satisfactorily on either type of current. Four Westinghouse 130 motors on each locomotive provided a total hourly rating of 1420 h.p. and a starting tractive effort of 42,000 pounds.

The locomotives could exceed 80 mph, and in tests, speeds as high as 89 mph were recorded.

A single locomotive was designed to handle the railroad's average consist, but multiple-unit control equipment permitted operation in pairs or threes whenever required for heavier trains. Although multiple-unit control was a feature of New York Central's new locomotives, it seldom was employed, and the New Haven locomotives were the first to regularly use M.U. control to assemble motive-power combinations in the "building block" concept that later became common with diesel-electric units.

The locomotives were equipped with a multitude of current-collection devices to permit operation over the dual power-supply systems. Eight third-rail shoes, two on each side of each truck, could be raised or lowered by the engineer. Two large overhead pantographs were provided for A.C. operation, while a third, small pantograph was used for current collection from short sections of overhead third rail installed at switches on the New York Central D.C. system. Control circuits permitted the transition from A.C. to D.C. operation without stopping. Interlocking controls prevented current-collection devices from being in contact with the D.C. third rail and the A.C. overhead at the same time.

A number of difficulties were encountered with the new A.C./D.C. locomotives during their first months of operation. One of the most serious was a lack of stability and a tendency of the four-wheel driving trucks to "nose," or oscillate from side to side, at high speed. After this problem had been corrected by the addition of a pair of non-powered guiding wheels at each end of the locomotive, and lesser electrical deficiencies were worked out, the New Haven's A.C./D.C. box-cab locomotives proved to be a highly successful design. By 1910, when almost every one of the EP-1 units had run more than 100,000 miles, the New Haven reported a maintenance cost per mile and a record of reliability for the electrics that were much more favorable than those previously experienced with steam power. In 1909, for example, the EP-1's averaged well over 12,000 miles between each locomotive-caused delay.

Soon after delivery of the 35-unit EP-1 order was completed in mid-1907, six more locomotives were ordered for delivery in 1908. The entire class served long lives in high-speed passenger service. By 1924 the EP-1 fleet had accumulated an average of over 1.25 million high-speed miles. A number of EP-1's were retired as early as 1936, but several, including prototype 01, wheeled New Haven varnish to as late as 1947.

CONSTRUCTION work on the New Haven electrification began in 1905. The overhead was energized from Cos Cob to New York in April 1907, and the first regular train to run behind electric power operated from Grand Central to New Rochelle, N. Y., on July 24, 1907. Service was extended to Port Chester, N. Y., the following month, and reached all the way to Stamford by October.

Although all trains operating over the New Haven electrification initially were powered by electric locomotives, the railroad in 1909 began to acquire multiple-unit passenger cars for its suburban services. The New Haven M.U. fleet, constructed by Standard Steel Car Company and Osgood Bradley Car Company, by 1931 reached a total of 221 cars, of which 129 were motor cars. Typically, motor cars were equipped with four

Westinghouse A.C./D.C. motors rated at 175 h.p. each, and they were geared for a maximum speed of 55 mph. M.U. control equipment, transformers, current-collection devices, and other electrical equipment were comparable to that installed on the railroad's locomotives. The cars were approximately 72 feet long, weighed from 84 to 88 tons, and seated 76 to 84 passengers. Trail cars were of equivalent size and capacity.

The New Haven's electrification came none too soon, for commuter traffic was increasing rapidly as the suburbs served by the railroad grew. In the decade from 1900 to 1910, New Haven commutation traffic into and out of Grand Central nearly doubled, and it more than doubled again from 1910 to the early 1920's. In 1916 New Haven handled 11.4 million passengers at Grand Central; by 1922 the number was 16.3 million, almost half again as much. Along with an increasing traffic volume, trains grew heavier, too, as steel cars replaced wooden equipment.

By 1910 the New Haven had completed plans for expansion of its electric operation, not only eastward from Stamford to New Haven, but also on the busy Harlem River line to its junction with the main line at New Rochelle. Although the original installation had been limited to passenger-train operation, the railroad decided to electrify freight and switching service as well. The electrification of this predominately nighttime traffic promised to improve the load factor on New Haven's power-supply and distribution system in addition to the general economy of operation that it would provide.

This expanded electrification, as well as steady traffic growth, required a substantial increase to the New Haven's electric motive-power fleet. Before placing a major locomotive order, the railroad ordered four experimental locomotives, each of widely varied design, from Baldwin-Westinghouse.

The first unit delivered, in 1910, was No. 071, a box-cab locomotive mounted on two four-wheel articulated trucks with a single unpowered guiding axle at each end. Instead of the gearless-type motors used on the previous New Haven locomotives, the 071 was equipped with a gear-and-quill drive. Each of the four traction motors — one for each driving axle — was mounted on the main frame of the locomotive above the driving axle. A gear-and-pinion arrangement drove a hollow quill enveloping the axle, which in turn powered the 63-inch driving wheels through the same type of flexible spring connections employed on the earlier EP-1 units. In addition to keeping unsprung weight on the driving wheels to a minimum in the same manner as the previous design, the higher motor position of the gear-and-quill drive raised the loco-

DEMONSTRATING its ability to draw power from the New York Central's 600-volt D.C. third rail as readily as it does from its own A.C. catenary, New Haven box-cab motor No. 027 rolls a six-car train south through Botanical Garden station in the borough of the Bronx in New York City on the Central's four-track Harlem Division on October 1, 1910. —Charles B. Chaney, collection of the Smithsonian Institution.

MULTIPLE-UNIT controls permitted the New Haven to assemble its EP-1 box-cab units into motive-power blocks of various capacities to meet traffic requirements. Here three of the 1420 h.p. units, with all six pantographs raised for current collection, have teamed up to move a 16-car train along the original 21-mile electrified section between Stamford and Woodlawn.—Industrial Photo Service.

motive's center of gravity. The low center of gravity of gearless designs was considered by most engineers to be hard on track because of higher lateral forces at curves.

The 140-ton 071 employed four Westinghouse motors rated at 315 h.p., and developed a maximum tractive effort of almost 47,000 pounds. The locomotive had control and current-collection equipment for both A.C. and D.C. operation, and was intended for either freight or passenger service.

Experimental locomotive No. 069, a box-cab also delivered in 1910, had an unusual structural arrangement. Deep steel girders the full length of the locomotive formed each side of the frame and carried the full weight of the cab. Four driving axles with 63-inch wheels were carried by the side girders, while an unpowered guiding axle at each end was connected to the frame through a radius bar that permitted lateral movement. The locomotive used a gear-and-quill drive generally similar to that installed on experimental unit 071. Instead of a single motor for each driving axle, however, two smaller motors were geared to each axle. The 069, like the 071, was equipped for both A.C. and D.C. operation in either freight or passenger service.

A third experimental unit, No. 070, delivered in 1910, employed a type of running gear different from any previous New Haven electric. The design was patterned after the side-rod DD1-class units that had entered service on the Pennsylvania Rail-

road's New York terminal electrification a short time previous. The 070 was made up of two articulated cab units and measured 53 feet 8 inches in length, considerably longer than any previous New Haven motors. Running gear consisted of two pairs of 57-inch driving wheels and a single guiding axle under each of the articulated cab sections. A single Westinghouse No. 406 motor rated at 630 h.p. was mounted on the locomotive frame inside each of the two cab sections. Connecting rods from cranks at each end of the motor armature drove a jackshaft, located between the guiding wheels and the first pair of drivers, which in turn drove the driving wheels by means of steam locomotive-type side rods. Weighing 136 tons and developing a maximum tractive effort of 36,000 pounds, the locomotive was equipped for both A.C. and D.C. operation and was designed for both freight and passenger service.

The New Haven found experimental unit 071 to be somewhat heavier than necessary and ordered a fourth unit of similar, but lighter construction. Delivered in 1911, No. 072 utilized the same running gear arrangement, cab design, and electrical equipment as 071, but was some 16 tons lighter.

Although all four New Haven experimentals were to have long service careers, their primary purpose was to test different ideas in electric-locomotive design. After extended testing the New Haven selected the best features of two of the ex-

ATTIRED in the standard engineer's cap of the time and displaying an appropriately serious countenance, a New Haven engineer grasped the controller of an EP-1 box-cab for a camera study around 1908.—*Library of Congress.*

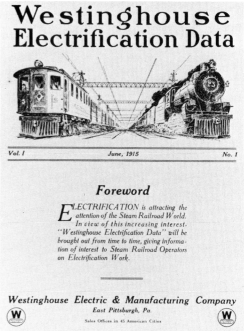

BOTH the New Haven and the Westinghouse company were intensely proud of the achievement represented by the railroad's electrification. For many years New Haven timetables featured an electric theme with a drawing that showed the view over the engineer's shoulder (top); the imaginative steam-versus-electric scene (above) appeared on a number of Westinghouse publications.—*Top, collection of Donald O'Hanley; above, collection of Donald Duke.*

perimental designs for its second large fleet of electric motive power. The resulting design employed the mechanical arrangement of No. 072 and the twin-motor gear-and-quill drive of locomotive No. 069. Thirty-nine units of the new design were ordered from Baldwin-Westinghouse for delivery during 1912 and 1913. The first three were equipped for A.C. or D.C. operation in either freight or passenger service, while the remainder, identified as Class EF-1, were equipped for A.C. operation in freight service only. The passenger version of the new design weighed 118.5 tons while freight units weighed just under 110 tons. Rated hourly horsepower for both types was 1600 h.p. Freight units were held to a maximum safe speed of 45 mph, while passenger units were geared for a maximum speed of slightly over 60 mph.

For electrification of its freight-yard operations, the railroad ordered 16 large steeple-cab locomotives, which were delivered from Baldwin-Westinghouse during 1911 and 1912. Weighing almost 80 tons, they developed a maximum tractive effort of 46,000 pounds. A double-truck articulated running gear was used, with a 163 h.p. traction motor driving each of the four axles through a geared quill drive. The switchers were equipped for A.C. operation from overhead catenary only since all freight yards were in New Haven's own A.C. territory.

Simultaneously with the locomotive develop-

ment program, work went ahead on extension of the railroad's electrified territory. The first addition to the initial electrification had been completed in 1908 when the short, 8-mile Stamford-New Canaan branch was converted to 11,000-volt A.C. power supply from the 600-volt D.C. trolley system installed in 1901. The six-track, 11-mile

THE New Haven began to acquire multiple-unit cars for its growing suburban service in 1909. The original M.U.'s, built by the Standard Steel Car Company, were distinguished from subsequent car orders by open platforms. The six-car train was photographed on a section of line near Glenbrook, Conn., which was equipped around 1909 with an experimental system of compound catenary supported by arch-shaped bents. Although no further overhead of this type was built, the design included many features later adopted for the remainder of the New Haven's mainline electrification as well as that of the New York, Westchester & Boston.—*Penn Central.*

(RIGHT) New Haven No. 069 was one of four experimental locomotives built by Baldwin-Westinghouse in 1910 and 1911. Although the locomotive's unusual girder side-frame design was not duplicated, No. 069 was the first locomotive to use the twin-motor gear-and-quill drive that subsequently was employed in virtually every New Haven electric locomotive until the advent of the GE rectifier units in the mid-1950's. The unique experimental operated in freight service for several decades.—*Theodore A. Martin.*

ANOTHER of the experimental locomotives was No. 070, built by Baldwin-Westinghouse. The articulated, side-rod-drive locomotive was similar in its mechanical arrangement to the Pennsylvania's DD1's. Connecting rods between the jack-shafts and the driving wheels had not yet been installed when this photograph was taken. Although the design was not repeated, the locomotive was successful enough to remain in service for a number of years. No. 070 originally was equipped for A.C. and D.C. operation, but later it was stripped of its D.C. gear and train-heating boiler and assigned to freight service.—*Collection of H. L. Broadbelt.*

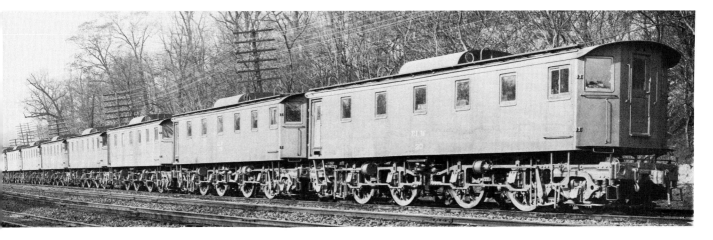

THE design for the New Haven's 110-ton, 1600 h.p. Class EF-1 box-cab freight motors was derived from the railroad's locomotive test program of 1910 and 1911. The locomotives had a 1-B+B-1 wheel arrangement and employed the twin-motor gear-and-quill drive which was to become virtually standard for all New Haven electric locomotives that followed. Ten units (above) were lined up after completion by the Baldwin Locomotive Works and before installation of their Westinghouse equipment. The front-end design (right) was strictly utilitarian. —*Above, collection of H. L. Broadbelt; right, Penn Central.*

ALTHOUGH one of the EF-1's is pulling a passenger train on the New Haven's main line, the class was intended for freight service, because neither train-heating boilers nor third-rail D.C. apparatus for operation into Grand Central Terminal were provided. Three almost-identical units classed as experimentals were equipped for passenger service.—*Collection of Charles B. Chaney, from the Smithsonian Institution.*

CLASS EF-1 freight motor No. 087 performs its accustomed task, hauling tonnage down the Harlem River line to the car floats at Oak Point in the Bronx.—*Collection of Charles B. Chaney, from the Smithsonian Institution.*

THE New Haven electrified its freight yards during 1911 and 1912 with 16 B+B steeple-cab switchers. Baldwin-Westinghouse-built No. 0200 (right), first of the series, weighed nearly 80 tons and developed a maximum tractive effort of 40,000 pounds.—*Smithsonian Institution.*

SWITCHER 0213 makes up a train in one of the New Haven's electrified yards. The untiring Baldwin-Westinghouse units regularly worked three full shifts every day and accumulated as many as 4500 miles a month. The original 16 switchers were supplemented by six more steeple-cabs built in 1927.—*Smithsonian Institution.*

Harlem River branch, which carried heavy freight and suburban passenger traffic between New Haven's Harlem River terminal at 138th Street in the Bronx and a junction with the main line at New Rochelle, began operating with electric power in July 1912. By June 1914 trains were running under catenary to New Haven, and a year later the A.C. wire was hot all the way through New Haven to Cedar Hill freight yard on the east side of the city at the junction between the New Haven's Shore Line and its New Haven-Springfield (Mass.) line. Freight yards at Stamford, Westchester, Harlem River, and Oak Point were electrified. The Oak Point yard in the Bronx, where New Haven interchanged freight traffic by car float with most of the principal eastern railroads, had 35 miles of track under catenary.

Unlike the original electrification between Woodlawn and Stamford, which employed the New Haven's novel triangular cross-section catenary, the subsequent installations used several compound-catenary systems of more conventional design. Fourteen new water-tube boilers and four additional 5000 kilovolt-ampere steam-turbine-powered generating units were added to the Cos Cob generating plant, increasing the station's total generating capacity to 35,400 kilovolt-amperes. The original power supply arrangement, under which 11,000 volts had been fed direct to the distribution system from the generators, was replaced by a 22,000-volt power supply system which reduced line losses over the longer distances. Transformers at the Cos Cob plant stepped up the power to 22,000 volts for distribution, while substations along the electrified lines reduced it to 11,000 volts for the contact wire. To supplement the Cos Cob supply, a 15,000-kilovolt-ampere substation supplied by the New York Edison Company was built at West Farms on the Harlem River branch.

EVEN as the New Haven proceeded with further electrification in the New York suburban area, the railroad embarked on an extraordinary project: the construction and electrification of an entirely new suburban railway, the New York, Westchester & Boston, serving much of the same Westchester County territory already served by New Haven lines or by the New York Central's Harlem Division.

The Westchester adventure was but one of a series of bold, expansionist moves that had characterized the New Haven since it had come under the control of financier J. P. Morgan in 1891. In scarcely two decades of Morgan management the New Haven grew from a relatively short, if highly prosperous, railroad linking New York and principal Connecticut points to a great transportation

system of nearly 10,000 miles operating throughout most of New England. Through merger or control, the New Haven held a virtual monopoly of the region's principal railroads. The principal steamship lines operating between New York and points in Connecticut, Rhode Island, and Massachusetts were brought under New Haven control, and by 1910 the railroad owned approximately 90 per cent of New England water transportation. In just a few years, between about 1904 and 1907, the New Haven invested something on the order of 120 million dollars to acquire control of virtually all the trolley lines in Connecticut, Rhode Island, and a large part of Massachusetts.

Much of this New Haven acquisition of rival transportation properties was the result of a Morgan predilection to avoid competition by eliminating it. Such was the case with the Westchester line. Incorporated in 1872, the New York, Westchester & Boston had spent nearly 30 years in receivership and never had built so much as a mile of line when it came to the New Haven's attention. Motivated by optimistic estimates of the road's suburban traffic potential and the need for relieving the growing burden of suburban traffic on the New Haven main line and Grand Central Terminal, as well as by the threat of the line's eventual construction through Danbury to Boston in competition with the New Haven, Morgan acquired control of the Westchester in 1907 in what would prove to be one of the most costly of New Haven's expansion projects. More than 14 million dollars were spent on the acquisition even before construction started. Just where the money went in that era of free-wheeling high finance is unknown to this day. By the time the first 12 miles of the Westchester opened in 1912, its construction had cost another 22.3 million dollars, more than 1.25 million dollars a mile.

Construction of the Westchester began in late 1909. The line was built to engineering standards no less demanding than those for the New Haven main line itself. Along its entire length the line was grade separated from roads or other railroads. Concrete or steel structures included three viaducts (one of them 2100 feet long), a 3940-foot subway tunnel, 43 bridges, and 23 highway overpasses. Stations and signal towers were almost all of concrete construction, with Spanish Mission or Italian Renaissance architecture predominating in the station designs. High-level platforms were built at all stations, except at a few Harlem River line stations used jointly with the New Haven. Curvature, gradients, and the track structure were suitable for high-speed operation.

From the Harlem River terminal shared with New Haven, the Westchester operated over the

TRAINS of the New Haven's subsidiary New York, Westchester & Boston operated from a Harlem River terminal at 133rd Street, where passengers made connections for Manhattan points via the trains of the Third Avenue El. A two-car train departs for Port Chester, N.Y., 21 miles distant, on October 31, 1937, two months before the Westchester was abandoned.—*George E. Votava.*

(BELOW LEFT) Westchester traffic never reached the grand level originally anticipated, and throughout its life one-car trains were adequate for off-peak schedules. A single car rolls along the four-track, rock-ballasted right of way north of 180th Street in the Bronx in 1933.—*A. P. Formanek.*

AT Westchester Avenue the NYW&B shared a massive six-track drawbridge over the Bronx River with the New Haven's Harlem River line. The two-car train in this 1937 photograph is southbound from New Rochelle, N.Y.—*George E. Votava.*

(BELOW CENTER) North of Mount Vernon, N.Y., the White Plains and Port Chester lines of the NYW&B were double track. Coach No. 101, one of the Westchester's original cars, heads north to White Plains, N.Y., through the rock cut at Wykagyl in December of 1937.—*George E. Votava.*

(BELOW) A single 80-ton locomotive was sufficient to handle freight traffic throughout the Westchester's history. Motor No. 701, shown at Mount Vernon Junction, N.Y., in 1937 with a freight for White Plains, became New Haven No. 224 after the NYW&B was abandoned.—*George E. Votava.*

tracks of New Haven's Harlem River branch for a distance of not quite 4 miles to 174th Street, where its own four-track main line began. A double-track branch extended from a junction at Columbus Avenue in Mount Vernon to White Plains, a total distance of 19.5 miles from the Harlem River, while the main line, reduced to two tracks, ran eastward to New Rochelle. Passengers reached Manhattan by changing to elevated or subway lines at any one of several interchange points between 180th Street and the Harlem River terminal.

The Westchester adopted an 11,000-volt, single-phase A.C. system almost identical to that of the New Haven main line. Design and installation of the Westchester facility, in fact, were performed by the New Haven under the direction of its engineer in charge of electric traction, P. J. Kearney. Power was supplied from the New Haven's Cos Cob power plant through a connection at New Rochelle, and the Westchester's overhead catenary was patterned after that being installed on the New Haven's Harlem River line electrification.

The Pressed Steel Car Company built an initial 30 multiple-unit passenger cars for the Westchester. Constructed entirely of steel, the cars were 72 feet ¾ inches long, weighed 60 tons, and seated 78 passengers. A single motor truck on each car was powered by two Westinghouse A.C. traction motors with an hourly rating of 175 h.p. each, providing sufficient power for a 1-mph-per-second acceleration rate and a top speed of 57 mph. A lone 80-ton locomotive, identical to the New Haven's new switching units, was supplied by Baldwin-Westinghouse for the Westchester's limited freight traffic.

The first section of the Westchester began regular operation on May 29, 1912, and the entire railway was operating by August 10. Between 1921 and 1929 the New Rochelle line was extended 8 miles to Port Chester. The double-track extension was laid alongside the New Haven main line, and the Westchester shared stations with its parent road at four of the eight stops on the extension. Between 1915 and 1928, 65 more multiple-unit passenger cars, identical except for minor refinements to the line's original equipment, were supplied by Pressed Steel Car and Osgood Bradley.

If the New York, Westchester & Boston was an engineering triumph, the railroad was a business disaster. Although considerable suburban traffic was diverted from the New Haven main line and from the New York Central's Harlem Division by the Westchester's much lower fares, the electric line developed neither the volume of business that had been forecast by its developers nor the volume its generous design standards would have accommodated. In 1913, its first full year of operation,

the Westchester carried 2,874,484 passengers and even in 1928, one of its best years, only 14,053,188 passengers rode the line, far fewer than the 100 million annual volume the line was said to be capable of handling. Single-car locals and two-car express trains generally sufficed for the line's traffic, and even during rush hours, four-car trains usually were ample.

In its first three years of full operation, from 1913 to 1915, the Westchester lost $4,354,000, and never once in the 25 years it operated did the line pay even its interest charges. Traffic fell after the beginning of the depression; by the mid-1930's traffic was down to 26,000 daily passengers from a 1928 level of 43,000. In 1935 the Westchester followed its parent New Haven into bankruptcy. Without New Haven help in meeting annual losses of 2 to 3 million dollars, the Westchester quickly expired. The last trains ran on December 31, 1937. A little money was recouped by the sale of most of the line as scrap; the City of New York bought 4 miles of the line in the Bronx and extended elevated service over it; and the New Haven reclaimed the line's lone freight motor and 50 cars that it had purchased and leased to the Westchester.

The venture had been a costly one for the New Haven. In financing the Westchester's construction and in meeting its losses, the New Haven had managed to lose close to 50 million dollars in one of the most ill-favored projects of the Morgan years.

EVEN as it lavished money on the unfortunate Westchester scheme, the New Haven proceeded with another expansion and electrification project that was to have far more lasting and beneficial results. As far back as 1892, the Pennsylvania Railroad's Samuel Rea had suggested an East River bridge and tunnel scheme that would provide a direct link with the New Haven for New England traffic. The connection was then being made either by a circuitous all-rail route via the New Haven's Poughkeepsie Bridge on the Hudson River, or by a time-consuming 14-mile car-float transfer across New York Harbor, which operated between the Pennsy's terminal at Greenville, on the New Jersey

IN a world that still was awed by each new technological triumph, the plans of the New Haven and the Pennsylvania for the 27-million-dollar Hell Gate Bridge project that would link New England with points south and west of New York City were received with appropriate wonderment. Readers of the September 18, 1909, issue of *Harper's Weekly* were treated to this aerial view of the proposed project drawn by artist Vernon Howe Bailey. A long, massive viaduct carried the New York Connecting Railroad's four-track line over Randall's Island, Little Hell Gate, and Ward's Island, and the great steel arch itself spanned the turbulent waters of Hell Gate to carry the rails to Long Island City and the Pennsylvania's East River tunnels. Electric traction, of course, made it all possible.—*Collection of William D. Middleton.*

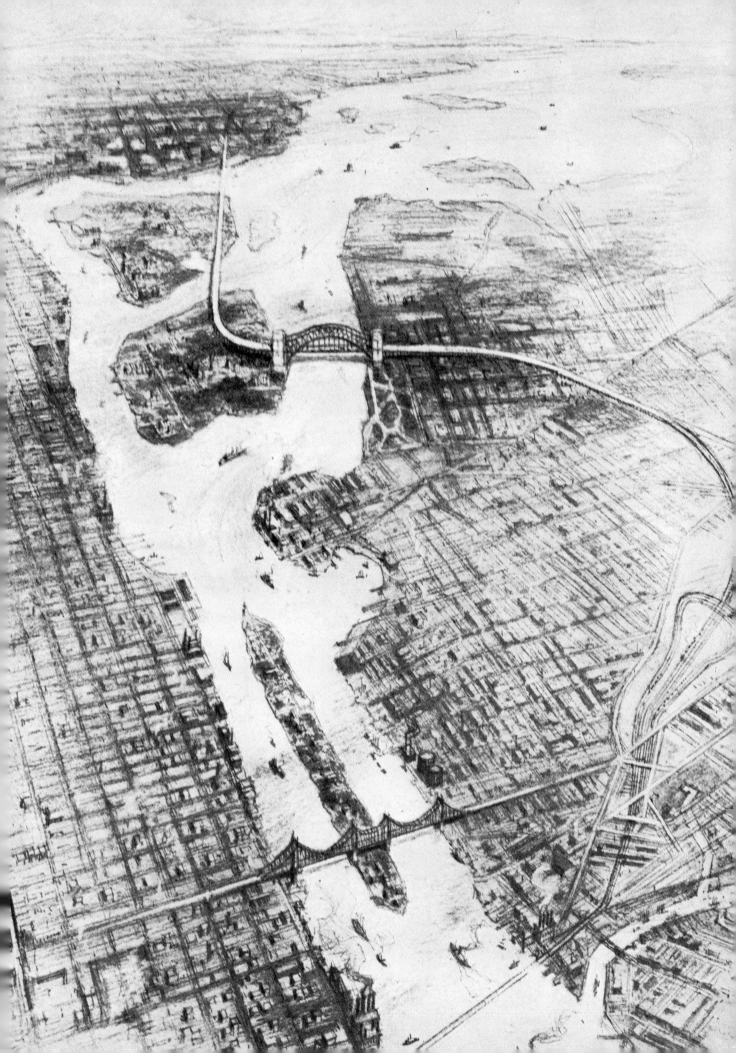

GUSTAV LINDENTHAL'S steel arch reaching 977 feet across Hell Gate was one of the engineering triumphs of its time, and even today the bridge is one of the wonders of New York City. This view looks northwest toward Ward's and Randall's islands.—*Electric Railroaders' Association.*

shore, and the New Haven's Harlem River line at Port Morris, N. Y.

Although the New York Connecting Rail Road (later Railroad) was organized in 1892 to construct an East River bridge at Hell Gate that would link the New Haven with the Long Island Rail Road, nothing came of Rea's idea until after 1900, when the Pennsylvania began its own New York terminal scheme. The Pennsy's project would bring tracks under the Hudson to the new Pennsylvania Station in Manhattan and then under the East River to a direct link with the Long Island Rail Road at Long Island City. In 1902 the New Haven and the Pennsylvania jointly acquired the stock of the New York Connecting and by 1912 had started construction of the project, which would connect the New Haven from a point near Port Morris on the Harlem River line to the Pennsylvania at Harold Avenue in Long Island City.

The New York Connecting Railroad cost 27 million dollars and stood as a remarkable engineering achievement. A high, curving viaduct carried the four-track line across Ward's and Randall's islands. Included in the structure were two 175-foot spans over the Bronx Kill and a bridge nearly 1200 feet

KNOWN as the "Bull Moose," No. 068 was an experimental freight locomotive built by General Electric in 1916. The locomotive operated for a number of years but remained a one-of-a-kind on the New Haven's roster.—*General Electric.*

FROM the time the New York Connecting Railroad was electrified in 1927 until well after World War II, the New Haven's workhorse EF-1 freight motors were a familiar sight on the route over Hell Gate Bridge to the car floats at Bay Ridge in Brooklyn. Two of the sturdy box-cabs were capable of taking half again as much tonnage over the 1.2 per cent maximum grade on the Hell Gate approaches as the heavy J-2 Mikados that they replaced. Four EF-1's led by No. 0111 accelerate a heavy eastbound train on the Long Island Rail Road-owned section of the Bay Ridge line at New Lots Avenue in 1943. The third-rail-equipped trackage at the lower right also belongs to LIRR.—*H. Fagerberg.*

NORTHBOUND with a Washington-Boston express, an EP-2-class locomotive crosses the Hell Gate Bridge some time in the mid-1920's. No. 0308 was part of the second order for a dozen EP-2's delivered by Baldwin-Westinghouse in 1923 and 1924.—*Collection of Donald Duke.*

A NEW class of passenger locomotives was added to the New Haven roster in 1919 with the arrival of five 1-C-1+1-C-1's such as No. 0303 from Baldwin-Westinghouse. The 69-foot, 175-ton locomotives were classified EP-2.—*Collection of Edward T. Francis.*

(ABOVE) Racing toward New York in 1933 with an express, most likely the *Mayflower*, EP-2 No. 0323 sprints along west of Stamford at close to its 70-mph top speed, its pantograph neatly framed for an instant by a pair of the New Haven's distinctive round-ended, left-handed semaphores. No. 0323, built by Baldwin-Westinghouse in 1927, was part of the third and final order for 10 EP-2's.—*Bruce D. Fales.*

UNLIKE all of the New Haven's earlier electric motive power, which employed series commutator motors capable of operation on either A.C. or D.C., seven General Electric locomotives delivered in 1926 used motor-generator sets and low-voltage D.C. traction motors. No. 0112 (above left) was one of five Class EF-2 1-B+B-1 freight locomotives. No. 0217 (left) was one of a pair of similarly equipped Class EY-3 switchers. Although the units served for many years, the New Haven later reverted to series commutator motors. —*Both photos, General Electric.*

THE New Haven's roster included more than 160 standard steel M.U. motor cars and trailers, most of which lasted more than 40 years in regular service. On a July afternoon in 1955 a train of them paused at New Rochelle on the way to Grand Central. The Y-shaped catenary is an interesting variation on New Haven's distinctive overhead; the theater poster is typical of New York-area suburban stations. —Paul J. Dolkos.

long across the Little Hell Gate. Designed by the noted bridge engineer Gustav Lindenthal, the Hell Gate Bridge itself was a massive steel arch structure of unprecedented dimensions. With a clear span of 977 feet 6 inches and a clearance of 135 feet above mean high water, it was longer and heavier than any previous arch bridge. Because of the turbulent Hell Gate currents and navigational requirements, it was impossible to use falsework for the construction and the great arch was built outward from its piers supported by huge temporary backstays until the two sections were brought together at the center. On the Long Island side of the bridge, the tracks were carried on a long steel-and-concrete elevated structure almost to the point where they joined the Pennsylvania.

The "Hell Gate Bridge Route" was opened for passenger service on April 1, 1917. By the end of the year the New York Connecting was joined to the Long Island's Bay Ridge line, affording direct access between the New Haven and a new car-float terminal at Bay Ridge that was only 3½ miles across New York Harbor from the Pennsylvania's Greenville terminal.

The new route was operated with steam power initially, but early in 1918 the passenger-train route was electrified with 11,000-volt A.C. catenary all the way to the junction with Pennsy third rail at Harold Avenue. Freight trains continued to run

behind steam until 1927, when the New York Connecting and the Long Island completed the installation of 11,000-volt A.C. catenary to Bay Ridge. Freight trains ran through to Bay Ridge from New Haven's Cedar Hill Yard behind New Haven motive power, while the Long Island acquired 14 79-ton, 570 h.p. electric locomotives for switching and transfer service.

Expansion of its electrification necessitated still more electric motive power for the New Haven. General Electric got a chance to break the Baldwin-Westinghouse monopoly of the New Haven's electric motive-power roster in 1916, when the Schenectady (N. Y.) firm landed a contract for a 145-ton experimental freight locomotive. Known informally as "Bull Moose," GE No. 068 consisted of two units, each with a four-wheel leading truck and four 54-inch driving wheels. Four 450 h.p. motors powered the driving wheels through a gear and side-rod drive. The design was not successful, and the locomotive was withdrawn from service after several years.

The New Haven returned to the Baldwin-Westinghouse team for its next locomotive order. Five EP-2 passenger units ordered in 1919 were enlarged versions of the successful freight and passenger units bought during 1912 and 1913. Length was increased to 69 feet, and one pair of driving wheels and a trailing axle were added to each of the two

GENERAL ELECTRIC finally achieved a major motive-power success on the New Haven in 1931 with its design for 10 Class EP-3 passenger locomotives. The EP-3's combined the 2-C+C-2 wheel arrangement developed by GE for the Cleveland Union Terminal electrics with the New Haven's time-tested twin-motor geared-quill drive. The 77-foot-long locomotives weighed 202 tons and had a continuous rating of 3000 h.p. They established a basic configuration for a heavy high-speed electric locomotive that was employed for several more orders of New Haven electrics as well as for the Pennsylvania's GG1. No. 0351 (above), first of the series, stands outside the builder's plant at Erie, Pa., for its official photograph. No. 0354 (below), the very locomotive that the Pennsy borrowed for the test program that led to the GG1, races through West Haven, Conn., with the eight cars of the Boston-to-Washington *Colonial.—Above, General Electric; below, H. W. Pontin.*

SIX Class EP-4 passenger locomotives built by General Electric in 1938 were almost identical to the EP-3's mechanically but had a streamlined carbody. At 216 tons and 3600 h.p. they were somewhat heavier and more powerful than their box-cab predecessors. In the view at the left the six locomotives are under construction at GE's Erie works. In the foreground the frame of one of them displays the twin motors on each driving axle and the articulated joint at the center. Beyond the farthest EP-4 and obscured by a nose section for one of the electrics hanging from a crane is one unit of GE's steam-turbine-electric of 1939.—*Above, General Electric; left, Smithsonian Institution.*

MOVING UP fast on the outside track, an EP-4 and its passenger train overtakes a brace of laboring EF-1's pulling a freight on the curve at Glenbrook, just east of Stamford, in the early 1940's.—*James D. Bennett.*

THE third and final order for 10 2-C+C-2 locomotives for the New Haven was divided between General Electric and Westinghouse in 1942 and 1943. Although they were similar in appearance to the EP-4's of 1938, the EF-3's weighed 30 tons more, were equipped for A.C. operation only, and normally were used only in freight service. In 1948 train-heating boilers were added to the five Westinghouse units, 150-154, permitting them to operate in passenger service on A.C.-only routes, such as New York (Penn Station)-New Haven. No. 0150 (above left) was one of the Westinghouse EF-3b's, and No. 0155 (above right), shown near Port Chester in May 1943, was the first of the five GE-built EF-3a's.—*Above left, Westinghouse Electric Corporation; above right, General Electric.*

articulated trucks, giving the new design a 1-C-1+1-C-1 wheel arrangement. The same type of traction motor and twin-motor geared quill drive were employed. Developing an hourly rating of 2460 h.p. and a maximum tractive effort of almost 50,000 pounds, the new units had a safe speed limit of 70 mph. Subsequent orders between 1923 and 1927 increased the class to 27 units.

General Electric got a second chance at the New Haven's electric locomotive business in 1926, when the railroad ordered five 1-B+B-1 freight units. The box-cab units weighed 141 tons and were rated at 1350 h.p. GE delivered a pair of 500 h.p. B+B switchers at the same time. Although similar to the New Haven's previous Baldwin-Westinghouse freight power in wheel arrangement, all seven locomotives employed a radically different electrical and mechanical configuration that was favored by GE as a means of combining the advantages of A.C. transmission with those of D.C. traction motors. A large motor-generator set within the carbody converted the New Haven's 11,000-volt, single-phase current to direct current which was supplied to low-voltage D.C. traction motors geared to each driving axle. All seven units operated for more than two decades, but the motor-generator arrangement was not repeated in later New Haven electrics. In fact, for a six-locomotive switcher order in 1927, the New Haven bought 90-ton units from Baldwin-Westinghouse that were

virtual duplicates of those delivered during 1911 and 1912.

General Electric finally displaced Westinghouse as the New Haven's prime electric-motive-power supplier in 1931, when the railroad bought 10 Class EP-3 passenger units that utilized the 2-C+C-2 wheel arrangement employed by GE two years before on its highly successful locomotives for the New York Central's Cleveland Union Terminal electrification. A dozen A.C. traction motors, arranged in the New Haven's favored twin-motor geared quill drive, gave the locomotives a rating of 3440 h.p. and a maximum tractive effort of 68,500 pounds. The box-cab units weighed almost 202 tons and were capable of a maximum safe speed of 80 mph.

Six more GE units, delivered in 1938 and designated as EP-4's, were similar to the EP-3's except for an increase in weight to 216 tons and the adoption of a streamlined carbody. Baldwin-Westinghouse received one last New Haven motive-power order during World War II, when the builder divided an order with GE for 10 Class EF-3 streamlined freight units that were delivered during 1942 and 1943. Although similar in appearance and arrangement to the EP-4 passenger units, the EF-3's were equipped for operation with A.C. power only. Weighing 246 tons and rated at 4860 h.p., the EF-3's had a maximum tractive effort of 90,000 pounds.

THE New Haven's main inspection and heavy overhaul point for electric motive power was the extensive Van Nest shops in the Bronx. EF-1 No. 083 is surrounded by a variety of disassembled trucks and motors in this 1938 view of the main shop floor.—*Charles A. Schrade.*

The New Haven's last orders for new electric motive power were placed during the mid-1950's. In 1954 Pullman-Standard built a fleet of 100 stainless-steel, air-conditioned, multiple-unit suburban cars which replaced 150 of the New Haven's original M.U. cars. The new cars were more than 86 feet long and seated 120 passengers in the coach version. Four 100 h.p. motors provided a 1-mph-per-second acceleration rate and a top speed of 80 mph. A year later General Electric delivered 10 Class EP-5 passenger locomotives. The locomotives had a C-C wheel arrangement, weighed 174 tons, and developed a maximum tractive effort of 87,000 pounds. Rated at 4000 h.p., they were allowed a maximum speed of 90 mph.

Both the 100 new M.U. cars and the 10 EP-5 lo-

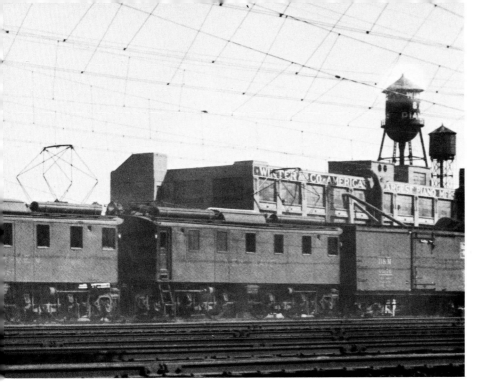

THREE of the New Haven's durable EF-1's head eastbound tonnage up the Harlem River line at Oak Point around 1940. From the time of its completion in 1917 until the late 1960's the New York Connecting Railroad and the Harlem River line formed one of the principal freight routes between New England and points south and west of New York.—*H. W. Pontin.*

THE EP-1 box-cab passenger motors, the first high-speed single-phase units built in America, remained in regular service as late as the end of World War II. Two of them, 016 and 030, head a New York-bound train near Stamford on the New Canaan branch in the 1940's.—*James D. Bennett.*

comotives employed ignitron rectifiers, which converted A.C. power to low-voltage D.C. far more efficiently than had GE's motor-generator experimentals of the 1920's, and permitted the use of more efficient D.C. traction motors.

Completion of the Bay Ridge electrification in 1927, together with a 24-mile electrification of the South Norwalk-Danbury (Conn.) line in 1925, marked the end of New Haven electrification expansion. For all that it had accomplished in putting one of America's most heavily trafficked main lines under wire, the New Haven fell far short of the expansive electrification goals that it once had held. As early as 1912 the company had announced a 7-million-dollar electrification and four-tracking project for the 44 miles of line between Boston and

AN EP-2 leads a train south over the New York Central's Harlem River drawbridge. Ahead is Grand Central; immediately behind the train is 138th Street station. The swing span was replaced in the early 1950's with a vertical lift bridge.—*New York Central.*

Providence, R. I., that would have placed 116 miles of the 229-mile New York-Boston main line under electric operation. At the time, eventual electrification of the entire Shore Line Route seemed assured.

New Haven's inability to extend electrification east of New Haven largely was owed to the railroad's worsening financial situation resulting from the extravagant diversions of the Morgan era. By 1913 the railroad's debt load had increased more than four-fold in scarcely a decade, the value of its stock had fallen by 75 per cent, and the losses of its unprofitable ventures were running to several million dollars a year. In 1913 — for the first time in 40 years — the New Haven passed a dividend. Never again would the New Haven be able to undertake projects of the magnitude required to achieve the dream of 11,000-volt A.C. catenary stretching unbroken from New York to Boston.

If it failed to achieve all of its original goals, the New Haven's pioneer A.C. electrification was a remarkable engineering accomplishment that was surpassed in scale among American railroad electrifications only by the Milwaukee Road's Pacific Extension electrification and the great Pennsylvania Railroad program of the 1930's.

Including the Westchester and the New York Connecting, the New Haven operated well over 600 miles of track under 11,000-volt A.C. catenary, and the traffic moved by electric traction was enormous. In 1924, for example, New Haven and its Westchester subsidiary hauled close to 2 million passengers into or out of New York every month, most of them during the two daily rush hours. Electric-powered freight trains moved in excess of 150 million ton-miles of freight every month. All told, the great New Haven electrification consumed 140 million kilowatt-hours of electric power

PANTOGRAPHS locked down and third-rail shoes picking up 600-volt direct current, EP-4 No. 365 thunders through Woodlawn station on New York Central's Harlem Division with a long eastbound express on a June afternoon in 1954. In a mile or so the train will swing east onto New Haven rails for the trip up the Shore Line to Boston. Summertime traffic has added a heavyweight parlor car to an otherwise all-stainless-steel consist.—*Herbert H. Harwood Jr.*

NO. 360, originally No. 0366, is on the inside track at Cos Cob, Conn., with an eastbound train. In the late 1940's, EP-3 No. 0360 was renumbered 0350 and EP-4 No. 0366 became 0360. In 1952 with the demise of steam, the leading zeros were dropped from the numbers of the New Haven's electric and diesel-electric locomotives.—*Jim Shaughnessy.*

annually to transport almost 2½ billion gross ton-miles of freight and passenger traffic.

Aided by the powerful new EP-4 and EF-3 locomotives, the New Haven's electrification carried the load of an enormous traffic increase during the World War II years. By 1944 New Haven freight traffic had almost doubled from the level of the mid-1920's, while passenger traffic had increased by more than 100 per cent. In 1945, even without the Westchester, New Haven's passenger traffic into or out of New York approached 36 million passengers, almost twice the number of 1924. Meas-

ured in terms of electrical energy required — 285 million kilowatt-hours in 1944 — the New Haven electrification carried a wartime traffic that was close to double the previous peaks of the 1920's.

Unprecedented in scale, and unequaled in the boldness of its innovation, the New Haven's pioneering A.C. installation was the proving ground for an electrification system and technology that endured as industry standards for close to half a century. It fulfilled every demand placed upon it and still is in regular operation nearly seven decades after its construction began.

(RIGHT) Three generations of New Haven electric passenger locomotives wait for assignments on the ready track at New Haven in September 1955. At the left is EP-2 No. 325, built by Baldwin-Westinghouse in 1927. In the center is EP-4 No. 364, outshopped by General Electric in 1938. At the right is EP-3 No. 352, GE class of 1931. —*Jim Shaughnessy.*

(LEFT) With a train of the New Haven's distinctive streamlined Pullman-built rolling stock, EP-4 No. 0360 rolls eastward through New Rochelle Junction in April 1949. The train is on the main line, which connects with the New York Central's Harlem Division at Woodlawn. The tracks of NH's Harlem River line in the foreground lead to Hell Gate Bridge.—*J. J. Farwell.*

(BELOW LEFT) An EP-4 awaits departure time at New Haven, Conn., while carmen, their lanterns bobbing, couple the air and steam lines. The flank of the big electric is bathed in the glow of the headlight of a train on the adjacent track. The year is 1960. —*Jim Shaughnessy.*

(BELOW) The 10 EF-4's were by a wide margin the most powerful electric motive power ever operated by the New Haven. Westinghouse-built No. 150, rated at 4860 h.p., rumbles west through Stamford with tonnage on its drawbar in 1957.—*Jim Shaughnessy.*

THE inlets and rivers along the Connecticut shore of Long Island Sound are spanned by more than a dozen major bridges along the New Haven's scenic Shore Line route. One of the largest is the Mianus River drawbridge at Cos Cob, Conn. For clearance reasons there is a gap in the catenary across the movable span; therefore the pantograph of the lead car of this eastbound M.U. train momentarily is reaching for empty air.—*Fred W. Schneider III.*

PULLMAN-STANDARD built 100 stylish ignitron-rectifier M.U. cars for the New Haven in 1954 at its Worcester (Mass.) plant. The order comprised 89 coaches, 7 baggage-coach combines, and 4 club cars for rental to commuter clubs. The exteriors of the new M.U.'s were corrugated stainless steel; amenities included blue plush seats in 3-2 configuration, air conditioning, and fluorescent lighting.—*Penn Central.*

(RIGHT) Crossing above the rails of the former New York Central's Harlem Division which it shortly will join, a Stamford-Grand Central M.U. train approaches the junction at Woodlawn. The train has just left the ex-New Haven A.C. catenary, the pantographs have been lowered, and the cars are drawing 600-volt D.C. from the third rail. When the photograph was taken on May 23, 1970, both railroads had become part of the Penn Central, and the lead car already bore PC's "mating worms" logo.—*Fred W. Schneider III.*

A COMBINE is in the lead as train 1908, a Grand Central-to-New Haven local, rolls across the Wepawaug River at Milford, Conn., on October 17, 1970. The M.U.'s originally had dark green ends, and Penn Central's livery was similar. In the 1960's, though, the car ends bore the black, white, and vermilion colors that were adopted by the New Haven during the presidency of Patrick McGinnis.—*William D. Middleton.*

TWO small boys watch from the bank of the Wepawaug River as GG1 No. 4890 heads the Washington-Boston *Colonial* through Milford in November 1970. With the inclusion of the New Haven in the Penn Central merger, GG1's began operating between New York and New Haven, eliminating the engine change at Penn Station and displacing the New Haven's much newer EP-5's.—*William D. Middleton.*

(RIGHT) The New Haven's final order for electric locomotives represented a radical departure from its previous locomotive designs. Ignitron rectifiers converted the A.C. from the overhead wire to direct current, and low-voltage D.C. traction motors were mounted on the axles in a C-C arrangement similar to diesel-electric locomotive practice. The EP-5's brought a note of flamboyance to the appearance of the New Haven's roster, introducing the McGinnis-designed paint scheme of black, white, and vermilion. No. 379 stands on the ready track at New Haven next to a 1931-built EP-3 in May 1960.—*Jim Shaughnessy.*

(RIGHT) During the late 1950's the New Haven was faced with a fleet of aging passenger diesels and an electrification that needed major overhaul. To solve the railroad's problem, Electro-Motive designed and built the FL9, a diesel-electric that also could operate as a straight electric, drawing current from New York Central's third rail in Grand Central, where only electric operation was permitted by law. With the coming of the FL9's, only the EP-5's and the M.U. cars remained in service, diesels assumed all freight duties, and predictions were rife that the catenary east of Stamford would be dismantled. One of the hybrid diesel-electric-electrics stands next to EP-5 No. 379 at New Haven in 1960.—*Jim Shaughnessy.*

ON its electrified single-track branches the New Haven sometimes conveyed the feeling of a rural interurban. The one-car shuttle that worked the Stamford-New Canaan branch stopped briefly to let off a pretty girl at Talmadge Hill, Conn., in October 1970.—*Fred W. Schneider III.*

FOURTEEN years of service, a number of them with red ink on its owner's ledgers, have taken their toll of the glossy paint on the flanks of EP-5 No. 376, shown crossing the Naugatuck River at Westport, Conn., with New Haven-bound train 606 in May 1969.—*Fred W. Schneider III.*

TRAILING a consist of heavyweight Pullmans (an overnight extra from Boston), rectifier electric No. 373 glides through Rye, N.Y., early on an August morning in 1959. The engineer has lowered the pantograph to coast past a highway overpass construction site.—*Don Ball.*

PENN CENTRAL train 171, the Boston-to-Washington *Colonial,* roars through Stratford, Conn., behind GG1 No. 4893 on October 17, 1970. Inclusion of the New Haven in the PC merger helped preserve an electrification that had come close to dismantling a decade before.—*William D. Middleton.*

IT'S early morning in Harlem as an inbound New Haven M.U. train meets an outbound train pulled by an EP-5 just south of the New York Central's Harlem River drawbridge. Clearly visible on top of No. 371 are the small D.C. pantograph and the Hancock air whistle; the locomotive is drawing power from the third rail and the A.C. pans are locked down. The cylindrical object just behind the pantograph on the roof of the M.U. car is a lightning arrestor.—*David Plowden.*

DISSATISFIED with the de-electrification of freight service during the late 1950's, the New Haven acquired ex-Virginian rectifier freight locomotives from the Norfolk & Western in 1963. Repainted vermilion, white, and black and classified EF-4, the former coal-haulers went to work pulling New Haven-New York freights. On an April morning in 1966 rectifier motors 308 and 307 accelerate New Haven-New York freight NG-1 out of Cedar Hill Yard.—*Stephen P. Buettner.*

AMTRAK'S *Southern Crescent* is just about at the midpoint of its journey from Boston to Washington as it crosses Hell Gate Bridge. In a few minutes the train will pause in Penn Station while coaches and sleepers to be forwarded to the Southern Railway at Washington are added to the train's consist. The graffito at the right must be one of the most inaccessible in New York City. —*Victor Hand.*

PENN CENTRAL GG1 No. 4897 rumbles across Hell Gate Bridge trailing the express cars, coaches, and parlor cars of the Washington-Boston *Senator* in May 1969.—*J. C. Smith Jr.*

UNDER the Amtrak banner, *Metroliners* turned up under former New Haven catenary during 1972. Led by Metroclub parlor car 885, a four-car New Haven-Washington *Metroliner* slowed for the station stop at Bridgeport, Conn., on a rainy day in June 1972.—*J. C. Smith Jr.*

RED-WHITE-AND-BLUE striped Metroliner cars heading toward Washington slice through the tranquility of a Sunday afternoon in July 1972 as they cross the Westport River at Westport. —*J. C. Smith Jr.*

COMMUTERS on the New Haven began riding a third generation of M.U. equipment in 1973 when the first of these M-2 Cosmopolitan cars went into service. Similar in appearance to the Long Island's Metropolitans, the 100-mph M-2's were built by General Electric's Erie plant, with carbodies supplied by Canadian Vickers. Ownership of the 144-car M-2 fleet was divided equally between the Connecticut Department of Transportation and New York's Metropolitan Transportation Authority. This two-car train was photographed at Greenwich, Conn., during tests in 1972.—*J. C. Smith Jr.*

EMERGING from the New Jersey portal of the Pennsylvania Railroad's twin tunnels under the Hudson River and Bergen Hill, DD1 No. 26 gathers speed for the dash across the Hackensack Meadows to Manhattan Transfer. The train is the 4 o'clock express to Philadelphia, and the date is June 22, 1913. The Pennsylvania's great New York terminal project has been complete for a little more than two and a half years.—*Charles B. Chaney, collection of the Smithsonian Institution.*

4. Under the rivers to Manhattan

EVEN as the New York Central began work on its New York suburban electrification project and its magnificent new Grand Central Terminal on 42nd Street, the rival Pennsylvania Railroad embarked upon an even greater New York terminal project of its own.

Of the railroads reaching New York City from the west, only the New York Central enjoyed direct access to a Manhattan terminal. All of the other lines were compelled to terminate their trains in New Jersey and rely upon Hudson River ferries to transport freight and passengers to and from Manhattan. The Pennsylvania Railroad, with its enormous passenger traffic, found the lack of a New York terminal an intolerable competitive dis-

advantage, and the company had considered a number of solutions to the problem from the early 1870's on.

One of the first serious attempts to replace the Hudson ferries was organized in 1873 by railroad builder and miner Dewitt Clinton Haskin, who began work in 1874 on a tunnel from Jersey City, N. J., to Manhattan. Legal problems soon halted the work, and five years elapsed before tunneling resumed. In 1880 an accident occurred that flooded the tunnel and 20 workers were drowned. Financial problems frequently interrupted the work, and construction went on intermittently for almost three decades before the tunnel finally was opened in 1908 as part of William Gibbs McAdoo's Hudson & Manhattan Railroad.

CHIEF ENGINEER for the Pennsylvania's New York terminal project was Samuel Rea. At the time a vice-president of the Pennsylvania, Rea ascended to the railroad's presidency in 1912 and served for a 13-year period that saw the beginning of what was to be the greatest of all North American railroad electrifications.—*Courtesy of Railroad Magazine.*

PRESIDENT of the Pennsylvania Railroad from 1899 to 1906, civil engineer Alexander Johnston Cassatt initiated the tunnel and terminal project that would extend the railroad into the heart of New York City and onto Long Island.—*The Historical Society of Pennsylvania.*

The Pennsylvania Railroad, however, was not interested in tunnel schemes, and apparently lent little or no support to Haskin's project. In the 1870's and 1880's electric traction was not available, and operation of a long tunnel with steam locomotives did not seem to be a practical idea.

The Pennsylvania was more interested in a proposal advanced in 1884 by the eminent engineer Gustav Lindenthal (who later designed the New York Connecting Railroad's splendid Hell Gate Bridge). Lindenthal proposed a high-level bridge across the Hudson, which would terminate at a point near Desbrosses and Canal streets in lower Manhattan. War Department opposition to the plan, which called for two piers within harbor lines, and the depression of 1884 combined to forestall approval of Lindenthal's proposal. Six years later Lindenthal was back with revised plans that conformed to War Department requirements. The bridge was planned to cross the Hudson at 59th Street with a Manhattan terminal on Sixth Avenue. It would have 14 tracks on two levels, 10 of them for steam trains and 4 for rapid-transit trains.

At about this time at least two tunnel projects also were being proposed. The Long Island Rail Road contemplated the construction of a tunnel under the Hudson from Jersey City to a point in Manhattan near the Battery, from which it would continue under the East River to a junction with the Long Island at Atlantic Avenue in Brooklyn. A second tunnel scheme proposed construction of a line 31.5 miles long which would leave the Pennsylvania Railroad near Rahway, N. J., cross Staten Island, and tunnel 3.5 miles under the Narrows to Brooklyn. A new bridge over the East River would carry the line into a Manhattan terminal on Madison Avenue.

Samuel Rea, then an assistant to Pennsylvania's President George B. Roberts in general charge of all construction work, real estate purchases, and promotion of new lines, was appointed in 1892 to study the various bridge and tunnel alternatives for the railroad's New York terminal project. Rea favored Lindenthal's bridge scheme, which was estimated to cost 100 million dollars and would have required that all of the lines terminating in New Jersey join with the Pennsylvania in its construction. Financial reverses following the panic of 1893 precluded any progress on the project. Around 1900 the idea was revived, but failed to gain sufficient support.

By 1900 progress in electric traction had made the idea of a tunnel more attractive. Samuel Rea had visited the pioneer City & South London electric subway in 1892; and B&O's successful 1895 electrification of its Howard Street tunnel in Baltimore had not gone unnoticed by the Pennsylvania.

The Pennsylvania had operated an experimental electrification of its own on the Burlington & Mt. Holly branch in New Jersey since 1895. Pennsy President Alexander J. Cassatt, at Rea's urging, attended the opening of a 3-mile electrified tunnel line on the Paris-Orleans Railway in Paris, France. Cassatt came home convinced that an electrified tunnel system was practical.

By 1900, too, the Pennsylvania had acquired control of the Long Island Rail Road, a move which only increased the need for a terminal in Manhattan. The Long Island already was developing the intense commuter traffic which characterizes it today and was actively seeking its own Manhattan terminal. Through the Long Island acquisition, the Pennsylvania was able to combine the terminal requirements of the two roads into a single, massive project.

In 1901 the Pennsylvania appointed a board of distinguished engineers to study the practicality of the tunnel and terminal project, to establish the best means of accomplishing it, to estimate its costs, and finally — if the project was to be carried out — to supervise its construction. Reporting to Samuel Rea, by then a vice-president, the board included Col. Charles W. Raymond of the Army's Corps of Engineers; Gustav Lindenthal, the noted bridge designer; Charles M. Jacobs, an English tunneling expert; Alfred Noble, an engineer with wide experience on large projects; and William H. Brown, the Pennsylvania's chief engineer. A year later, electric traction authority George Gibbs, who also was active in the New York Central's terminal electrification project, was added to the board.

Late in 1901 the Pennsylvania organized two subsidiary companies, later consolidated into the Pennsylvania Tunnel and Terminal Railroad Company, to carry out its great New York terminal project. The massive undertaking would include the construction of a new double-track line diverging from the Pennsy main line near Newark, N. J., crossing the Hackensack Meadows on a high fill, and extending through Bergen Hill and under the Hudson River in two single-track tunnels to a new Manhattan station. Four tubes under the East River would join the new station with the Long Island Rail Road in Queens and a new coach yard at Sunnyside, in Long Island City. The new route would be electrified from its junction with the original main line at Manhattan Transfer all the way to a junction with the Long Island, a distance of 13.4 miles. More than 5 miles of the route were underground, including 1½ miles under the two rivers. Total cost for the project at the time of its completion in 1910 was almost 113 million dollars.

Initial contracts for what engineering historian James Kip Finch called "one of the boldest and most courageous undertakings ever conceived by the creative imagination of man" were awarded in March of 1904. A contract for construction of the Hudson River tubes was awarded to the noted New York engineering and construction firm headed by John F. O'Rourke, while S. Pearson and Son of London, England, contracted to construct the four East River tunnels.

In both cases, the tunnels were driven by the shield method to as much as 70 feet below high-water level, and were made up of 23-foot diameter cast-iron shells lined with 2 feet of concrete.

The two Hudson tubes were completed in record time, despite formidable problems presented by tunneling through the soft Hudson River silt. Working under the direction of Charles M. Jacobs, one of the members of the Pennsylvania's board of engineers, the O'Rourke firm started tunneling operations in February 1905. The shields for the north tube were brought together under the river in September 1906, and the south tube was joined a month later.

Porous sand and gravel, bits of ledge rock, and pockets of a red quicksand known as "bull's liver" made the driving of the East River tubes a difficult and hazardous undertaking. The Pearson firm, supervised by Alfred Noble, another member of the railroad's board of engineers, holed through the first of the East River tunnels in February 1908, with the remaining three following in March of the same year.

WORK on the railroad's Manhattan station began on May 1, 1904, soon after the award of contracts for excavation and construction of retaining walls. More than 100 houses were cleared from the 8-acre site. Nearly a half million cubic yards of earth were excavated from the area. The subterranean track level of the station covered 28 acres and included some 16 miles of track. Eleven platforms served 21 tracks.

The station building, designed by architects McKim, Mead and White, was to rank as one of the world's greatest railroad terminals. The structure covered two full blocks, bounded by 31st and 33rd streets and Seventh and Eighth avenues, an area 430 feet by 789 feet. The design was Roman Doric. The main waiting room, a great vaulted hall patterned after the Baths of Caracalla at Rome, was the largest railroad station waiting room in the world, with a floor area of more than 30,000 square feet and a ceiling 150 feet high. The latter, it just so happened, was 25 feet higher than the ceiling in the concourse of the rival New York Central's new Grand Central Terminal. The station's great concourse, an area 210 by 340 feet covered by a lofty roof of iron and glass, derived its architectural in-

THE principal features of the Pennsylvania's planned New York tunnel and terminal project were depicted by artist H. M. Pettit for the center spread of the November 12, 1904, issue of *Harper's Weekly*. (Top) The route of the tunnels and the location of the terminal are shown from an imaginary vantage point above New Jersey. The lower half of the spread shows (left) the Long Island portals of the East River tunnels, (center) a general view of Pennsylvania Station, and (right) a section of the Hudson River tunnels.—*Collection of William D. Middleton.*

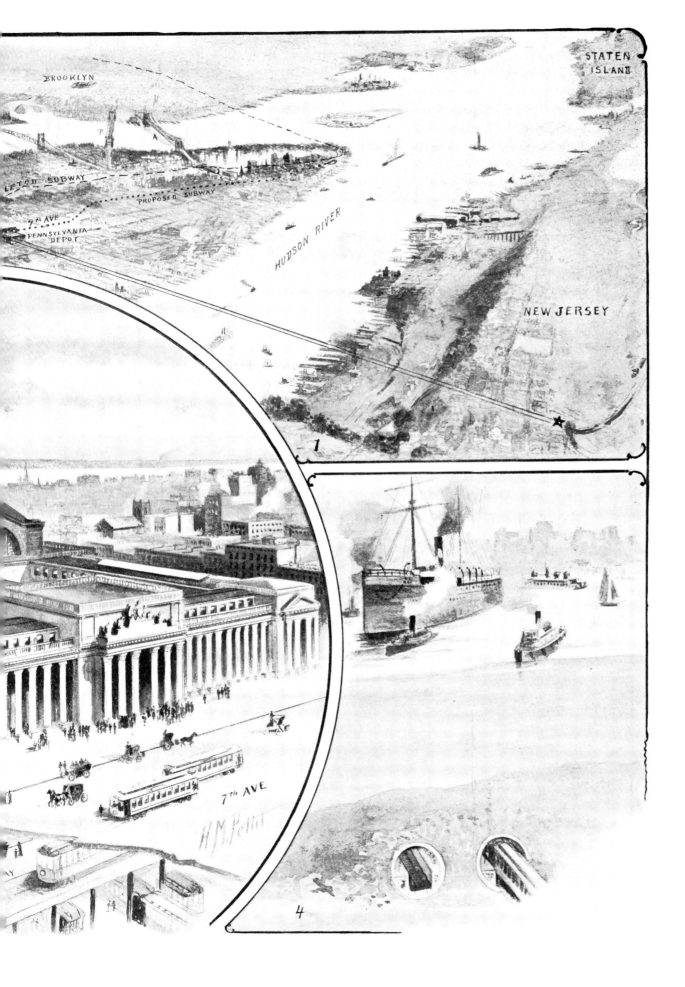

BROOKLYN

STATEN ISLAND

LETED SUBWAY

PROPOSED SUBWAY

7TH AVE

PENNSYLVANIA DEPOT

HUDSON RIVER

NEW JERSEY

1

7TH AVE

H.M.Petit

4

ARTIST Pettit also detailed the inner workings of the Pennsylvania's New York station for the readers of the May 9, 1908, *Harper's Weekly*. The sectional view showed the main waiting room, the glass-roofed concourse, and, underneath it all, the trains.—*Collection of William D. Middleton.*

FLASH POWDER illuminated the scene and flags waved in celebration on January 4, 1907, as the eastbound and westbound tunnel headings met beneath 32nd Street and Third Avenue, completing the section between Fifth Avenue and the East River.—*Collection of William D. Middleton.*

THE Vernon Howe Bailey drawing above appeared in the October 20, 1906, issue of *Harper's Weekly* titled "The Immense 'Culebra Cut' in the Heart of New York City." (The reference is to the Panama Canal, which was under construction at that time.) Made from a vantage point at the corner of Ninth Avenue and 33rd Street, the drawing shows the tremendous excavation that was required for Pennsylvania Station. In the distance a trestle carries the traffic of Eighth Avenue across the construction site.—*Collection of William D. Middleton.*

spiration from the Basilica of Constantine. A separate waiting room and concourse were provided for the Long Island Rail Road.

Sunnyside Yard, situated in Long Island City just beyond the end of the East River tunnels, was the supporting passenger-train servicing and storage facility for Pennsylvania Station. Occupying an area 1500 feet wide by 2 miles long, the yard was able to clean, service, and store more than 1400 passenger cars. It was said to be the largest coach yard in the world.

ELECTRIFICATION, of course, was the key to the success of the Pennsylvania's New York terminal project. The railroad's experience with electric traction went back to its 1895-1901 experimental electric operation of the Burlington & Mt. Holly

A LATER illustration by G. W. Peters, titled "Moles of Manhattan," from the March 7, 1908, *Harper's Weekly*, shows the falsework that carried Ninth Avenue and the elevated over the 75-foot-deep hole.—*Collection of William D. Middleton.*

THIS view eastward from Ninth Avenue and 32nd Street in 1908 shows the huge hole for the terminal trackage nearly complete and the steel framework for the station building rising at Seventh Avenue and 32nd Street. In the middle distance Eighth Avenue crosses the excavation on a steel and concrete bridge.—*Library of Congress.*

THE classic Roman Doric facade of Pennsylvania Station had begun to take shape when the photograph above was taken from the Seventh Avenue side of the structure. Just to the left of the center appears the Italianate vaulted arcade of the main entrance, which led to a stairway that descended to the main waiting room.—*Courtesy of Railroad Magazine.*

MOST of the tunnel and terminal project was hidden underground; Pennsylvania Station was the visible part of the undertaking. Clean and white in its newness, it was an appropriate monument to its owner's aspirations for a New York terminal. The Seventh Avenue main entrance was flanked by two block-long colonnades of Doric columns surmounted by attics that rose to a height of 76 feet above the sidewalk. Beyond, the lofty hall of the great waiting room, patterned after the Baths of Caracalla, rose to a height of 150 feet.— *Library of Congress.*

120

INSPIRED by the Basilica of Constantine, the great concourse of Pennsylvania Station was covered by a striking vaulted roof of iron and glass. The photograph at the left predates the opening of the station in 1910, to judge by the scaffolding and the absence of the clock and the chandeliers, which appear in the view above that is far more typical of the almost continuous activity in the concourse during the half century it served the public.—*Left, Library of Congress; above, Pennsylvania Railroad,* TRAINS *collection.*

(RIGHT) Until the floor of the concourse was extended to the west over the track area, the arrival and departure of the trains was a fascinating part of the scene at Penn Station. The absence of the overhead wires of Pennsy's A.C. electrification dates the photograph as having been taken before 1933. —*Thomas Emden.*

(LEFT) The main waiting room of Pennsylvania Station was a somber and majestic place, with a vaulted ceiling even higher than that of the concourse of the Grand Central Terminal a few blocks uptown.—TRAINS *collection.*

THIS striking nighttime view of Penn Station from a tall building on Eighth Avenue clearly delineates the relationship of the station's principal areas. To the right is the iron-and-glass roof of the 210 x 340-foot main concourse. In the center the roof of the main waiting room rises to almost twice the height of the rest of the building. Beyond the waiting room is the entrance arcade.— *Pennsylvania Railroad, courtesy of Railroad Magazine.*

CABIN A, which controlled the tracks at the west end of the station, was originally in open air. Beyond the cabin can be seen the structure that carried Ninth Avenue and the Ninth Avenue El over the Pennsylvania's tracks, and in the distance are the portals of the Hudson River tunnels. The steel girders over the tracks support an overhead power conductor where gaps in the third rail were necessary through complicated trackwork.—*Collection of W. R. Osborne.*

WHEN the terminal and tunnel project was completed, the New Jersey countryside near the west portal of the Hudson River tunnels was still essentially rural in aspect, and the catenary of the Pennsylvania's A.C. electrification was more than 20 years in the future.—*Pennsylvania Railroad,* TRAINS *collection.*

branch with a 500-volt D.C. trolley system. In 1904 the Pennsylvania began to electrify the Long Island with a 600-volt D.C. third-rail system similar to rapid-transit practice. Opened in June 1905, the Long Island's initial 38-mile third-rail installation was one of the first major steam railroad electrifications. Because operation of Long Island electrics into Penn Station was among the goals of the New York terminal project, the selection of an identical D.C. third-rail system for the New York terminal electrification was a logical choice.

Operating conditions for the New York terminal electrification were going to be extremely demanding. To avoid the hazards of wooden equipment in case of a tunnel accident, the Pennsylvania planned to use only steel passenger cars into Penn Station. The much greater weight of all-steel trains, combined with the maximum tunnel grades of 1.93 per cent, necessitated powerful locomotives. Equally important, the limited number of tunnel tracks and the dense traffic required high speed and fast acceleration. With characteristic thoroughness, the Pennsylvania set out to design a locomotive that would meet these exacting technical requirements.

Shortly after construction work had started on the terminal project, Pennsy President Cassatt appointed an electric locomotive committee to design the motive power. Chairman of the committee was George Gibbs, who was chief engineer of electric traction and station construction for the terminal project. Gibbs had designed both the electrical installation and the rolling stock for the Long Island's initial electrification, and was a consultant to the New York Central for its New York electrification project. Members of the committee included Alfred W. Gibbs (a first cousin of the chairman) and David F. Crawford, general superintendents of motive power, Pennsylvania Lines East and Lines West, respectively, and Axel S. Vogt, the Pennsylvania's mechanical engineer.

As the first step in developing a suitable design, two experimental electric locomotives were designed and built in 1905 at the Pennsylvania's Juniata Shops in Altoona, Pa. Both were B+B box-cab units employing articulated trucks and Westinghouse electrical equipment. No. 10001 was an 88-ton unit equipped with four nose-suspended, 350 h.p. traction motors. No. 10002 weighed 98 tons and had four traction motors of the gearless quill type, an arrangement similar to that used on the B&O's 1895 units and adopted in 1905 for the A.C./D.C. locomotives built for the New Haven electrification. Both locomotives were designed for D.C. third-rail operation and a top speed of 45 mph.

The two units performed well in a series of tests

on the Long Island Rail Road. Originally the Pennsylvania had planned to confine electric operation to the haul through the tunnels between Bergen Hill and Sunnyside Yard. Later, after it had been decided to extend electrification to Manhattan Transfer and Jamaica, adding about 10 miles of electric operation at each end, both experimental units were modified for operation at speeds up to 65 mph.

In subsequent tests on the Long Island at higher speeds the two locomotives displayed an alarming tendency to nose or hunt from side to side and produced severe lateral forces on the rails. To correct this problem, the Pennsylvania's locomotive committee carried out tests near Franklinville, N. J., in 1907. The test site included sections of both curved and tangent track on the West Jersey & Seashore Railroad, a Pennsylvania subsidiary between Camden and Atlantic City that had been electrified in 1906 with a 650-volt D.C. third-rail system.

A third experimental unit was included in the test program along with Nos. 10001 and 10002. This was an 11,000-volt, 25-cycle, single-phase A.C. locomotive, No. 10003, built by Baldwin-Westinghouse in 1907. Weighing 70 tons, No. 10003 was a 2-B unit fitted with 72-inch driving wheels. Its wheel arrangement was like that of an American-type steam locomotive. Two 375 h.p. traction motors powered the two driving axles through a gearless quill drive. Following the Franklinville tests, No. 10003 was tested on a 5-mile section of the Long Island equipped with A.C. catenary. Special equipment carried in a separate car powered the A.C. unit on the third-rail D.C. West Jersey & Seashore.

In addition to the three Pennsylvania experimental units, one of the New Haven's new Class EP-1 Baldwin-Westinghouse A.C./D.C. locomotives — No. 028 — was tested. To provide a comparison with the tracking qualities of steam locomotives, two standard Pennsylvania locomotives were included in the tests. ·One was a Class D16b American, No. 6032, with 68-inch driving wheels; the other was a Class E2 Atlantic, No. 6020, which had 80-inch driving wheels.

To record the effect on the track of the locomotives operating at speed, 80 special cast-steel recording ties supporting a 165-foot length of track were installed, first on a 1-degree curve and then on a tangent section. A recording device at the outer end of each tie employed a hardened steel ball, which was pressed into a steel plate by the movement of the rail, to measure the lateral forces imposed by the locomotive. Precise measurement of the depth of the indentation made by the ball permitted accurate calculation of the forces. A hydraulic device designed by railroad mechanical engineer George

EXPERIMENTAL electric locomotive No. 10001 was designed and built by the Pennsylvania's Juniata Shops in Altoona, Pa. Electrical equipment was provided by Westinghouse. The locomotive was operated extensively on the Long Island and the West Jersey & Seashore in the exhaustive test program that ultimately produced the design for the DD1. No. 10001 remained the lone example of its type on the rosters of the Pennsylvania, where it operated for more than a decade, and the Long Island, on which it continued in service as No. 323 until 1957.—*Collection of Edward T. Francis.*

THE most successful of the three experimental electric locomotives tested by the Pennsylvania in 1907 was No. 10003, whose 2-B wheel arrangement was the same as that of an American-type steam locomotive. Because of the unit's superior tracking qualities, its wheel arrangement was adopted for the DD1. Instead of No. 10003's gearless quill drive, however, the DD1 had a jackshaft and side-rod drive. No. 10003 is shown in the fall of 1908 with a two-car test train on a 5-mile section of the Long Island near Hempstead on which experimental A.C. catenary had been erected.— *Collection of Edward T. Francis.*

WITH a determined-looking engineman at the controller, brand-new DD1 No. 3977 posed for a classic low-angle view that clearly showed the steam-engine wheel arrangement, rods and all, that the Pennsylvania's engineers borrowed for the historic electric locomotive design. No. 3977 was one of a final batch of nine DD1's completed in July 1911.—*Smithsonian Institution.*

L. Fowler measured the effect of wheel impact on turnouts.

Each locomotive was tested at a wide range of speeds, operating both singly and in multiple. Both of the experimental units with articulated trucks showed extremely bad sidesway and nosing characteristics at high speed and developed lateral impact forces on the rail at least twice as great as those developed by steam locomotives at the same speed. No. 10002 was particularly hard on the track, kinking rails at high speed even on tangent track.

The New Haven EP-1, which was similar in arrangement to the two original Pennsylvania experimental units except for the use of non-articulated swivel trucks, proved to be a much superior performer except for a tendency to nose on tangent track. To correct this tendency, New Haven later added two-wheel guiding trucks at each end of the EP-1's.

By far the best performer among the electrics was the 2-B unit, No. 10003, which equalled the steam locomotives included in the test program in tracking qualities and stability. The Pennsylvania's engineers attributed the superior performance of No. 10003 to its non-symmetrical wheel arrangement and its high center of gravity. Although it had once been thought that a low center of gravity contributed to stability at high speed, motive-power engineers had found that a locomotive with a high center of gravity acted as an inverted pendulum and reduced lateral forces on the rails.

IN 1908, the committee, using the test program results, completed the design of a locomotive for the New York tunnel and terminal electrification that was radically different from any previous electric locomotive design. The design featured the same steam-locomotive-type wheel arrangement used on experimental unit No. 10003, with a four-wheel guiding truck and four 72-inch driving wheels. Two such box-cab units were permanently coupled back-to-back by a drawbar.

In designating its electric locomotive classes, the Pennsylvania continued the classification system used for its steam power. Since the letter D represented the 4-4-0 American type, the new electric design, with its back-to-back 4-4-0 arrangement, became the DD1 class.

Instead of the gearless quill drive used on the experimental unit, the DD1 employed a single large spring-supported traction motor carried on the frame of each unit. Power was transmitted to the driving wheels through connecting rods, a counterbalanced jackshaft, and side rods, an arrangement that further heightened the DD1's resemblance to steam-locomotive design. This arrangement not only permitted the use of extremely large and powerful traction motors but also raised the locomotive's center of gravity, improving its high-speed riding qualities. The Westinghouse 315A motor in each unit was rated at 2000 h.p.

The DD1 was a locomotive of impressive size and capacity. Each of the double-unit locomotives was almost 65 feet long and weighed 313,000 pounds in running order. Starting tractive force, rated at the standard 25 per cent adhesion, was almost 50,000 pounds. The DD1's proved to have exceptionally good adhesion, however, and in a dynamometer test, the initial DD1 developed a tractive force of 79,200 pounds. Maximum safe speed of the locomotive was 80 mph. In actual operation the DD1 was capable of easily handling trains of 1000 tons and could start an 850-ton train on the 1.93 per cent tunnel grades.

A noteworthy feature of the DD1 design was the completely independent construction of the cab, which could be lifted free from the running gear, leaving the floor and control equipment undisturbed. This arrangement enabled rapid and easy access to the huge 42,000-pound traction motors and driving equipment for overhaul and undoubtedly contributed to the DD1's low maintenance cost.

Two third-rail shoes were mounted on a wooden beam on each side of the guiding truck. A small pantograph on the top of each cab permitted uninterrupted current collection from an overhead conductor where the trackside third rail had to be broken for turnouts. Cable jumpers permitted operation of DD1's in multiple. No more than two of the locomotives normally were run in tandem, and even this was done only infrequently, since the great power of a single DD1 usually was ample.

Two prototype DD1's were built. The Pennsylvania's Juniata Shops constructed the mechanical parts, while the locomotive's electrical equipment was built and installed by Westinghouse. The first DD1 was ready for service in October 1909, and the second locomotive was completed the following April. The production units which followed later

126

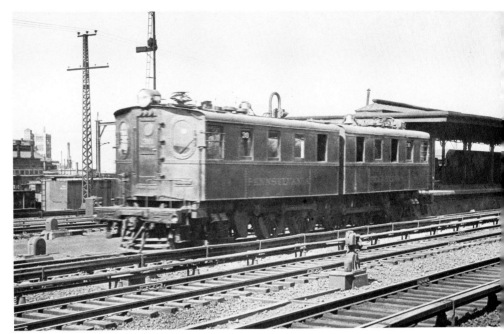

ON an August afternoon in 1930 DD1 No. 30 uncouples from the westbound *Broadway Limited* at Manhattan Transfer and pulls ahead. In a few moments a K4 Pacific will take the DD1's place at the front of the Pennsylvania Railroad's premier train.—*Rail Photo Service: H. Cotterell Jr.*

MANHATTAN TRANSFER, 9 miles from Penn Station at Harrison, N. J., was the point where steam locomotives and the DD1's traded places. Motor No. 12 has just arrived with a westbound express that includes four steel Pullman parlor cars and a pair of Pennsy's P70 coaches. A steam engine will couple on, and the train will resume its journey toward Philadelphia. — *Pennsylvania Railroad: P. L. Mahaffey.*

(BELOW) Racing across the Hackensack Meadows toward the west portal of the Hudson River tunnels, DD1 No. 36 heads train 20, the *Keystone Express* from St. Louis, through Union City, N. J., in November 1911. Although each unit carried its own four-digit road number, the Pennsylvania assigned a two-digit Electrified Zone Number to each two-unit DD1.—*Charles B. Chaney, collection of the Smithsonian Institution.*

TRAILING the 10 cars of train 56, DD1 No. 13 dives into the portal of the Hudson River tunnels after the sprint across the meadows from Manhattan Transfer. The date is October 11, 1914, and the buildings, roadbed, and landscaping still have a look of newness about them.—*Charles B. Chaney, collection of the Smithsonian Institution.*

ITS passengers discharged at Penn Station, train 56 has moved through the East River tunnel behind DD1 No. 36 toward Sunnyside Yard at Long Island City, where the train will be readied for another trip. The photograph was taken on October 4, 1914. No. 36, made up of units 3936 and 3937, has been preserved.—*Charles B. Chaney, collection of the Smithsonian Institution.*

INTENDED to be a successor to the DD1, elongated steeple-cab unit No. 3929 was one of two prototype Class L5 locomotives built by the Pennsylvania's shops, with Westinghouse electrical gear, in 1924 and 1925. Another 21 L5's followed during the next three years.—*Courtesy of Railroad Magazine.*

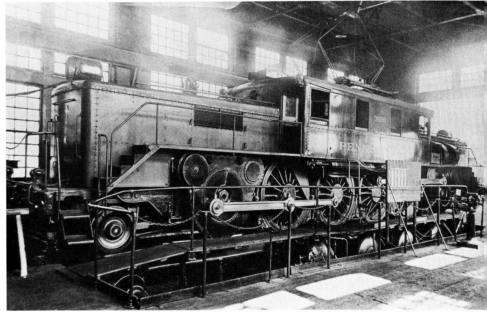

ONE L5, No. 3930 (above) was equipped for operation from A.C. catenary. It remained on the Pennsylvania's roster until 1944. An important part of the Pennsy's locomotive testing program was the Altoona test plant, where locomotives could be tested under load. No. 3930 stands ready for testing (right), with its pantograph raised to a special contact overhead.—*Both photos, collection of Charles B. Chaney, from the Smithsonian Institution.*

in 1910 were virtually identical to these two prototype units except for being somewhat lighter. Including the prototypes, Pennsylvania's initial order was for 24 DD1's. Nine more DD1's were delivered in July 1911. All were built at the Juniata Shops and equipped with Westinghouse electrical equipment.

After some balancing problems with the locomotives had been worked out, the Pennsylvania was ready to open its New York terminal. The Long Island, which began operating trains under the East River to Penn Station on September 8, 1910, was actually the first to make regular use of the station. The Pennsylvania commenced regular operation that November.

To ensure that all would begin smoothly, the Pennsylvania placed the entire new terminal into full operation two weeks before its scheduled opening date. Every man was at his post, every scheduled train was run, steam and electric motive power were exchanged at Manhattan Transfer, trains were inspected and serviced, train sheets were kept and delays were recorded and explained. All that was lacking were passengers, baggage, mail, and express. It was a two-week-long dress rehearsal. The new station opened on November 27, 1910. Service began without the slightest difficulty as local train No. 375 departed at 12:02 a.m. for Perth Amboy, N. J.

THE remarkable DD1's were the key to the success of the Pennsylvania's terminal electrification. When Penn Station opened in 1910, about 600 of its 1000 daily trains were Pennsy schedules handled by the side-rod electrics. The combination of reverse signalling on both tracks and the speed and acceleration of the DD1's permitted the Pennsylvania to handle as many as 144 train movements an hour on the double-track line under the Hudson to Manhattan Transfer.

The speed of the ungainly box-cabs was phenomenal. Not only were they able to make 80 mph with ease, but unofficial claims placed their top speed as high as 90 mph. On the last leg of the *Lindbergh Special*'s dash from Washington to Manhattan in 1927, a DD1 made the nearly 9 miles from Manhattan Transfer to Penn Station in 9 minutes flat.

The DD1's were reliable and rugged. In their first four years of service, during which they accumulated nearly 4 million miles, the DD1's experienced only 45 failures. Total detention time was only 271 minutes. A number of the DD1's had run 90,000 to 112,000 miles before general repairs were required. Maintenance costs during the first four years averaged 7.2 cents per locomotive mile, a figure that dropped to 3.5 cents in 1915 and 1916.

The DD1's were versatile motive power, too. Because of their short rigid wheelbase, they performed well in switching service at Penn Station and Sunnyside Yard. During World War I, when Pennsy moved heavy coal trains through the New York tunnels, which normally carried only passenger trains, the DD1's hauled tonnage just as successfully as they pulled passenger trains.

For a decade and a half, the DD1's remained the Pennsylvania's only motive power for the New York terminal electrification. In 1924 and 1925 they were joined by two prototypes of a planned Class L5 "Universal" electric locomotive. The Pennsylvania was planning extensive single-phase, 25-cycle A.C. electrification, and the L5 was designed so it could be modified to operate on either D.C. from a third rail or A.C. from overhead wire. The L5 was intended for both freight and passenger service.

The 200-ton L5's were provided with a pair of guiding wheels at each end and eight 80-inch-diameter driving wheels driven through a geared jackshaft and side-rod drive similar to that of the DD1's. Although driving-axle pairs were separately driven, all four driving axles were carried on a single rigid frame, giving the locomotive a 1-D-1 wheel arrangement. A large center cab and a low equipment hood at each end gave the 68-foot 3-inch L5's an elongated steeple-cab appearance.

Each pair of driving axles was driven by two Westinghouse 418 series-commutator motors geared to a single jackshaft which in turn drove the driving wheels through the side rods. The L5's had an hourly rating of 4170 h.p. and a maximum

speed in passenger gearing of 70 mph. A pair of third-rail pickup shoes was mounted on both sides at each end of the locomotive, and two miniature pantographs were provided for overhead power collection at third-rail breaks.

The Pennsylvania also constructed a third L5 prototype equipped for A.C. operation. All three units were built at the railroad's Juniata Shops at Altoona, and equipped with Westinghouse electrical equipment. During 1926 and 1927, Juniata delivered another 10 Westinghouse-equipped L5's arranged for third-rail operation. A further 11 units, with General Electric or Brown Boveri electrical equipment, were completed at Juniata in 1927 and 1928.

The L5's were not notably successful despite the large number of units built. The single A.C. prototype was never repeated, and the Pennsylvania abandoned rod drive for its later A.C. locomotive designs. The 23 D.C. units were placed in New York terminal service, displacing some DD1's. Although the L5's performed satisfactorily, they were never able to match the DD1's for all-around efficiency and low maintenance cost. Because of their long rigid wheelbase (22 feet 3 inches), the L5's were inferior in tracking qualities to the DD1's, which had a rigid wheelbase of only 7 feet 2 inches.

After the L5's arrived, 16 DD1's were transferred to the Long Island Rail Road, where they operated in both freight and passenger service. Another seven units followed at various dates during the 1930's and 1940's, while the remainder of the fleet continued to operate in Pennsy's New York terminal third-rail zone.

The entire D.C.-equipped L5 fleet was withdrawn from service and scrapped early in 1942, but the untiring DD1's rolled on. Most of the remaining Pennsylvania DD1's were scrapped during the late 1940's, and the Long Island's 23 DD1's were scrapped between 1948 and 1952. Two of the Pennsylvania DD1's, however, rounded out a half century of service before they were retired in the early 1960's. One locomotive, made up of units 3936 and 3937 (Juniata-Westinghouse 1911), survives in the Railroad Museum of Pennsylvania at Strasburg. It is a fitting place for this most notable locomotive. For it was the remarkably successful DD1 — and electrification — that permitted the unprecedented tunnel and terminal project that afforded the Pennsylvania Railroad its long-coveted Manhattan terminal.

DD1 No. 36 waits on the ready track at Sunnyside Yard in the late 1950's. At the time the locomotive was assigned to wire-train service. A few years later the 1911-built electric was withdrawn from duty and retired to the Railroad Museum of Pennsylvania at Strasburg.—*Jim Shaughnessy*.

SHADOWS are long as the sun sets on September 25, 1932, and L5 motor No. 7814 hurries train 218, a Philadelphia-New York express, through Union City on the way from Manhattan Transfer to Pennsylvania Station. The catenary is up and the substation is in, and soon A.C. locomotives will power the "Clockers" between the two cities.—*Collection of Charles B. Chaney, from the Smithsonian Institution.*

CAT'S-WHISKER stripes decorate 30-year-old DD1 No. 36, which has just arrived at the New York World's Fair on July 29, 1939, with the first eastbound trip of the Pennsylvania's all-coach Chicago-New York streamliner, the *Trail Blazer.* During the World's Fair the train ran through New York and Penn Station to the fairgrounds at Flushing. —*Charles B. Chaney, collection of the Smithsonian Institution.*

THE first major tunnel operation to be converted to electric power was that of the Grand Trunk Railway's St. Clair Tunnel Company. After several months of operation by the contractor, Westinghouse Electric & Manufacturing Company, the 3300-volt single-phase system was turned over to the Grand Trunk on November 12, 1908. This early photograph taken at the Port Huron (Mich.) portal of the tunnel is believed to show the special train that carried an inspection party of dignitaries, railroad and Westinghouse officials, and the press. After the tour, the party repaired to the Hotel Vendome in Sarnia, Ont., for a luncheon and a number of speeches.—*Canadian National Railways.*

5. Taming the tunnels

IF BY 1905 the relative economies of steam and electric operation remained open to debate, electrification clearly had established itself as a practical alternative in operating situations where the smoke and gases resulting from the use of steam locomotives posed particular problems and handicaps. The Baltimore & Ohio's successful Baltimore tunnel electrification was 10 years old. The New York Central and New Haven railroads, impelled by public pressure, were electrifying terminal facilities at New York City, and the Pennsylvania Railroad had embarked on a tunnel and terminal project that would have been impractical without electrification.

Electrification's early success as a smokeless alternative to steam soon inspired its adoption at several tunnels where steam presented severe operating problems.

The Saint Clair Tunnel Company

THE first major tunnel operation to convert to electric power was that of the St. Clair Tunnel Company, a subsidiary of the Grand Trunk Railway.

The St. Clair Tunnel broke a serious traffic bottleneck on the Grand Trunk when it opened between Sarnia, Ont., and Port Huron, Mich., in

133

1891. Following acquisition of its own route into Chicago in 1879, the Grand Trunk by 1883 was moving a third of all traffic between Chicago and New England. This success created operating problems at the St. Clair River, where carferries connected the Grand Trunk's Canadian lines at Sarnia with its Chicago & Grand Trunk subsidiary at Port Huron. During one 12-month period 197,500 cars were ferried across the river, requiring around-the-clock crossings at an average rate of one every 48 minutes. Winter ice jams in the river frequently disrupted the heavy water traffic and the railroad's yards became crowded to capacity. River traffic between lakes Huron and Erie made the construction of a bridge an impractical solution to the problem. A tunnel seemed to provide the only satisfactory answer.

The Grand Trunk first studied the feasibility of a tunnel in 1882. In 1884 the subsidiary St. Clair Tunnel Company was formed, and a year later boring of test tunnels began under the direction of project engineer Joseph Hobson, who would see the St. Clair Tunnel project through to completion. Work started on the actual tunnel in 1888, utilizing the newly developed shield tunneling method. The bore was holed through in 1890, and traffic began using the 6032-foot tunnel the following year.

Four extraordinary Baldwin 0-10-0T Camelback locomotives were used to haul trains through the St. Clair tube. Weighing 90 tons, they were the world's largest steam locomotives at the time of their construction. Anthracite was burned to minimize the smoke and gases, and special operating rules eliminated some of the hazards of steam operation in the long tunnel. Firemen were instructed not to place green coal on their fires when running through the tunnel; train operations were spaced to permit gases to clear from the tunnel; and the use of air brakes was prohibited in order to avoid a break-in-two that might stall a train in the tunnel.

The St. Clair Tunnel was successful. Elimination of the ferry operation saved the railroad $50,000 a year, and travel time between New York and Chicago was cut by 2 hours. Steam operation, however, had shortcomings. Despite the railroad's elaborate safety precautions, two serious asphyxiation accidents occurred in little more than a decade. In 1893 three men in a freight-train crew were overcome by gases and killed in a mishap resulting from a break-in-two. In 1903 a similar accident claimed several lives.

By 1900 increasing freight tonnage began to tax the ability of the steam engines to move traffic through the single-track tube. Despite their record-breaking size, the tunnel company's locomotives were limited to a train weight of 760 tons on the 2

per cent grade of the tunnel approaches on both the Michigan and Ontario sides, and barely managed a speed of 3 mph. Moreover, the number of trains that could be dispatched through the tunnel was limited by the need to allow gases to clear between trains.

By about 1904 the Grand Trunk was seriously exploring the subject of electrification. At this time the great A.C. versus D.C. debate was at its height, and the railway engaged the noted electrical engineer Bion J. Arnold, one of the consultants for New York Central's Grand Central Terminal electrification project, to study each alternative. Competitive proposals for both A.C. and D.C. systems were received, and the Grand Trunk finally chose the single-phase system advanced by the Westinghouse Electric & Manufacturing Company. The Grand Trunk's choice, along with the almost simultaneous decision of the New Haven Railroad to adopt a similar A.C. system, was a major victory for the single-phase electrification system advocated so vigorously by Westinghouse. Both decisions to adopt A.C. undoubtedly were influenced by the experimental two-unit single-phase locomotive built by Westinghouse in 1904 and tested at the company's East Pittsburgh (Pa.) works. The design subsequently adopted for the St. Clair Tunnel units was almost identical to that of the experimental locomotive.

The electrification installed by Westinghouse employed a simple-catenary overhead supported by steel catenary bridges spaced 250 feet apart. Within the tunnel, double overhead wires were supported by steel messenger cables, which in turn were carried on iron brackets bolted directly to the cast-iron tunnel shell. Overhead was installed over 4 miles of line, from the west end of the freight yards and passenger station in Port Huron to a point east of the Sarnia station and yard. The necessary yard trackage on both sides of the tunnel also was electrified. Altogether 12 miles of track were electrified. Because of limited clearances within the 19-foot-diameter tunnel, the trolley wire was energized at 3300 volts rather than at the 6600- or 11,000-volt potential usually favored for single-phase installations.

In addition to providing single-phase power for train operation, the electrical system furnished three-phase power for the pumps installed at each portal of the tunnel to remove tunnel seepage and rain water runoff from the approaches. Power also was supplied to an extensive system of tunnel lighting and to station, shop, and roundhouse buildings in Sarnia and Port Huron.

A new railroad-owned power plant on the Port Huron bank of the St. Clair River furnished the power. Four coal-fired, quick-steaming Babcock &

A SERIES of drawings in *Scientific American* illustrated the shield tunneling method employed to bore the St. Clair Tunnel. (Top left) The vertical and horizontal partitions on the cutting edge of the shield gave rigidity to the shield and provided platforms for the workmen. (Top right) On the rear of the shield was a bulkhead with emergency doors that could be dropped to seal off the cutting face from the tunnel in the event of a major leak. (Above left) The 60-ton shields were assembled and then rolled into the approach cuts at each end of the tunnel. (Above right) From the platforms behind the cutting edge of the shield the diggers excavated the river-bottom clay, which was then passed back to be carried to the surface in dump cars drawn by mules. An erector arm was used to raise the sections of the cast-iron shell into place. They were then bolted together. A system of 24 hydraulic jacks pushed the shield forward into the clay.—*All drawings, collection of Jerry A. Pinkepank.*

ON the front page of the September 13, 1890, issue of *Scientific American* an imaginative drawing appeared depicting the historic moment when the two St. Clair Tunnel shields, advancing
from the American and Canadian shores, met on August 23, 1890.—*Library of Congress.*

Wilcox water-tube boilers, along with a separately
fired Foster superheater, supplied superheated
steam at 200 pounds pressure to a pair of 1250-kilo-
watt Westinghouse-Parsons turbogenerators which
generated 25-cycle, three-phase power at 3300 volts.
Because of the great variation in the load on the
power plant, an automatic control system regu-
lating both stoker equipment and air supply to the

boilers was installed to maintain a constant steam
pressure.

Six Baldwin-Westinghouse box-cab locomotives
were delivered in 1908. Each 66-ton unit had three
pairs of 62-inch driving wheels. Three Westinghouse Type 137 geared traction motors gave the
units a continuous rating of 720 h.p. A single
transformer reduced voltage from the 3300-volt po-

tential at the trolley wire to the 235 volts required for the traction motors. The transformer and the three traction motors were cooled by air delivered through ducts from a single electrically driven blower inside the cab. The locomotive units were equipped to operate independently or in multiple. Specifications required that a two-unit locomotive be able to start a 1000-ton train on the 2 per cent tunnel grade without taking slack. Rated tractive effort for a two-unit pair was 50,000 pounds at 10 mph, sufficient to maintain speed with a 1000-ton train. Maximum speed was 30 mph.

The St. Clair Tunnel electrical installation was completed early in 1908, and an initial trial trip was made through the tunnel with a 700-ton train on February 28, 1908. After a transition period, all steam operation through the tunnel ended on May 17, 1908. Westinghouse, as the contractor, operated the electrification until November 12, 1908, when the Grand Trunk formally accepted the work with considerable ceremony. A party of invited railroad officials, electrical and railway engineers, and members of the press was transported through the tunnel in a special electric train. After a thorough

THE Baldwin-Westinghouse locomotives normally worked in pairs to haul freight through the St. Clair Tunnel. Units 1308 and 1309 stood still for the photographer soon after they arrived from the builder in 1908. The interior of the box-cabs (below) was strictly utilitarian. Hatches in the floor allowed access to the traction motors.—*Both photos, collection of the Pennsylvania Railway Museum Association.*

SHORTLY after electricity displaced steam in the St. Clair Tunnel, two of the new Baldwin-Westinghouse motors posed with one of the extraordinary steam locomotives they replaced. Baldwin built four such steam engines in 1891 expressly for service through the tunnel. They were built as 0-10-0T's and later were converted to tender engines. —*Michigan Historical Commission.*

inspection of the work, the guests adjourned to the Hotel Vendome in Sarnia where a luncheon was served and speeches were made by Grand Trunk officials, Westinghouse representatives, and other railway men.

The Westinghouse installation exceeded many design requirements. A single-unit 66-ton locomotive developed a maximum drawbar pull of 45,000 pounds, and a two-unit combination was able to maintain 12 mph on the 2 per cent grade with a

1000-ton train. Running time for the 2¼-mile summit-to-summit distance was reduced from an average of 15 minutes with steam to 10 minutes with electric power, and the maximum permissible train weight was increased from 760 tons to 1000 tons. Tunnel capacity was increased by at least a third with electrification.

Considering the limitations imposed by both the single track and the 2 per cent grades, the volume of traffic handled through the electrified tunnel

READY to roll east into Canada through the St. Clair Tunnel, a pair of 66-ton box-cab motors head a freight train in the Port Huron yard. Two of these units were rated for 1000 tons on the tunnel's 2 per cent ruling grade. —*Collection of the Pennsylvania Railway Museum Association.*

THE circular cross section of the St. Clair Tunnel's 19-foot diameter cast-iron shell is evident in this view of motor No. 2659 approaching the Port Huron portal. The double overhead wire assured ample current-carrying capacity for the heavy power demands of the tunnel service. A system of incandescent lamps, installed at the time of the electrification, rendered the tunnel, according to a contemporary account, "as well lighted as a city street." —*Collection of the Pennsylvania Railway Museum Association.*

(LEFT) With No. 1305 in the lead, two of the 720 h.p. Baldwin-Westinghouse box-cab motors head a westbound passenger train out of the Port Huron portal of the 6032-foot tunnel. —*Library of Congress.*

represented a significant achievement for the time. Soon after electrification, traffic was averaging 26 freight trains with an average train weight of 924 tons every 24 hours. In addition, 15 passenger trains averaging 281 tons each ran through the tunnel during the same period. No wonder, then, that in 1908 the St. Clair Tunnel operation was regarded as the heaviest railway service handled by electricity in the world.

Electrification yielded attractive financial results.

Locomotive fuel costs were cut by 60 per cent and maintenance costs were reduced by half. Over a six-year period the average cost per car handled through the tunnel was reduced to 17.2 cents from 26.6 cents with steam power. The entire $500,000 cost of the electrification, it was estimated, was liquidated by savings in the first five years of operation.

Once again, electrification had come through handsomely.

(ABOVE) While a lineup of four electrics waits on the adjacent track, a Grand Trunk Western 0-6-0 switches head-end cars on the westbound *Inter-City Limited* at Port Huron. No. 175 was one of two Baldwin-Westinghouse locomotives acquired second-hand from the Chicago South Shore & South Bend Railroad in 1927 after the interurban converted from a 6600-volt single-phase system to D.C. Within a few years after this photograph was taken in October 1955, steam and electric power gave way to diesel. —*Thomas C. Van Degrift Jr., from the Electric Railroaders' Association.*

(ABOVE RIGHT) Multiple-unit control gave the Baldwin-Westinghouse box-cabs of 1908 the ability to cope with substantial increases in freight-train weight during the half century that they operated through the tunnel. Originally a pair of the 720 h.p. units was ample for the average Grand Trunk freight train. As train length and weight increased over the years, four-unit blocks of the durable motors became commonplace. No. 154 leads a four-unit consist into Port Huron in 1955.—*Thomas C. Van Degrift Jr., from the Electric Railroaders' Association.*

CAREFULLY working the air brake lever, the engineer of a St. Clair Tunnel motor eases his train up to the tower at the west end of the tunnel in March 1950.—TRAINS: *W. A. Akin Jr.*

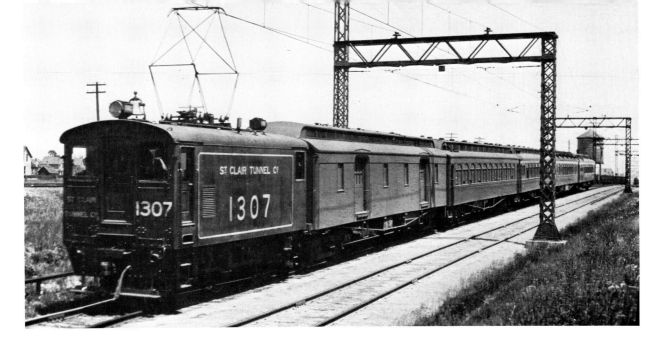

(ABOVE) In the early years of the St. Clair Tunnel electrification, a single unit was adequate for the typical passenger train. No. 1307 heads a five-car varnish into the tunnel from Sarnia, Ont.—*The Public Archives of Canada.*

POWERED by three of the original tunnel motors and a secondhand unit from the South Shore, Canadian National train 6, the eastbound *Inter-City Limited,* pulls up past the waiting passengers at Sarnia (right). The electrics are being cut off (below), and in a few minutes a big CN 4-8-4 will take over for the run to Toronto.—*Both photos,* TRAINS: *A. C. Kalmbach.*

The Detroit River Tunnel

AT DETROIT, MICH., the Michigan Central Railroad was confronted with an operating problem equal to that which the Grand Trunk overcame with its St. Clair Tunnel. The Michigan Central possessed one of the principal rail routes from the Midwest to the Northeast and Eastern Canada, but its main line across Michigan and southern Ontario was interrupted at the Detroit River, where traffic was ferried between Detroit and Windsor, Ont. The operation was costly and time-consuming under the best of circumstances, and during the winter months river ice conditions imposed severe handicaps.

By the turn of the century, an alternative to the carferry crossing at Detroit was urgently needed. In 1875 less than 174,000 cars had been ferried across the river. The annual traffic had reached a half million cars before the end of the 1890's, and by 1909, the last full year of ferry operation, it would reach 735,753 cars.

To accommodate its traffic, the Michigan Central was obliged to operate a fleet of 10 carferries. The time required to break up trains, cross the river, and reassemble the cars delayed freight trains from 3 to 8 hours. During the winter, ice conditions periodically interrupted traffic, and diversions to the railroads to the north and the south occurred annually.

As early as 1867 the Michigan Central and the other railroads reaching Detroit or Windsor had considered an alternate means of crossing the Detroit River in place of carferries. In 1872 the Michigan Central and the Great Western Railway (a Grand Trunk predecessor) began construction of a tunnel. The tunneling methods of the day could not cope with the problems posed by the blue clay of the river bottom, and the effort was halted the following year. During the next 30 years at least five plans for construction of a bridge across the river were considered. On four occasions the Army Corps of Engineers, which had jurisdiction over the waterway, raised objections and the railroad companies were unable to obtain legislative approval.

In 1904 the bridge proponents finally seemed near success, and the Michigan Central and the Grand Trunk jointly engaged a consulting engineer to select a site for a high-level bridge that

A MICHIGAN CENTRAL tunnel motor emerges from the Detroit portal of the 1.6-mile Detroit River Tunnel with a westbound passenger train. On the upper level a K-80-class Pacific parallels the electric-powered train into MC's new Detroit station.—*Library of Congress.*

REPRODUCED from the front page of a 1907 issue of *Scientific American*, this drawing depicts the trench-and-tube method of tunnel construction first employed for the Detroit River Tunnel. The prefabricated twin-tube steel tunnel section has been floated into position and sunk into the tunnel trench dredged in the river bottom. Concrete to be placed around the exterior of the tubes is being mixed aboard the barge, which is held in position by spuds lowered to the river bottom. The concrete will be placed through tremie chutes. The ends of each tunnel section are plugged with wood. After all the tunnel sections are in place and concreted, the plugs will be removed and the tunnel will be lined with concrete.—*Collection of William D. Middleton.*

THE six 100-ton steeple-cab locomotives constructed by Alco-GE in 1910 for the Michigan Central's Detroit River Tunnel electrification were so successful that subsequent orders over the next 15 years were built to an almost identical design. Maintenance costs for these locomotives were particularly low. From 1916 to 1924, during which time they averaged more than 26,000 miles a year, repair costs averaged less than 9 cents a locomotive mile. —TRAINS *collection.*

LOCOMOTIVE No. 7505, photographed at the point of a freight train shortly after the Detroit River Tunnel was opened, shows off the features borrowed from NYC's New York electrification: underrunning third-rail shoes and a roof-mounted miniature pantograph to collect power from an overhead conductor through complex trackwork.—*Library of Congress.*

would best serve the needs of all railroads interested in a Detroit River crossing. Hardly had the consultant's report been received, however, when the successful development of heavy electric traction for the New York Central's New York terminal project served to eliminate the problem of locomotive smoke and gases, one of the greatest objections to construction of a tunnel.

Late in 1904, then, the Michigan Central, since 1879 a part of Vanderbilt's New York Central System, set aside the bridge scheme and appointed a commission to investigate the feasibility of a tunnel and to make specific recommendations concerning its construction. Civil engineer William S. Kinnear served as chairman of the commission, which included E. A. Handy, chief engineer of the Lake Shore & Michigan Southern, and William J. Wilgus, vice-president of the New York Central & Hudson River and the engineer who had conceived

the brilliant design for the railroad's new Grand Central Terminal in New York City.

The commission soon reported favorably on the tunnel proposal and recommended an 8373-foot double-track tunnel with maximum grades of 2 per cent for westbound traffic and 1.5 per cent for eastbound traffic. Unlike the Grand Trunk's St. Clair Tunnel, which initially was operated with steam power, the Detroit River Tunnel was planned for electric operation from its inception.

A subsidiary company, the Detroit River Tunnel Company, was formed in 1905 to carry out the project, and the Michigan Central appointed a three-member Advisory Board of Engineers to supervise the construction and electrification of the tunnel. Two members of the board were carried over from the previous advisory commission. Wilgus became chairman of the board, while Kinnear was appointed both a member of the board and chief engineer for the tunnel company. Howard A. Carson, a civil engineer, was the third member of the board.

Plans were prepared during the latter part of 1905, and early in 1906 the company solicited proposals from construction contractors. Plans for the open-cut and tunneled approaches on both sides of the river were based upon established construction methods, but a novel variation was proposed for the underwater portion of the tunnel.

Four alternative construction methods for the underwater tunnel were presented in the preliminary plans made available to contractors, who had the option of proposing still other construction methods. Three of the methods proposed by the tunnel company were variations of a scheme developed by Wilgus. All required the dredging of a trench in the bottom of the river, followed by the positioning of either prefabricated concrete tunnel sections or some type of tunnel section forms, which then would be filled with concrete placed under water.

The fourth alternative contemplated shield-driven construction, the method first used on a large scale for the St. Clair Tunnel. This method was not considered desirable because it would have required tunneling with only a thin layer of material above the level of the tunnel — inviting the danger of a blowout into the river from the high air pressures — or tunneling at a lower alignment, which would have carried the shield into solid rock for at least 1200 feet and would have increased the gradient.

The method selected by the successful contractor was still another variation of the Wilgus scheme. A trench first was dredged in the blue clay of the river bottom along the alignment of the tunnel. Large steel tunnel sections, constructed at a shipyard some 60 miles upstream at St. Clair, Mich., were floated into place over the trench and sunk into position. The 262-foot twin-tube steel sections served as a form for exterior concrete, which was placed through tremie tubes from a barge positioned above the tunnel section. The tunneling method pioneered by the Detroit River Tunnel was highly efficient and subsequently was adopted for a number of major projects elsewhere.

Construction of the tunnel itself was finished in 1909, but completion of the approaches, as well as tunnel-lining, tracklaying, electrification, and related work continued through 1910. The overall project included construction of new yards at Detroit and Windsor, a new union passenger station in Detroit, a new station at Windsor, and the installation of connecting tracks for the various railroads which would use the facility.

Considering Wilgus' position as head of the ad-

visory board, it was not surprising that the electrification system adopted for the tunnel was virtually identical to the D.C. third-rail system used for the New York Central's New York terminal project.

All trackage between the Detroit and Windsor passenger stations, a distance of 4½ miles, was electrified with a Wilgus-Sprague underrunning third rail. Including the yard and station trackage as well as the tunnel line, nearly 30 miles of track were electrified.

Most railroads up to the time built their own powerhouses to supply new electrifications, but Michigan Central contracted with Detroit Edison for its power supply. A substation built near the Detroit end of the tunnel was supplied with three-phase, 60-cycle, 4400-volt power from the Edison Company. Two 1000-kilowatt motor-generator sets delivered the 650-volt D.C. power that was supplied to the third rail. To even out the load on the substation, and to provide an emergency source of power in the event the commercial supply was interrupted, the substation was equipped with a 2520-ampere-hour 650-volt storage battery capable of operating the electrification for 30 minutes. The electrical installation also powered sump pumps at five locations in the tunnel and its approaches, and an incandescent lighting system in the tunnel.

Six 100-ton locomotives completed early in 1910 for the Michigan Central by the American Locomotive Company and General Electric were substantially different in arrangement from the motive power supplied by the same builders to the New York Central's New York terminal electrification. Drawbars at each end were attached directly to heavy four-wheel trucks, which were articulated at the center of the locomotive. This arrangement permitted tractive-force loads to be carried directly by the running gear. Four nose-suspended GE-209-A traction motors, each rated at 300 h.p., were geared to 48-inch driving wheels. Blowers, control equipment, and auxiliaries were installed within either a main operating cab or one of two equipment hoods which were located at each end in a steeple-cab design. Designed to handle a 900-ton trailing load on a 2 per cent grade at 10 mph, each of the locomotives had a maximum tractive effort of 67,000 pounds.

Construction was completed on July 1, 1910, and the first electric train ran from Detroit to Windsor on July 26. Regular freight operation through the tunnel started on September 15, following completion of terminal work in Detroit. Passenger traffic began a month later.

Perhaps because it involved an electrical system that already had been proven at New York, the Detroit River Tunnel electrification operated une-

A PAIR of Michigan Central electrics grind up the 2 per cent grade from the Detroit portal of the tunnel with a long mail-and-express train in June 1952. No. 170, in the lead, was built by Alco-GE in 1926, one half of the final order of electrics for the tunnel.—*Thomas J. Dworman*.

AT several points on the Michigan Central's trackage in the Detroit terminal overhead conductor was needed because of long gaps in the third rails at slip switches.—*Thomas J. Dworman*.

ON a hot June day in 1952 New York Central Hudson No. 5356 accelerates a noon express to Chicago out of the Detroit station, overtaking a pair of steeple-cab motors still working hard to pull a long freight up the grade from the tunnel.—*Thomas J. Dworman.*

DURING the final years of electric operation six of the New York Central's big R-2-class C+C box-cab locomotives were transferred to Detroit from New York City. Units 303 and 306 pull a freight up the 1.5 per cent grade into Windsor, Ont., in June 1953. Several tri-power units also were moved west for the last years of the electrification.—*Thomas J. Dworman.*

ventfully from the beginning. Freight trains of 2000 to 2100 tons normally were operated on the 2 per cent westbound grade, while trains of up to 2500 tons rolled up the 1.5 per cent eastbound grade — the direction of Michigan Central's heavier traffic flow. Two electric units at the head end, with a third as a pusher, normally were used. Running time through the tunnel was less than 6 minutes.

The original electrical installation soon was expanded because of steadily increasing traffic. Four locomotives were added to the roster in 1914. Except for an increase in weight to 120 tons, they were similar to the 1910 units. Two more units were added in 1926.

By 1925 the capacity of the tunnel company's substation had been tripled to 6000 kilowatts and the capacity of the tunnel was estimated to be

IT'S 2:10 on a July afternoon in 1935 as a string of Boston & Maine's box-cab 1-B+B-1 tunnel motors leads Lima Berkshire No. 4003 and westbound tonnage into the east portal of the 25,081-foot Hoosac Tunnel to pierce the solid granite of the Hoosac Range.—*Ken L. Henderson.*

247,000 tons per day. Freight traffic through the tunnel was running at approximately 58 million ton-miles annually. Passenger-train movements accounted for 320,000 car-miles.

The Hoosac Tunnel

ANOTHER major tunnel was electrified in 1911, when the Boston & Maine Railroad installed a single-phase electrification through the 4¾-mile Hoosac Tunnel in northwestern Massachusetts.

Hoosac Tunnel, opened in 1875, was one of the greatest achievements of 19th-century railroad builders. Fully 22 years in the drilling, the 25,081-foot tunnel was carved out of the solid granite of the Hoosac Range of the Berkshire Hills, first by primitive brawn-and-black-powder methods, and later by some of the earliest pneumatic-drill and nitroglycerine tunneling. The project cost 195 lives and 14 million dollars, and it was the source of bitter political controversy throughout the long period of its construction. Hoosac reigned as the world's longest tunnel for nearly a decade, and it was the longest tunnel in America for more than 40 years.

Hoosac Tunnel afforded the Boston & Maine and its predecessors a crossing of the Berkshires 600 feet lower than that of the rival Boston & Albany to

the south, a competitive advantage that remains as valid in the 1970's as it was a century before.

As traffic through Hoosac increased during the latter part of the 19th century, the usual problems caused by the smoke and gases of steam operation in a long tunnel became more severe. The tunnel, which was built on ascending 0.5 per cent grades from each portal that met at a summit near the center of the bore, originally depended upon natural ventilation through a 1028-foot ventilating shaft drilled near the center point. Increased traffic through the tunnel made natural ventilation inadequate, and in 1899 a steam-driven fan was installed at the top of the central ventilating shaft. Next, oil-burning locomotives were tried, but the problems remained.

Although the division's ruling grades were located elsewhere, B&M was obliged to assign helper engines to many trains because of bad rail conditions inside the tunnel caused by condensing steam. Delays to trains while crews waited for smoke and gases to clear made the tunnel the limiting feature to the traffic capacity of B&M's Fitchburg Division. Engine exhausts shattered rock and

brickwork, and acid gases corroded telephone and signal lines. Track gangs were limited to only 2 hours of effective work in a daily shift because of the undesirable conditions inside the tunnel.

By 1910 close to 100 trains a day traveled over the Hoosac Tunnel Route and the railroad decided to electrify. At this time the monopolistic expansion of the New Haven Railroad into much of New England transportation under J. P. Morgan and Charles S. Mellen was at its peak. In 1909 the B&M had come under the control of the New Haven, with Mellen as B&M president. It was no wonder, then, that the electrification adopted for Hoosac Tunnel was almost identical to the 11,000-volt, 25-cycle, single-phase system installed a few years before on the New Haven main line.

The B&M electrification was designed by New Haven's engineering department. Construction started on November 1, 1910, and on May 27, 1911, all Hoosac Tunnel traffic was moving behind elec-

MOTOR No. 5001 emerges into the sunshine and heat of an August 1940 afternoon. The heavy wooden doors at the west portal of Hoosac Tunnel are wide open now, but when winter comes to the mountains of western Massachusetts they will be swung closed between the passages of trains to keep snow from drifting into the tunnel.—*George B. Dutton Jr.*

tric power. The 7.9-mile electric zone extended from the west end of the North Adams yard through the tunnel to a yard just beyond the east portal. Altogether, 21.4 track-miles were placed under electric operation.

Power was supplied to the electrification from a 6000-kilowatt steam generating plant at Zylonite, Mass., 2½ miles south of North Adams. Single-phase, 25-cycle power was transmitted at 11,000 volts to a switch house at the west portal of the tunnel, which, together with a switch house at the east portal, controlled the flow of power to the sectionalized overhead system.

Power was distributed through a compound-catenary overhead system supported at 150-foot intervals by steel bridges or, where four or more tracks were spanned, by cross-catenary construction supported by steel towers. Within the tunnel the catenary was supported at 100-foot intervals, and a double contact wire was provided.

The overhead system within the tunnel was installed under difficult conditions. One track at a time in the double-track tunnel was turned over to the contractor, who performed the work from platform cars on two work trains. Trains operated on the single track in use at frequent intervals. Work had to be suspended for 10 to 20 minutes after the passage of each train while the smoke and gases cleared. Every third platform car was equipped with an air lock, into which the installation crew retreated during and after the passage of a train. Clean air was pumped into the air locks at a sufficient pressure to keep out the smoke and gases. A coach on each work train outfitted as a dining car also had an air lock. Each train carried an oxygen tank and an air helmet to aid anyone overcome by gas.

In 1911 B&M purchased five locomotives from Baldwin-Westinghouse which were near duplicates of experimental New Haven box-cab locomotive No. 071, delivered by the same builder the previous year. Each 130-ton locomotive had two articulated four-wheel trucks with a single unpowered guiding axle at each end. Four 315 h.p. Westinghouse Type 403 motors were geared to 63-inch driving

THREE electrics lead the Troy-to-Boston *Minute Man* out of the "Great Bore" into the valley of the Deerfield River. The large off-center headlight, which replaced a smaller roof-mounted light soon after the locomotives were delivered, was an eccentricity of B&M's electrics.—*R. E. Tobey.*

A SINGLE box-cab motor rolls a Boston-bound passenger train into the yard at Hoosac Tunnel station, just across the Deerfield River from the east portal of the tunnel.—*Collection of the Pennsylvania Railway Museum Association.*

WITH both pantographs reaching for 11,000-volt alternating current, motor No. 5003—and a 2-8-0 road engine—drift downgrade trailing a freight into the yard at North Adams, Mass., the west end of the electrified zone.—*Collection of the Pennsylvania Railway Museum Association.*

CONVENTIONAL compound catenary ended at the portals of the Hoosac Tunnel. Inside the tunnel an unusual system of catenary-suspended double contact wire transmitted power to the locomotives. A pair of brand-new locomotives pose outside the east portal in December 1912 in this view illustrating the hardware of electrification.—*Collection of Jim Shaughnessy.*

wheels through a gear-and-quill drive. Maximum starting tractive effort was 72,000 pounds.

Three units were geared for freight service. Each was capable of hauling a trailing load of 1600 tons up the tunnel's ruling 0.5 per cent grade at 20 mph. The remaining two units were geared for somewhat higher speeds for the operation of passenger trains. Two almost identical units were added in 1917.

The transition to electric operation of the tunnel was executed without any significant difficulties. The 20 locomotive crews selected to operate the electrics spent three weeks or more in training on similar New Haven equipment, and then spent several weeks in practice operation of the B&M equipment.

In service the electrics moved freight trains of 1600 tons through the tunnel in 15 to 20 minutes

THE first electrically hauled passenger train through the Hoosac Tunnel left North Adams in the predawn darkness of May 18, 1911. The view at the left of motor No. 5002 trailing a 4-6-0 and a train of open-platform wooden coaches standing at the east portal may well depict the official first trip with electric power, to judge by the straw-hatted, name-tagged dignitaries.—*Collection of Charles B. Chaney, from the Smithsonian Institution.*

TWO Baldwin-Westinghouse motors ease a long freight and its 2-8-0 out of Hoosac Tunnel yard and across the Deerfield River toward the east portal of the tunnel in the early days of the electrification.—*Collection of the Pennsylvania Railway Museum Association.*

and passenger trains of 400 to 500 tons in 7 or 8 minutes. Steam locomotives, with fires banked, were pulled through with their trains.

ALL THREE of these early tunnel electrifications operated for long periods with few modifications to the original installations. Supplemented by a few later units added to accommodate increased traffic, the original electric motive power continued to perform well for 35 to 50 years.

Mainline dieselization displaced electrification in these tunnels during the decade following World War II. Initial savings notwithstanding, the operating and maintenance costs for the short electrified tunnel sections were always something of a burden above normal operating costs to the railroads. As long as steam power survived, there was no suitable alternative to electric tunnel operation. But the railroads found that with improved ventilating systems they could operate diesel motive power right through the tunnels, and the electrics were soon out of a job. Boston & Maine, an early convert to mainline dieselization, discontinued its Hoosac Tunnel electrification in 1946. The Detroit River Tunnel electrification closed in 1953 following dieselization of the Michigan Central. The Grand Trunk, like its parent CN a late starter in dieselization, continued to operate electric motive power until 1958, when the St. Clair Tunnel, too, gave way to dieselization.

6. Conquering the Cascades

NOT LONG after the Grand Trunk Railway initiated its electrification project for the troublesome St. Clair Tunnel in 1905, James J. Hill's Great Northern Railway, too, turned to electrification to solve an even greater tunnel problem in the railroad's crossing of the Cascade Mountains of Washington.

The Cascades had been a problem for Great Northern ever since the early 1890's, when the indomitable Jim Hill pushed the nation's northernmost transcontinental westward to the Pacific Coast. In 1889 Hill's masterful engineer, John F. Stevens, discovered an easy crossing of the Rockies for GN in Montana's Marias Pass, the lowest of the Northwest railroad passages at an elevation of 5213 feet. Nearly 600 miles to the west of the Rockies, however, the much lower Cascades were a far more formidable barrier confronting Stevens.

After surveying a number of routes through the Cascades, Stevens decided on the 4000-foot elevation pass that was soon to carry his name. The route selected over the pass afforded a maximum grade of 2.2 per cent to an elevation of 3382 feet. Confronted with even more difficult terrain at this point, the railroad's builders planned a 2½ mile tunnel. Construction of such a tunnel would have required years, however, so the GN was rushed to completion in 1893 with an interim switchback route over the pass that necessitated grades as severe as 4 per cent.

While a succession of heavier and heavier steam locomotives struggled to keep GN tonnage moving over the rugged switchback route, tunneling crews bored the Cascade Tunnel through the solid granite of Jim Hill Mountain. The single-track tunnel, opened in December 1900, extended 2.63 miles from its West Portal at Wellington on a steady 1.7 per cent ascending grade to the East Portal at Cascade Tunnel station. Completion of the tunnel enabled the maximum grade in Stevens Pass to be reduced from 4 per cent to 2.2 per cent, eliminated the eight switchbacks of the old route over the top, shortened the line by 9 miles, and cut the running time through the pass by 2 hours.

The advent of still heavier steam power permitted a steady increase in the tonnage of GN trains moving over the Cascades. By 1908 Class L 2-6-6-2 Mallets, as road engine and pusher, handled trains of 1600 tons over Stevens Pass; in 1893 trains on the old switchback route had been limited to 600 tons.

Although steam was moving the tonnage, conditions in Cascade Tunnel were difficult and hazardous, and they limited Great Northern's capacity to handle through freight.

Heavy freight trains were unable to exceed 7 or 8 mph because of the severe grades and conditions in the tunnel. Traffic density was so great that the tunnel often was choked with smoke and gases. Temperatures in locomotive cabs were almost unbearable, sometimes rising to 200 degrees. Condensing steam and smoke coated the rails with a damp, greasy soot that caused drivers to slip, making the arduous eastbound climb up the tunnel's 1.7 per cent grade even more difficult.

GN locomotives burned a high-grade Crow's Nest coal which was supposed to be free of sulphur and gas-forming materials, and firemen were instructed to maintain clean fires. Stack extensions were installed on some locomotives, and engine crews were provided with gas masks. Such measures helped the situation but by no means solved the problem.

The hazard of steam operation through the tunnel was illustrated by a near-catastrophe in 1903, when a trainload of more than 100 passengers narrowly escaped asphyxiation. After the train had been stopped in the tunnel by a break-in-two between the helper and road engines, the engine crew was overcome by smoke. Only the quick action of a fireman riding on the train as a passenger averted disaster. He released the engine brakes, enabling the train to coast to safety outside the tunnel.

THE practicality of electric operation under similar difficult operating conditions was being demonstrated at several important installations elsewhere, and a decision to electrify provided GN with an obvious solution to the GN's problems in Cascade Tunnel.

At the time, heavy-duty railroad electrifications in the U. S. had been limited to either low-voltage D.C. third-rail or high-voltage single-phase A.C. systems. However, Dr. Cary T. Hutchinson, the consulting electrical engineer engaged by GN to plan the Cascade Tunnel electrification, selected a three-phase A.C. system. GN's installation was the first and only three-phase electrification in America, but the system had achieved considerable success on several European railways. In Switzerland a light three-phase electrification had operated between Burgdorf and Thun since 1899. In Italy the first section of a three-phase electrification system that would eventually power more than 1000 route-miles of Italian railway had opened on the Valtellina line in 1902. In 1906 the 14.3-mile Simplon Tunnel opened between Switzerland and Italy with a three-phase electrification.

Considering the state of development of electrification technology, the three-phase system seemed to afford advantages over either a D.C. or a single-phase A.C. installation for the heavy traffic and severe mountain operating conditions that typified GN's Cascade line.

Three-phase induction motors and their controls were characterized by mechanical and electrical simplicity, and they were able to withstand a great deal of rough use. Electrical efficiency of the motors was high, and they could develop a greater continuous output than other types of motors of the same size. The more uniform torque of a three-phase motor helped to prevent wheel slip at starting and gave a three-phase locomotive better adhesion than other types.

Because of its electrical characteristics, a three-phase motor operates at a constant speed, regardless of load. This characteristic normally was considered to be disadvantageous in railroad electrification, but it was regarded as an asset in a mountain installation such as GN's, and was considered particularly important in limiting the speed of trains on a descending grade.

Again because of its electrical characteristics, the three-phase motor could act as a generator to return power to the distribution system when a locomotive was operating downgrade. Great Northern was the first U. S. railroad to employ regenerative braking.

Although GN planned to later electrify the entire 57 miles between Leavenworth and Skykomish, which comprised all Stevens Pass trackage with a grade in excess of 1 per cent as well as the tunnel itself, the initial three-phase installation was confined to Cascade Tunnel, its immediate approaches, and the yards at both ends of the tunnel.

General Electric Company supplied the entire electrical installation for the project. A hydroelectric plant was built on the Wenatchee River just west of Leavenworth. Two 4000 h.p. waterwheels each drove a 2500-kilowatt generator which produced three-phase 25-cycle A.C. at 6600 volts. A bank of four transformers in the powerhouse stepped up the voltage for transmission over a 33,000-volt line to the substation at Cascade, 30 miles away. A single step-down transformer in the substation reduced the voltage to 6600-volt three-phase power for the electric locomotives.

Three-phase distribution to locomotives was accomplished through two overhead wires, with the running rails serving as the conductor for the third phase. The overhead wires were suspended from the roof of the tunnel; outside, a simple trolley-wire suspension system was utilized, with cross-catenary or bracket supports every 100 feet. Heavy steel anchorage bridges for the overhead system were installed at intervals of 1000 feet.

An obvious disadvantage of three-phase electrification was the complexity of this overhead distribution system. The overhead wires had to be carefully insulated from each other at supporting points, and complicated section insulators were required where wires of opposite phase crossed at turnouts.

GN needed motive power that could pull a 2000-ton train at 15 mph over the entire mountain divi-

FOUR 115-ton, three-phase locomotives were built for Great Northern's original Cascade Tunnel electrification by American Locomotive Company and General Electric. Rheostats for the traction motor controls were placed in the roof monitor. Air that had cooled the transformer was exhausted through the grilles in the sides of the monitor to also help cool the rheostats. No. 5001 was photographed on the GE test track at Schenectady, N.Y.—*General Electric.*

THREE-FOURTHS of Great Northern's original electric roster waits at Tye (formerly Wellington) in May 1913, ready to move eastbound freight up the 1.7 per cent grade through the first Cascade Tunnel. Three-phase power required three conductors, two wires overhead plus the running rails. Pairs of trolley poles were used to collect current from the overhead wires. Visible in this photograph are the complicated system of insulators required to separate the overhead wires and the dual cross-catenary system that supported the contact wires.—*Collection of the Washington State Historical Society.*

MOUNTAIN railroaders and mountain electrics are arranged for the camera at Tye, a few years before World War I. Electric power took eastbound trains, steam locomotives and all, through the Cascade Tunnel from here.—*Collection of the Washington State Historical Society.*

THREE-PHASE locomotives drift downgrade out of the West Portal of the original Cascade Tunnel into Tye after taking an eastbound train through the tunnel. Above the portal can be seen three tiers of the roadbed that carried GN over Stevens Pass before the tunnel was opened in 1900. —*Collection of the Washington State Historical Society.*

MORE than three years in construction, Great Northern's 7.79-mile-long second Cascade Tunnel was a massive undertaking that was carried out at unprecedented speed. Entire camp towns such as the one near Scenic (above) were erected to house the hundreds of men employed on the project. Working at multiple faces opened up by the vertical Mill Creek shaft and the pioneer tunnel parallel to the main bore, drillers and blasters (above right) excavated nearly a million cubic yards of rock and earth. Air-operated power shovels (right) and mucking machines (below right) loaded the excavated material into narrow-gauge electric trains, which removed it from the tunnel (bottom right) and also transported the workmen and their supplies in and out of the tunnel (below).—*Above and right, courtesy of Railroad Magazine; other photos,* **TRAINS** *collection.*

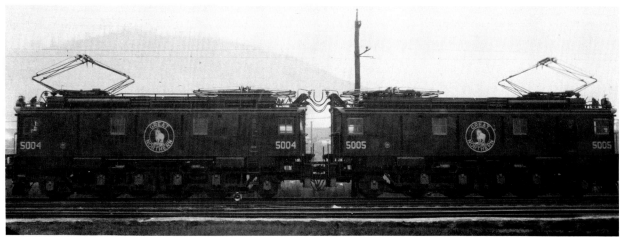

THE Great Northern's first Z-1-class locomotive, comprising semi-permanently coupled 1-D-1 units 5004 and 5005 (later renumbered A5004 and B5004), was photograped on the Westinghouse test track at East Pittsburgh, Pa., after its completion in November 1926. One of the Z-1's was billed as the "Colossus of the Rails" by its proud builder and exhibited to an estimated 65,000 persons on a tour from Chicago to Seattle in early 1927. It was, according to the *Electric Railway Journal*, "a triumphant tour, rivaling that of some royal personage." At the left is the motor-generator that converted the 11,000-volt A.C. from the catenary to low-voltage D.C. for the traction motors.—*Both photos, collection of the Pennsylvania Railway Museum Association.*

sion between Leavenworth and Skykomish. To accelerate such a train on the 2.2 per cent ruling grade, four locomotives with a maximum tractive effort of 37,500 pounds each would be required.

Four locomotives, with carbodies and running gear built by American Locomotive Company and electrical equipment by General Electric, were delivered in early 1909. The 44-foot-long, 115-ton box-cab units greatly exceeded the railroad's specifications. Each could produce a maximum tractive effort of nearly 80,000 pounds and was able to accelerate an 885-ton train on the 2.2 per cent grade. The smooth torque of the three-phase motors gave the locomotives a 35 per cent coefficient of adhesion.

Each locomotive was mounted on a pair of four-wheel cast-steel trucks, which were articulated at the center of the locomotive. Drawbars at the ends of the locomotive were mounted directly on the trucks, permitting tractive forces to be carried directly through the running gear rather than through the carbody.

Four GE-1506 three-phase induction motors provided a horsepower rating of 1500 h.p. for each locomotive. The motors were truck-mounted in a nose-suspended arrangement and were geared to 60-inch driving wheels through twin drive gears. The motors had eight poles and operated at a synchronous speed of 375 rpm on 25-cycle power, giving a locomotive speed of 15.7 mph.

To accommodate a wide variation in trolley-wire height, current collection was accomplished through trolley poles. Two pairs were installed on each locomotive to permit bidirectional operation. Two 400-kilowatt air-blast transformers in each locomotive reduced the trolley-wire voltage to 500 volts for the traction motors. The locomotives were equipped with a rheostatic control system and Sprague-GE multiple-unit control.

Electric operation of all eastbound traffic began on July 10, 1909. Steam locomotives were hauled through with their trains. At first, westbound trains were not electrically operated downhill through the tunnel. A short time later, however, electric locomotives began handling westbound passenger trains in order to provide the smoother operation afforded by regenerative braking.

The electrical installation experienced a few initial difficulties. Poor regulation of power generation at the hydroelectric plant obliged GN to work the Mallet road engines in order to smoothly start eastbound trains out of the Wellington yard. The railroad attempted to limit this to the use of just sufficient steam to turn the Mallet itself over, and steam was shut off at the tunnel portal. Also, it was found that smoother starts could be obtained by maintaining a slight braking pressure on the locomotives. Pressure was gradually reduced as the train was started.

The complicated trolley-wire crossings at turn-

Z-1-CLASS unit A5006 led the *Oriental Limited* on its first electric-powered trip from Wenatchee to Skykomish on December 4, 1928.—*Collection of the Pennsylvania Railway Museum Association.*

outs created another problem. On several occasions dewirement of the trolley poles cut off the power to electric locomotives being used as pushers. Such occurrences suddenly increased the pull on the drawbars of the lead locomotives and trains were sometimes pulled apart. This problem was temporarily overcome by using a Mallet pusher to assist a train through the area of the trolley-wire crossings in the Wellington yard. Improvements to the wire crossings, as well as increased experience in starting trains on the part of engine crews, corrected this particular problem and the Mallet pushers were soon discontinued.

The constant-speed characteristics of three-phase motors resulted in a novel mishap in GN's three-phase electrification some years later. An eastbound freight train, with two electric units on the head end and two more pushing, entered the tunnel. After the lead locomotives were in the tunnel, the two pushers suddenly lost power. The engineer in the lead unit was unaware that anything was wrong, since the synchronous motors continued to grind away at their usual speed. The train gradually slowed to a stop, with the wheels of the lead locomotives continuing to turn. The engineer, unaware that his train had stopped, held the controller in the power position until the usual time for a trip through the tunnel had elapsed. When

daylight failed to appear he finally shut down the locomotive, went to investigate, and found that the wheels of his stationary locomotive had ground through two-thirds of the rail web.

Great Northern's provision for power regeneration by locomotives operating downhill produced the anticipated results. In one test, a 1550-ton train with three electrics returned 950 kilowatts of power to the overhead distribution system when operating down a 1.7 per cent grade at 15 mph. There was no actual opportunity to utilize the power returned to the system by regeneration, however, because of the short length of GN's initial electrification through Cascade Tunnel. To gain the advantages of regenerative braking, an automatically controlled water rheostat was installed at the Leavenworth power plant to dissipate the returned energy. When electrification was extended to Leavenworth and Skykomish, regenerated power from descending trains was expected to assist ascending trains elsewhere in the electrified section.

During its first 33 days of full operation the GN electrification handled 212 eastbound train movements through Cascade Tunnel, representing a daily average of 8350 tons. Freight trains hauled by the electrics averaged more than 2000 tons. Studies by GN's superintendent of motive power indicated that the electric locomotives handled the traffic at approximately double the efficiency of the Mallet steam locomotives used previously.

A month and a day after it opened, the electrification was shut down abruptly on August 11, 1909, when both waterwheels failed at the Leavenworth power plant. Electric operation resumed on September 9, and later in the month the railroad formally accepted the installation.

More trouble struck the new electrification in its first winter of operation, in one of the greatest tragedies in Great Northern history. Throughout the latter part of February 1910 the GN had been plagued by snow slides in Stevens Pass. The situation at Wellington was particularly bad because a forest fire during the previous summer had destroyed the timber which normally held the heavy snows in place.

Early on the morning of March 1, an avalanche, triggered by an unseasonable rainstorm the previous evening, roared down from the hillside above Wellington. The wall of snow and debris slashed

into the GN yards at Wellington, carrying into the valley a mail train and a passenger train (which had been stranded at Wellington because of blockages elsewhere on the line), all four electric locomotives, a rotary snowplow, three steam locomotives, much of the overhead wiring, and a large part of the town of Wellington. All told, 101 persons were killed in the avalanche. Not until March 11 did traffic move through Cascade Tunnel again, and not until summer was the electrification back in service. After that, operations on America's only three-phase electrification were relatively uneventful.

GREAT NORTHERN'S electrification ended the railroad's Cascade Tunnel operating problems, but the entire crossing of the Cascades constituted an operating handicap of growing severity for GN. The arduous Stevens Pass crossing simply was out of place on a railroad that boasted the least curvature, the lowest grades, and the shortest route be-

IN one of the most spectacular areas on GN's original Cascade Tunnel line, the motive power of a 72-car westbound freight passes below its caboose as the train negotiates Horseshoe Tunnel and the lower Martin's Creek trestle on the west slope of the Cascades. The regenerative braking power of the two-unit Baldwin-Westinghouse motor-generator locomotive holds back the heavy train on the 2.2 per cent grade.—*Collection of the Pennsylvania Railway Museum Association.*

EACH two-unit Z-1-class locomotive weighed more than 371 tons, had an hourly rating of 4330 h.p., and could develop a continuous tractive effort of 88,500 pounds. A pair of Z-1's, four units in all, could move a 2900-ton train over the 2.2 per cent maximum grade of the Cascade line. Units B5006 and A5006 are shown here delivering handsomely on the Jim Hill maxim, "maximum ton-miles with minimum train-miles," rolling a 5000-ton, 104-car freight eastward over the new Chumstick Cutoff on the east slope of the Cascades in March 1929. —*Right, Burlington Northern; below, Great Northern.*

EASTBOUND passenger train No. 4 was the last regular train over the old Cascade Tunnel line on January 12, 1929. GE motor-generator unit No. 5012 did the honors. Jim Hill's grandson, Louis W. Hill Jr., on the left, rode the locomotive on the historic occasion. —*Library of Congress.*

SNOW covered the ground in early January 1929 when Baldwin-Westinghouse units A5006 and B5006 appeared at Scenic with what photographer Lee Pickett captioned as the "first train at the West Portal" of the newly completed Cascade Tunnel.—*Library of Congress.*

tween the Great Lakes and the Pacific Coast. In addition, snow slides menaced the line in the high elevations around Cascade Tunnel. Although little trouble with snow slides originally was encountered on the heavily timbered slopes, the loss of timber cover owing to lumbering and forest fires made slides a growing problem that required constant extension of the railroad's snowsheds.

Increasing freight-train tonnages also caused operating problems over the electrification. With the advent of GN's heavy Class O1 Mikados, trains of 2500 tons were operated over the 2.2 per cent ruling grade of Stevens Pass with two 2-6-8-0 Mallets assisting the 2-8-2 road engine. The three-unit electric locomotives used through the tunnel were inadequate to relay this amount of tonnage. The addition of a fourth unit overloaded the power plant, so for a time trains were worked through the tunnel in two cuts. Later, GN electrical engineers installed a new control arrangement known as "concatenation" or "cascade control" which permitted the synchronous motors to operate at half their normal speed. Cascade control enabled GN to use a four-unit locomotive to haul a 2500-ton train through the tunnel without overtaxing the power plant, but train speed was reduced from 15 mph to 7.5 mph.

As early as 1917 Great Northern studied the economies of a longer tunnel at a lower elevation. Such a tunnel would eliminate the menace of slides and avalanches; combined with an extension of the electrification it would cut operating costs. World War I and other problems delayed the project, but in 1925 John F. Stevens, the conqueror of the pass that carried his name, was appointed to study the tunnel proposal. Stevens recommended the tunnel, and on Thanksgiving Day 1925 GN's board of directors approved a 25-million-dollar project to give the railroad a new crossing of the Cascades.

The principal feature of the project was a 7.79-mile tunnel between Berne and Scenic. The new Cascade Tunnel would be the longest railroad tunnel in the Western Hemisphere. On the east slope of the Pass a cutoff following Chumstick Creek on a greatly improved grade and alignment would replace more than 17 miles of the original line between Peshastin and Winton, and substantial revisions were to be made to the original line between Winton and Berne. Electrification would be extended to Wenatchee and Skykomish.

The projected benefits of the project were enormous. The length of the Cascade crossing would be reduced by 8.7 miles, and the summit elevation would be 502 feet lower at 2881 feet. The number and severity of curves would be reduced. Altogether GN would reduce its total curvature in the Cascade crossing by 3365 degrees, the equivalent of more than nine complete circles. Although several miles of 2.2 per cent ruling grade would remain, 21 miles of 2 per cent grade or worse would be eliminated.

The new alignment and tunnel would afford the railroad permanent protection from the hazards of snow slides and winter operating costs would be reduced by moving the railroad below the heavy snow belt of the Cascades. The higher portions of the Cascade line avoided by the new tunnel received the heaviest snowfall on the Great Northern system — as much as 670 inches a season. All 6 miles of GN's Cascade snowsheds, which cost nearly a half million dollars annually to maintain, would be eliminated by the new line.

Electrification of the entire Cascade crossing would improve both the speed and economy of operation. Electric power would operate through one entire motive-power division, and freight-train running times over the Cascades would be reduced by 3½ to 4 hours.

To avoid further maintenance expense for the deteriorating snowsheds, the new tunnel had to be completed before the winter of 1928-1929. To meet this completion date, the railroad's contractor, A. Guthrie & Company of St. Paul, Minn., would have to complete the tunnel in approximately three years. Such a schedule was unprecedented.

Work was started in December 1925. A 622-foot-deep shaft was sunk to the level of the tunnel from the deep valley of Mill Creek, 2½ miles from the tunnel's east portal. This shaft made it possible to advance the tunnel from additional headings. Still more points of attack were provided by the boring of a small preliminary tunnel parallel to the main tunnel from the west portal to Mill Creek shaft. Lateral tunnels at intervals provided access to additional drilling faces.

The pioneer tunnel, which was advanced more rapidly than the main tunnel because of its smaller size, was used to accommodate an air supply for the tunnelers, power and compressed air lines for lighting and machinery, pipes for the removal of water from the main tunnel, and narrow-gauge trains for hauling workmen, supplies, and excavated rock.

The contractor built entire camp towns to house the hundreds of men working on the project. More than 10 miles of electrically powered narrow-gauge railway were laid in the main and pioneer tunnels. The builders' record-breaking pace was sustained by work that went on around the clock, seven days a week. In all, 934,600 cubic yards of earth and rock were removed and 263,000 cubic yards of concrete were placed.

On May 1, 1928, President Calvin Coolidge

AT the time of their construction the Great Northern's Y-1-class 1-C+C-1 box-cabs were the largest single-unit motor-generator locomotives ever built. Weighing 259 tons and rated at 3300 h.p., a Y-1 was almost half again as heavy and powerful as a single unit of the earlier Baldwin-Westinghouse Z-1's. One of the first two units, No. 5011, is shown on GE's test track at Erie, Pa., in 1927. Two more Y-1's were built in 1928, and another four in 1930.—*General Electric.*

SOON after the Great Northern conquered the Cascades with extended electrification, a major line relocation, and what is still the longest railroad tunnel in the Western Hemisphere, the *Empire Builder* began operating between Chicago and the Pacific Northwest as GN's premier train. The *Builder* is shown emerging from the West Portal of the new Cascade Tunnel. The narrow-gauge tracks are remnants of the construction railway.—*Courtesy of Railroad Magazine.*

pressed a key which set off a blast opening the first connection between the pioneer tunnel and the Mill Creek shaft. By October 20, 1928, the main tunnel was holed through. At this time 6½ miles of tunnel already had been lined with concrete, another mile had been enlarged to full size, and 5 miles of electrical installation had been completed. A construction period of 3 years 47 days elapsed

from the date the contractor was told to proceed until the day that the first train ran through the great tunnel. The average progress rate, 36 feet per day, was a new record for speed in tunneling.

Even before the new Cascade Tunnel was completed, Great Northern elected to proceed with the west slope portion of its extended electrification on 21 miles of line between the original tunnel and Skykomish. Although 8 miles of this electrification were located on a line that was to be abandoned upon completion of the new Cascade Tunnel a few years later, so great were the anticipated economies of electrification that the railroad still found it advantageous to proceed with the work.

Experience both favorable and unfavorable with the original three-phase electrification as well as a number of advances in electrification technology since 1909 led Great Northern to abandon the three-phase system and to install a 25-cycle, single-phase A.C. system for its extended electrification.

The key to GN's adoption of the single-phase system was the success of a locomotive tried in 1925 on an electrification of Henry Ford's Detroit, Toledo & Ironton Railroad. This experimental locomotive successfully combined the efficiency of high-voltage, single-phase A.C. for power transmission and distribution with the advantages of low-voltage D.C. traction motors. A large motor-generator set in the locomotive employed a synchronous A.C. motor to drive a D.C. generator, which supplied the low-voltage current required for the traction motors.

The first two locomotives of this type completed for GN were delivered by Baldwin-Westinghouse in 1926. Each locomotive was made up of a pair of semi-permanently coupled 1-D-1 box-cab units. The locomotive pairs weighed more than 371 tons, had an hourly rating of 4330 h.p., and developed a maximum starting tractive effort of 189,000 pounds. One Westinghouse 356-A traction motor was geared to each driving axle. The new locomotives, like the original GN three-phase units, were fitted for multiple-unit control and regenerative braking.

Power was supplied to the new electrification from both the railroad's original hydroelectric plant at Leavenworth, which was modified to provide 25-cycle single-phase power, and from the network of the Puget Sound Power & Light Company, which operated a number of hydroelectric plants in the Cascades. The 60-cycle commercial power was converted to 25-cycle power by 7500-kilovolt-ampere frequency changers at Skykomish and, later, Wenatchee. Power was distributed to the electrification through a 44,000-volt transmission line to seven substations, which fed 11,000 volts to the overhead catenary system.

(LEFT) Motor-generator unit No. 5013 has just coupled onto one of GN's handsome Baldwin-built P-2-class Mountains at Skykomish and is ready to pull the steam locomotive and its passenger train over the Cascade electrification in October 1928.—*Burlington Northern.*

(RIGHT) Proudly carrying the Great Northern emblem on a cab-door drumhead, Y-1 No. 5011 emerges from the West Portal of the new Cascade Tunnel with the Seattle-bound *Cascadian.* The date is March 15, 1930, and the Cascades still are heavily blanketed with the snow of winter.—*General Electric.*

(BELOW) The shrouds over the headlight and the classification lights confirm the 1944 date of this view of the eastbound *Cascadian* at Skykomish. Just behind No. 5012 is the steam generator car that was carried on passenger trains when heat was required, since GN's electrics lacked train-heating boilers. The protruding contact at the end of the roof, similar to that on Reading M.U. cars, served to connect 11,000-volt A.C. between locomotives operating in multiple. It was a GN modification to the original General Electric design.—*Hedrich-Blessing,* **TRAINS** *collection.*

An estimated 65,000 people viewed one of the new locomotives during a tour of principal GN points early in 1927. On March 5, 1927, the two new Baldwin-Westinghouse locomotives were placed in service between Skykomish and East Portal of the original tunnel, and the original three-phase electrification was abandoned.

The new electrification registered remarkable improvements in operations. Whereas a Mikado road engine with two Mallet helpers formerly had required 4 hours to take a 2500-ton eastbound train over the 20 miles from Skykomish to Tye, a Mike and two of the new electrics could cover the same run in 1 hour 45 minutes with a 3500-ton train. No wonder Great Northern didn't wait until the new tunnel was opened to extend its electrification.

The two Baldwin-Westinghouse electrics ran up more than 50,000 miles of mountain railroading each during their first year of operation. Virtually no problems were encountered with the locomotives. Three more of the Z-1-class two-unit Baldwin-Westinghouse locomotives were acquired during 1928.

In 1927 and 1928 the General Electric Company delivered four locomotives, which at the time were the world's largest single-unit motor-generator locomotives. The Y-1-class GE box-cab units were almost 74 feet long and weighed 259 tons. They had an hourly rating of 3300 h.p. and could exert a maximum tractive effort of 120,600 pounds. An air-blast transformer in the locomotive stepped down the catenary voltage to 2300 volts, which was supplied to a synchronous motor driving two 750-volt D.C. generators operating in series. One GE-290-A traction motor was geared to each of six pairs of 55-inch driving wheels. The cast-steel frames were articulated; the six driving axles and two guiding axles were arranged in a 1-C+C-1 pattern. As in the Baldwin-Westinghouse locomotives, multiple-unit control and regenerative braking were provided. Another four identical units were delivered in 1931.

The expanded electrification permitted GN for the first time to obtain the economies of regeneration. In the event that regenerated power from a descending train was not required by another train, the power fed back into the utility company's system could be metered and credited to the railroad.

IN a 1946 view of "standard" electric railroading, train 5, the Spokane-Seattle *Cascadian*, occupies the siding at Monitor, a few miles west of Wenatchee, while train 6, its opposite number, thunders by with three Z-1 units on the point. In a moment train 5 will resume its climb to Cascade Tunnel. Its brass-railed observation car and oil-burning marker lamps will disappear to the west, and the wind will once again be the loudest sound at Monitor.—*Burlington Northern.*

Following completion of the Chumstick Cutoff on the east slope of the pass, GN finished the electrification between Wenatchee and the East Portal of the new tunnel. For a few months at the end of 1928 some trains were operated electrically over this section, and then were hauled, electric locomotive and all, over a 4.5-mile section of unelectrified line by a Mallet to reach catenary again at the old tunnel. By January of 1929 GN was ready to open the new Cascade Tunnel and conquer the Cascades once and for all.

The tunnel opened on January 12, 1929, with a gala celebration. A national radio hookup reached an estimated 15 million people. Among the dignitaries who took part in the broadcast were President-elect Herbert Hoover; J. B. Campbell of the Interstate Commerce Commission; Gen. William Wallace Atterbury, president of the Pennsylvania Railroad; and, of course, Great Northern President Ralph Budd.

The westbound *Oriental Limited,* drawn by a two-unit locomotive, made the official first trip through the tunnel. After a stop at East Portal for ceremonies, the train proceeded to West Portal, where it burst through a paper cover as a radio announcer described the scene for his nationwide audience.

GN traffic soon rolled through the new Cascade Tunnel routinely, and the old line and tunnel were abandoned. With the worst of the climb over the Cascades eliminated, the electrics were able to climb the west slope with trains of 5000 tons — double the tonnage common to steam operation over the old line. Moreover, the electrics performed the task in much less time than steam took.

FOR more than a quarter of a century GN's electrification continued to give a good account of itself. During the traffic-heavy World War II years, GN moved some phenomenal trains over the pass. One common practice of the war years, when the electric locomotives were taxed to their limits, was to tie three of the big GE electrics on the head of a

LATE-AFTERNOON sun illuminates the running gear of Z-1 locomotive 5008 as it waits with pantographs down in the siding at Dryden, in the apple-growing country along the Wenatchee River near the east end of Great Northern's electrification. The year is 1940.—TRAINS: *Linn H. Westcott.*

IT'S dusk and the classification lamps are lit as No. 5000 leads a five-unit block of 1-D-1's east toward Cascade Tunnel. —*Rail Photo Service: William J. Pontin.*

6000-ton train, cut a four-unit 5400 h.p. diesel helper into the middle, and put a 2-8-8-2 pusher behind the caboose. A combination like this usually made 17 mph climbing the 2.2 per cent grade to the tunnel.

After World War II, increasing traffic and heavier trains obliged GN to supplement its fleet of 13 electric locomotives. Two W-1-class locomotives were built by General Electric's Erie (Pa.) plant and were delivered to GN early in 1947. The W-1's extended 101 feet between couplers, weighed 360 tons, and possessed a continuous rating of 5000 h.p. Billed as the most powerful single-unit electrics in the world, they readily qualified as "the

FRESHLY PAINTED Y-1 No. 5017 and sisters 5012 and 5010 have the 5263 tons of eastbound time freight 402 in tow crossing the Foss River near Tonga in May of 1941. Out of sight to the rear, steam power in the form of an O-4-class 2-8-2 is helping the three electrics keep the train's 99 cars moving on the 2.2 per cent grade.—W. R. McGee.

Big Boys of North American electrification." Capable of a starting tractive effort of 180,000 pounds, a W-1 could outpull any two 4-8-4's and could exceed the pulling power of even a Union Pacific "Big Boy" by one third.

Regenerative braking gave the big electrics a continuous braking capacity of 5750 h.p., and should a train be too heavy for even the largest of all electrics, the two W-1's could be run in multiple.

The W-1's employed the same motor-generator arrangement of earlier GN electrics to convert high-voltage A.C. power from the trolley wire to low-voltage D.C. for the traction motors. A single 11,000/1350-volt transformer supplied power to a pair of 25-cycle synchronous motors, which in turn drove the locomotive's D.C. traction generators.

The big locomotives were equipped with a pair of cast-steel main frames connected by a pin at the center of the locomotive. Each frame carried four pairs of driving wheels and a four-wheel guiding truck. In a departure from most previous electric-locomotive designs, every axle on the W-1's was powered, giving the locomotives a B-D+D-B wheel arrangement. A dozen nose-suspended GE-746 series-wound D.C. traction motors, one for each axle, were geared to the 42-inch drivers.

The streamlined body was of welded steel construction and had a diesel-style operating cab at each end. Transformers, main motor-generator sets, blowers, and controls were housed in the long center section; air compressors and auxiliary motor-generators were installed in the nose sections.

The giant electrics added a substantial new ca-

AFTER suffering extensive damage in a fire, Y-1 No. 5011 was rebuilt by GN's St. Paul shops in 1945. The reconstruction included (right) EMD diesel cabs and the Omaha orange and Pullman green livery of GN's new streamliners. (Above) The one-of-a-kind Y-1a arrives at Skykomish with the westbound *Cascadian*, the daytime Spokane-Seattle local.—*Above, Rail Photo Service: William J. Pontin; right, Burlington Northern.*

pacity to GN's Cascade electrification. In passenger service they were good for a top speed of 65 mph. In freight service they could pull a 2000-ton train up the line's 2.2 per cent ruling grade without a helper, and their great regenerative braking capacity permitted downgrade operation of tonnage trains without the use of train air brakes.

Despite the remarkable performance of these new electrics, Great Northern's mountain electrification was eclipsed by diesel-electric motive power less than a decade after the W-1's entered service. The reasons for de-electrification were much the same as those that displaced electric traction from the St. Clair, Detroit River, and Hoosac tunnels during the same period. Diesels could run straight through over several divisions, offering substantial economies in time and operating costs. Stops to ex-

change diesel and electric motive power for a relatively short run were inconsistent with this kind of operation. By comparison with steam, internal-combustion power created only minor operating problems in long tunnels — problems that could be corrected with improved ventilation systems.

Thus, when Great Northern completed a high-capacity ventilating system for Cascade Tunnel in 1956, diesel-electric motive power moved into the Cascades and the wires of GN's remarkable mountain electrification came down. Seven of the Y-1-class 1-C+C-1 GE locomotives were sold to the Pennsylvania Railroad, where they saw service as helper engines in eastern Pennsylvania, while one of the W-1's was rebuilt by Union Pacific as an experimental coal-fired gas-turbine engine. Everything else was scrapped.

TIPPING the scales at 360 tons, GN's W-1 was 46 tons heavier than a Union Pacific "Big Boy" and weighed about the same as a Northern Pacific Yellowstone, the heaviest steam locomotive in North America. The awesome dimensions of the largest single-unit electrics built in North America are evident in the broadside view (above) of No. 5018 at Wenatchee and the view of the running gear (left) on the assembly floor of General Electric's Erie plant. The head-on view and the photo of the cab interior show the influence of diesel-electric practice in the styling of the locomotive.—*Above, Great Northern; other photos, General Electric.*

GIANT motor-generator locomotive No. 5018 rolls downgrade along the Wenatchee River toward
the city of the same name with the Mid-Century edition of GN's flagship, the *Empire Builder*.
In passenger service the W-1's were allowed a maximum speed of 65 mph.—*Great Northern*.

SOON after W-1's entered service the Great Northern undertook a major line relocation in the Cascades. Several miles east of Cascade Tunnel a new tunnel and a new bridge were built and a mile of line was relocated along Nason Creek Canyon, all at a cost of 1 million dollars. The project reduced the grade of the line from 2.2 to 2.09 per cent, eliminated 207 degrees of curvature, avoided a treacherous rockslide area, and cut running times by 5 minutes. (Above) A westbound train drawn by Y-1 No. 5014 pops out of tunnel 14.7 in 1949, shortly after the new line was opened. (Right) One of the W-1's leads eastbound time freight No. 442 across the new Nason Creek Canyon bridge.—*Both photos, Great Northern.*

ON a June evening in 1956 representatives of GN's three classes of electrics gathered at the Wenatchee enginehouse, seemingly to discuss their futures. W-1 No. 5018 eventually would become part of an experimental Union Pacific gas-turbine, and seven of the Y-1's would don Pennsy's red keystone emblem and begin a new career as helpers. (PRR also purchased Y-1a No. 5011 for parts.) For No. 5019 and the Z-1's, the future held only the scrapyard.—*Stan Kistler.*

THE GE-built Y-1's received GN's many-striped orange-and-green streamliner livery after World War II. A trio of them lift an eastbound freight up the grade near Scenic, assisted by another batch of electrics cut in farther back in the train.—*Joseph Sweeney.*

LAST RUN: On July 31, 1956, No. 5018 emerged from the East Portal of Cascade Tunnel towing a string of older electrics from Skykomish to Wenatchee. Soon afterward the new tunnel ventilating system was activated, power to the catenary was turned off, and diesels began to operate straight through from the east to Seattle.—*Wenatchee Daily World, courtesy of Railroad Magazine.*

BIG MOTORS in the Appalachians: Virginian "squareheads" —No. 106 on a train of empty hoppers returning to West Virginia mines and No. 110 heading mixed eastbound traffic— meet near Glenvar, Va., on April 19, 1956.—*John E. Pickett.*

❖❖❖❖❖❖❖❖❖❖❖❖❖❖❖❖❖❖❖❖❖❖❖❖❖❖❖❖❖

7. Big motors in the Appalachians

❖❖❖❖❖❖❖❖❖❖❖❖❖❖❖❖❖❖❖❖❖❖❖❖❖❖❖❖

SHORTLY before World War I, electric traction successfully met one of railroading's toughest operating challenges when the Norfolk & Western Railway electrified its crossing of the Appalachians over Elkhorn Mountain. The project eased a severe traffic blockage on N&W's rugged main line.

Since 1883 high-grade bituminous coal had been mined from the Pocahontas coal fields of eastern Kentucky, western Virginia, and West Virginia and shipped to tidewater on the Norfolk & Western; coal traffic on this route increased steadily over the years. On the western slope of the Appalachians this traffic was confronted by the most severe operating conditions on the entire railroad.

Over a distance of 40 miles, from Iaeger, W. Va., to the east portal of Elkhorn Tunnel, eastbound Pocahontas Division traffic encountered steadily increasing grades that reached a maximum of 2 per cent near the summit. Sixty per cent of the long climb beside Tug Fork River and Elkhorn Creek was on curves; some of the curves were as tight as 13 degrees. Just before reaching the summit of the Elkhorn Mountain climb the rails passed through the 3014-foot Elkhorn Tunnel on a 1.4 per cent ascending grade.

As coal traffic grew, N&W hurled larger and larger steam power against the Elkhorn grade. During the first decade of the century as many as

181

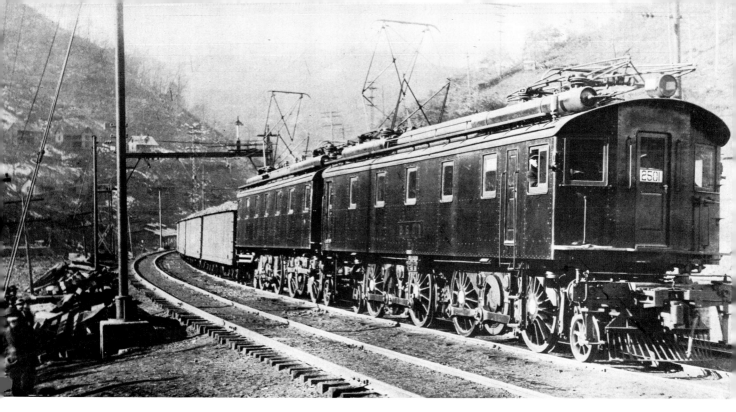

THE quiet hum of traction motors and the whoosh of blowers have replaced the furious sound of Mallets as Norfolk & Western motor 2501 moves West Virginia coal up Elkhorn grade. Out of sight at the end of the drag another set of the 300-ton electrics assist the train in maintaining its steady 14-mph pace. These N&W LC-1's were North America's largest electric locomotives when this photo was taken in the spring of 1915.—*Smithsonian Institution*.

ALTHOUGH designed primarily for coal drag service, N&W electrics also boosted steam-powered passenger traffic over the arduous Elkhorn grade. In fact, a 1916 report states, "it [was] a common occurrence to pick up a train twenty minutes late at North Fork and put it into Bluestone Junction on time." Neither the exact locale nor the reason for 2506's missing pilot in this early view are known.—*Norfolk & Western*.

six 2-8-0 Consolidations could be found struggling over the grade with a 2000-ton train. Around 1910 N&W introduced 2-6-6-2 and 2-8-8-2 Mallet compounds, equipped with mechanical stokers and superheaters. Three of these big engines could move a 3250-ton coal train over the grade.

Despite the increased capacity afforded by the new Mallets, N&W desperately needed further improvement to its Appalachian crossing. A daily eastbound coal traffic of as much as 65,000 tons required at least 20 coal extras each day over the grade, in addition to other freight and passenger traffic. Steam-powered coal trains were able to maintain speeds of only 7 to 8 mph on the grade, and further delay was encountered every time a train had to be halted on the grade for fuel and water. Winter weather, which dropped the tonnage rating for steam power by as much as 10 per cent, further aggravated the problems.

The real "neck of the bottle" on Elkhorn grade, however, was the single-track Elkhorn Tunnel. Elsewhere, the line was double or triple track. Smoke and gas problems in the tunnel prevented steam-powered trains from traveling faster than about 6 mph, and 7 minutes were required for a train to clear the block that included the tunnel. Frequently, during periods of peak traffic, trains were backed up at each end of the tunnel waiting to get through. Elkhorn Tunnel limited the capacity of N&W's main line.

Enlargement of Elkhorn Tunnel to accommodate a second track would have been a formidable undertaking for the railroad. Instead, after several years of study, N&W in 1912 decided to electrify Elkhorn grade.

Contracts between Norfolk & Western and the Westinghouse companies for locomotives and other electrical equipment were signed in 1913. Construction work for the 3 million dollar project, much of which was carried out by a specially organized N&W force, started later the same year.

The initial electrification extended over an entire engine division, from Vivian, W. Va., eastward for 27 miles over Elkhorn grade to Bluefield, W. Va., the location of a major classification yard. Including second and third mainline tracks, sidings, yard tracks, and branches into coal mines, track under catenary totaled 90 miles.

The electrical system developed by the railroad's consulting engineers, Gibbs & Hill of New York, was a radical departure from the D.C. and A.C. systems that had been used in previous railroad electrifications. For the heavy-tonnage mountain operation that characterized the proposed electrification, N&W's consultants believed that the constant-speed three-phase induction motor, with its ruggedness and simplicity, high output, uni-

form torque, and adaptability to regenerative braking, would be superior to both single-phase and D.C. motors.

For the power distribution system, however, the engineers preferred an 11,000-volt, 25-cycle, single-phase A.C. system similar to that which had been used in the New Haven and Boston & Maine electrifications. A single-phase system avoided the complexities of the two-wire overhead distribution required for three-phase power distribution. Moreover, a single-phase installation would afford the highest efficiency in transmitting the great amount of power required for N&W's exceptionally heavy traffic.

Recognizing the potential advantages of both systems, General Electric and Westinghouse for several years had been experimenting with phase converters or phase-splitting devices that would permit single-phase power distribution to be used with three-phase induction motors. Aside from a small experimental unit tested by General Electric several years previous, this concept remained untried. Norfolk & Western's decision to adopt the split-phase system for what was then one of the most important electrifications yet undertaken was an important victory for this new concept in railroad electrification.

Power for the N&W installation was distributed through a simple-catenary overhead system supported by steel bridges at 300-foot intervals. Power was generated in a railroad-owned plant constructed at Bluestone, W. Va., 10.8 miles west of Bluefield. A dozen 200-pound Stirling-type boilers supplied steam to three 10,000-kilowatt Westinghouse turbogenerators. A fourth generator was added later. The generators delivered power at 11,000 volts, which was transformed to 44,000 volts for transmission to five substations, where it was reduced back to 11,000 volts for trolley-wire distribution. The section of overhead wire nearest the power plant was supplied at 11,000 volts directly from the generators.

The most important technical feature of the N&W electrification, of course, was its split-phase locomotives. Each of the dozen Class LC-1 locomotives Baldwin-Westinghouse delivered to N&W in 1914 consisted of a pair of semi-permanently coupled 1-B+B-1 box-cab units. Each 300-ton pair was 105 feet 8 inches long. With an hourly rating of 3200 h.p. and a maximum starting tractive effort of 125,000 pounds, the two-unit LC-1's were the largest and heaviest electric locomotives in the United States at the time they were placed in operation.

Current collection was by pantograph, and a single transformer on each locomotive unit stepped down the single-phase current from 11,000 to 750

PORTRAIT of power: Class LC-1 No. 2500 hums eastbound up Elkhorn grade past the Appalachian Power & Light Co. plant at Ennis, W.Va., with a steam locomotive and its nine-car passenger train.—*Norfolk & Western.*

volts. The 750-volt current powered the rotating phase converter, which supplied 750-volt, three-phase power to the traction motors.

The Baldwin-Westinghouse design utilized steam-locomotive-type side rods driving 62-inch wheels. Each four-wheel driving truck was powered by a pair of Westinghouse 450A motors geared through jackshafts located midway between the driving axles. This design had the advantages of low unsprung weight and a high center of gravity, thereby reducing lateral forces against the rail, a problem common to electric locomotives with motors at axle level.

The two trucks on each unit were connected by a Mallet-type hinge, and a two-wheel, radial leading truck was provided at each end of the unit. Tractive loads were transmitted through the truck frames by means of draft gear mounted directly on the main trucks at each end of the locomotive.

Windings for either four- or eight-pole operation and a provision for cascade connection enabled the constant-speed induction motors to be operated to provide running speeds of 7, 14, and 28 mph. Regenerative braking also was possible. An unusual feature of the N&W locomotives was the use of liquid rheostats, which employed iron electrodes raised or lowered in a solution of anhydrous sodium carbonate to vary the resistance in the motor-control circuits. First used on N&W electric locomotives, the liquid rheostat afforded exceptionally precise motor control. Multiple-unit control permitted operation of each locomotive pair from a single operating cab.

Electric operation over a portion of the division began in early 1915, and the entire division was electrically operated by late spring. Aside from a few weaknesses in various locomotive components, problems which were readily solved by the builders, the new installation performed flawlessly from the start, with operating results that met or exceeded the railroad's expectations.

To ensure that locomotives would be able to overcome the severe loads associated with starting heavy coal trains, N&W had specified that the locomotives be able to deliver their maximum drawbar pull for a period of 5 minutes with the wheels at rest — that is, stalled under full load. In dynamometer tests the LC-1's exceeded this requirement by 20 per cent. In one test an LC-1 developed a tractive effort of more than 170,000 pounds, over a third more than its rated maximum. In starting a maximum-tonnage coal train a pair of LC-1's (four units) was able to develop 11,000 h.p. and proved capable of a continuous output of 8000 h.p. when running with a train. With regenerative braking kicked in, a single LC-1 was able to hold a full-tonnage train to 14 mph on the 2.4 per cent descending grade east of Elkhorn Tunnel.

The improvement in operating conditions on Elkhorn grade brought on by electrification was substantial. Under steam, a 3250-ton coal train required two Mallets to move it over the engine division, with a third Mallet added as a pusher on the 1.5 and 2 per cent grades west of the tunnel. A two-unit LC-1, with a second electric operating as a pusher on the maximum grades, was able to take the same train over the division. Moreover, a pair of LC-1's could take 3250 tons up a 2 per cent grade at 14 mph, double the speed that three Mallets could make with the same tonnage. In one test,

LOW-LEVEL, head-on view of motor 2501 towing an eastbound passenger train dramatizes the work performed by the LC-1's in mountain duty. This 1920's scene is just above Maybeury, W.Va., on the 2 per cent approach to Elkhorn Tunnel.—*Fred Eidenbenz.*

three of the electrics successfully handled a 4800-ton train over the division.

At congested Elkhorn Tunnel, where steam-powered trains had required 7 minutes to clear the single-track block, electrics rolled a train through in 3 minutes. During the first year of operation, N&W reported that the electrics daily handled up to 50 per cent greater tonnages eastbound over Elkhorn grade than the maximum set by steam power.

Electrification had other advantages, too. The greater speed and capacity of the electric units, as well as their capability to be turned quickly at the end of a run, permitted N&W to increase its loco-motive utilization tremendously; the 12 LC-1's per-formed the same work that formerly had required 33 Mallets. The greater efficiency of the electrics cut N&W's fuel costs a third from what they would have been with steam operation. By the early 1920's the railroad reported that electrification was saving an estimated $15,000 a month on its coal bill and that overall motive-power costs were 12.5 per cent less with electricity than with steam.

The initial Norfolk & Western electrification had hardly started operation when the railroad began constructing extensions. During 1915-1916 cate-nary was extended 6 route-miles over the Clift Yard and Pocahontas branches, extending north and south respectively from Bluestone Junction. Shortly after World War I, catenary was built west-ward over the main line from Vivian to Farm and over the Welch-Wilcoe (W. Va.) branch. Even be-fore this work was completed in 1923, N&W direc-tors voted still another extension westward over the main line from Farm to Iaeger, 52 miles west of

Bluefield. By the time this final extension was completed in 1925, N&W had doubled the mileage of its original electrification.

To provide sufficient motive power for the ex-tensions, N&W ordered four more two-unit split-phase locomotives from Westinghouse and the American Locomotive Company. Similar in design to the LC-1's, the new Class LC-2 locomotives had nearly a third greater capacity than the earlier machines. Each of the 414-ton, two-unit locomo-tives had an hourly rating of 4750 h.p. and a max-imum starting tractive effort of 168,000 pounds. Two of the new locomotives could take a 4000-ton train up Elkhorn grade's 2 per cent eastbound climb.

The mechanical drive and running gear of the new locomotives varied somewhat from the pre-vious design. Although the jackshaft and side-rod drive was retained, the LC-2's employed a rigid 1-D-1 wheel arrangement and a spring arrange-ment identical to that of a Mikado-type steam locomotive. Two jackshafts, one at each end of a unit, drove two driving axles each. A single West-inghouse 452 inductive motor was geared to each jackshaft.

For more than three decades N&W's huge split-phase, side-rod electrics continued to hoist West Virginia soft coal over the backbone of the Appala-chians. Even during the height of World War II, when N&W moved an all-time record of 54 million tons of coal in 1943, the big electrics kept traffic fluid over the toughest engine division on the railroad.

Soon after World War II, however, N&W em-barked on an ambitious 5-mile, 11.9-million-dollar

185

THE most important technical advancement of N&W's electrification project was its split-phase locomotives. First were 12 Class LC-1's (above left) delivered by Baldwin-Westinghouse in 1914. These two-unit locomotives had a 2 (1-B+B-1) wheel arrangement and an hourly rating of 3200 h.p. In 1924 N&W expanded its electric power roster with four more split-phase locomotives, the LC-2's (left) built by Alco-Westinghouse. The LC-2's had a jackshaft and side-rod drive similar to the LC-1's, but employed a rigid 1-D-1 wheel arrangement on each unit of the pairs. The LC-2's had an hourly rating of 4750 h.p. and were one third heavier than the LC-1's.—*Both photos, Norfolk & Western.*

(FAR LEFT) All is not downhill from Elkhorn Tunnel: LC-2 No. 2513 eases hoppers loaded with soft coal mined from the Pocahontas region into the 1.2 per cent grade just west of Graham, Va. The tonnage is bound for tidewater, but the electric locomotives will be removed at the Bluefield (W.Va.) yard at the eastern end of the catenary just 4 miles ahead.—*Norfolk & Western.*

NEARING Elkhorn summit, an LC-2 (left) acting as a pusher assists a coal drag up the 2 per cent grade. The 414-ton LC-2's were only a few years old when Swiss photographer Eidenbenz recorded this scene of electric railroading.—*Fred Eidenbenz.*

AWAITING helper duties on Elkhorn grade, an LC-2 stands at North Fork, W.Va. Out of North Fork eastbound trains faced 5 miles of 1.5 per cent grade and then 4 miles of 2 per cent on the way to Elkhorn Tunnel.—*Wilhelm Vutz*.

A MIX of LC-2's and LC-1's stand on the ready track at N&W's Eckman (W.Va.) yard on June 17, 1949. The big box-cabs were scrapped in the summer of 1950.—*Richard J. Cook*.

188

STRETCHING the drawbars of Extra 2504 East, two LC-1's—6400 h.p. worth of power—move upgrade through Powhatan, W.Va., in June 1949 with a string of loaded hoppers. Scenes like this were typical until the end of N&W electrification in 1950.—*Richard J. Cook.*

tunnel and line-relocation project to improve operating conditions over Elkhorn Mountain. A new 7052-foot, double-track Elkhorn Tunnel pierced the mountain at a substantially lower elevation. In addition to eliminating the single-track bottleneck of the old tunnel, the relocation lowered the summit of N&W's Appalachian crossing by nearly a hundred feet, eliminated much of the severe curvature of the old route, and reduced the maximum eastbound grade from 2 per cent to 1.4 per cent.

The combination of improved operating conditions and the availability of N&W's magnificent fleet of modern articulated steam power largely offset the advantages of retaining electrification. Catenary never went up on the relocated Elkhorn grade, and the big box-cabs were cut up for scrap after the new line opened in the summer of 1950.

The Virginian Railway

WHILE the Norfolk & Western was completing the final section of its Appalachian electrification during the mid-1920's, another Pocahontas region coal hauler, the Virginian Railway, was embarking on an even more ambitious electrification program.

Constructed by financier Henry Huttleston Rogers during the first decade of the century, the Virginian had been built almost exclusively to transport coal from West Virginia coal fields to ports on Chesapeake Bay. Originating at Deepwater, W. Va., the railroad tapped both the Pocahontas and New River region coal mines, and moved their output across the Appalachians through Roanoke, Va., to the company's own coal piers at Norfolk, Va.

East of Roanoke the Virginian main line had a maximum grade eastbound of only 0.2 per cent, but in the Appalachians between Roanoke and Elmore, W. Va., the principal collecting yard for coal traffic, far more difficult operating conditions were encountered. The maximum eastbound grade, between Elmore and Clarks Gap, W. Va., exceeded 2 per cent, and track curvature was as sharp as 12 degrees. Except for double track on the railroad's heaviest grade between Mullens, W. Va., and Clarks Gap, the entire Virginian was single track.

From the very beginning the Virginian was designed, built, and equipped to accommodate exceptionally heavy traffic. Track was rock-ballasted and laid with 100- and 130-pound rail, and bridges were built to the heaviest loading standards. Even before World War I the railroad was building six-wheel-truck gondola cars that had an imposing capacity of 120 tons of coal. Between 1909 and the early 1920's the Virginian took delivery of some of the most powerful steam locomotives of that time.

The Virginian put its first Mallet, a 150-ton 2-6-6-0, in service in 1909, and within a decade had progressed through several series of 2-8-8-2's to a batch of 342-ton 2-10-10-2 Mallets. In 1917 the railroad even tried out the famous "Triplex" locomotive, an extraordinary 2-8-8-8-4 that had a maximum tractive effort of 200,000 pounds.

Virginian steam power handled some remark-

ably heavy tonnage. Regularly, trains of 5500 tons were moved up the 2.11 per cent grade between Elmore and Clarks Gap by a 2-8-8-2 Mallet road engine and two 2-10-10-2 Mallet helpers. The three locomotives exerted a combined tractive effort of 409,400 pounds. East of Princeton, W. Va., trains of 8000 tons regularly were operated with only one road engine, with a pusher used only to help trains out of Princeton yard and on the 0.6 per cent grade between Whitethorne and Merrimac, Va. On one occasion, in 1921, one of Virginian's 2-10-10-2's, aided by a 2-8-8-2 helper on the Merrimac grade, took a train of a record 17,050 tons over the road from Princeton to Norfolk.

By the early 1920's, despite the exceptional capabilities of its steam power, the Virginian — like the Norfolk & Western — had recognized that its potential for traffic growth was limited by the section of line over the Appalachians. By this time the railroad was hauling 7 million tons of coal a year, and with development of new mines and expanded production at existing mines, a traffic increase of 100 per cent was forecast. The line east of Roanoke and the Norfolk coal piers could accommodate increased traffic, but the line over the mountains was approaching the limits of its ability to handle tonnage.

Adding more trackage and steam motive power

was one solution to the problem, but it promised to be a costly one. An economical alternative, according to Virginian studies, was electrification, and early in 1923 the railroad announced a 15-million-dollar electrification project that would put 134 miles of line between Mullens and Roanoke under catenary.

The electrical system and motive power adopted for the Virginian's electrification project were virtually identical to those developed a decade earlier with such success by the Norfolk & Western for similar mountain service. Eleven-thousand-volt, 25-cycle A.C. was supplied through a heavy-duty catenary system supported by steel H-section poles at 320-foot intervals. The overhead distribution system was designed to deliver exceptionally large amounts of power for the immense horsepower demands imposed by the high speeds and heavy tonnages contemplated by the Virginian. For example, 14,000 kilowatts of power was required to start a 6000-ton coal train on a heavy grade.

Determined that "traffic movement should not be subordinated to power demand," the Virginian constructed its own power plant to assure that ample power at low cost always would be available. Located beside the New River at Narrows, Va., midway between Mullens and Roanoke, the steam turbogenerator plant supplied all power for

THE first Virginian box-cab electrics, completed by Alco-Westinghouse in 1925, were impressive pieces of machinery. Virginian proudly called these 640-ton, 7125 h.p., 152-foot, triple-unit EL-3A electrics "the world's most powerful locomotives," and there was nothing on rails at the time that could challenge the claim.—*Collection of Edward T. Francis.*

VIRGINIAN men called them flatnoses and squareheads and anything except beauties, but the three-unit, split-phase motors were as impressive as anything in railroading. Richard J. Cook photographed No. 103 at Rich Creek, Va., running along the New River with an eastbound extra in September 1953. —*Richard J. Cook.*

LEANING hard on No. 103's regenerative braking, eastbound tonnage descends the 1.5 per cent grade into the New River valley in September 1953 near Oakville, W.Va.—*Richard J. Cook.*

MOTOR 101 rumbles eastbound through Narrows, W.Va., in 1948. With all the furious motion of their jackshafts and side rods, the squareheads had almost as much visual excitement as a steam locomotive. As David P. Morgan once wrote, "they allowed Mallets to retreat from the battlefield with dignity intact."—*Ben F. Cutler.*

the railway's electrification. Five 1521 h.p. Springfield cross-drum boilers, fed on a diet of pulverized coal, supplied steam to four 25-cycle, three-phase, 11,000-volt turbogenerators, which delivered a maximum of 15,000 kilowatts each. Three of the generators were capable of supplying the maximum anticipated power demand of 43,000 kilowatts. A water rheostat at the plant absorbed excess power returned through the distribution system by regeneration from descending trains.

Four 10,000-kilovolt-ampere transformers at the plant increased the voltage to 88,000 volts for transmission to seven step-down transformers located at various intervals between Mullens and Roanoke. The transformers reduced voltage back to 11,000 volts. An 88,000-volt transmission line installed in 1928 between the Virginian at Matoaka, W. Va., and N&W's Bluestone power plant permitted the two railroads to interchange power in the event of an emergency.

The distribution system and the locomotives were designed to operate at either 11,000 or 22,000 volts. A change to the higher voltage was contemplated when traffic increased to the point where the additional capacity became necessary.

Electric motive power for the Virginian included 36 locomotives built by Alco-Westinghouse during 1925 and 1926. They were near duplicates of N&W's split-phase LC-2's delivered by the same builders in 1924. Each of the 50-foot 9-inch-long box-cab units weighed over 212 tons. Power from the overhead entered the locomotive and passed through a single oil-cooled transformer and a phase converter to two Westinghouse 452-A induction-type traction motors, which provided synchronous speeds of 14 and 28 mph. Each traction motor powered two pairs of 62-inch driving wheels through a jackshaft and side-rod drive. Acceleration to either running speed was accomplished by a liquid rheostat. Electropneumatic multiple-unit control permitted up to four units to be operated from a single cab. Maximum tractive effort for each box-cab unit was 92,500 pounds, with an hourly rating of 2375 h.p. at 28 mph.

Like Norfolk & Western's LC-2's, the Virginian locomotives automatically regenerated power when descending a grade. In addition to saving electricity, the regenerative feature allowed trains to descend grades at a fixed speed without the use of air brakes. This meant reduced wear on brake shoes and rigging.

Six of the box-cabs were arranged for single-unit operation, but the remainder were semi-permanently coupled into three-unit sets, said to be the largest locomotives in the world. Weighing more than 640 tons, each of these mammoth motive-power blocks had a starting tractive effort of

VIRGINIAN electric 103 has a running start for the Clarks Gap grade as she comes grinding through Alpoca, W.Va., on a summer day in 1950.—*H. W. Pontin.*

TRIPLE-UNIT motor 104 emerges from a tunnel at Algonquin, W.Va., in August 1948, running left-handed on the double track up Clarks Gap grade.—*Ben F. Cutler.*

277,500 pounds and an hourly rating of 7125 h.p.

The initial 14-mile section of Virginian electrification, on the severe 2.11 per cent grade between Elmore and Clarks Gap, was opened in September 1925. A few weeks later the electrification was extended another 20½ miles to Princeton. After a delay while unsuccessful merger talks were held with N&W, work resumed on the installation early in 1926, and the electrics began running all the way to Roanoke on September 18.

Operation of the first electric-powered coal train eastbound up Clarks Gap grade was attended with suitable fanfare. For the occasion, Virginian assembled a 62-car, 6050-ton train of loaded 50- and 116-ton-capacity hoppers. Two of the new three-unit electrics, one pulling and one pushing, hauled the train, which weighed more than 8000 tons including locomotives, caboose, and a business car for Virginian brass hats on the end.

To provide a dramatic comparison between the steam locomotives and the new electrics, a similar train was assembled and three Mallets were coupled on. It was given a 15-minute head start up the double track of the grade. The electric locomotives overtook and passed the laboring steamers

long before they reached the midpoint of the grade, where a battery of motion-picture cameramen were waiting to film the event. The electric train had almost passed the cameramen before the steam train came into view.

The running time of the electrics for the 14-mile drag up to Clarks Gap was only 1 hour, compared to an average of 2½ hours for somewhat lighter steam-powered trains. Needless to say, Virginian was pleased with the results. "All the preliminary tests have indicated that our expectations as to the value of electric operation will be met," declared Virginian President Charles H. Hix.

With electrification into Roanoke completed the following year, electric movement of coal traffic assumed a regular pattern. At Elmore yard, the gathering point for coal traffic from West Virginia mines, trains of 6000 tons were assembled, and moved up Clarks Gap grade by two three-unit EL-3A's, one pulling and one pushing. At Clarks Gap, trains were filled out to 9000 tons and moved to Roanoke behind a single set of EL-3A's.

In contrast, it had taken a 2-8-8-2 road engine and two 2-10-10-2 helpers to conquer Clarks Gap grade with a 5500-ton train. A single 2-8-8-2 then

JUNE 1949 miner's vacation had Virginian coal traffic in the doldrums, explaining why photographer Cook found so many idle units at Mullens, W.Va.—*Richard J. Cook.*

could move the tonnage from Clarks Gap to Princeton. There, trains were filled to 10,000 tons for the remainder of the run to Roanoke, although steam trains required helpers at two points east of Princeton. Moreover, the big "squarehead" electrics could move tonnage over the road in less than half the time it took with steam.

The electrics went into operation just in time to handle a surge in Virginian's coal traffic. In 1924, the last year Virginian trains were handled with steam power exclusively, the railroad handled a net coal traffic of 7,440,832 tons. In 1927, when the electrification was in full operation, the railroad moved 11,825,101 tons of coal.

For two decades Virginian's original electrics proved equal to the task of moving the coal down to tidewater. Traffic dropped off for a while during the great depression but came back stronger than ever during World War II, reaching an annual level of nearly 13 million tons. After the war, an increase in export coal tonnages raised Virginian's traffic to even higher levels. By 1948 the railroad was hauling 15.5 million tons of coal yearly.

By the end of World War II Virginian's aging squareheads were beginning to feel the strain of

the growing traffic, and in late 1945 the railroad placed an order with General Electric for four new electric locomotives. True to the Virginian motive-power traditions that had produced the colossal Triplex of 1917, the largest-anywhere 2-10-10-2's of 1918, or the "world's most powerful" EL-3A-class electrics of 1925, the new Class EL-2B units established still another motive-power record for the Virginian.

The new EL-2B's consisted of two semi-permanently coupled cab units, stretching 150 feet 8 inches between coupler faces and weighing almost 517 tons (or, as the press-release copywriters seemed to prefer, "a million pounds"). Each locomotive pair was rated at 6800 h.p. and developed a starting tractive effort of 260,000 pounds. A continuous tractive effort of 162,000 pounds made them the most powerful continuous-rated locomotives in the world.

Except for their prodigious size and capacity, below the pantographs there was little similarity between Virginian's new GE locomotives and the original Alco-Westinghouse box-cabs. The new EL-2B's, with diesel-inspired streamlined carbodies dressed in glossy black with racy yellow striping,

LOOKING every bit of her 150-foot 8-inch length in this overhead view, motor 125 slams through Princeton, W.Va., in 1949 with a train of empty hoppers.—*Ben F. Cutler.*

MOTOR 128 moves an eastbound coal extra across the Norfolk & Western at one of many locations where competing N&W followed Virginian rails. The GE EL-2B's were about two years old when this scene was recorded in 1950.—*H. W. Pontin.*

THE dimensions and capacity of the million-pound, 6800 h.p. EL-2B's were noteworthy even on the Virginian, a railroad accustomed to setting motive-power records. No. 125 (left) was the first EL-2B off the production line in 1948. The construction view (above) was taken at GE's Erie (Pa.) works.—*Left, General Electric,* TRAINS *collection; above, General Electric, courtesy of Railroad Magazine.*

DAWN greets two generations of Virginian electric power meeting at Princeton at 5:45 a.m. on Friday, June 13, 1958. EL-2B No. 128 heads westbound empties; the new rectifier unit is leading a coal extra.—*J. P. Lamb Jr.*

HIGH above the New River valley near Glen Lyn, Va., on one of Virginian's spectacular trestles, GE motor 127 vaults across the Virginia-West Virginia state line with a westbound train of empty hopper cars in July 1948.—*C. A. Brown.*

BLACK-AND-YELLOW EL-2B's whirl along the north bank of the New River near Pembroke, Va., in July 1949 with an eastbound coal extra. One-year-old No. 128 could take a 9000-ton train from Clarks Gap, W.Va., to Roanoke, Va., without assistance.—*H. Reid.*

NOCTURNAL camera study by Jim Shaughnessy portrays the impressive proportions of Virginian's GE rectifiers awaiting assignments at Roanoke in 1958.—*Jim Shaughnessy.*

were quite a contrast to the boxy, utilitarian squareheads.

Internally, the difference was even greater. In place of the phase-converter system employed by the original split-phase units, the new power had a motor-generator system like that used by electric locomotives on the Great Northern Railway's Cascade Tunnel electrification. Each unit contained a transformer to reduce the A.C. voltage going to a synchronous motor which drove a pair of D.C. traction generators and D.C. exciters.

Instead of the massive jackshaft and side-rod drive of the earlier electrics, the new locomotives were equipped with four four-wheel trucks in a B-B+B-B arrangement. A GE-746 traction motor in the nose-suspended arrangement customary in diesel-electric practice was geared to each pair of 42-inch driving wheels.

Delivered in 1948, the EL-2B's were splendid performers. Unassisted, one of them could take a 3000-ton train up a 1.3 per cent grade at a steady 35 mph, or could handle a 10,000-ton train at higher speeds on level track. Equipped for regenerative braking, the new locomotives had a braking horsepower of 7800 to 7900 h.p., sufficient to control heavy trains on grades without the use of air brakes. Maximum speed of the EL-2B's was 50 mph, 22 mph faster than the split-phase units. Nine years after the EL-2B's went into service, the Virginian figured that maintenance costs for the motor-generator units had averaged only 5 cents per thousand gross ton-miles.

Besides ordering new electric motive power Virginian also upgraded its power supply. The Narrows power plant was rehabilitated in 1946, and a new Foster-Wheeler boiler, a 10,000-kilowatt GE turbogenerator, and other electrical equipment were added to the plant in 1949 and 1950, increasing its capacity by 25 per cent.

By the mid-1950's replacement of the split-phase units no longer could be deferred, and the Virginian took a hard look at the future of its electrification. Elsewhere on the system, diesel-electric locomotives had replaced steam power, and dieselization of the electric district as well was considered. Instead, the railway elected to retain electrification and placed an order with General Electric for a dozen new electric units, which would permit retirement of the aging squareheads.

Delivered in late 1956 and early 1957, the new

RECTIFIERS slice through a deep rock cut east of Princeton in June 1958 with export coal bound for the piers at Norfolk, Va.—*Both photos, Herbert H. Harwood Jr.*

(ABOVE RIGHT) Shortly after delivery from GE's Erie plant in the mid 1950's, EL-C's 130 and 131 swing onto the high trestle at Covel, W.Va., on the eastbound climb to Clarks Gap with loaded hoppers.—*General Electric, courtesy of Railroad Magazine.*

THREE ex-Virginian rectifier units (right) apply their 9900 h.p. to moving westbound freight out of Roanoke in October 1961. N&W-VGN merger is evident: Two units still carry Virginian yellow and black; one is repainted in Norfolk & Western colors.—*Don Wood.*

GE locomotives, designated as EL-C's, represented still another approach to A.C. motive power for the Virginian. The EL-C's were based upon the ignitron-rectifier concept that had evolved in the post-World War II decade, a concept used in several experimental Pennsylvania units and in New Haven's 1955 GE passenger motors. The Virginian locomotives were equipped with a bank of 12 ignitron-rectifier tubes to convert A.C. to D.C. A single transformer reduced the 11,000-volt A.C. trolley-wire voltage and the output of the rectifier tubes was passed through an iron-core smoothing reactor before being fed to the D.C. traction motors.

The new EL-C electrics looked very much like large diesel-electric road-switchers; indeed, they were designed for both road and switching service. Each unit was mounted on two six-wheel trucks, with a series-wound, axle-hung D.C. traction motor — the same type used on diesel-electric locomotives — geared to each of the six axles. Multiple-unit control permitted as many as four units to be operated from one cab, and also enabled the EL-C's to M.U. with the 1948 GE motor-generator locomotives.

The 69-foot 6-inch EL-C's each weighed 174 tons, had a starting tractive effort of 98,500 pounds, and delivered 3300 h.p. Maximum speed was 65 mph. Instead of the regenerative braking systems installed in previous Virginian electric power, the EL-C's were equipped for dynamic braking.

The rectifier units proved to be capable performers. During acceptance trials two of them hauled a 3140-ton train up Clarks Gap grade, and then went on to Roanoke with 10,000 tons on the drawbar. Soon after the last of the new units arrived on the property, the Virginian began taking the 30-year-old split-phase units out of service.

By the end of the 1950's Virginian was in the enviable position of operating a thoroughly modernized electrification. In one decade the railroad had rehabilitated and enlarged its power supply, and replaced its entire electric motive-power roster. It appeared that the new electrics would be looking forward to a long and prosperous future. Merger with the Norfolk & Western changed all that.

Operating essentially parallel routes between the West Virginia coal fields and port facilities at Norfolk, the two railroads long had been considered likely candidates for merger. Indeed, the two had been operated in this fashion under the United States Railroad Administration during World War I. An attempt to merge the two lines in 1925 failed, but in 1959 the two roads tried again, and by the end of the year merger was accomplished.

Merger drastically changed the flow of traffic over the former Virginian main line. Much of the

WHAT the 3300 h.p. GE EL-C's lacked in beauty (Virginian historian H. Reid compared them to "misshapen bricks") they made up for in performance.—*General Electric.*

heavy coal traffic from the Pocahontas and New River fields now followed the Guyandot River line west from Elmore, bypassing the Clarks Gap climb in favor of easier grades of N&W's main line. East of Princeton, the combined eastbound traffic of both railroads followed the superior profile of the former Virginian's main line while the westbound traffic in empty coal hoppers used the old N&W. The Virginian electrics were now deprived of their toughest job, Clarks Gap grade, and had only what was largely a one-way eastbound traffic on the eastern end of the electrification.

Under these post-merger conditions, then, the N&W was confronted with a choice of either greatly expanding electrification for efficient utilization of electric motive power, or of abandoning the electrification entirely. N&W chose the latter course, and on June 30, 1962, the last electric run tied up at Roanoke and the Narrows power plant was shut down for good. The big GE motor-generator units of 1948 were scrapped soon afterward. The almost-new rectifier units sat idle for more than a year until the New Haven bought them for a bargain price of $25,000 each and put them back to work in late 1963 between New York and Cedar Hill Yard in New Haven, Conn.

AFTER merger with N&W in 1959, the combined eastbound traffic of both roads began moving over the former Virginian main line east of Princeton. Three rectifier electrics (above) were pulling more than 200 loaded N&W hoppers on December 30, 1960, as they eased across the New River bridge at Glen Lyn.—*J. P. Lamb Jr.*

JUNE 30, 1962, was the last day of operation of former Virginian electrification. We're looking forward from the rear cab of a three-unit set of rectifier locomotives (Nos. 236, 230, and 233) only hours before catenary was de-energized.—*J. P. Lamb Jr.*

203

THE arid hills of Montana form a backdrop for Butte, Anaconda & Pacific box-cab motors 64 and 60 as they pull a train of hopper cars loaded with copper ore bound for the smelter out of the yard at East Anaconda.—*Donald Sims.*

8. Montana copper carrier

DESPITE the ascendancy of single-phase A.C. for heavy railroad electrification during the first decade of the 20th century, the General Electric Company, which had developed a full range of equipment for A.C. traction, continued to maintain its interest in direct-current traction.

The customary 600- to 700-volt D.C. installation presented some serious shortcomings for heavy railroad electrification, although it had been used successfully for such major electrifications as the New York terminal projects of the New York Central and the Pennsylvania, as well as for several important suburban electrifications. The heavy current demands of railroad service necessitated the use of third-rail power distribution, creating obvious hazards to the public and railroad employees and introducing potential equipment clearance difficulties. The need for heavy feeders and frequent spacing of substations to preclude excessive voltage drops made low-voltage D.C. an uneconomic system for long-distance electrification of heavy railroad loads.

While Westinghouse vigorously promoted the use of single-phase A.C. for railroad electrification, General Electric just as vigorously advocated the use of higher-voltage D.C. systems which obviated many of the shortcomings of the standard 600-volt D.C. system. In 1907 GE had equipped an interurban railway between Indianapolis, Ind., and Louisville, Ky., with a 1200-volt D.C. overhead system, in which the size of the feeders and the number of substations were both reduced from what would have been necessary with a 600-volt system. So successful was this installation that within a

TWO 1000-kilowatt motor-generator sets in the Butte substation supplied 2400-volt D.C. power to the BA&P catenary. The small unit in the foreground is a 125-volt exciter. A similar installation was housed in the Anaconda substation. In 1967 when the railroad discontinued its electrification this equipment was still in use after 54 years of service.—*General Electric.*

few years virtually every major new interurban railway employed 1200- or 1500-volt D.C. systems. No interurban railway installed a single-phase A.C. system after 1910, and many that originally had used single-phase power later converted to high-voltage D.C.

The first application of a higher-voltage D.C. system to steam railroad electrification was a General Electric 1200-volt D.C. installation on Southern Pacific's suburban lines out of Oakland, Calif., completed in 1911. This, however, was not much different in its technical details from a typical interurban railway installation. Two years passed before General Electric had a significant opportunity to demonstrate the efficiencies it claimed for high-voltage D.C. electrification of steam railroads, using as its example the newly completed 2400-volt D.C. electrification of the Butte, Anaconda & Pacific Railway in Montana.

The BA&P electrification was a particularly significant one on at least two counts. It was the first major steam railroad electrification to be carried out with a high-voltage D.C. power system. Even more important, it was the first electrification that was done purely for economic reasons. Previous electrification projects had been motivated, at least in part, by such considerations as tunnel operation, smoke abatement in major terminals, and the special demands of dense suburban traffic. On the BA&P, however, none of these special considerations were present, but one other one was. Because railroad electrification represented a sizable

market for copper, the BA&P's parent, Anaconda Copper Mining Company, had a considerable interest in demonstrating the benefits of electrification.

The BA&P was built in 1892 to transport copper ore from the mines at Butte to the Washoe smelter, located 26 miles west of Butte at Anaconda, where an ample supply of water for the ore reduction process was available. Cuts of ore cars loaded at a number of different mine shafts were consolidated into trains at the Butte Hill and Rocker yards and then moved over the main line to the Anaconda smelter. Heavy 2-8-0 Consolidation and 4-8-0 Twelve-Wheeler steam locomotives were used in the service.

During the first decade of the 20th century the Anaconda company electrified much of the machinery and equipment in its mining and smelting processes. The results were so satisfactory that electrification of the railroad itself was considered. An ample supply of power was available from hydroelectric plants on the Missouri River watershed, precluding the need to construct a railroad-owned power plant. Once a decision to electrify was reached, the BA&P was able to negotiate an advantageous power contract with the Great Falls Power Company, which not only relieved the railroad of the cost of developing a power plant but actually provided power at a lower unit cost than would have been possible with an independent railroad-owned plant.

A contract for the BA&P electrification was

IN a classic scene of Western railroading a pair of BA&P 80-ton box-cab motors crosses the Clark Fork River in Silver Bow Canyon with 60 cars of copper ore bound for Anaconda. The nearer of the two railroads across the river is the Northern Pacific; beyond it is the Milwaukee Road, which would soon electrify with a similar D.C. system.—*General Electric.*

awarded to GE in December 1911. Included in the contract, together with locomotives and the required substations, was the electrification of 90 miles of track, including the main line and all spurs and yards between Butte and Anaconda, the Missoula Gulch line between Rocker and the Butte Hill yard, and lines at Smelter Hill in Anaconda. Work was started in the spring of 1912, and electric operation began a year later.

Substations at Butte and Anaconda housed the 2400-volt motor-generator equipment which powered the railway. Two 1000-kilowatt sets were installed at each location. Each set consisted of a three-phase, 1450-kilovolt-ampere synchronous motor, powered from the 2400-volt, three-phase A.C. supply, and two 500-kilowatt, 1200-volt D.C.

generators connected in series to provide 2400 volts.

Power was distributed to trains through a simple-catenary overhead system supported by Idaho cedar poles spaced 150 feet apart. A separate feeder wire was connected to the trolley wire at 1000-foot intervals. A negative return wire, connected to the rails at 1000-foot intervals, was installed between Rocker and East Anaconda. Section breakers permitted isolation of individual sections of the overhead system.

The 17 locomotives constructed by GE for the BA&P were similar in mechanical design to units built earlier for the Great Northern, the New York Central's Detroit River Tunnel electrification, and the Baltimore & Ohio. Each of the 80-ton box-cab

BOX-CAB motor No. 46 was part of a 1914 order for four 80-ton locomotives identical to the 17 original units that General Electric had delivered the year before. The task of retraining BA&P's engineers was made easy by the simplicity of the controls (below).—*Above, General Electric; below, Gordon W. Rogers.*

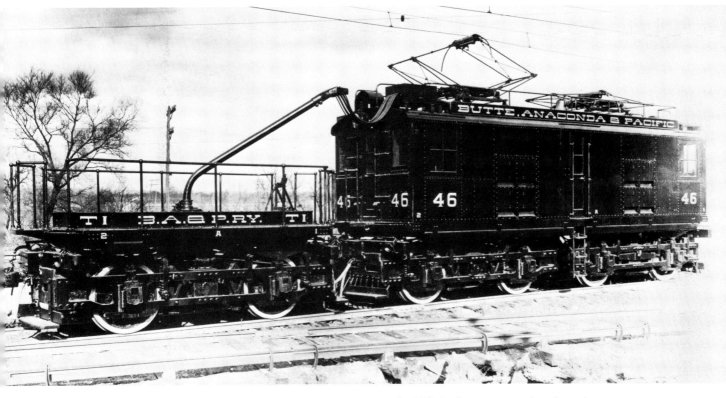

UNIQUE to the BA&P were the tractor trucks, one of which is shown connected to box-cab No. 46. They were an early counterpart of the diesel-switcher "slug" unit.—*General Electric.*

units was mounted on a pair of articulated four-wheel trucks. Draft gear was attached directly to the truck frames, permitting tractive forces to be carried directly through the running gear.

Each pair of 46-inch driving wheels was driven through twin gears by a GE-229-A motor with an hourly rating of 320 h.p. The motors were wound for 1200-volt operation, and were permanently paired in series. Blowers, controls, and other auxiliary equipment were installed in the box-cabs. Operating controls were provided at both ends. A pneumatically operated roller-type pantograph collected the current. For multiple-unit operation an insulated 2400-volt bus was installed along the center of the cab roof, with provision for connection between two units so that power could be obtained from either unit's pantograph.

Fifteen locomotives were geared for freight service with a free running speed of 35 mph. Rated maximum tractive effort for a 5-minute period was 48,000 pounds. Two units geared for passenger service were capable of a free running speed of 55 mph and could maintain 45 mph with a three-car train on level track.

The first locomotive was run in Anaconda on May 14, 1913, and two weeks later a pair of electrics took over a regular assignment hauling ore from the East Anaconda yards to the concentrator yards, a run of 7 miles on a 1.1 per cent ruling

grade. The previously assigned Twelve-Wheeler steam locomotive had normally made six trips with 16 loaded ore cars during a regular shift, a total of 96 loads per shift. The electric locomotive pair could make eight trips with 25 cars each, or a total of 200 cars during a shift, an increase of more than 100 per cent. Since loaded ore cars weighed about 70 tons each, the two electric units were handling a train of approximately 1750 tons on the 1.1 per cent grade.

Gradually, as steam-locomotive crews were trained on the electrics and additional sections of the electrification were readied for operation, the BA&P converted to electric operation. By early October 1913, the entire mainline passenger and freight operation had been taken over by electric power, and the last of the new locomotives entered service in late November.

The transition from steam to electric was an easy one for the BA&P's enginemen because of the simplicity of the electric-locomotive controls. Despite the lack of any formal training, the steam crews quickly became proficient in the operation of the electric power and soon preferred it to steam.

"Contrary to the general rule, there was no carefully studied program of instructions nor was there an instruction book prepared for the enginemen's use," wrote the railroad's electrical superintendent, Fred W. Bellinger. "Electric operation started with

ALTHOUGH hauling ore was BA&P's reason for existence, two of its electrics had 55-mph gearing for handling the two daily passenger trains each way between Butte and Anaconda. No. 66 is shown in Silver Bow Canyon with an eastbound varnish run.—*General Electric.*

AN eastbound passenger run pauses at Durant around 1914. The electric lines on the car roofs carried 2400-volt D.C. for heat and 600-volt D.C. for lighting. The BA&P shared Silver Bow Canyon with Northern Pacific, Milwaukee Road, and the Clark Fork River.—*General Electric.*

STILL delivering ton-miles reliably in 1957 after more than four decades of service, BA&P box-cabs 55 and 45 pull a string of loaded hoppers from one of the mines located on the rich hill of copper ore that stands above Butte.—*Donald Sims.*

A TRIO of box-cabs brings a long train of empties through Silver Bow Canyon on the way to Rocker yard. At this point the BA&P and the Milwaukee shared roadbed and span wires.—*Donald Sims.*

one experienced man . . . No road foreman of engines was provided to assist these men . . . The principal trouble they had was with the controller. The habit of pulling the throttle out to most any position is one that is hard to break."

The BA&P electrification produced some of the most dramatic economies and improvements to operations achieved anywhere during railroad electrification's early years.

With electrification of the around-the-clock operation between East Anaconda and Smelter Hill, for example, three engine and train crews did the same work that had required four with steam operation. On the main line between Rocker and East Anaconda a Twelve-Wheeler had been capable of hauling 50 to 55 loaded ore cars, with a gross train weight of 3500 to 4000 tons, over the line in an average running time of 2 hours 25 minutes. With electric power, gross train weight was increased to an average of 4800 tons, and average running time was reduced to 1 hour 45 minutes.

When BA&P compared its steam performance of June 1913 with the electric operation of June 1914, the railroad found that it had reduced the number of mainline trains by nearly 26 per cent while increasing the average tonnage per train by 35 per cent. Crew hours on the entire railroad had been cut by more than 29 per cent. Train delays from all causes were reduced by 42 per cent.

The financial payoff from electrification was equally favorable. Between 1913 and 1914 the railroad cut its total locomotive costs, including fuel, power, and enginemen's wages, by 40 per cent and its trainmen's wage costs by more than 21 per cent, an overall savings of more than 36 per cent. At the same time the gross ton-miles handled increased almost 8.8 per cent.

Including allowance for depreciation, BA&P found that its net operating savings from electrification were running slightly over $242,000 annually, an amount equal to 20 per cent of the railroad's total electrification cost of $1,211,000. Thus

212

READY to roll with a string of loaded hoppers, a pair of electrics wait for the highball at East Anaconda in 1955.—*Donald Sims.*

the electrification paid for itself in only five years.

Only a few teething problems hampered the electrics in their first months of operation. The traction-motor brushes chipped badly, resulting in flashovers and blown fuses. Replacement with a different type of brush and other modifications increased the average life of brushes from 3000 to 30,000 engine-miles.

The roller pantographs also presented some initial problems. Originally, the rollers were mounted on oil-lubricated brass bushings. The oil soon was thrown out and the rollers stuck, damaging both the overhead system and the pantograph. A change to roller bearings corrected this trouble. Modifications to the overhead structure and pantograph mountings solved a problem of excessive trolley-wire wear caused by a hammering effect of the rollers. Eventually, the rollers were replaced entirely with graphite contacts. But these were all minor problems, and the BA&P's electrics settled down into a long and productive service life that revealed the basic design to be an extraordinarily sound one.

Armature failures were so infrequent that sometimes none occurred on the railroad for two years. The motor commutators were not turned during the first 20 years. Rheostat contact tips lasted an average of more than eight years. Gear pinions had a life of 90,000 miles, and gear rims lasted 300,000 miles. After six years of operation BA&P found that it was spending from 4.9 to 6.8 cents per mile to maintain its electric locomotives; steam-locomotive maintenance costs had been about 16.1 cents a mile. Typically, the electric motors operated at least two shifts daily, six days a week, year after year. So little time out was required for maintenance that the electrics were reported as being available for service an average of 355 days a year.

The electrification was so productive that only a year after it opened, Anaconda Copper Mining Company diverted to the Anaconda smelter some 3000 tons of ore daily which previously had been going to a Great Falls (Mont.) smelter. To handle this 25 per cent increase in tonnage, BA&P added a motor-generator set at the Anaconda substation and ordered four freight locomotives identical to those in the original order.

Along with the new locomotives, BA&P purchased two novel "tractor truck" units. The tractor truck, a duplicate of the power trucks under the locomotives, was ballasted to a weight of 40 tons and was equipped with the necessary mechanical and electrical equipment to operate in multiple with a standard locomotive. Operated this way a tractor truck increased total tractive effort by 50 per cent over that of a standard locomotive at the same power input, with a reduction of about one-third in the free running speed. This early "cow-and-calf" arrangement was used in spotting service on Smelter Hill, where it allowed for an increase of 56 per cent in the weight of the trains taken up the hill.

A third tractor truck was received in 1915, and seven more locomotive units were ordered during 1915-1916. Another motor-generator set was added at each substation, bringing the total power capacity to 3000 kilowatts at Butte and 4000 kilowatts at Anaconda. Thus equipped, BA&P easily absorbed the tonnage growth that came with the World War I copper demand, handling as much as 5 million tons of ore in some years.

The original BA&P installation operated with little variation for more than 40 years, except for the electrification of another 30 miles of mining spurs. In 1957 two additional locomotives were ordered from General Electric. Weighing 125 tons and arranged in a double-truck road-switcher configuration, they developed half again as much tractive effort as the original locomotives and had regenerative braking, a feature the original units lacked. Along with new motive power, BA&P installed a new 2500-kilowatt ignitron-rectifier auto-

matic substation at Dawson, about midway between the two original substations.

With the capacity thus augmented, and the original electrical equipment still giving yeoman service at low cost, electric traction seemed assured of many more years of service on the Montana copper carrier. But scarcely a decade after new motive power went on the line, the installation of a new

ON a winter day in the early 1950's, box-cab No. 48 and tractor truck T1 teamed up for switching chores.—*Donald Sims.*

(RIGHT) In 1957 BA&P received two new General Electric locomotives that bore a family resemblance to the builder's industrial diesels. They are shown at Rocker with two older units in tow. The two types could not M.U.—*Philip C. Johnson.*

BA&P's two original passenger locomotives head into the Milwaukee Road station in Butte some time in the early 1950's with a single combine to begin the daily passenger round trip, a franchise run, to Anaconda. The train will pick up loaded ore hoppers at West Butte and Rocker; hence the seeming excess of power.—*Donald Sims*.

A MARCH DAY in 1953 saw the passenger train arriving Anaconda, having dropped its ore cars at East Anaconda.—*Donald Sims*.

ore concentrator at Butte drastically cut the movement of ore from Butte to Anaconda. A single train rolled over the line where more than a dozen daily trains had been required, and changes in ore handling methods at Butte Hill eliminated most of the local switching. Diesels handled what little traffic remained and the electric power ran for the last time in 1967.

Throughout its long and useful existence the BA&P electrification was a showplace of high-voltage D.C. traction. The BA&P electrification led to the adoption of high-voltage D.C. systems for a number of important electrifications in the U. S. and overseas, among them that of the Milwaukee Road, which was to be one of the longest and greatest of all North American electrifications.

THE second section of train 261, the *XL Special*, accelerates westward through Pacific Junction in Butte, Mont., behind an electric and diesel motive-power mix that was characteristic of the waning years of Milwaukee electrification. At one time the span wires here also held catenary for the Butte, Anaconda & Pacific (left track). The tower of the former Milwaukee Road station can be seen against the backdrop of the Continental Divide.—*Richard Steinheimer.*

9. Catenary over the mountains

EVEN before the Butte, Anaconda & Pacific placed its pioneer high-voltage D.C. electrification in operation, the Chicago, Milwaukee & St. Paul Railway had adopted an almost identical system for electrification of its Western mountain crossings. Reaching a total length of 647 route-miles when completed into Tacoma, Wash., in 1920, the Milwaukee electrification was the greatest single electrification project undertaken anywhere in the world until that time. Save for the great Pennsylvania Railroad electrification of the 1930's, the Milwaukee's installation was the longest electrification ever constructed in North America.

During the last decades of the 19th century, the Milwaukee Road developed into one of the strongest of the Midwestern granger lines. Around the turn of the century the Milwaukee's officers became interested in building their own rail outlet to the Pacific Coast. Traffic to and from the Pacific Coast, as well as the Orient, was growing. With Northern Pacific, Great Northern, and Burlington under the control of the Hill-Morgan interests, and Union Pacific firmly controlled by the Harrimans, Milwaukee officials believed themselves to be at the mercy of their competitors in gaining a share of the rich Western trade.

The railroad first studied the feasibility of building its own line west to Puget Sound in 1901. The decision to expand westward was reached by the board of directors in late 1905, and construction began scarcely four months later.

Construction of the Milwaukee's Pacific Extension proceeded simultaneously at a number of locations, and the monumental project was completed in record time. From the existing western railhead on the Missouri River in South Dakota, the railroad's engineers crossed five mountain ranges and laid some 1400 miles of line to reach the western terminal at Tacoma. The original estimated cost of 60 million dollars was exceeded by more than 300 per cent. Reports indicated that at one time more than 20,000 men were helping to build the line. Service was established to Butte, Mont., 717 miles west of the Missouri River, in August 1908. Barely three years from the date construction started, the last rail of the Pacific Extension was spiked into place at Garrison, Mont. — on May 14, 1909.

The Milwaukee began to consider electrification before the line was completed. Indeed, Milwaukee President Albert J. Earling had seen to it that the land acquisition had provided for the later construction of power supply installations.

Interest in electrification gained support in 1909 when John D. Ryan was added to the railroad's board of directors. Ryan, the president of Anaconda Copper Mining Company, was interested in electrification for reasons beyond the operating efficiencies it promised. Electrification represented an important new market for Anaconda copper (the Milwaukee's project ultimately required nearly 12,000 tons of copper, an average of 17.4 tons per mile). Moreover, Ryan was interested in

THE initial motive power for the Milwaukee electrification was a fleet of 42 two-unit motors whose riveted box-cab design epitomized no-nonsense, utilitarian industrial styling. No. 10200 was photographed on builder GE's test track in September 1915.—*General Electric.*

new markets for the several hydroelectric plants in Montana in which he and his associates had substantial interests. These dual considerations were instrumental in the 1911 decision to electrify the Butte, Anaconda & Pacific, an Anaconda subsidiary, as a showplace of what electrification could accomplish.

The mountain operating conditions the Milwaukee hoped to tame with electric traction were formidable. Long steep grades and sharp curves characterized the most difficult stretches of the Pacific Extension. The grade ascending the west slope of the Belt Mountains in Montana, for example, was a steady 1 per cent for 49 miles. Between Beverly and Boylston, Wash., westbound traffic operated against 18.8 miles of 2.2 per cent grade. Curves as sharp as 10 degrees were encountered at a number of points. There were 45 tunnels on the Extension's main line. The longest on the original line, at the summit of St. Paul Pass, was 8771 feet long. Another, to be completed in 1914 as part of a major line relocation in Snoqualmie Pass, would be 11,890 feet long.

Although the railroad used modern, oil-burning steam locomotives, severe winter weather made efficient motive-power operation difficult. Temperatures sometimes fell to 40 degrees below zero; locomotives frequently failed, and some simply could

not make sufficient steam. The mountain operating conditions were so difficult for steam power that the Milwaukee had to set up its engine divisions to accommodate average locomotive runs of only 113 miles.

The Milwaukee ordered electrification surveys made under the direction of its electrical engineer, Reinier Beeuwkes. In late 1912 the railroad signed a 99-year power contract for its Rocky Mountain Division with the Great Falls Power Company of Montana, and four months later concluded a similar contract with the Thompson Falls Power Company for the adjoining Missoula Division. John Ryan held an interest in both power companies, which shortly afterward were merged into the Montana Power Company, in which Ryan also maintained an interest.

Initial Milwaukee plans involved electrification of 438 route-miles from Harlowton, Mont., to Avery, Ida., which included the crossings of the Belt Mountains, the main range of the Rockies, and the Bitter Root Mountains. An Electrification Department, headed by C. A. Goodnow, assistant to the president, and Beeuwkes, was formed in March 1914 to direct the work. Construction started in April, and the first regular electric operation began a little more than one and a half years later.

The Milwaukee's installation essentially was

identical to that of the Butte, Anaconda & Pacific, except for an increase in trolley-wire potential to 3000 volts. A simple-catenary overhead supported by bracket arms from wooden poles was employed. The use of a double heavy copper trolley wire helped to assure current collection with a minimum of sparking. Both a heavy copper positive feeder and a "negative feeder," connected at intervals to the return circuit in the running rails, were used.

The Montana Power Company supplied power to the Milwaukee electrification from existing hydroelectric plants, and construction began on new plants to assure adequate capacity for both the railroad load and other commercial development. At the time the Milwaukee contracted for its power supply, more than 70,000 kilowatts in installed hydroelectric generating capacity was already available on the Missouri River and its tributaries; within the next few years another 140,000 kilowatts in generating capacity was placed on the line.

From several interchange points with the power company's distribution network, the Milwaukee distributed three-phase, 60-cycle power at 100,000 volts over its own transmission line parallel to the electrified section. Fourteen substations, erected at an average spacing of 32 miles, converted the power to 3000-volt D.C. for the trolley wire. Principal substation equipment included 100,000/2300-volt transformers and synchronous-motor-driven motor-generator sets of 1500- or 2000-kilowatt capacity. Each substation was equipped with either two or three motor-generator sets, providing substation capacities that varied from 4000 to 6000 kilowatts.

A power-indicating and -limiting system maintained a record of net power consumption, automatically deducting regenerated power returned to the power company and limiting the power supplied to a division by lowering the trolley voltage when a predetermined maximum load was reached. The system also equalized the demand on individual substations by reducing voltage on a heavily loaded station to transfer part of the load to adjacent substations.

A group of 42 two-unit box-cab locomotives was built by the American Locomotive Company and the General Electric Company during 1915 and 1916 for the Montana electrification. Thirty locomotives intended for freight service were geared for a maximum speed of 30 mph. The remaining 12, intended for passenger operation, were identical except for 60-mph gearing, oil-fired train-heating boilers, and train-lighting panels.

Each locomotive was made up of two identical semi-permanently coupled box-cab units. Each unit was mounted on two articulated frames. The

THE grandeur of Montana Canyon in the Belt Mountains near Lombard, Mont., awed passengers aboard a box-cab-powered *Olympian* in July 1916.—*Asahel Curtis, collection of the Washington State Historical Society.*

DESCENDING the 1 per cent grade in Montana Canyon in 1916, box-cab 10103 treats *Olympian* patrons to a ride "as smooth and jerkless as that of a powerful ship on a summer sea." Such copy typified promotion of the new electrics and their regenerative-braking features.—*Asahel Curtis, collection of the Washington State Historical Society.*

lead frame, at the control end of the unit, had a four-wheel guiding truck and two pairs of 52-inch driving wheels, while the rear frame had two pairs of driving wheels only, resulting in a 2-B+B wheel arrangement for each unit. This flexible running-gear arrangement was ideally suited to the sharp curvature of much of Milwaukee's mountain trackage. Although the length of a two-unit locomotive was 112 feet, the maximum rigid wheelbase was only 10 feet 6 inches. Draft gear was mounted on the truck frames, permitting tractive stresses to be transmitted directly through the trucks rather than through the carbody.

Each pair of driving wheels was driven by a GE Type 253-A traction motor with a 1-hour rating of 430 h.p. and a continuous rating of 375 h.p. A nose-hung mounting was employed for the motors, with twin gearing to the driving axles. The use of both a spring gear drive and a spring nose suspension minimized shock on the motors from the high tractive forces. A blower in the cab provided forced ventilation for the traction motors.

An operating cab was located at one end of each unit. The locomotives were equipped with a Sprague-GE M.U. control system. Control and auxiliary equipment were housed within the carbody. Each unit had a single air-operated pantograph and an auxiliary trolley pole for current collection.

A two-unit locomotive weighed 288 tons, with 225 tons carried on the driving wheels. At continuous output each locomotive was rated at 3000 h.p., with an hourly rating of 3440 h.p. Maximum starting tractive effort was 135,000 pounds.

One of the most important features of the locomotives was the capability for regenerative braking on descending grades. The engineer, using the auxiliary handle on the master controller, could employ the traction motors as generators to return power to the trolley wire in the amount required to maintain a desired speed.

The Milwaukee's new electrics shattered every previous record for power and tractive effort, and the publicity men made the most of it. The first locomotive completed, No. 10200, was shipped from GE's Erie works in late September 1915 with 40-foot banners on each side that immodestly proclaimed it to be the "largest electric locomotive in the world." At Chicago, the first stop on an exhibition tour that included every major point on the Milwaukee all the way to Seattle, Wash., an estimated crowd of 10,000 viewed the locomotive during the 4 hours it was on display near Union Station.

Shortly after its arrival at Butte on the transcontinental tour, the big electric was coupled to a Milwaukee business car and dispatched on a 30-

"ONE-ARMED BANDIT" was just one of the many nicknames applied to the Milwaukee Road's four Alco-GE steeple-cab switchers. The two 70-tonners built in 1916 were rated at 670 h.p.; the pair built in 1919 weighed 82 tons and developed 726 h.p.—*General Electric.*

mile round trip to Durant under Butte, Anaconda & Pacific catenary with President A. J. Earling and other Milwaukee brass on board.

At Spokane and Seattle the crowds viewing the locomotive were so large that the exhibition period was extended to two days in each city. When the tour ended, an estimated 60,000 persons had seen the locomotive.

Following exhibition at Tacoma, No. 10200 was shipped back to Butte in November for trial runs with a second locomotive, No. 10201, over the BA&P, since the Milwaukee's own electrification was not ready for operation. The testing program emphasized the regenerative braking feature. In one test on November 13 with No. 10201, regenerative braking was used to control a 5000-ton ore train on 1 per cent gradient between Rocker and Anaconda, Mont. Regenerative braking was applied at 25 mph and smoothly reduced train speed to 7 mph, returning as much as 2100 kilowatts to the trolley wire in the process. The feature was an obvious success.

THE first 113 miles of Milwaukee catenary, between Three Forks and Deer Lodge, Mont., were energized by the beginning of December. On December 2 the locomotives thus far received began

exhaustive tests on this section of the Milwaukee's electrification. In one test, conducted on December 6, two locomotives took a 2800-ton train over the Continental Divide from Butte to Piedmont, 39 miles, in 2 hours 15 minutes. The run included some 10 miles of ascending grade with a maximum gradient of 1.66 per cent and a 21-mile descent on the eastern slope of the Divide with grades as steep as 2 per cent. The two locomotives maintained a 14-mph average speed on the climb up to the Divide, and on the descending grade regenerative braking held the train to an almost uniform speed of 17 to 18 mph.

On December 8 the new electrics were matched against steam power in a spectacular test over the Continental Divide from Butte to Piedmont. A large party of railroad officials and other spectators, headed by Milwaukee President Earling, witnessed the test. Conveyed by a special train of six Pullman cars drawn by one of the new electric locomotives, the party preceded the test trains out of Butte to observe the tests from Janney, partway up the 1.66 per cent grade to the Divide.

First, two of the 288-ton electrics coupled onto a 48-car freight train of 3000 tons in the Butte yard and started over the grade. Shortly after, two 2-8-2 Mikados and a Mallet pusher locked couplers with

UNIQUE among electrics were Milwaukee's Class EP-2 bipolar gearless locomotives built by GE in 1918. Their superstructures consisted of three articulated sections carried on four articulated power trucks. The rounded contours afforded good visibility.—*General Electric.*

a 37-car, 2200-ton train and followed the electrics out of town. By the time the two electrics reached the waiting brass hats at Janney, they were traveling 16 mph with ease. The steam power, however, struggled upgrade at less than 10 mph.

"The men in the cabs," reported the Butte *Miner,* "were doing their utmost to make a showing; but the best they could do in the ascent was nine miles an hour. There was something almost pathetic in the game fight which steam put up against the new power. But it was visibly outclassed. Even a child could have picked the winner. Not one of the spectators could avoid the feeling that he had witnessed the overwhelming triumph of the new against the old, and that a tried friend that had faithfully served mankind for nearly a century in the field of transportation had been defeated."

The first few electric locomotives were placed in helper service, and during 1916 the Milwaukee gradually converted its Rocky Mountain and Missoula divisions to electric operation as additional sections of catenary were completed and the remainder of the locomotives were delivered.

The winter of 1915-1916, when the first electrics entered service, was one of the worst ever recorded

in Montana. Again and again the reliability of the electric locomotives and their indifference to temperature and weather conditions helped the Milwaukee to keep traffic moving when steam power died in the bitter cold. On one occasion two freight trains, with a total of three steam locomotives and 75 cars, stalled on the main line east of Three Forks in 40-below-zero weather. With only a few minutes notice an electric locomotive was on the way to the rescue. The electric coupled the 75 cars and the three locomotives into one train and pulled them into Three Forks without the slightest difficulty.

"Our electrification has been tested by the worst winter in the memory of modern railroaders," said C. A. Goodnow, the Milwaukee's assistant to the president in charge of the electrification. "There were times when every steam locomotive in the Rocky Mountain district was frozen, but the electric locomotive went right along. Electrification had in every way exceeded our expectations. This is so, not only as respects tonnage handled and mileage made, but also the regularity of operation."

By April 1916, 226 miles — or about half — of the planned Montana electrification was operated

222

IT was in an era of unabashed press agentry that CM&StP unveiled its new bipolars—with a pushing contest between bipolar 10254 and 2-6-6-2 No. 9520 at Kent, Wash., on February 22, 1920: Steam and cinders hurtle skyward as the Mallet's dozen 57-inch drivers claw the rails. From the electric there's little more than the whoosh of blowers and a soft humming of electrical equipment. Gradually, the forward push of the Mallet slows, then stops; drivers spin futilely. Almost imperceptibly, and seemingly without effort, the bipolar inches forward and the furiously working Mallet is unceremoniously shoved offstage. Traction has triumphed! Steam is dead!—*Asahel Curtis, collection of the Washington State Historical Society.*

ANOTHER triumph: Bipolar 10253 wins tug-of-war with a 2-6-6-2 and a 2-8-0 (over 110,000 pounds of steam tractive effort) near Garcia, Wash.—*General Electric, TRAINS collection.*

CASCADE MOUNTAINS and catenary combine to create this breathtaking setting in which bipolar 10251 sweeps downgrade with a westbound Elk's special in 1925 near Garcia.—*Asahel Curtis, collection of the Washington State Historical Society.*

entirely with electric power. The electrics ran through from Harlowton to Deer Lodge, effectively consolidating two engine divisions into one. On the 2 per cent grades over the Rockies one passenger locomotive could haul a train of 10 or 11 steel cars at 20 to 30 mph. An electric, with one helper locomotive, could take 3000 tons over the ruling grade at 15 mph, and a single locomotive could make double that speed on level track with the same tonnage.

Electric power cut the running time of passenger trains from 1 hour 5 minutes to only 40 minutes up the 21-mile, 2 per cent westbound grade from Piedmont to Donald. Between Deer Lodge and Butte 30 minutes were cut from the 1-hour 20-minute passenger-train running time of steam power.

In freight service steam power required from 10 to 12 hours to cover the 115 miles over the Continental Divide between Deer Lodge and Three Forks; the electrics did it in 7 to 8 hours.

The regenerative braking equipment controlled passenger and freight trains with exceptional smoothness, and the virtual elimination of air braking in mountain operation saved enormous wear and tear on wheels and braking equipment. Savings of approximately 15 per cent in power consumption were attributed to regenerative braking.

The ease and smoothness of operation of the electrics, reported the railroad, made it "practically impossible to pull out drawbars except through an extreme degree of carelessness." Although their de-

READY to conquer the Cascades, bipolar 10250 stands at Seattle (Wash.) Union Station prior to departure for Chicago with an orange-and-maroon *Olympian* in July 1927, shortly after catenary had been extended into Seattle from Black River Junction, Wash.—*General Electric.*

WESTBOUND *Columbian* poses near Rockdale, Wash., just west of the 11,890-foot Snoqualmie Tunnel in 1925.—*Asahel Curtis, collection of the Washington State Historical Society.*

THE *Olympian* accelerates east out of Ellensburg, Wash., in the Kittitas Valley in June 1925. The lush flatland separating the Cascade and Saddle ranges gave the bipolars a chance to display a 60-mph top speed.—*Asahel Curtis. collection of the Washington State Historical Society.*

sign was new, the electrics operated in the demanding mountain service without significant maintenance problems.

"Electrification has been such a tremendous success on the Milwaukee Road that it is difficult to state the results without seeming exaggeration," wrote C. A. Goodnow of the first year's experience, "but I think it quite within the fact to say that the Milwaukee Road has forgotten that the Continental Divide exists."

The entire 438-mile electrification between Harlowton and Avery was in operation by the end of 1916. Despite an increased traffic over the Milwaukee's transcontinental main line resulting from World War I and the closing of the Panama Canal, the 42 electric locomotives, together with two 70-ton steeple-cab B-B switchers added to the roster in early 1917, were able to replace 112 steam engines of various types in use on the two divisions prior to electrification.

The railroad's board of directors was delighted with the Montana electrification and on January 25, 1917, authorized a further 207 miles of electrification between Othello and Tacoma, Wash. —

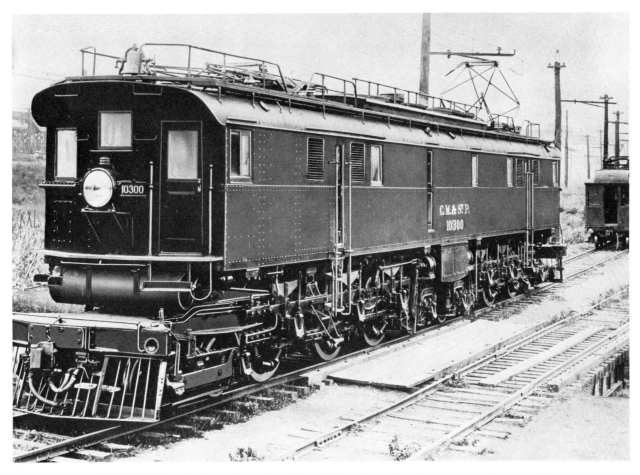

CONCEALED by the simple lines of the Class EP-3 carbody (above) was power almost equal to two USRA 4-8-2's. CM&StP's 10 EP-3's were delivered in 1920. The Pullman-car proportions of the EP-3's 78-foot cab are evident (below) in this view at Baldwin Locomotive Works.—*Above, collection of the Smithsonian Institution; below, collection of H. L. Broadbelt.*

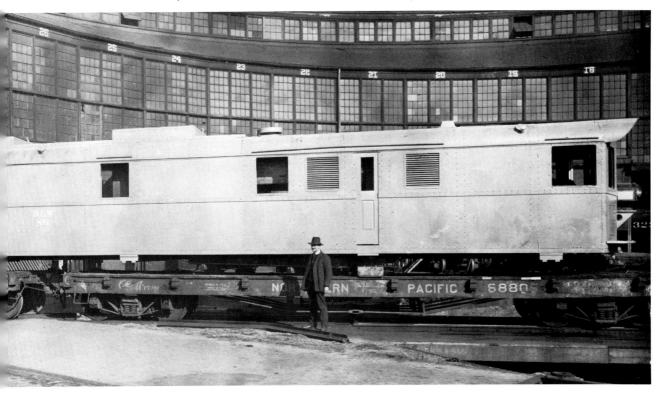

PASSENGERS aboard the eastbound *Columbian*, powered by a Baldwin-Westinghouse motor, enjoy the splendid scenery along the North Fork of the St. Joe River a few miles east of Avery, Ida., in October 1929.—*Asahel Curtis, collection of the Washington State Historical Society.*

EP-3 No. 10300, in command of the eastbound *Columbian*, pauses at Falcon, Ida., on the 22-mile climb from Avery to St. Paul Pass Tunnel. Presently the train will pass along the tracks in the background.—*Asahel Curtis, collection of the Washington State Historical Society.*

Columbia and Coast division trackage that included arduous crossings of the Saddle Mountains and the Cascades. The two electrifications were separated by the 216-mile Idaho Division which, because of relatively easy grades, continued to operate with steam power.

In March 1917 the railroad negotiated a 98-year power contract with the Intermountain Power Company, another Ryan company, which later was incorporated into the Washington Water Power Company. Actual electric operation was delayed by the war until the fall of 1919, when electric locomotives went into freight pusher service on the steep Cascade Range grades. Full electric operation began the following year.

The Coast line's electrical installation was similar to that of the Montana system. Eight substations, spaced at an average distance of 28 miles, were each equipped with one or two 2000-kilowatt motor-generator sets that supplied 3000-volt D.C. power to the trolley wire. The substations were supplied from a 100,000-volt Intermountain Power Company transmission line running parallel to the railway. Power was supplied from hydroelectric plants of the Washington Water Power Company and the Puget Sound Power & Light Company.

Additional motive power for the expanded electrification included two more switching units, of 82 tons, from General Electric in 1919, five bipolar passenger locomotives for Cascade Range service

WITH the safety valve of the train-heating boiler popping, Baldwin-Westinghouse passenger motor 10307 drifts downgrade across spidery Clear Creek bridge toward Avery in 1929 with the westbound *Columbian.—Asahel Curtis, collection of the Washington State Historical Society.*

MORNING shadows are long, and only a few early risers are on hand as the eastbound *Olympian* halts at the handsome Missoula (Mont.) station in June 1926. In the diner it's "First call to breakfast."—*Asahel Curtis, collection of the Washington State Historical Society.*

SAFE from Montana Canyon's rattlesnake population, passengers inside the westbound *Olympian* are treated to magnificent Belt Mountain scenery in June 1926. The train is emerging from Eagle Nest Tunnel.—*Asahel Curtis, collection of the Washington State Historical Society.*

POLLUTION-FREE bipolars and EP-3's enabled Milwaukee Road to make the most of the fine mountain scenery through which its electrified lines passed—by adding to summertime trains open-air observation cars, such as the one bringing up the rear of the westbound *Olympian* near Hyak, Wash., in August 1923.—TRAINS *collection.*

THE traditional open-platform observation car still complemented the *Columbian* when CMStP&P's secondary Chicago-Seattle train was photographed slowing for Missoula in 1949. Meanwhile, box-cabs departed for Avery with westbound freight.—*Frank McKinlay.*

PREVIEW of coming attractions: Demonstrator GE 750 departs Bearmouth, Mont., while testing on CMStP&P's electrified lines in 1949. Twenty of these "Little Joes" were built for the USSR, but orphaned by Cold War politics; CMStP&P adopted 12 of them and GE 750 became Milwaukee Road No. E-70 in 1950. *Rail Photo Service, Frank McKinlay.*

built by GE in 1918, and 10 passenger locomotives for the Rocky Mountain and Missoula divisions delivered by Baldwin-Westinghouse in 1920. The 12 GE box-cab units equipped for passenger service were regeared for freight operation, and the original box-cab fleet of 42 locomotives was divided between the two electric divisions.

The Milwaukee's five Class EP-2 bipolar gearless passenger electrics delivered by General Electric's Erie plant at the end of 1918 were unorthodox in wheel arrangement and unforgettable in appearance. The EP-2's, rated at a maximum hourly output of 3480 h.p., were capable of a starting tractive effort of 114,450 pounds. Length was 76 feet and weight exceeded 260 tons. The locomotives were supported by 28 wheels carried on four articulated frames in a unique 1-B+D+D+B-1 wheel arrangement. A dozen GE-100 motors of the bipolar type, with armatures mounted directly on the driving axles, powered 44-inch driving wheels — an arrangement identical to that developed a decade and a half before by GE's Asa F. Batchelder for the original New York Central electric locomotives. There was a single unpowered guiding axle at each end of the locomotive.

The carbody was made up of three sections. The center section housed an oil-fired train-heating boiler and fuel and water tanks. The two end sections each included an operating cab and a long, round-topped hood, housing electrical equipment, which gave the bipolars their distinctive appearance. Control equipment was provided for multiple-unit operation and regenerative braking.

In service the EP-2's could move a train of a dozen all-steel cars weighing 1000 tons up the Cascade line's ruling 2.2 per cent grade at 25 mph without a helper, or they could roll the crack *Olympian* at 60 mph on the level. In the words of a contemporary GE blurb, the bipolars provided "a hitherto unknown assurance that passenger trains will be run on schedule time, regardless of temperature changes, independent of rail conditions and free from the vagaries of firemen and steaming qualities of fuel."

Although designed to meet the same operating conditions and requirements as the GE bipolars, the 10 Class EP-3 passenger locomotives delivered by Baldwin-Westinghouse a little over a year later represented a different design approach. "From an inspection of the finished locomotives," reported *Railway Age*, "it would appear that the two types could hardly be more different."

The EP-3's were more orthodox in appearance and arrangement than the Milwaukee's famous GE bipolars, but they were larger and more powerful. Each of the box-cab units weighed an even 300 tons and extended 88 feet 7 inches between coupler faces. The EP-3's were rated at an hourly output of 4200 h.p. and developed a maximum starting tractive effort of 105,000 pounds. Like all of the Milwaukee's mainline electric power, the Baldwin-Westinghouse units were equipped for regenerative braking.

The running-gear arrangement of the EP-3's was comparable to that of two back-to-back Pacific-type steam locomotives connected by a drawbar, or in electric notation: 2-C-1+1-C-2. Each pair of 68-inch driving wheels was driven by twin Westinghouse 348 motors through a gear-and-quill drive similar to that employed for several New Haven Railroad electric-locomotive designs. The cab housed electrical, control, and auxiliary equipment; a large train-heating boiler; fuel and water tanks; and a control position at each end.

Like the bipolars, the EP-3's could take a 1000-ton train up a 2.2 per cent grade at 25 mph. Maximum speed was 65 mph. Normal operating assignments of the EP-3's were arduous, requiring that they run the length of the 438-mile Montana electrification without change, covering three mountain ranges and what had been four separate steam-engine divisions.

The completed Milwaukee Road electrification was a resounding success. The railroad found that it could dispense with helpers for passenger trains, which had required assistance at a number of points with steam operation. The great power and the regenerative braking of the passenger locomotives contributed to exceptionally smooth operation when ascending or descending mountain grades. Compared with steam-powered passenger trains, electrically powered trains showed a higher standard of on-time performance and often made up time lost on other divisions.

The advantages of electric operation were even more evident in freight service. Speed was materially improved over that experienced with steam, and the Milwaukee was able to almost double the tonnage handled in a train. In 1918, for example, the engine-miles per thousand ton-miles for the Missoula Division were reported as only 55 per cent of what they had been during steam operation. The electric freight locomotives regularly ran with trailing loads of 2500 tons at 16 mph on grades of up to 1 per cent. With one helper, trains of 3000 tons were handled eastbound on 1.66 per cent gradients, and westbound trains of 2800 tons were hauled on 2 per cent gradients. With two helpers, 4500- to 5000-ton trains of 100 or more cars were lifted over the Milwaukee's most severe grades. The electric locomotives, because of their smooth operation, greatly reduced the frequency of damaged draft gear and break-in-twos.

Probably no feature of the electrification, how-

A BIG Baldwin-Westinghouse passenger motor wheels the eastbound *Olympian* along the Clark
Fork River at Bonner Junction, Mont., on a summer day in the early 1940's.—*R. V. Nixon.*

ever, was more popular than regenerative braking. The strain on drawbars and couplings incurred through air braking was eliminated with the entire train bunched behind the locomotive at a uniform speed. Severe wheel and brake-shoe wear from normal braking was almost eliminated, and the Milwaukee also reported less track wear, particularly on sharp curves. Regenerative braking offered substantial savings in power costs. The energy of a 2500-ton train descending a 2 per cent grade at 17 mph, for example, represented about 3500 kilowatts. With regeneration this energy largely was returned to the power system rather than dissipated as heat by the friction of brake shoes, as it would have been with ordinary air braking.

On at least one occasion, however, the vaunted regenerative braking of the box-cabs failed to operate as advertised, with spectacular and costly results. Soon after the Cascade electrification opened, an eastbound train of 59 loaded cars, powered by an electric motor and a Mallet helper, crested the summit of the Saddle Mountains and started down the 18 miles of 2.2 per cent grade to Beverly, Wash. Air brakes were not applied and the engineer allowed his train to reach a speed of about 30 mph before trying to cut in the regenerative braking. The breakers promptly blew. Another attempt was made, and again the breakers blew. Service air braking was tried with negligible results, followed by an emergency application, but the train was

SOARING for a moment high above the conifers of the Cascades, box-cab E50 (nee 10200) rumbles across Hanson's Creek bridge near Bandera, Wash., with an eastbound freight train. The Milwaukee Road renumbered its electric locomotives in 1939.—*The Milwaukee Road.*

moving too rapidly to be controlled. The consist, restrained slightly by the engine brakes of the electric and the Mallet helper as well as by some hand brakes that had been set before the train started down, stayed on the rails as far as Doris, 11 miles down the grade. There, the Mallet's tender derailed on a bad switch and the helper separated from the train. Rolling downgrade through 10-degree curves at an estimated 50 mph, the runaway train traveled a few miles more before 28 carloads of shingles left the rails — tearing out the 100,000-volt transmission line — and began burning. Thirteen more cars left the rails within the next few miles. Finally the remaining block of cars separated from the locomotive, derailed, and burned. The electric locomotive came to a halt with flat spots on every wheel.

In the future, the Milwaukee decided, trains would be kept under the control of the air brakes before gaining sufficient speed for regenerative braking.

THE financial results of electrification were as impressive as the operating results. Maintenance costs for the electric locomotives were only a third of those for steam power of equal capacity. Annual savings approached 1 million dollars. The heavier trains and higher operating speeds made possible with electric power reduced train-crew expenses. Low-cost hydroelectric power and the greater efficiency of electric locomotives produced estimated annual savings over steam-locomotive fuel costs of nearly $600,000.

In 1923, when 59 electric locomotives handled freight and passenger traffic of nearly 3 million gross ton-miles that would have required an estimated 167 steam locomotives, the Milwaukee reported a net saving in operating costs of $1,271,793. In a 1925 report that detailed the results of electric operation from its start in 1916 through the end of 1924, the Milwaukee showed a net saving over steam operation of 12.4 million dollars, including allowance for interest and depreciation on its electrification investment. Considering that the cost of the electrification had been some 23 million dollars, these were sizable savings indeed.

The Milwaukee's satisfaction with its choice of the 3000-volt D.C. system was reflected by the endorsement of an important French railway commission, which spent three months visiting electrified railways in the U.S. during the early 1920's.

"On account of the remarkable results obtained by the Chicago, Milwaukee & St. Paul Railway with 3000 volts direct current," wrote M. Maudit, secretary of the commission, "the writer does not hesitate to formally conclude in favor of the adoption of this system, and he believes it to be actually the only system suitable for the electrification of heavy traction lines."

Although French railroads failed to follow M. Maudit's advice, high-voltage D.C. systems were chosen during the next decade for important electrifications elsewhere in North America and in South America, Africa, Western Europe, and the Soviet Union.

The Milwaukee Road electrification captured the public fancy as had few other comparable engineering achievements. To an age not yet jaded by the latest advances of technology, there was something wondrous about trains that preserved dwindling reserves of coal and oil by taking their energy from the "white coal" of rushing mountain streams ("making nature drive the wheels"), made no smoke or cinders, and frugally returned electricity to the wires by the magic of regenerative braking.

Sunday supplements and popular magazines extolled electrification's advantages. Milwaukee Road publicists blurbed the wonders of the "giant electric motors, the largest and most powerful type of motor in existence," and pitted straining Mikados and Mallets against the seemingly invincible power of the GE bipolars in great tug-of-war contests that produced reams of copy. Celebrities eagerly posed in the cabs of the big electrics.

Thomas Edison wrote, ". . .no grinding, no jerking, no puffing, no pulling, no straining, no disturbed slumbers — just a keen sense of moving swiftly, of being propelled by power vastly in excess of requirements. You ride with ease — you are at ease — it is the very last word in transportation."

To Americans in the 1920's, the image of a massive, riveted Milwaukee "King of the Rails" box-cab, or the rendering of a distinctive bipolar posed with a pumpkin-orange *Olympian* against a Cascade backdrop, became a harbinger of a not-too-distant future when swift, clean electric power would vanquish steam.

Milwaukee catenary was extended 10 miles from Black River Junction to Seattle in 1927, but no other expansion ever was undertaken. The 216-mile gap across Idaho between the two electric divisions might have been closed during the 1920's, but the railroad entered receivership in 1925, a condition brought on largely by the huge debts accumulated in building the Pacific Extension. The railroad was reorganized as the Chicago, Milwaukee, St. Paul & Pacific Railroad Company in 1927.

The Milwaukee's electrification, little changed from the original installation of 1915-1920, showed a remarkable capacity to meet the demands placed upon it in the half century or more following its completion. The versatile GE box-cab locomotives adapted easily to the challenge of increasing train tonnages. Operating cabs and guiding trucks were removed from a number of the units, and the locomotives were reassembled into three- or four-unit consists to provide greater power at the head of trains than was provided by the original two-unit consists.

For a time in the decade following World War II

FAMOUS personages were eager to pose with Milwaukee's new electrics: (Left) Mary Garden (in the cab), general director of the Chicago Opera, and members of her company pose on motor 10302 at Drexel, Mont., in 1922. President Warren G. Harding (center) was photographed on motor 10305 on July 2, 1923, near Avery. Wearing his famous cap, baseball's legendary Babe Ruth (right) shakes hands with the engineer of bipolar 10252 in 1926. *Left and right, Asahel Curtis, collection of the Washington State Historical Society; center, The Milwaukee Road.*

it appeared that the Milwaukee's electrification would be displaced by dieselization. The failure to close the electrification gap across Idaho had created motive-power utilization problems that were only compounded when diesels, with their ability to run long distances without change, replaced steam power in non-electrified territory. When the diesel-hauled *Olympian Hiawatha* began operation in 1947, the motive power ran from Chicago to Tacoma without change.

But instead of abandonment, the electrification was modernized in a course of events that resulted in part from the political tensions of the post-World War II Cold War.

In 1946 the General Electric Company had accepted an order from the Soviet Union for 20 of the most powerful electric locomotives ever built in North America. Designed for operation under 3300-volt D.C. catenary on the Russian 5-foot broad gauge, the 2-D+D-2 locomotives weighed 273 tons, stretched 88 feet 10 inches between coupler knuckles, and delivered a continuous rating of 5500 h.p. Before GE's Erie plant had completed work on the locomotives, deteriorating East-West relations precluded their shipment to the USSR. GE decided to complete the order anyway, and started looking for other buyers. Fourteen had been completed to the Russian broad gauge; the last six were built for standard gauge.

Three of the "Little Joes," as they soon became known, were sold to the Chicago South Shore & South Bend in 1949, and five went to Brazil's Paulista Railway in 1951. The best potential customer, however, was the Milwaukee Road, with its long 3000-volt D.C. electrification and an elderly motive-power fleet. The first standard-gauge unit completed was modified for operation on the Milwaukee and was shipped west in December 1948 for a four-month trial. An offer to purchase all 20 units was rejected by GE, but an agreement finally was reached in 1950 for the sale of 12 units in an "as is" condition, and the Milwaukee's own shops made the necessary modifications. Two units were equipped with train-heating boilers for passenger operation; the remainder were employed in freight service. All were assigned to the Rocky Mountain Division.

The new electrics, with a starting tractive effort of 110,750 pounds and capable of M.U. operation, increased the Milwaukee's tonnage-hauling capacity. During the late 1950's the railroad's electrical engineer, Lawrence Wylie, developed a control modification that enabled the electrics to be run in multiple with diesels. The typical combination of two Little Joes and GP9 diesel could take a 3600-ton westbound train or a 5800-ton eastbound train over the division without helpers.

Along with the acquisition of new motive power, the Milwaukee upgraded its electrical distribution system. The capacity of substations and feeders at key locations was increased, and substation equipment in general was modernized. Many of the original locomotives were overhauled and upgraded, and several box-cab freight units were regeared and altered for passenger service as electric power again was assigned to the point of passenger trains.

A comparison of running times over the 438-mile Avery-Harlowton electric division indicates how well the Milwaukee electrification met the greater demands of mid-20th century railroading. In 1918 the fastest passenger train covered the division in 15 hours; by the mid-1950's electric power moved the *Olympian Hiawatha* over the run in just 10 hours 40 minutes. In 1918 eastbound freight trains were limited to a maximum of 2800 tons and took 36 hours 45 minutes to make the run; by the mid-1950's eastbound freights were covering the distance with 5800 tons in less than 24 hours.

By the beginning of the 1970's, however, electrification was again in decline on the Milwaukee. Renewed dieselization of passenger service, followed by its discontinuance altogether on the Milwaukee's Pacific Extension, had permanently idled the passenger electrics during the early 1960's. By the end of the decade freight diesels had become commonplace under the catenary, and more than half of the original box-cab units, by this time more than a half century old, had been scrapped.

WESTBOUND train 263, rolling across the prairies of the Columbia Basin, enters the Coast Division electrification near Othello in July 1972. The Othello-Tacoma (Wash.) electrification was shut down later that year.—*Ted Benson.*

THE Little Joe leading Second 262 spits fire and water as its pantograph shatters ice on the catenary inside a tunnel near Adair, Ida. The resulting miniature thunderstorm lights up the bore's rough rock walls rushing past the locomotive.—*Richard Steinheimer.*

Only the Little Joes, frequently in multiple with two or three high-horsepower diesel units, continued to operate with any degree of regularity.

For a time the future of Milwaukee catenary was reported to be "under study," and there were hopeful rumors of possible renewal and modernization of the electrification. But this was not to be. During 1972 electric locomotives were withdrawn from the Coast Division. Finally, on February 20, 1973, the Milwaukee formally announced that the pan-

tographs were coming down for good. The remaining electrics would be retired as they came due for overhaul, and diesel power would gradually take over the remaining Rocky Mountain Division electric territory.

On Saturday, June 15, 1974, double Joes and three diesels arrived in Deer Lodge at 7:50 a.m. with the last electrically powered train on the Milwaukee — eastbound freight No. 264. Joes E-73 and E-20 were set out, and an era came to an end.

ENOUGH snow for even the most ardent of skiers blanketed the ground at Hyak, the site of the Milwaukee Road's Ski Bowl, where a bipolar-powered ski special waited to take passengers back to Seattle and Tacoma on February 6, 1949. The bipolar sported an experimental color scheme, one of several tried out before the railroad finally settled on yellow and gray colors for the aging locomotives.—*Wade J. Stevenson*.

OLD MAN WINTER has not yet relinquished his grip on the Bitter Roots as train 263 plunges through a mid-May snowstorm near Falcon in 1974.—*Ted Benson*.

240

ELDERLY box-cabs E-22 and E-23 were modernized for passenger service in 1953 by Tacoma shops. E-22 (below) makes a trial run over the Rocky Mountain Division in 1953.—*The Milwaukee Road.*

ON rare occasions electrics supplemented — rather than supplanted — steam. Three-unit motor E-39 assists Class S-1 4-8-4 No. 250 eastbound near Othello in August 1951.—*Wade J. Stevenson*.

HELPERS on the *Hi*? No. To avoid wyeing at Seattle, the *Olympian Hiawatha* was pulled backwards from Tacoma to Seattle, where locomotives changed ends. From there the train retraced its tracks to Black River Junction before heading east to Chicago—*John C. Illman*.

REPAINTED in orange and maroon (but still unmistakably bipolars), M.U.'ed E-2 and E-4 race under a covered bridge south of Seattle with the eastbound *Olympian Hi* in 1953.—*John C. Illman*.

VERSATILITY was a virtue of the box-cabs whether they were on freight or passenger schedules, in helper service, or performing switching duties. E-33 shunts cars of westbound freight 263 at Othello in July 1958 before escorting the train to Tacoma.—*Fred Matthews.*

LITTLE JOE No. E-21, one of two Joes (E-20 was the other) equipped with steam generators for passenger operation, descends the 1 per cent grade through Montana Canyon around 1951 with No. 15, the westbound *Olympian Hiawatha.*—*The Milwaukee Road.*

243

DESPITE their utilitarian design, the venerable old "Pelicans" were fascinating pieces of machinery. Even idle, they could keep a photographer busy for an hour. (Above, left to right) Classification lamp of the E-50A . . . a door with paint alligatored by age . . . trolley pole used to activate the air compressors to raise the pantographs. (Below, left to right) Orderly intricacies of truck side frames revealed in an Avery sunset . . . roller-bearing journal on an ancient truck . . . builder's plate to remind us who created these unforgettable box-cabs.—*Below left, Ted Benson; all other photos this page, Richard Steinheimer.*

GE'S BOX-CABS astounded steam operators in 1915; in the early 1970's their active longevity still amazed a dieselized world. Eastbound for Deer Lodge, Mont., E-50 on train 266 swings away from Burlington Northern right of way west of Drummond, Mont., in July 1972.—*Ted Benson.*

244

FREIGHT haulers of two generations—almost five decades separate their birth dates—stand at Tideflats Yard in Tacoma on an overcast afternoon in July 1972.—*Ted Benson.*

LUGGING 91 cars of eastbound freight, three-unit box-cab No. 10504 approaches the west portal of Pipestone Pass Tunnel on the Continental Divide in August 1938.—*Otto C. Perry.*

A HOT bearing on the rear box-cab made doubling the hill at Hyak mandatory on this July day in 1970. Alas, one can't expect perfect health from a 55-year-old locomotive.—*Tom Brown.*

IMPOSING proportions of Joe E-73 and box-cab E-34A dominate the Geep at the far end of the inspection bay at Avery engine terminal in July 1972.—*Ted Benson.*

(ABOVE RIGHT) Golden moment at Gold Creek: GE motor E-50A hums past the remotely operated substation at Gold Creek, Mont., with train 266 bound for Deer Lodge. This classic scene of Milwaukee electrification in the Rockies was photographed in 1972, but for all practical purposes it could have been 1922.—*Ted Benson.*

(CENTER RIGHT) The sun sets on E-50B, the Milwaukee's original 1915 box-cab, as it waits out a meet with an eastbound train at Haugan, Mont., in July 1972.—*Ted Benson.*

(RIGHT) During their last days on the Rocky Mountain Division, the Pelicans often were relegated to helper service. Here box-cabs working as midtrain helpers are about to duck into St. Paul Pass Tunnel (photographer Brown was standing on the portal) as they assist double Joes—already in the bore—on a westbound freight in September 1971. —*Tom Brown.*

(LEFT) The waters of the St. Regis River, swelled by melting snow on a warm spring day in the late 1950's, rush past Extra E-27 West climbing the east slope of the Bitter Roots near St. Regis, Mont.—*Richard Steinheimer.*

SNOW clings to the upper elevations of the Flint Creek Range as box-cab E-38 rolls an eastbound extra between Deer Lodge and Butte in the 1950's. The 6750 tons on the drawbar will require a helper from Butte to Piedmont.—*Richard Steinheimer*.

(BELOW LEFT) The awesome expanse of the Columbia Basin dwarfs four-unit E-36 as it rolls a freight train eastward near Taunton, Wash., 10 miles west of Othello.—*Fred Matthews.*

(BELOW CENTER) Maroon-banded Little Joes on a westbound extra slip into the siding to meet a 128-car freight holding the main at Bearmouth in the 1950's.—*Richard Steinheimer.*

A MAY 1974 sunset paints the flanks of box-cabs E-57B/E-34C in golden hues as the crew returns to Harlowton (Mont.) depot after working industries on the Lewiston branch.—*Ted Benson.*

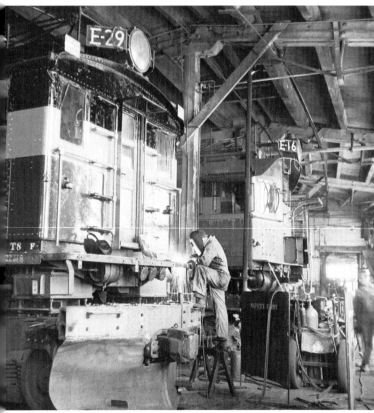

THOSE funny little electric engines had been around as long as she (above) could remember . . . A young cyclist ignores the last survivor of Milwaukee's little fleet of steeple-cab switchers, the E-82, as it breaks up train 264 at Deer Lodge in May 1974. (Right) Steeple-cab E-81 charges back to Butte with payloads after making a turn to Silver Bow, Mont., on the last day of June 1972.—*Above, Ted Benson; right, Fred W. Schneider III.*

DEER LODGE, situated in a wide valley in the Montana Rockies, is a maintenance base for the Rocky Mountain Division. (Above left) A worker fits a locomotive wheel with a new tire in Deer Lodge shops. (Far left) A welder repairs freight motor E-29 in Deer Lodge roundhouse in 1958. Baldwin-Westinghouse passenger motor E-16, beyond, is being scrapped after a long and productive life under catenary. (Left) Rebuilt box-cab E-23 and a Little Joe await assignments at Deer Lodge in 1958.—*Three photos, Richard Steinheimer.*

AIR rushes through blowers, traction motors hum, and slack is gently taken up on No. 263's 60 cars as the westbound manifest departs Harlowton in 1958. Sixteen traction motors will soon battle mountain ranges as Little Joes E-71 and E-70 take train 263 on a 15-hour dash across the rugged Rockies to Avery. —*Richard Steinheimer*.

TWIN Little Joes—dressed in Milwaukee Road's handsome orange, maroon, and black color scheme—proudly roll westbound tonnage across the span at Saltese, Mont., in 1958. Simplified orange-and-black livery was applied in the 1960's.—*Richard Steinheimer*.

PULLED by a pair of the 273-ton, 5500 h.p. Little Joes, a westbound Milwaukee Road freight cruises along the Clark Fork River on its way into the Bitter Root Mountains of western Montana.— *The Milwaukee Road*.

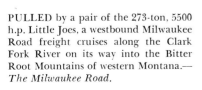

LIFE was hell for the crew of eastbound freight 266 on the afternoon of June 15, 1972. Little Joes reconstruct 266 at East Portal after doubling to the summit at St. Paul Pass Tunnel from Avery. On the way up, two of the three box-cab helpers in the middle of the 103-car train failed and had to be tucked behind the Joes to be forwarded to Deer Lodge.—*Ted Benson.*

RUNNING as an extra on St. Patrick's Day, 1958, train 263 pauses for orders at Two Dot, Mont., site of the first substation west of Harlowton.—*Richard Steinheimer.*

SYMBOL of an era when CMStP&P trains were "propelled by a power vastly in excess of requirements." Box-cab pantograph reaches for 3000-volt catenary.—*Ted Benson.*

THE Teslow grain elevator in Deer Lodge symbolizes the vast agricultural riches of Big Sky country as Joe E-71 on No. 263 waits to meet No. 264 in 1974.—*Ted Benson.*

MILKING TIME and Little Joes were a way of life in Montana. Farmer Bill Stratton milks his Jersey cow to the sounds of 263 working up Butte Hill.—*Ted Benson.*

IN the late 1950's the Little Joes were modified to M.U. with diesels, thereby creating motive-power blocks of prodigious capacity. Here two Joes team up with a GP9 on westbound 263 at Three Forks, Mont.—*William D. Middleton*.

(BELOW LEFT) Friday, July 14, 1972, at Avery finds box-cabs getting ready to assist train 264's GP40's over the summit because of the freight's malfunctioning Locotrol helpers. GE U28B No. 5507 will go west on 265.—*Ted Benson*.

EVEN as an all-diesel 264 (below) climbed the gnarled 1.7 per cent grade along the North Fork of the St. Joe River in 1972, rumors sparked that Milwaukee might electrify the gap between Avery and Othello. Ultimately, the railroad chose GP40's and Locotrol units as the more economical alternative to rebuilding its aging electrification system.—*Ted Benson.*

YARD engineer Ken Boynton gives steeple-cab E-82 a couple of notches of juice while switching Deer Lodge.—*Ted Benson.*

LITTLE JOE, diesels, and diesel smoke of eastbound 264 burst from Pipestone Pass Tunnel at the summit of the Continental Divide in August 1971. Milwaukee's crossing of the Divide is 17 miles east of Butte.—*Tom Brown.*

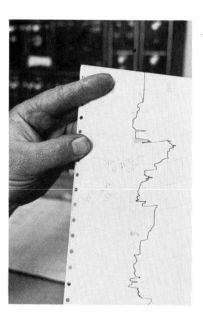

LIKE something out of a Frankenstein movie, sinister-looking electrical apparatus (above left) in the immaculately clean transformer room of East Portal substation reaches high into the rafters. Substation operator Bob Williams (above center) opens the main breaker that starts the "white coal" flowing. The substation's prowess in moving tonnage over St. Paul Pass is recorded on the transmission graph (above right).—*Three photos, Ted Benson.*

LITTLE JOES on Butte Hill near Newcomb, Mont., make a valiant last stand in May 1974. A month later, on June 15, 1974, electric operation ended.—*Ted Benson*.

APPROACHING their fallen comrades, Joes E-73 and E-20 on train 264 arrive in Deer Lodge yard on June 15, 1974, with the last electric-powered Milwaukee Road train.—*Jim Farrell*.

IT COULD BE Reading Terminal or Randolph Street or Oakland Pier—anywhere commuters stream off electric trains and head for the street, subway, or ferry. (It is Hoboken, and the trains are Erie Lackawanna's.)—*Fred W. Schneider III.*

❖❖❖❖❖❖❖❖❖❖❖❖❖❖❖❖❖❖❖❖❖❖❖❖❖❖❖❖❖

10. Electrifying the 5:15

❖❖❖❖❖❖❖❖❖❖❖❖❖❖❖❖❖❖❖❖❖❖❖❖❖❖❖❖❖

T HE multiple-unit control system developed by Frank J. Sprague in 1897 was quickly adopted for rapid-transit services. The system was ideally suited to rapid-transit operation for a number of reasons. By permitting two or more units of electric equipment to be operated from one control point, multiple-unit control made possible the economical operation of trains of almost any length, allowing a much more frequent service than was possible with locomotive-hauled services. M.U. control also enabled the motors for tractive effort to be distributed throughout a train. Thus rapid-transit trains, with a better power-to-weight ratio, could accelerate faster than could locomotive-hauled trains.

These advantages of M.U. control made the system equally applicable to the electrification of heavily trafficked steam railroad suburban and commuter services. Suburban services operated with multiple-unit equipment were a feature of the early electrification projects of the New York Central and New Haven railroads into New York's Grand Central Terminal. Before either of these services was started, though, several other steam railroad suburban operations in North America had begun to electrify with multiple-unit equipment for the economy and efficiency that electric operation offered.

263

A TWO-CAR train of the steel-and-aluminum M.U.'s acquired by Northwestern Pacific in 1929 and 1930 races through Alto toward Sausalito, Calif.—*Charles D. Savage, collection of Donald Duke.*

PICKING its way through the turnouts of the yard, a three-car train of NWP's original St. Louis-built wooden M.U.'s arrives at the Sausalito ferry terminal.—*B. H. Ward.*

NWP's *Eureka*, the largest ferry on San Francisco Bay, steams toward San Francisco from Sausalito on February 28, 1941, the last day of NWP train and ferry service. Beyond is the Golden Gate Bridge, which caused the demise of NWP's commuter business.—*Southern Pacific.*

North Shore

THE earliest electrification of suburban railroad service was carried out in 1903 by California's North Shore Railroad. Originally known as the North Pacific Coast Railroad, the steam-powered narrow-gauge line operated to points in Marin and Sonoma counties from Sausalito, where it connected with railroad-owned ferries from San Francisco. At the turn of the century the pleasant surroundings and excellent climate north of the Bay were attracting many new residents, who relied on the narrow-gauge trains and ferries to reach their daily work in San Francisco.

Recognizing the potential in Marin County's modest commuter business, a group of San Francisco investors secured control of the NPC in 1902, reorganized it as the North Shore Railroad, and began to rebuild and modernize its suburban division. A new ferry slip and depot were constructed at Sausalito. Between Sausalito and San Rafael a standard-gauge rail was added, and almost all of the 12-mile line was double-tracked. An automatic block signal system was installed, and the suburban service was electrified.

The North Shore adopted a 550-volt D.C. third-rail system similar to that already in use on several elevated, subway, and interurban railways. The principal power supply was a combination substation and generating plant constructed by the railroad at Alto, 4 miles north of Sausalito. Three-phase power was supplied to the substation at 50,000 volts, transformed down to 4500 volts, and converted to D.C. by two motor-generator sets. A steam boiler and a generator were also provided as a reserve supply. A 560-ampere-hour storage battery at Alto helped meet peak power demands on the system, and a 225-kilowatt motor-generator set in a second substation near San Rafael boosted power supply to a section of 2 per cent grade.

Rolling stock for the suburban service included nine new combination baggage-passenger motor cars and 12 coach trailers built by St. Louis Car Company. Additional motor and trailer coaches were rebuilt by the railroad from existing cars, both standard gauge and narrow gauge. The wood cars were similar in overall size and arrangement to typical interurban railway equipment rather than steam railroad cars. Motor cars were mounted on one Hedley motor truck, with two GE No. 66 motors rated at 125 h.p., and one trailer truck. Multiple-unit control permitted operation of the equipment in trains. Maximum speed was between 50 and 60 mph.

Standard-gauge electric trains began running in 1903 over 10 miles of North Shore's main line between Sausalito and San Anselmo, and into Mill Valley on a short branch line. Two lines into San Rafael were opened to electric operation the following year, and a final 2-mile extension of electrification from San Anselmo to Manor was opened in 1908. In 1907 the North Shore became part of the Northwestern Pacific Railroad, jointly owned by the Santa Fe and the Southern Pacific until 1929, when it became exclusively an SP subsidiary.

Another 12 motor cars, similar to the original equipment, were purchased by NWP at the time of the 1908 extension. Soon after the SP took control of the NWP in 1929, the railroad ordered 19 new 72-foot, 55-ton cars from the St. Louis Car Company. Although similar in dimensions and appearance to equipment operated in the Southern Pacific's East Bay electric services, the NWP cars were distinguished by the extensive use of aluminum in their carbodies.

Northwestern Pacific's suburban service was hard hit by the depression and it suffered a further setback with the completion of the Golden Gate Bridge in 1937. Marin County commuters could reach San Francisco either in their own automobiles or by means of through bus services in competition with the NWP's rail-ferry service. The NWP suffered severe losses and filed for abandonment of suburban service the following year, and the electric trains and the ferries ran for the last time in February 1941.

Long Island Rail Road

THE first major commuter railroad to begin conversion to electric operation was the Long Island Rail Road, which opened its first electric lines in 1905. Although it was chartered in 1834 as a link in a rail-and-ferry route to Boston, by the turn of the century the Long Island had developed into a commuter-oriented railroad serving the Long Island (N. Y.) communities that were fast becoming "bedroom" suburbs of New York City.

Development of LIRR's commuter traffic was handicapped, however, by the lack of a direct entrance into Manhattan. Long Island trains terminated at Flatbush Avenue in Brooklyn and at Long Island City in Queens, where passengers were obliged to transfer to elevated lines or ferries to cross the East River to Manhattan. In 1900 the Pennsylvania Railroad acquired control of the Long Island, and within a year began to plan its New York tunnel and terminal project that would

provide a Manhattan terminal for both itself and the Long Island Rail Road. Because of the long East River tunnels, electrification of the Long Island was mandatory.

Before the Penn Station project was completed, the Long Island began an electrification program as part of improvements to its Atlantic Avenue line in Brooklyn, which included a long tunnel under Atlantic Avenue and a new underground passenger terminal at Flatbush Avenue.

Totaling 38 route-miles, this initial LIRR electrification ran from Flatbush Avenue east to Belmont Park, Queens, and south from Woodhaven Junction across Jamaica Bay to Rockaway Park and to Valley Stream via Far Rockaway. Power was distributed by a 650-volt D.C. third-rail system identical to that later chosen for the New York terminal project. Power was generated in a plant built by the Pennsylvania Railroad at Long Island City to supply both the Long Island and its own New York tunnel and terminal trackage. An 11,000-volt, three-phase A.C. transmission system delivered power to LIRR substations, where it was converted to 650-volt D.C. by motor-generator sets.

During 1905 and 1906, 134 steel M.U. cars were built for this initial Long Island electrification. Designed by consultant George Gibbs, the 51-foot, 40-ton cars were each powered by two Westinghouse No. 113 motors rated at 210 h.p. Unusually small for a railroad electrification, the cars were virtually identical to equipment designed at the same time by Gibbs for New York's first sub-

THE Long Island's original electrification was opened in 1905 as part of the Atlantic Avenue line improvements. This 1910 view, taken at the corner of Atlantic and Stone avenues in Brooklyn, N.Y., shows, at the left, a train of new MP54 cars outbound from Flatbush Avenue as a Jamaica express and, right, a train of older subway-size "Gibbs cars" operating as an inbound local.—*Collection of Ron Ziel.*

TWO of the Long Island's original MP41 "Gibbs cars" spliced by an open-platform wooden trailer form the first train over the third-rail extension to Hempstead, N.Y., in a photograph taken at Floral Park on May 26, 1908. At the time the Long Island Rail Road, with nearly 50 electrified route-miles, had one of the most important electrifications in the U.S.—*Collection of W. S. Boerckel.*

A BAND greeted the first electric train to Babylon, N.Y., on May 21, 1925. The celebration marked what was to be the last major extension of LIRR third rail for 45 years.—*James V. Osborne.*

way, since operation of Long Island trains through the IRT subway from Brooklyn to Manhattan was planned. This joint operation never materialized, and later Long Island cars were constructed to more liberal dimensions.

Long Island third rail was extended to Hempstead and Mineola in 1908. In 1910 trackage from Jamaica into Penn Station was opened to electric trains, along with track from Glendale to Ozone Park and from Valley Stream to Long Beach. Within another three years the Long Island's entire North Shore Division to Whitestone Landing and Port Washington was being electrically operated.

To prepare for the expanded service that would follow the opening of Penn Station, the Long Island ordered 222 steel motor cars from American Car & Foundry Company in 1909 and 1910. The cars closely followed new standards developed by the Pennsylvania for suburban passenger cars. Constructed entirely of steel, the Class MP54 LIRR cars measured 64 feet 6 inches over buffers, weighed just under 54 tons, and seated 72 passengers. Each car was mounted on one motor truck and one trailer truck, and was powered by two Westinghouse No. 308 motors rated at 225 h.p.

By 1913 the Long Island was operating 89 route-miles and 188 track-miles of electrified main line. More than 400 steel M.U. cars were in service. By then the Pennsylvania Railroad had advanced more than 20 million dollars to the Long Island to finance electrification, grade-crossing eliminations, and other related improvements.

Electrification combined with the new Manhattan terminal to increase Long Island's ability to handle commuter traffic. The traffic growth that had motivated the Pennsylvania's massive investment quickly followed, and the Long Island was soon the nation's foremost commuter hauler.

During the first 10 months of operation into Penn Station the Long Island's passenger loadings increased by 92 per cent. During the 15 years from 1905, when its first electric line opened, to 1919, the Long Island's passenger traffic increased by 353 per cent to more than 64 million passengers annually, as Manhattanites flocked to the Long Island communities made convenient by the electric train service. In the decade from 1910 to 1920, for example, the population of the Borough of Queens increased almost 65 per cent.

Electrification also cut operating costs for the Long Island. In 1910 the railroad was operating its electric trains at a cost of less than 18 cents a car-mile; steam-hauled services cost almost 28 cents a car-mile. By 1919, when total electric car-miles exceeded 18 million, the savings would be sizable indeed.

By 1925 third rail extended east to Babylon on

the Montauk branch, 38 miles from Penn Station. Still more rolling stock, virtually identical to the MP54-class cars built at the time of the Penn Station electrification, were added to the roster in subsequent orders. By 1930 the Long Island owned more than 1000 electric cars.

The Long Island transported the greatest traffic in its history during the World War II period. Passenger traffic, more than 70 per cent of it carried by the electric trains, reached a peak of some 116 million passengers in 1946.

Financially troubled, bankrupt (in 1949), and badly run down from the demands of its enormous wartime traffic, the Long Island went through three major postwar rehabilitation programs. A 16.5-million-dollar Pennsylvania Railroad improvement program immediately after the war paid for 50 new 134-seat, double-deck M.U. cars and some substation improvements. In 1954 the railroad began operating under a 12-year redevelopment plan that provided 140 new M.U. cars, rebuilding of older equipment, and improvements to the electrical distribution system.

A TRAIN of new double-deck M.U.'s bound from New York City to Babylon lets off passengers at Rockville Centre on a sunny afternoon in 1948.—*Collection of W. S. Boerckel.*

DOUBLE-DECK trailer car 200 (above) was built for **LIRR** in 1932 by parent Pennsylvania's Altoona shops. Passengers stepped up or down from the aisle to reach the seats. (Left) The upper-level seats utilized space that normally was wasted.—*Both photos, Long Island.*

ARCH-ROOFED MP54 M.U.'s from Port Washington pass along the south edge of Sunnyside Yard on Pennsy rails as they head toward Penn Station, New York. The overhead wire furnishes 11,000-volt power to New Haven trains on the Hell Gate Bridge route.—*James G. La Vake.*

AN owl-eyed MP54 leads a train of several types of LIRR M.U. cars through a January snowstorm near Jamaica in 1964.—*Ron Ziel.*

DEEP underneath Penn Station in New York a train of Long Island M.U.'s waits for the homeward rush of commuters. The open windows of the cars attest to hot, muggy summer weather. —*William D. Middleton.*

Still another overhaul of the Long Island began in 1965, when the State of New York's new Metropolitan Transportation Authority took title to the railroad from the Pennsylvania and began a rehabilitation and modernization that would ultimately make it one of the most technologically advanced of all commuter railroads.

At the heart of the MTA program was a 620-car fleet of new stainless-steel M-1 Metropolitan M.U. cars to replace the railroad's older electric equipment. Delivered by the Budd Company during 1968-1971, the 85-foot, 46-ton stainless-steel cars operated in semi-permanently coupled pairs. The new cars provided radically improved passenger comfort, with air conditioning and 3-2 seating for 118 or 122 passengers.

The M-1's were equipped with trucks of the Budd *Pioneer III* design, fitted with rubber cushioning and an air-suspension system, while four 160-h.p. GE traction motors and a combination of dynamic and conventional air brakes gave the M-1's radically improved performance characteristics, with a 100-

mph maximum speed and a 2.1-mph-per-second acceleration rate that was more than a third faster than even the fastest earlier LIRR M.U.'s.

Equipped with the combination of dynamic and conventional air brakes, the M-1's had a maximum braking rate of 3.2 mph per second, exceeding the performance of older cars by 60 per cent. An Automatic Train Operation control system maintained train speed automatically in accordance with signal indications.

Delivery of a follow-on order from General Electric brought the M-1 fleet to a total of 770 cars by the end of 1972, while Budd delivered another 174 similar M-3 cars in 1985, permitting retirement of all of the railroad's older electric equipment.

MTA capital support also enabled the Long Island to begin a massive renovation of its physical plant. Expansion of the railroad's electric power system more than doubled the power supply to the third rail. Track and signal systems were upgraded to permit 100-mph operation by the new M-1 fleet. Stations were improved and a new car repair shop

THE Long Island abandoned its double-deck car design with a 1953 order for 20 Pullman-Standard M.U.'s that seated 128 passengers in 3-and-2 seats on one level. The same basic arrangement was specified for subsequent orders that reached a total of 190 cars in 1963.—*Long Island.*

LONG ISLAND shopmen rework an elderly MP54 in the Morris Park shops in 1970. Many of the durable cars served LIRR commuters for more than 50 years before they were replaced by the Metropolitans.—*Metropolitan Transportation Authority: Ted Kell.*

NEGOTIATING one of the elevated grade separations characteristic of the Long Island's busiest lines, a New York-Babylon train stops at Seaford on a warm May morning in 1970.—*William D. Middleton.*

JAMAICA—all change! Hub of the Long Island is Jamaica station in the borough of Queens. A typical moment on a May afternoon in 1970 saw MP54's arriving and a train of Metropolitans awaiting departure on two of the station's eight tracks.—*William D. Middleton.*

HEADING toward New York from Long Beach, an M.U. train passes through a pleasant wooded area west of Lynbrook in the spring of 1970.—*William D. Middleton*.

THE time and the place are the same as in the photo at the left: A long string of M-1 Metropolitans heads east toward Babylon.—*William D. Middleton*.

HALF a century of LIRR M.U.-car evolution is represented in this 1970 view at Jamaica. At the right a train of M-1's approaches from Flatbush Avenue. In the background arriving from Penn Station is a train with a mixture of three types of older cars.—*William D. Middleton*.

AN old WJ&S wooden baggage motor bears the markers of a Millville-Camden train racing through Woodbury, N. J., in 1947. Two newer steel cars carry the passengers.—*David H. Cope.*

was built at Hillside. As traffic into Manhattan continued to grow, LIRR completed extensive expansion and improvements to its Penn Station facilities and added a new car storage yard on Manhattan's west side.

In 1970 the Long Island expanded its electrification for the first time in nearly 40 years when trains began operating over 16.2 miles of new third rail from Mineola through Hicksville to Huntington. A second major expansion of electric territory came in 1988 with the completion of a 23.5-mile extension of third rail from Hicksville to Ronkonkoma.

West Jersey & Seashore

ONLY a year after the Long Island Rail Road opened the first section of its suburban electrification, another Pennsylvania Railroad subsidiary, the West Jersey & Seashore Railroad, completed a third-rail electrification between Camden, across the Delaware River from Philadelphia, and Atlantic City, N. J. Comprising 75 route-miles and about 150 miles of track, the West Jersey & Seashore electrification was at the time of its opening in 1906 the longest steam road electrification in North America.

One of two routes operated between Camden and

Atlantic City by WJ&S, the line converted to electric operation did a brisk suburban business out of Camden and carried heavy traffic to and from the New Jersey coast during the summer. The line was double track for its entire length between Camden and Atlantic City, with a third running main between Camden and Woodbury.

The 650-volt D.C. third-rail system used by the Long Island was adopted for the WJ&S electrification. Because of numerous road crossings, overhead trolley wire was installed for a distance of 4.4 miles between Haddon Avenue in Camden and South Gloucester; current collection was by trolley poles. A 10-mile branch between Newfield and Millville also was operated with an overhead trolley system from the time of its electrification in 1906 until 1909, when it was converted to third rail.

Like other installations of comparable magnitude the West Jersey & Seashore was obliged to construct its own power plant to assure an adequate power supply. A coal-fired steam plant was built on Big Timber Creek just north of Westville. A dozen 358 h.p. Stirling water-tube boilers delivered superheated steam at 175 pounds pressure to three 2000-kilowatt, 6600-volt, 25-cycle, three-phase

TAKE a walk on the Boardwalk: First advance to Tennessee Avenue in Atlantic City, N. J., location of West Jersey & Seashore's depot, shown in a quiet moment on a June day in 1926. Could it be that the WJ&S was the Short Line Railroad that has mystified railroad-knowledgeable Monopoly players all these years?—*Leonard Rice, collection of LeRoy O. King.*

SHORTLY after the West Jersey & Seashore electrification opened, a dapper train crew posed at the Camden (N. J.) terminal with their wooden M.U.'s. The two trainmen at the left seem confident of the strength of the board shielding the third rail.—*Collection of Richard S. Clover.*

SACKS of mail are loaded aboard a 1906-vintage baggage-mail car at Woodbury in December 1948. PRSL electric cars carried an illuminated number board and a locomotive-type bell on their roofs.—*E. F. Wiegand.*

Curtis turbogenerators. Nine 700-kilowatt transformers at the power plant converted the power supply to 33,000-volt, three-phase A.C. for transmission to eight substations.

Each of the substations was equipped with transformers to reduce the A.C. voltage and two motor-generator sets of 500-kilowatt or 750-kilowatt capacity to provide the 650-volt D.C. power supply. Power was supplied directly to the 100-pound third-rail sections, while parallel copper feeders were used for the overhead trolley-wire sections.

Simultaneously with electrification, much of the WJ&S was relaid with heavier running rail, and new passenger terminals were built at Camden and Atlantic City. At Camden the construction included both a new station that adjoined the Delaware River ferry terminal and a ¾-mile, double-track elevated approach. At Atlantic City a new terminal, similar to that at Camden, was connected with the WJ&S line by 2 miles of new right of way which included a drawbridge over the Thoroughfare, the neck of tidewater separating Atlantic City from the mainland, and an elevated structure crossing the tracks of the Philadelphia & Reading Railway.

A fleet of 68 multiple-unit cars was built by American Car & Foundry, J. G. Brill, and Wason. Six were combination baggage-mail cars; the remainder were coaches seating 58 passengers. Weighing 44½ tons fully equipped, the cars were 55 feet 5½ inches over buffers. Each car was provided with two GE-69 motors rated at 200 h.p. and Sprague-GE M.U. control. Unlike mechanically similar equipment then being constructed for the New York Central and the Long Island, the West Jersey & Seashore cars were built of wood, an unfortunate choice that rendered them obsolete almost from the day they entered service.

Electrification of the WJ&S was carried out in record time. Only two days after a powerhouse site was selected in mid-January 1906, for example, construction was under way, and by July 1 the plant was supplying power to the newly electrified tracks.

Initial schedules showed express trains running between Camden and Atlantic City at hourly intervals, making the 65-mile run in only 90 minutes. Local trains operated between Camden and Glassboro every 15 minutes during rush hours, with every fourth train continuing to Millville. Within a few months service was expanded to provide an Atlantic City express every 15 minutes. Camden-Millville trains were run every half hour, and 10-minute service was operated between Woodbury and Camden.

During the summer of 1910 through service was operated from Camden to Ocean City, with WJ&S

A PAIR of Pennsylvania-Reading Seashore Lines wooden M.U.'s roll south through Gloucester City, N. J., under trolley wire in 1947. The WJ&S became part of the PRSL in a 1933 merger with Reading's Atlantic City Railroad.—*David H. Cope.*

RUNNING as Millville-Camden local 766, a pair of PRSL steel cars cross Mantua Creek, just south of Wenonah, N. J., in 1947. The 1912-built cars were among the few steel cars operated by the third-rail line.—*David H. Cope.*

277

trains operating from Pleasantville to Ocean City over the rails of the Shore Fast Line interurban.

Only a few months after it opened, the WJ&S electrification suffered a major wreck. On October 28, 1906, a three-car M.U. train from Camden to Atlantic City derailed on the Thoroughfare drawbridge at Atlantic City. The derailment, it later was determined, resulted from the failure of the drawbridge operator to lock the rails upon closing the span after the passage of a boat. The entire train plunged into the deep water. Two cars were entirely submerged, while a portion of the third remained above the water. The loss of life was aggravated by a patent handle on the car doors, which could be opened only by members of the train crew and couldn't be opened at all if they were sprung or bent. The casualty list for the wreck totaled 57 dead and 32 injured.

As traffic on the third-rail line grew, more rolling stock was added. By 1912 more than 100 M.U. cars were in service. Some of the cars were built of wood, but a number of the later cars were of steel construction, like the equipment operated by parent PRR and its Long Island subsidiary.

Electric train traffic to Atlantic City suffered from the effects of private automobile ownership after World War I, and electric operation was discontinued between Newfield and Atlantic City before 1932. The electric trains continued to haul a sizable commuter traffic as far as Millville through World War II. After a 1948 order of the New Jersey Public Utilities Commission sidelined the aging wooden M.U. cars, steam-hauled trains displaced some former electric schedules, and in August 1949 electric operation ended altogether.

Hudson & Manhattan Railroad

THE Hudson & Manhattan Railroad began operating between Manhattan and Hoboken, N. J., in 1908. Strictly speaking, the H&M was not a steam railroad electrification. Powered from the very beginning by electricity, the H&M's tunnel lines under the Hudson River resembled subway lines in their general characteristics more than they did an electrified steam railroad.

The H&M could trace its beginning to the Hudson tunnel project organized in 1873 by Dewitt Clinton Haskin. Work started in 1874, but more than 30 years of injunctions, accidents, and financial reverses intervened before the first train operated through Haskin's tunnel.

The idea of a railroad under the Hudson to connect Manhattan with the suburban communities and railroad terminals on the New Jersey shore was finally realized by William Gibbs McAdoo, a New York lawyer and businessman who subsequently became Woodrow Wilson's Treasury Secretary and headed the wartime United States Railroad Administration. Long intrigued by the tunnel project, McAdoo in 1902 organized what was to become the Hudson & Manhattan to complete the long-dormant tunnel project. At the time McAdoo revived the project, a half mile of completed tunnel had been untouched since work was suspended 10 years before.

Using the shield method, the 5650-foot tunnel was holed through early in 1904, and a second, parallel tube was completed the following year. While work progressed on the tunnels, construction was started on the subway that would carry trains from the Manhattan end of the tubes at Christopher Street to a new terminal at 19th Street and Sixth Avenue. On the New Jersey side, the H&M was extended north to the Lackawanna Railroad's Hoboken terminal.

Even before the first tunnels were completed, the H&M had started work on a second pair of tubes that would carry trains under the Hudson from Jersey City to a new Hudson Terminal at Cortlandt Street in lower Manhattan. On the New Jersey side the tube trains served both the Pennsylvania Railroad's Exchange Place station and the Erie Railroad's station, and connected with the original two tubes at Hoboken.

A third New Jersey terminal was added in 1906, when the H&M concluded an agreement with the Pennsylvania Railroad to operate a joint service between Hudson Terminal and Newark, using PRR tracks for a portion of the run.

The H&M's first line between New York and Hoboken opened with gala ceremonies on February 25, 1908. As a crowd of 400 invited dignitaries waited in the railroad's 19th Street station, President Theodore Roosevelt pressed a button on his White House desk that turned on the power. A special train carried the guests through the tunnel under the Hudson, stopping at a circle of red, white, and blue lights on the state line while the New York and New Jersey governors, Charles Hughes and Franklin Fort, shook hands. A cheering crowd of 20,000 attended the ceremonies at Hoboken, where the usual round of speeches was made. The official party then returned to Manhattan for a banquet at Sherry's.

In July 1909 the Hudson Terminal in lower Manhattan was opened, and by September trains were serving the three Jersey City and Hoboken steam road terminals through both pairs of Hudson tubes. In 1910 the uptown Manhattan line was extended to Sixth Avenue and 33rd Street. Traffic on the H&M grew rapidly. From an average of 32,000 passengers each day in the summer of 1909, traffic increased to a daily average of 130,000 before the end of 1910. In 1911 service was extended over

THE November 1, 1890, *Scientific American* illustrated the shield tunneling method used to dig the first Hudson River tunnel. Financial problems halted the work in 1892; a decade elapsed before the work was resumed by the Hudson & Manhattan Railroad.—*Library of Congress.*

ARTIST H. M. Pettit's drawing (above) illustrates one proposal that was made for the H&M station at Journal Square in Jersey City, adjacent to the Pennsylvania's tracks. The photograph below shows the Journal Square yard as it appeared in 1911.—*Both illustrations, Port Authority Trans-Hudson, collection of Electric Railroaders' Association.*

RUNNING east on Pennsylvania Railroad trackage, a Hudson & Manhattan train passes PRR's Waldo Tower at Journal Square in 1954. Both 600-volt third rail and 11,000-volt catenary serve these tracks.—*Herbert H. Harwood Jr.*

PENNSY'S keystone decorated the sides of 30 air-conditioned cars purchased in 1958 from St. Louis Car Company for joint PRR-H&M service between Manhattan and Newark, N.J. H&M owned 20 identical cars.—*St. Louis Car Company.*

the Pennsylvania into Newark, completing the H&M system.

Power was produced in the H&M's own steam generating plant in Jersey City, which was equipped with two 6000-kilowatt and two 3000-kilowatt Curtis turbines. Power was distributed at 11,000 volts A.C. to substations, where it was converted to 600 volts D.C. for the railroad's third-rail system.

Pressed Steel Car and American Car & Foundry delivered 50 multiple-unit passenger cars early in 1908. Constructed to dimensions more typical of the New York subway system than of railroad practice, the cars were 48 feet 3 inches long, weighed 35 tons, and seated 48 passengers. Orders delivered by Pressed Steel Car and American Car & Foundry between 1909 and 1911 added 176 passenger cars to the H&M roster, while the Pennsylvania Railroad acquired 60 nearly identical MP38 cars for operation in the joint service to Newark in 1911. More than 100 additional cars constructed to similar specifications were acquired during the 1920's.

Aside from a shift of its Newark terminal to the new Pennsylvania Station in 1938 and the addition of 50 air-conditioned cars in 1958, the H&M operated with little change into the 1960's. But plagued by operating losses during the postwar period, the railroad entered bankruptcy and in 1962 was taken over by the Port Authority Trans-Hudson Corporation (PATH), a subsidiary of the Port of New York Authority.

A PATH overhaul of the system included 252 air-conditioned aluminum cars delivered by the St.

(RIGHT) Ownership by the Port of New York Authority brought 206 new cars to the former Hudson & Manhattan in 1965 and 1967. The new cars completed the upgrading of H&M rolling stock that was begun in 1958.—*Port Authority Trans-Hudson, from Electric Railroaders' Association.*

Louis Car Company and Canada's Hawker Siddeley between 1965 and 1972, while another 95 similar cars came from Japan's Kawasaki Heavy Industries in 1986. Stations, tunnels, tracks, electric power, and signal systems were rehabilitated, and a new maintenance shop was opened in 1990. Completion of the World Trade Center in 1971 gave the railroad a new lower Manhattan terminal, while a new Journal Square Transportation Center in Jersey City was completed in 1975.

Southern Pacific

THE first railroad to adopt a high-voltage D.C. overhead system was the Southern Pacific Company, which in 1911 electrified the suburban services it operated out of Oakland, Calif. The SP electrification employed the 1200-volt D.C. system that had been introduced for interurban railway construction in 1907 by General Electric.

Because of the higher voltage, the 1200-volt system reduced by half the amperage required for the same load at 600 volts, with corresponding savings in the size and cost of feeders and overhead systems and in reduced line losses. Indeed, as long as 600-volt D.C. was used, the power demands of heavy railroad loads made any system other than third

SOUTHERN PACIFIC M.U.'s coil down into San Francisco's East Bay Terminal from the San Francisco-Oakland Bay Bridge. The bridge trackage had catenary for SP and Sacramento Northern trains and third rail for the Key System.—*Arthur R. Alter, collection of Donald Duke.*

THREE of SP's big red electric cars roll along a four-track right of way shared with steam trains in East Oakland, Calif. Gates instead of doors were characteristic of both these cars and Northwestern Pacific's cars of 1929 and 1930.—*Charles D. Savage, collection of Donald Duke.*

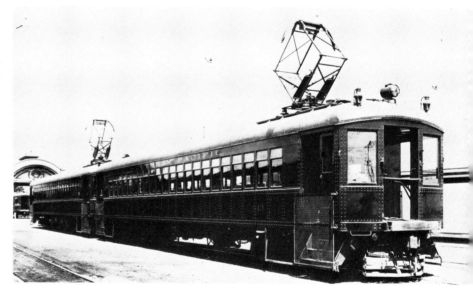

PORTHOLES later replaced the large rectangular end windows of SP's electric cars, shown between runs at Oakland Pier.—*Smithsonian Institution.*

A ONE-CAR train bound for San Francisco via the Bay Bridge emerges from the Northbrae Tunnel on the Shattuck Avenue line in Berkeley. By April 1940, when the picture was taken, operation of the electric line had been assumed by SP's subsidiary Interurban Electric Railway. Key System later took over operation of this line.—*Arthur R. Alter, collection of Donald Duke.*

rail impractical. Since much of the SP suburban system operated in the streets of the East Bay communities, a third-rail installation was out of the question.

The decision to electrify the SP lines was the result of steady growth in the railroad's commuter traffic which traveled between residential communities in the East Bay area and San Francisco by means of the SP train services and connecting ferry services from the Alameda and Oakland moles. Over 50 miles of line were electrified to Berkeley, Oakland, Alameda, and San Leandro.

For its overhead distribution system, SP employed a catenary system supported by either steel catenary bridges or center poles and brackets. Power for the electrification was generated in the SP's Fruitvale power plant, which was equipped with two 5500-kilowatt, three-phase turbogenerators. Power was transmitted to substations at West Oakland and Berkeley at 13,200 volts. The two substations, together with a third located at the power plant, used rotary converter equipment with a capacity at each substation of 4500 to 6000 kilowatts.

Initial rolling stock for the SP electric system included 60 steel M.U. cars built by the American Car & Foundry Company. The cars measured almost 73 feet over buffers, and the motor cars weighed 55 tons. The 10-foot 4-inch width over side sills permitted 3-2 seating, which gave the cars a seating capacity of 116 passengers. Motor cars were mounted on Baldwin trucks and were equipped with four GE-207-A motors rated at 125 h.p. and geared for a maximum speed of 40 mph. Sprague-GE multiple-unit control was installed. A roller-type pantograph was employed for current collection.

Subsequent orders, built by AC&F and Pullman, expanded the SP M.U. fleet to more than 140 cars.

Traffic on the SP electrified lines increased steadily, reaching a peak of 22 million passengers in 1920. By 1936 auto ferries and other competition had reduced SP electric traffic to 14 million passengers per year. The opening of the San Francisco-Oakland Bay Bridge further reduced traffic, even though the electric trains, operated after December 1, 1938, by SP's subsidiary Interurban Electric Railway, ran via the bridge into San Francisco. By 1939 fewer than 10 million passengers a year were using the service. Abandonment was requested, and the last trains ran in early 1941. Portions of the system were taken over by the rival Key System, which integrated the SP trackage with its own electric rail service.

Canadian Northern Railway

CANADA'S only suburban electrification was conceived in the decade before World War I as part

MOTOR 9185, built by English Electric, eases a heavy through train out of Canadian National's new Central Station in 1943. The new approach from the south connected main lines to the east, southeast, and west of Montreal, Que., with the new station built at the south end of the Mount Royal tunnel. Catenary extended as far south as Turcot Yard and Victoria Bridge.—*Canadian National Railways.*

283

EXCEPT for minor details, six box-cab locomotives built by Canadian GE in 1914 and 1916 for Canadian Northern's Montreal terminal electrification were identical to the passenger units built in 1913 for the Butte, Anaconda & Pacific.—*General Electric*.

NINE British-built box-cabs were acquired secondhand by CN in 1942 for the new Central Station in Montreal. They were built in 1924 and 1926 by English Electric for a Montreal operation of the National Harbours Board. —*Canadian National Railways*.

WOODEN coaches trail behind motor 9103, one of the original locomotives built in 1916, near Mount Royal, Que., in June 1948.—*J. P. Ahrens*.

of a Montreal (Que.) tunnel and terminal project of the Canadian Northern Railway, a Canadian National predecessor that was rapidly evolving into a major transcontinental system.

Approaching Montreal from the west, Canadian Northern had access only to an inconveniently located downtown terminal via a roundabout route skirting the north side of 769-foot-high Mount Royal. The arrangement placed the railroad at a competitive disadvantage with the rival Grand Trunk and Canadian Pacific systems, both of which had terminals in the heart of the city. Henry K. Wicksteed, CN's chief engineer of surveys, advanced a proposal for driving a 3-mile tunnel under Mount Royal to a new terminal in the heart of Montreal.

Tunneling started in July 1912, with work progressing from headings at each portal and from a shaft driven at Maplewood Avenue. By the end of 1913 the entire 3.2-mile tunnel had been driven through, although excavation work continued well into the following year. More than 400,000 cubic yards of earth and rock were removed during the tunnel excavation. The double-track tunnel had a steady 0.6 per cent grade ascending to the west.

A passenger terminal was built at the tunnel's east portal. Near the opposite end of the tunnel the railroad undertook the development of the "model city" of Mount Royal, which was expected to become a choice residential area only a few minutes from downtown Montreal by electric train.

Canadian Northern had planned from the outset for electric operation of its tunnel and terminal. Although both low-voltage D.C. and single-phase A.C. systems were considered, the railroad adopted the more recently developed high-voltage D.C. system advocated by General Electric. Technically the Canadian Northern installation was similar to that

BOX-CAB No. 188, one of the English Electric units, brings a train out of the south portal of Mount Royal tunnel into Central Station in August 1956. Beyond, a northbound M.U. train disappears into the tunnel.—*Jim Shaughnessy.*

TRAIN 33 from Hervey, Que., leaves Eastern Junction for Central Station behind No. 9187. Pacific 5579 heads "around the Horn" to Turcot Yard in 1948.—*Philip R. Hastings.*

AMONG the oldest locomotives still operating in regular line-haul service in North America are Canadian National box-cabs 6714 and 6713, seen pulling commuters homeward at Eastern Junction on July 2, 1971. CN's electrics have undergone several renumberings during their long and useful lives. —*All photos, William D. Middleton.*

TWO of CN's 1950 GE steeple-cabs bring a morning rush-hour train in from Deux-Montagnes through lush summer foliage near A-ma-Baie in 1971. The Erie-built units were similar in general appearance to GE's industrial diesel switchers—with pantographs added.

(LEFT) An M.U. train inbound from Cartierville, Que., clatters across the diamond at Eastern Junction, where the St. Laurent subdivision crosses the electrified suburban line.

STREAMLINING was not yet in vogue when English Electric's Dick Kerr works riveted together these box-cabs in the 1920's. Two of them pull a morning rush-hour train at Roxboro, Que.

TRAIN 920 from Cartierville stops for passengers at Portal Heights, at the north portal of the Mount Royal Tunnel. The 3.2-mile double-track tunnel affords CN a superb route to Montreal's northern suburbs.—*William D. Middleton.*

WAITING passengers look up as a northbound train comprising a third of CN's M.U. fleet rolls into Val-Royal station. Canadian Car & Foundry built six M.U. motor cars and twelve trailers for CN in 1952.—*William D. Middleton.*

FOR a few moments a small boy interrupts the serious job of filling the river with rocks. thrown one by one, to watch CN M.U.'s thunder across the Rivière des Prairies bridge at Île-Bigras.—*William D. Middleton.*

EIGHT box-cabs sun themselves south of Central Station. CN's power distribution system employs compound catenary and double contact wire supported by alternate clips from the secondary messenger.—*Jim Shaughnessy.*

A SUBURBAN train from Cartierville to Montreal joins the main line from Deux-Montagnes just west of Val-Royal station. GE box-cab No. 6710, 57 years old when the picture was taken in 1971, is in the lead.—*William D. Middleton.*

of the Butte, Anaconda & Pacific. Like the BA&P, CN employed an overhead catenary system energized at 2400 volts D.C. Power was supplied by the Montreal commercial power company and converted from 11,000-volt, three-phase A.C. to D.C. by a pair of 1500-kilowatt motor-generator sets in a substation near the tunnel's west portal.

Six B+B box-cab electric locomotives constructed for CN by the Canadian General Electric Company's Peterborough (Ont.) works in 1914 and 1916 were virtually identical to the BA&P units. Weighing 85 tons, the locomotives had a continuous rating of 1100 h.p. and were designed for a 45-mph free running speed. Each locomotive was fitted with M.U. control and two pneumatically operated pantographs. Two locomotives running in multiple could handle a 16-car passenger train.

Canadian Northern also placed an order with the Pressed Steel Car Company for eight all-steel multiple-unit cars for the planned suburban service to the new town of Mount Royal.

Delayed by World War I, the new tunnel and terminal finally were opened in late 1918, when the electrics began operating over a 8-mile route between the downtown terminal and suburban Cartierville. The M.U. car order, deferred by the war, was never delivered, and both suburban trains and through services to Ottawa and Toronto were operated through the tunnel by the electric locomotives.

In 1925, soon after Canadian Northern had become part of the new Canadian National system, catenary was extended another 9 miles to St. Eustache. Two "home-built" wooden M.U. cars, each capable of handling two trailer cars, were added to the electric roster to accommodate the additional traffic.

CN's electrification, previously confined largely to suburban service, took on a greatly expanded role in 1943 when the railroad completed its long-planned consolidated Montreal terminal at the site of the original tunnel terminal. Trackage throughout the area of the new Central Station was electrified, and all CN mainline traffic entering and leaving the terminal and almost all switching was handled with electric power. An ambitious earlier plan, which contemplated CN electrification throughout Montreal and its environs, never was carried out.

Nine box-cab locomotives, built by the Dick Kerr Works of English Electric during the mid-1920's for a Montreal operation of the National Harbours Board, were added to the CN electric roster in 1942.

A final addition to CN electric territory was completed in 1946, when suburban catenary was extended to Montreal Nord. Postwar modernization added to CN's roster three General Electric

B-B steeple-cab locomotives in 1950, and 18 Canadian Car & Foundry M.U. cars in 1952.

CN's electric operation declined in the postwar years. Dieselization virtually ended the need for electric motive power on through trains using Central Station, and the Montreal Nord suburban route was discontinued in 1969. With its original World War I era electric locomotives still in service, the line continued to operate much as always well into the 1990's, when the Société de transport de la Communauté urbaine de Montréal, or STCUM, the regional transit operator, carried out a complete rebuilding and re-equipment of Montreal's aging 2400-volt D.C. electrification.

The Staten Island Rapid Transit Railway

NEW YORK CITY'S electric suburban service, already the most extensive in North America, was increased further in 1925 when the Staten Island Rapid Transit Railway, a Baltimore & Ohio subsidiary, converted its steam-operated service to a third-rail electrification.

The borough of Richmond, on Staten Island, is separated from New York City's other four boroughs by New York Harbor. Nevertheless the island had a large population of commuters who used ferry services between the Battery and St. George. The Staten Island Rapid Transit operated a system of three suburban lines from the St. George Ferry terminal. In 1907 the railway carried

RAIL service on Staten Island, the least populous borough of New York City, is provided by Staten Island Rapid Transit. A two-car SIRT train rolls south through Grasmere on a wintry day in the late 1960's.—*Electric Railroaders' Association.*

2.5 million passengers. By 1921 traffic exceeded 13 million passengers annually.

At this time there was great interest in the idea of a tunnel under the Narrows linking the Staten Island rail system with the New York subway system in Brooklyn. In 1920 six possible tunnel routes were proposed by a special transit commission.

Work on tunnel headings was started on Staten Island and in Brooklyn in 1925. Political and financial troubles soon intervened, however, and the tunnel never was built. When a link across the Narrows finally was completed in 1964, it was by means of the Verranzo-Narrows Bridge, with no provision for rail operation.

BUNTING decorated the official first electric train over SIRT's St. George-Tottenville line on July 1, 1925. At stations along the way the train paused while bands played and politicians discoursed on the prosperity that would accompany the improved transit service.—*Collection of Louis Siscorett.*

AT the St. George terminal SIRT passengers transferred to ferries to Manhattan. This terminal burned in the late 1940's and was replaced by a modern structure.—*Baltimore & Ohio.*

(FAR LEFT) A two-car Staten Island Rapid Transit train bound for Tottenville halts for passengers at Hugenot Park on December 9, 1961.—*John J. Bowman Jr.*

(LEFT) The South Beach line was operated with one-car trains during off hours in its last years. A crossing watchman, complete with regulation cap, protects a single car as it crosses a street at South Beach. The car simply coasted through the third-rail gap.—*Stephen L. Meyers.*

IN 1972 New York's Metropolitan Transportation Authority upgraded SIRT service with cars borrowed from the Long Island Rail Road as a stopgap until the arrival of new equipment. Three MP72's pull alongside the platform at Grasmere on a rainy summer afternoon.—*Daniel Milone.*

But in anticipation of the forthcoming tunnel link with New York's rail rapid-transit system, as well as to better accommodate its growing traffic, the SIRT completed the electrification of its entire suburban service in 1925. The railway's principal electric line extended from St. George to Tottenville, where a connection was made with ferry services to Perth Amboy, N. J. A short branch, also electrified, served South Beach on Lower New York Bay. A third electrified line went from St. George to Arlington along the Kill Van Kull on the west side of the island.

The railway selected a standard overrunning third-rail system which was identical to that of the

New York subway system. Power was supplied from the Staten Island Edison Company at 33,000 volts and distributed through five substations, each equipped with two Westinghouse 1000-kilowatt rotary converters to produce 600-volt D.C. for the third rail.

Along with electrification, the railway installed a new signal system and rebuilt its track. High-level station platforms were already in use under steam operation.

During 1925 and 1926 the Standard Steel Car Company built 100 multiple-unit cars for SIRT that were essentially identical to those of the Brooklyn-Manhattan Transit Company. The cars therefore would be able to operate anywhere on the BMT subway system following the completion of the Narrows tunnel. The 67-foot-long cars were equipped with subway-style air-operated sliding doors at each end and at the center. Two 200 h.p. GE-282 motors powered each motor car, providing a maximum speed of more than 50 mph. Multiple-unit control allowed operation of up to 10 cars in a train. Dynamic braking was an unusual feature of the cars.

Construction work started in August 1924, and the installation on 28 miles of line from St. George to South Beach and Tottenville was completed in 10 months. Electric operation to South Beach started in June 1925; the main line to Tottenville was opened amid gala celebrations on July 1; and the M.U. cars began running on the Arlington line on Christmas Day.

The Staten Island line was able to reduce its running times by 10 minutes and cut operating costs significantly as a result of electrification. The big increase in traffic never came, however. Even in 1945, the peak World War II year, SIRT carried only 14.8 million passengers, not much more than had been carried by steam in 1921. The South Beach and Arlington passenger services, hard hit by motor-bus competition, were discontinued in 1953. The Tottenville line continues to operate, since 1971 under the ownership of New York State's Metropolitan Transportation Authority. Beginning in 1973, a fleet of 52 MTA Class R-44 subway cars began to displace SIRT's aging original rolling stock.

Illinois Central Railroad

ONCE electric traction proved itself in heavy steam railroad applications, electrification as a means of smoke abatement became a favorite rallying cry of civic improvers. Nowhere was there greater interest in electrification for this purpose than there was in Chicago, the national railroad capital. With an unparalleled density of railroad operations, Chicago's interest in smoke abatement

292

IT'S summertime, and all the windows are open as a Matteson-bound Illinois Central suburban train rolls into the station at Roosevelt Road, Chicago.—*William D. Middleton.*

WASHINGTON PARK racetrack was one of IC's biggest sources of seasonal revenue. Horseplayers board a racetrack special at Kensington in 1956.—*William D. Middleton.*

A NORTHBOUND mainline train rattles across the South Shore crossing at Kensington (115th Street, Chicago); behind it a local swings onto the main from the Blue Island branch. IC's suburban line is completely separate from the through-train tracks.—*William D. Middleton.*

A TRAIN of special platform cars enabled the men installing the catenary for IC's suburban electrification to work safely and easily. As on several other D.C. electrifications, double contact wire was used.—*Illinois Central.*

was understandable. A 1911 study revealed the enormity of the problem. Within the city limits 40 railroad companies operated over 2800 miles of track, 105 yards, and almost 1700 steam locomotives. In 1915 it was estimated that electrification of the railroads' Chicago terminal operations would cost 188 million dollars and take six years to complete. No wonder total electrification of the Chicago terminals never took place.

No Chicago railroad was more a target of the smoke abatement forces than the Illinois Central. The IC operated one of the largest suburban services in the U. S., carrying 18 million passengers annually by 1917, and without question was a major contributor to the problem. Moreover, the railroad's lakefront entrance at Chicago's "front door" made it one of the most conspicuous sources of smoke and cinders.

Even before the smoke problem had become a topic of public interest, IC had considered electrifying its suburban traffic. In 1891 the railroad hired Frank Sprague to study the practicality of electrifying in time for the 1893 World's Columbian Exposition. But electric traction, Sprague concluded, was not yet sufficiently advanced to be practical.

In 1897 a special committee appointed by the IC concluded that suburban electrification had become feasible, but nothing came of the committee's findings. Ten years later the railroad's president, J. T. Harahan, reported to the stockholders that a Chicago terminal electrification was receiving the "most earnest and thorough consideration." But again, nothing happened.

In 1919 the City of Chicago forced the issue with an ordinance which required electrification of IC's suburban service by 1927, freight operation north of Roosevelt Road by 1930, major freight operations within the city by 1935, and all through passenger service by 1940.

A massive IC electrification and terminal improvement program was begun in 1921. The electrification included the 29-mile Chicago-Richton (Ill.) suburban main line, which varied from two tracks at its southern end to a maximum of six, as well as a double-track branch to South Chicago and the single-track Blue Island branch.

All grade crossings, both rail and road, were eliminated from the Chicago-Richton suburban line, which paralleled IC's north-south main line. Most of the IC tracks in the terminal area south of Chicago were relocated and reconstructed. New shop facilities were built. Freight and passenger yards were built or relocated. Bridges and subways, 250 miles of new track, and thousands of feet of retaining wall were constructed. New interlocking plants and block signals were installed. Suburban

stations and platforms were relocated and new ones were built. At the peak of construction work, 4000 men were engaged in the project. The suburban improvement alone, including new rolling stock, cost IC an estimated 24 million dollars.

IC selected a 1500-volt D.C. system for its electrification. The overhead catenary system was supported by steel catenary bridges or bracketed poles. An unusual feature of the overhead system was the use of a double trolley wire to permit staggered joints at section breaks, eliminating arcing. Power was supplied by Chicago's Consolidated Edison Company through seven substations installed at an average of 6 miles apart. Substation capacity totaled 42,000 kilowatts, with individual stations varying from 1500 kilowatts to 9000 kilowatts. Substations were equipped with both rotary converters and mercury-arc rectifiers, one of the first major railroad applications of the latter. Remote-control breakers enabled the entire system to be controlled from a central power office at Randolph Street.

To operate its electric service, the IC ordered a

THE weatherman's 1970 April Fool joke on Chicago was a heavy, wet, sticky snowstorm. IC's electrics, seen rolling into 53rd Street station, were undaunted.—*Stanley Jacobson.*

A NORTHBOUND train of M.U.'s was just 3 minutes away from its terminal at Randolph Street in Chicago as it passed IC's Central Station.—*William D. Middleton.*

DURING the summer of 1926, when both steam and electricity powered IC suburban trains, new M.U. cars shared the tracks at Randolph Street station (left) with slide-valve 2-4-4T's and wooden coaches. (Above) Four bunting-draped special trains running a-breast inaugurated electric commuter service on August 7, 1926. —*Left, Chicago Historical Society; above, Illinois Central.*

SIGNAL installers were still at work when a train of IC's new M.U. cars posed for the company photographer. The cars were designed specifically for high-level platforms, and they had Tomlinson couplers with M.U. and air connections for fully automatic coupling.—*Illinois Central.*

A FOUR-CAR train races north toward Randolph Street in 1928 past some of the apartment towers near 51st Street that good suburban service helped to build.—*Illinois Central.*

(BELOW LEFT) Inbound and outbound Illinois Central trains meet on the South Chicago branch on a warm June afternoon in 1956. The electric trains encounter highway crossings only on the South Chicago and Blue Island branches.—*William D. Middleton.*

A SOUTH CHICAGO express emerges from the underground Randolph Street terminal and picks its way through the slip switches toward the main line. At the right a Chicago South Shore & South Bend train awaits departure from the upper level of the station.—*William D. Middleton.*

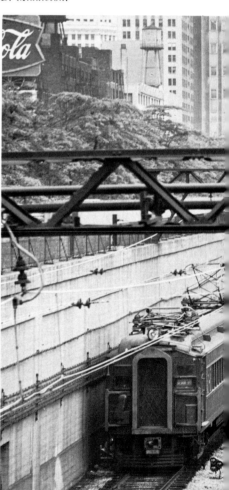

fleet of 280 steel-and-aluminum M.U. cars, which were constructed by Pullman and the Standard Steel Car Company between 1921 and 1929. The cars incorporated such advanced features as fully automatic couplers, electropneumatic braking, and electrically operated sliding doors for high-level platform loading. The cars were semi-permanently coupled in motor and trailer pairs and were able to multiple in trains of up to 10 cars. Four 250 h.p. traction motors on each motor car delivered a 64-mph balancing speed and a 1.5 mph-per-second acceleration rate.

The official opening of IC's suburban electrification on August 7, 1926, was the occasion for a civic celebration. The festivities got under way with the arrival at Central Station of four gaily decorated Electrification Specials, running abreast along the suburban tracks, from Matteson, Blue Island, and South Chicago. One of them was piloted by Illinois Governor Len Small, an *ex officio* IC director. On board the four specials were IC officials and 2000 invited guests. A parade of 450 floats followed the historic arrival at Central Station and a Pageant of Transportation was presented to 100,000 spectators in Soldier Field. The celebration was climaxed that night with a banquet at the

IN 1971 IC's suburban electrification was modernized with air-conditioned, double deck High-liners built by the St. Louis Car Division of General Steel Industries.—TRAINS: *J. David Ingles.*

Palmer House in Chicago's Loop, where IC entertained 1200 prominent guests.

Electrification permitted reductions of as much as 30 per cent in the running times of suburban trains. With steam IC had operated its suburban service at an annual deficit of well over $300,000; the first year of all-electric suburban service returned a net operating profit of $400,000. The improved service provided by smokeless electric power soon attracted new passengers to the IC's suburban trains. Even before its completion, electrification had set off a large-scale real estate boom throughout the IC suburban zone. IC suburban traffic climbed from 20 million passengers in 1920 to 36 million by 1929.

Electrification of the Chicago South Shore & South Bend Railroad was closely related to that of the Illinois Central. The South Shore was completed in 1909 between South Bend, Ind., and a junction with the IC at Kensington, Ill. The 6600-volt, single-phase A.C. interurban line was in poor physical and financial condition when it was acquired by Samuel Insull's Midland Utilities Company in the mid-1920's. Insull scrapped the South Shore's single-phase electrical system and installed a 1500-volt D.C. system identical to that adopted by the IC. A fleet of heavy, steel M.U. cars was purchased, and arrangements were made for South Shore trains to operate into Chicago's Randolph Street station over the new IC electrification. Traffic on the one-time interurban grew rapidly, and the South Shore assumed a position as an important Chicago commuter railroad.

The Illinois Central's electrification has been one of the most successful of all suburban electrifications. Transporting a traffic second only to that of the Long Island Rail Road on a system of only 38 route-miles, IC's electrics have enjoyed a reputation for superior performance and reliabil-

ity. The original 280-car M.U. fleet was capable of handling a World War II era traffic surge that reached a peak of 47 million passengers in 1946.

Except for a limited electric switching operation, the planned expansion of IC catenary for freight and through passenger service never took place. Instead, electrification came in the form of diesel-electric motive power.

A new generation of Illinois Central electric M.U. cars began arriving in 1971, when St. Louis Car delivered the first of a 130-car fleet of air-conditioned Highliner cars, while another 36 followed from Canada's Bombardier, Inc. during 1978-1979. Each of the 85-foot, bi-level gallery cars seated 156 passengers. Four 160-h.p. traction motors provided a maximum speed of 75 mph.

The Boston, Revere Beach & Lynn

ALTHOUGH electrification of railroad commuter services was a much-discussed topic in Boston, only one railroad serving the city electrified its lines. This was the 3-foot-gauge Boston, Revere Beach & Lynn, which converted its steam-operated services to 600-volt D.C. operation in 1928.

The BRB&L, which opened in 1875, had evolved into an important suburban line extending 9½ miles northward along the shore of Massachusetts Bay from East Boston to Lynn. A connection with the railroad's own ferry services at East Boston carried passengers across Boston Harbor to downtown Boston. The BRB&L was popular both as a commuter carrier and as a route to the beach resorts along the Bay. By 1927 it was carrying more than 13 million passengers annually.

Steam power always had been ill-equipped to handle traffic on the short-haul BRB&L, where stations were closely spaced and the frequency of service approached that of a rapid-transit line. Con-

FRESHLY painted in bright green and white, two coaches converted from steam-hauled cars made the first run over the electrified Boston, Revere Beach & Lynn in late 1928.—*Collection of Stephen D. Maguire.*

ELECTRIC trains of the 3-foot-gauge BRB&L ended their runs at a ferry terminal in East Boston, Mass. Railroad ferries carried passengers across Boston Harbor to Rowes Wharf in Boston. —*General Electric.*

sequently a new management, which took control of the railroad in 1927, decided to electrify the line to improve its operating economy and efficiency. Contracts were awarded to the General Electric Company, and work was started in April 1928.

Unlike most 600-volt electrifications, that of the BRB&L employed an overhead catenary system supported by steel catenary bridges spaced a maximum of 300 feet apart. Both the double-track main line and a branchline loop through Win-

throp were electrified. Power was purchased from public utility companies and supplied to the overhead system through 2000-kilowatt and 1000-kilowatt synchronous converter substations at Orient Heights and Lynn.

The railroad remodeled and re-equipped 60 of the 96 wood passenger cars that had been used in steam service instead of purchasing new rolling stock. One truck on each car was replaced with an electric motor truck powered by two GE-295A 60

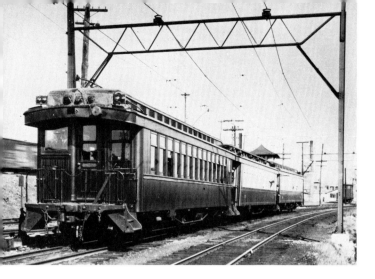

A THREE-CAR electric train bound for Boston stands at West Lynn in 1928. Beyond, a freight passes on the parallel Boston & Maine.—*Industrial Photo Service.*

OUTBOUND on the Winthrop Loop, a BRB&L electric train takes the switch at Pleasant Street for a counterclockwise circuit of the loop.—*William H. Butler Jr.*

STATIONS on the BRB&L were arranged for prepayment of fare, much like a rapid-transit system. The depot at Winthrop Centre was typical of the structures on the line.—*General Electric.*

h.p. motors. Operating cabs and multiple-unit controls were installed, and the cars were equipped with the various appurtenances required for electric operation. Trolley poles were installed for current collection.

At the same time the line was electrified, a number of improvements were made to its signal system and stations.

BRB&L service improved substantially following electrification in 1928. Express service was in-augurated during rush hours, and trains were operated on shorter headways throughout the day. Running times between East Boston and Lynn were cut by 10 to 15 minutes, a reduction of one-third.

Despite the improved service, the Boston, Revere Beach & Lynn's 1.4-million-dollar electrification was an ill-advised investment. New highways and competing Boston & Maine services paralleled the line; a new vehicle tunnel under Boston Harbor gave motorists a direct route into the city; and the railroad's ferry connection, which left passengers at some distance from the heart of downtown Boston, was more of a handicap than ever.

Traffic declined severely during the depression, and the railroad was abandoned in January 1940. Interestingly, electric train service was restored over the same right of way during the early 1950's by an extension of Boston's rapid-transit system to Revere Beach. A subway tunnel into downtown Boston eliminated the competitive disadvantages that had handicapped the electric narrow gauge.

The Delaware, Lackawanna & Western

THE last major commuter railroad in the New York metropolitan area to electrify was the Delaware, Lackawanna & Western, which completed electrification of 70 route-miles of its New Jersey suburban lines in 1930 and 1931.

The DL&W operated its suburban services out of Lackawanna Terminal in Hoboken, where it connected with both the Hudson & Manhattan tubes and the railroad's own ferry services to New York. The Lackawanna carried 60,000 passengers daily by the late 1920's, largely on its Morris & Essex Division, which served a number of New Jersey residential communities. Eventually, the Lackawanna was confronted with the need to expand its rush-hour capacity. The problem was particularly severe at Lackawanna Terminal, where both the terminal and the train yard were congested during rush periods by the large number of switchers and road locomotives required to make up and clear trains with steam operation. Also, needed track expansion along the Morris & Essex Division would have been prohibitively expensive because of the urban development that tightly hemmed in the railroad's right of way through Newark and the Oranges.

In 1928, then, the Lackawanna decided to electrify its Morris & Essex Division as far west as Dover, and its branch lines extending from Newark to Montclair and from Summit to Gladstone.

The Lackawanna selected the 3000-volt D.C. system that had worked so successfully on the Milwaukee Road's Pacific Extension electrification. A compound-catenary overhead system was supported by catenary bridges fabricated of steel H sections, except on the single-track Gladstone branch, where wood poles were used. Normal spacing of catenary supports was 300 feet.

Three different power companies supplied power for the electrification. Five mercury-arc rectifier substations, ranging from 4000 kilowatts to 12,000 kilowatts in capacity, supplied 3000-volt D.C. power to the overhead system. Normally, the entire overhead system was tied together through

THIRTEEN Erie Lackawanna M.U. cars curve through the prosperous Short Hills section of Millburn, N.J., bound for Hoboken on a June morning in 1970.—*Fred W. Schneider III.*

301

THE Lackawanna did not stint on quality in its New Jersey suburban electrification, which featured heavy steel M.U. cars and sturdy H-section catenary supports. The view of the engineer's cab reveals the simplicity of the controls: controller, air brake, whistle cord, and switches.—*Both photos, Delaware, Lackawanna & Western: William B. Barry Jr.*

LACKAWANNA freight transfer runs between the Secaucus (N.J.) freight terminal in the Hackensack Meadows and the Jersey City yard were drawn by two tri-power locomotives built by General Electric in 1930. The units could take power from the catenary or storage batteries. A 300 h.p. Ingersoll-Rand diesel engine powered a generator that charged the batteries. —*Courtesy of Railroad Magazine.*

A WINDOW of the abandoned interlocking tower at South Orange, N. J., frames a Hoboken-bound M.U. train on a summer morning in 1970.—*Steve King.*

EVENING electric: An eastbound M.U. speeds beneath a concrete arch overpass between Morristown and Convent, N. J., in September 1969.—*Tom Kelcec.*

THE single-track Gladstone (N. J.) branch, with its wooden poles and rural surroundings, is reminiscent more of an interurban than of a mainline electrification.—*Fred W. Schneider III.*

SOME of the raincoated, briefcased, newspapered commuters look up as their Dover-Hoboken express grinds to a stop at Convent in May 1970. Others continue reading, expecting constancy and dependability rather than surprise from EL's 40-year-old electrification.—*Fred W. Schneider III.*

ALMOST to Dover, the end of the electrified zone, a four-car train rolls west along the shore of a lake near Denville, N.J., in 1963. Two of the cars bear evidence of DL&W's 3-year-old merger with Erie; the other two look essentially as they did when they were built.—*Donald Duke.*

UNTIL 1967 EL commuters had a choice of routes from Hoboken to Manhattan: the Hudson & Manhattan (later PATH) tubes and EL's vintage ferries. *Elmira,* built in 1905, heads across the Hudson in 1967.—*Gerald Newman.*

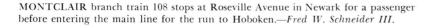

MONTCLAIR branch train 108 stops at Roseville Avenue in Newark for a passenger before entering the main line for the run to Hoboken.—*Fred W. Schneider III.*

TRAIN 433 emerges from the west end of Erie Lackawanna's Bergen Hill tunnels into a maze of switches and signals on its way to Gladstone in June 1970. EL's M.U. cars usually operate in motor-and-trailer pairs, with the motor car on the east (or Hoboken) end.—*Fred W. Schneider III.*

INTO the setting sun of a June day in 1970 accelerate two trains of commuters making their five-days-a-week trek to the suburbs. Train 639, on the left, is destined for Dover, on the Morris & Essex Division main line, and train 129 is heading for the Gladstone branch.—*Fred W. Schneider III.*

the substations and tie stations. Automatic switches, however, could isolate any overhead section in which trouble had occurred.

A fleet of 141 M.U. motor cars was constructed by Pullman for the new service. Each of the 71-foot-long cars weighed 74 tons and seated 84 passengers. Four 230-h.p. GE traction motors on each car furnished an acceleration rate of 1.5 mph per second. The motor cars were paired with trailer cars, which were modified from steel cars previously used in steam-hauled commuter trains. Multiple-unit controls permitted the pairs to operate in trains of up to 12 cars.

Contracts for the electrical installation and equipment were awarded in 1929. M.U. trains were running to Montclair and South Orange by the following September, and the entire installation was in service by February 1931.

The quality of the Lackawanna's suburban service improved substantially because of the superior performance characteristics and operating economies of the M.U. cars. Running times were reduced by an average of 25 per cent, and trains were operated much more frequently.

By the early 1970's planning was underway for a federal- and state-funded modernization and conversion of the aging electrification. Completed in 1984, soon after the system became part of NJ Transit, the work included a fleet of 180 new stainless-steel Jersey Arrow III M.U. cars and a complete rehabilitation and conversion of the electric power system from 3000 volts D.C. to a 25,000-volt, 60-cycle, single-phase A.C. system that would allow through operation into New York's Penn Station over the A.C. electrification of Amtrak's Northeast Corridor.

The Reading Company

IN 1929, almost simultaneously with the Lackawanna's decision to electrify its New Jersey suburban services, the Reading Company's board of directors approved the expenditure of 20 million dollars for the electrification of the Reading's Philadelphia suburban services. The Reading had been transporting passengers between Philadelphia and its suburbs ever since the 1830's; by the latter part of the 1920's commuter traffic on the railroad's suburban routes radiating from Reading Terminal at 12th and Market streets had become extremely heavy. Electrification offered an attractive means of increasing capacity and improving the efficiency and economy of the operation.

The initial plan announced by the Reading in October 1928 included electrification of lines from Reading Terminal to Lansdale, Hatboro, Langhorne, and Chestnut Hill, Pa. The following year the Norristown (Pa.) line was added to the Reading's electrification program, and in 1931 extensions to Doylestown, Pa., and West Trenton, N. J., were authorized.

The Reading adopted the 11,000-volt, 25-cycle, single-phase system, which by the late 1920's had emerged as the most popular of the several electrification systems advanced over the previous 25 years. Power was supplied under a long-term contract with the Philadelphia Electric Company, which constructed a frequency-changer station at Wayne Junction, Pa., to supply the power. Two 15,000-kilowatt motor-generator sets initially were installed in the station, with provision for four more when required for increased power demand. Power was distributed through a railroad-owned 36,000-volt transmission system, and autotransformer substations at 19 locations supplied 11,000-volt power to the trolley wire. A supervisory control system permitted the remote operation of

A PAIR of Reading M.U.'s speed north through a rock cut near North Wales, Pa., bound for Lansdale. H-section poles support the 11,000-volt catenary and the high-voltage transmission lines.—*Fred W. Schneider III.*

READING'S M.U. cars, built by the Bethlehem Steel Company, had several unique features: extensive use of aluminum in construction, Taylor trucks, and a high-voltage bus connector, which permitted power distribution to all cars in a train from just two pantographs.—*Reading Company.*

A MID-MORNING local receives Philadelphia-bound passengers at Jenkintown, Pa., the junction of the West Trenton (N. J.) and Doylestown (Pa.) routes.—*William D. Middleton.*

A THREE-CAR train of Reading M.U.'s speeds along the double track south of Jenkintown toward Philadelphia in the spring of 1964.—*William D. Middleton.*

CARS 9121 and 9120 leave Manayunk for Norristown in March 1970. The two cars were among those rebuilt and refurbished under a City of Philadelphia rail passenger service improvement program of the mid-1960's.—*Fred W. Schneider III.*

BLUE-AND-WHITE No. 9121 appears again, this time with a different companion, No. 9110, on the Chestnut Hill branch in Philadelphia, rolling through the aftermath of a March 1969 snowstorm.—*Robert Trennert.*

circuit breakers and sectionalizing disconnects located between substations.

Two types of overhead catenary were used. The outlying sections of several lines had a two-wire copper and bronze simple-catenary system supported at 250-foot intervals. Elsewhere a compound-catenary system, supported at 300-foot intervals, was used. On the four- and five-track section of line between Reading Terminal and Wayne Junction, catenary- and transmission-line supporting structures were made up of fabricated steel trusses carried on H-section steel columns. Elsewhere H-section crossbeams were used.

In 1930 orders were placed with the Wilmington (Del.) plant of the Bethlehem Steel Company for 70 M.U. motor cars. Although conventional in appearance and arrangement, the Reading M.U.'s incorporated a number of advanced features. A roof-mounted 11,000-volt bus connector permitted all cars in a train to be electrically interconnected. Electropneumatic braking systems and cab signals were provided. The Reading estimated that the extensive use of aluminum in the construction of the cars reduced the weight of each car by 6640 pounds; annual power savings for the lighter cars were estimated at more than $11,000.

Each of the cars was 72 feet 11½ inches over couplers and weighed 63 tons. The 70-car order

included 61 coaches, seating 86 passengers each, and nine combination cars seating either 62 or 38 passengers.

Each car was equipped with two General Electric, Westinghouse, or American Brown Boveri motors rated at 300 h.p. each. Automatic control systems provided a 1.25-mph-per-second acceleration rate, and the cars were capable of a 72-mph maximum speed.

Another 20 trailer cars, converted from former steam-hauled cars, were added to the Reading M.U. fleet in 1931, and 30 more motor cars were placed on order in 1932.

Construction work started in June 1929, and regular electric-train service began two years later between Philadelphia and Doylestown, Hatboro, and West Trenton. Service to Norristown and Chestnut Hill began early in 1933.

Reading's electrification improved the quality of the railroad's suburban services. Running times between Reading Terminal and suburban points were reduced by 20 to 25 per cent. The 10.8-mile run to Chestnut Hill, for example, which had taken from 40 to 44 minutes for a steam-hauled local, was made in only 29 minutes by an electric train in the same service. The economies of M.U.-car operation also permitted substantial increases in the frequency of service. In some cases service

TRAIN 479 pulls away from the station at Glenside, Pa., bound for Lansdale on the Doylestown line on May 13, 1970. Just ahead of the three-car train is the junction of the line to Hatboro.—*Fred W. Schneider III.*

(BELOW) The hub of Reading's commuter service is the arched trainshed of Reading Terminal at 12th and Market streets in Philadelphia. In May 1970 the tracks held old and new M.U. cars and a Budd RDC.—*Howard V. Pincus.*

was increased by as much as 300 per cent; in the entire suburban zone service was increased by an average of 35 per cent.

Aside from the addition of eight motor-trailer car pairs to the M.U. roster in 1949, the Reading's suburban electrification operated without change until the late 1950's. In 1958 the City of Philadelphia began providing public support to the money-losing service, which was ultimately taken over by the regional Southeastern Pennsylvania Transportation Authority. New equipment began joining the Reading fleet in 1963, when the City of Philadelphia financed 17 new 85-mph Budd Silverliner M.U.'s. These were joined in 1974 by 14 General Electric Jersey Arrow M.U.'s financed by the State of New Jersey, while subsequent SEPTA Silverliner orders ultimately permitted replacement of the entire original Reading M.U. fleet.

In addition to rehabilitation and re-equipment of the former Reading system, public financing and ownership brought a five-mile extension of the Newtown branch suburban catenary to Fox Chase, Pa., in 1966, and a two-mile extension of the Hatboro line electrification to Warminster, Pa., in 1974. A far more significant SEPTA project was the completion in 1984 of the Center City Commuter Tunnel and a new Market East station between Reading Terminal and Suburban Station, enabling SEPTA to tie together the former Reading and Pennsylvania suburban lines into a unified, all-electric regional rail system.

READING received 17 Budd-built Silverliner M.U. cars in 1963. They employed silicon-diode rectifiers to convert A.C. power from the catenary to D.C. for the traction motors. No. 9001, the first of the fleet, rolls south into Jenkintown past banks of forsythia in 1964.—*William D. Middleton.*

310

A SNOWY 1963 evening at the throat of Reading Terminal provides a contrast between the
Budd-built Silverliner M.U.'s, left, and Reading's older electric cars, right.—*R. S. Short.*

❖❖❖❖❖❖❖❖❖❖❖❖❖❖❖❖❖❖❖❖❖❖❖❖❖❖❖❖❖❖❖❖❖❖❖

11. The great Pennsy electrification

❖❖❖❖❖❖❖❖❖❖❖❖❖❖❖❖❖❖❖❖❖❖❖❖❖❖❖❖❖❖❖❖❖❖❖

THE Pennsylvania Railroad system was a pioneer in railroad electrification in North America. Its experimental electrification of a 7-mile branch line between Burlington and Mount Holly, N. J., in 1895 was one of the first electrification projects carried out by any steam railroad company. The third-rail electrifications of two Pennsylvania subsidiaries, the Long Island Rail Road and the West Jersey & Seashore Railroad, were among the most important electrification projects yet undertaken when they were completed in 1905 and 1906. The Pennsylvania's own New York terminal electrification, which opened in 1910, was as significant an application of electric traction as those of the New York Central and the New Haven.

Although all of these early Pennsylvania installations employed a low-voltage D.C. system, the Pennsy had developed an early interest in single-phase A.C. electrification. The three prototype electric locomotives tested on the West Jersey & Seashore Railroad in 1907 included a single-phase unit built by Baldwin-Westinghouse. A.C. power was supplied to the locomotive from a motor-generator set carried in a separate car during the tests on the third-rail D.C. WJ&S installation. Earlier the Pennsylvania had operated the experimental A.C. locomotive on a 5-mile A.C. installation on the Long Island near Garden City, where it was used to test different types of overhead systems and

313

HEADING from Paoli, Pa., to Philadelphia, MP54's cross over the old Philadelphia & Western line of the Philadelphia Suburban Transportation Company at Radnor, Pa., in 1964. The scene had changed little since 1915 when the first MP54's went into service.—*Donald Duke.*

current-collection devices. Although D.C. electrification was chosen for the New York terminal project, the A.C. equipment had given a good account of itself in the Pennsy's testing program.

Only a few years after its New York terminal electrification was completed the Pennsylvania again turned to electric traction to solve another operating problem.

At Philadelphia, the railroad had developed an exceptionally heavy suburban traffic on several routes radiating from Broad Street Station. By 1913 traffic in and out of the stub-end terminal had grown to more than 500 daily trains. Congestion in the busy terminal had become severe. Because of light-engine movements and switching operations for making up trains, each arrival or departure required an average of eight movements through the interlocking plant at the terminal throat. To relieve this congestion, the Pennsylvania in 1913 authorized the electrification of the two heaviest suburban routes operating out of Broad Street at a cost of more than 5 million dollars. The two lines were the railroad's Main Line 20 miles westward to Paoli and a 12-mile route which provided service to Chestnut Hill in northern Philadelphia. More than 150 daily trains operated over these two routes alone.

By 1913, too, the Pennsylvania was considering an eventual electrification of part of its long-haul mainline system. Consequently the electrification system adopted for the Philadelphia suburban lines had to be suitable for this purpose as well. The railroad was naturally predisposed toward the third-rail D.C. system in use at its New York terminal. By this time, however, the superior characteristics of single-phase A.C. electrification for heavy mainline service were well established by the New Haven's six years of experience, and the Pennsylvania chose the A.C. system for its Philadelphia suburban lines.

Power was supplied to this electrification from the main generating station of the Philadelphia Electric Company on the Schuylkill River through a substation at Arsenal Bridge, Pa. Power was delivered to the railroad at 13,200 volts, 25 cycles, and was transformed to 44,000 volts for transmission to substations at West Philadelphia, Bryn Mawr, Paoli, and Chestnut Hill, Pa., where it was stepped down to contact-wire voltage. Each of the substations was equipped with two 2000-kilowatt-ampere step-down transformers. Substations were remotely controlled from nearby interlocking plants, and the entire electrical system was under the control of a power director located at the West Philadelphia substation.

A simple-catenary overhead system was supported by a cross-catenary system carried on tubular steel poles spaced 300 feet apart. Along the main line the cross-catenary system spanned four tracks, and in yard and terminal areas as many as nine tracks.

For the initial Main Line electrification to Paoli the Pennsylvania put into service 93 all-steel Class MP54 multiple-unit passenger cars. Originally built for steam-hauled suburban trains, the cars were equipped with the necessary electrical equipment at the Pennsylvania's Altoona (Pa.) shops. Each of the 64-foot-long cars was equipped with one pantograph, a transformer to step down the trolley-wire voltage, and two 225 h.p. Westinghouse single-phase traction motors, both mounted on the same truck. Multiple-unit control equipment provided automatic acceleration at a rate of 1 mph per second. Balancing speed of the cars was 60 mph. Braking equipment was of the electropneumatic type.

Highly successful in the initial suburban electrification, the MP54 class was to remain the Pennsylvania Railroad's standard M.U. car for over 40 years. Additional cars of the same type were equipped for electric operation as subsequent suburban electrifications were completed, and the MP54 fleet eventually numbered more than 500 cars.

Construction work on the Main Line electrification started early in 1914, and regular electric operation began in September 1915. The use of bidirectional M.U. equipment on the Main Line's 78 daily suburban trains eased the congestion at Broad Street Station by eliminating the many shifting movements that had been necessary with steam-powered trains. The faster acceleration of the electric equipment also permitted the reduction of running times for the 20-mile Paoli run by as much as 7 minutes.

Electrification of the Chestnut Hill line, a project which included extensive grade separation work, was completed early in 1918. A 6-mile, single-track branch extending from the Chestnut Hill line to Whitemarsh, Pa., was electrified in 1924. Catenary was extended southward 27 miles to Wilmington, Del., between 1926 and 1928. Also in 1928, the Pennsy completed electrification of its Philadelphia-West Chester (Pa.) suburban line. The final extensions of suburban electrification out of Philadelphia were completed in 1930 when the suburban route to Norristown, Pa., and the New York Division as far north as Trenton, N. J., were equipped for 11,000-volt, single-phase operation.

Until 1930 the Pennsylvania's single-phase electrification had been installed exclusively for multiple-unit suburban trains. Through passenger and freight services continued to operate with steam power. From the beginning, though, the Pennsylvania had been planning for electric operation of all classes of service. As early as 1913, for example, the company's annual report advised the stock-holders that electrification of 35 miles of the Pennsy main line across the Allegheny Mountains, between Altoona and Conemaugh, Pa., was being considered.

The first tangible evidence of the Pennsylvania's plans for mainline electrification was an experimental locomotive, a prototype for the Allegheny electrification, that appeared under the catenary of the Paoli line in 1917. Constructed by the railroad's Juniata Shops, with electrical equipment supplied by Westinghouse, the Class FF1, 1-C+C-1 locomotive had much in common with the single-phase units built by Baldwin-Westinghouse several years before for the Norfolk & Western. It employed the same type of rotating phase converter used on the N&W units to obtain three-phase power for the traction motors. Four Westinghouse Type-451 induction motors drove the 72-inch driving wheels through jackshafts, cranks, and side rods at synchronous speeds of 10.3 or 20.6 mph.

The FF1, dubbed "Big Liz" by Pennsy men, was a mammoth machine, 76 feet 6 inches long and weighing 258 tons. Hourly rating of the locomotive was 4800 h.p. and 88,000 pounds tractive effort, with a maximum starting tractive effort of 140,000 pounds.

The experimental locomotive operated successfully in trials on the Main Line in August 1917, and ultimately spent a number of years in pusher service to Paoli. The Pennsy's plans for mountain electrification were deferred about this time, however, and the FF1 design never was repeated. When the railroad finally was ready for a heavy-duty electric freight locomotive, technical advances had overtaken the phase-converter concept.

A second experimental appeared under Main Line catenary in 1924, when one of the Pennsylvania's three experimental Class L5 "Universal" lo-

CLASS FF1 ("Big Liz") was the biggest thing around when tested on the PRR in 1917. Although never duplicated, Liz worked in pusher service until 1940.—*Courtesy of Railroad Magazine.*

comotives was equipped for A.C. operation. Although 23 D.C.-equipped L5's eventually were built, the A.C. version was not repeated.

By the mid-1920's, the Pennsylvania's interest in electrification had shifted primarily to its eastern main lines, which carried perhaps the densest rail traffic in America. Both freight and passenger traffic on the New York-Washington route were increasing rapidly. Despite a multiple-track main line, with at least four main tracks available for the entire distance between New York and Wilmington, the railroad foresaw a day when track capacity would be inadequate. Greater capacity, through the use of either additional tracks or electric power, would be required.

PENNSY President (from 1925 to 1935) William Wallace Atterbury launched the PRR on what, in 1928, was the world's greatest electrification project.—*Historical Society of Pennsylvania.*

FOLLOWING studies of the motive-power needs for the projected traffic growth in its eastern territory, the Pennsylvania's board of directors authorized an electrification program of unparalleled magnitude.

The statistics for Pennsy's electrification were overwhelming. Announced by Pennsylvania's President William Wallace Atterbury on October 13, 1928, the program included the extension of 11,000-volt, single-phase catenary over the railroad's principal lines between New York and Wilmington, as well as westward from Trenton, N. J., to Columbia, Pa. Altogether some 325 miles of railroad — and 1300 track-miles — would be electrified. A total of 365 new electric freight and pas-

senger locomotives would be purchased. More than 500 daily passenger trains would operate with electric power. Planned for completion over a period of six to seven years, it was estimated that the electrification program would cost 100 million dollars. It would be the greatest single railroad electrification project yet undertaken anywhere in the world.

Within the next few years even this ambitious program had been enlarged and accelerated. Following negotiations with the City of Baltimore in October 1929 to permit substantial improvements to the railroad's main line through the city, the Pennsylvania announced expansion of its electrification program to extend catenary all the way to Washington, D. C., including a connection to Potomac Yard at Alexandria, Va., where freight traffic was interchanged with railroads operating to the south.

Total cost for the expanded electrification program was estimated at 175 million dollars. On this electrified track, it was estimated, 60 freight trains and 830 passenger trains would operate daily. Annual traffic would be approximately 10 billion gross freight ton-miles, almost 134 million passenger car-miles, and nearly 18 million electric locomotive-miles. At the conclusion of the program, the Pennsylvania Railroad and its subsidiaries would be operating 800 route-miles and 2800 track-miles with electric power — an electric system rivaled elsewhere in the world only by those of the German and Italian federal railway systems.

Early in 1931, despite the deepening depression, President Atterbury announced that electrification work originally planned for the next four years would be completed in only two and a half years.

A number of other major improvements closely related to the electrification were planned for completion during the same period. A new station was begun at Newark, N. J. At Philadelphia a new Suburban Station was built adjacent to the old Broad Street Station, and a new station for north-south through trains was constructed at 30th Street in West Philadelphia. The extensive improvement program at Baltimore included the elimination of a number of grade crossings, and new double-track tunnels were built north and south of the Baltimore station, supplementing existing tunnels of restricted dimensions and capacity. To prepare for the higher speeds that would be possible with electrification, many miles of line were reballasted and relaid with the Pennsylvania's new 152-pound rail section.

The Pennsylvania's decision to press on with its great electrification project despite the effects of the depression proved to be a wise one. The reduced traffic level helped to minimize the interference of

SINGLE-PHASE catenary went up between Wilmington, Del., and Philadelphia during the 1920's. This Pennsylvania M.U. train raced south toward Wilmington in 1928 soon after the project was completed.—*Pennsylvania Railroad.*

PASSENGERS board MP54's at Norristown, Pa., in 1934. Electrified in 1930, PRR's Norristown line competed with electrified service to Philadelphia over the Reading and the Philadelphia & Western.—*Courtesy of Railroad Magazine.*

IN this illustration reproduced from the July 31, 1915, *Scientific American,* Pennsy linemen prove that catenary is stronger than it looks.—*Collection of Donald O'Hanley.*

POWER transmission and distribution to Pennsy electrification was controlled from four locations. This is the power director's room at Harrisburg, Pa.—*Penn Central.*

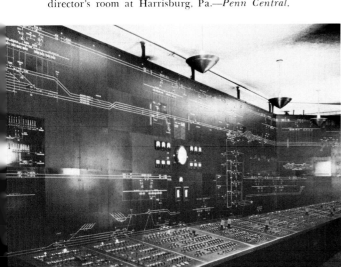

THIS 1932 view of a portion of Pennsylvania's newly completed New York-Washington electrification shows the heavy H-section steel supports that carried 132,000-volt transmission lines, 6600-volt signal power lines, and the supporting systems for the compound overhead.—*Pennsylvania Railroad.*

train movements with construction work. Labor and material prices were low, and skilled labor was plentiful. Through 1931 the Pennsylvania was able to finance the project entirely with its own resources. In 1932 a 27.5-million-dollar loan from the Reconstruction Finance Corporation helped to keep the electrification work going. Another loan of 80 million dollars from the Public Works Administration in 1934 helped to finance the electrification to Washington.

From the time of the Paoli electrification onward, the Pennsylvania followed a policy of purchasing all the power required by its electrified operations from public utility companies. With the exception of the Long Island City (N. Y.) plant jointly serving the New York terminal electrification and the subsidiary Long Island Rail Road, the railroad by 1930 had sold all of its own generating plants to the utility companies.

The Pennsylvania's mainline electrification project created a massive new market for several eastern power companies with which the railroad negotiated long-term power contracts. By the time the Washington electrification was completed in 1935, it was estimated that the railroad's annual energy consumption would total about 1.2 billion kilowatt-hours.

Initially, from New York as far south as Perryville, Md., power was supplied by the steam and hydroelectric generating stations of the Philadelphia Electric Company. In addition to a generating capacity of a million kilowatts in its own system, the Philadelphia company had access to an equal amount through power pools with two neighboring utility companies.

South of Perryville the electricity was supplied by the Consolidated Gas Electric Light & Power Company of Baltimore and associated hydro-electric companies, which possessed a combined capacity of some 600,000 kilowatts.

The railroad received the power at four locations. At Richmond in Philadelphia, Chester, Pa., and Loudon Park, Md., the utility companies supplied single-phase, 25-cycle power at 13,200 volts from frequency-converter installations ranging in capacity from 45,000 kilowatts to 60,000 kilowatts. At Perryville the supply point received 25-cycle power from frequency converters installed at the power company's Safe Harbor hydroelectric plant several miles up the Susquehanna River.

Railroad-owned transformer stations at each location stepped the power supply up to 132,000 volts for transmission to substations located 8 to 10 miles apart along the right of way, where the power was stepped down to the trolley-wire voltage of 11,000 volts.

When the electrification reached its full extent at the end of the 1930's the railroad was being supplied at seven different locations from four utility companies. Well over 1000 miles of 132,000-volt transmission lines transmitted power to 67 substations and switching stations. The entire system was under the control of the Central Load Dispatching Office at Philadelphia, which co-ordinated the operations of four railroad power directors, at New York, Philadelphia, Baltimore, and Harrisburg, Pa., and the four utility companies that supplied power.

The overhead distribution system was an improved version of the one designed for the electrification of the Paoli line. Generally, a cross-catenary support system was used to carry a compound-catenary distribution system. This was carried on steel H-section poles which were tall enough to carry 132,000-volt transmission lines and 6600-volt signal-power lines. Where right-of-way clearances prevented the use of the guy wires needed for the cross-catenary system, braced cross-beams were used to support the overhead system. Crossbeams also were installed to carry signals. Normal spacing of the poles was 285 feet.

Both the magnitude of the work and the extremely heavy traffic carried on the Pennsylvania's lines made construction of the power distribution system an exceptionally difficult task. Before the electrical system could be installed, extensive alterations had to be made to the track, roadbed, and structures. To provide adequate clearances for pantograph operation and to maintain sufficient clearances for high freight loads, grade and alignment alterations were required at a number of locations. Many bridges over the tracks had to be raised, some as much as 3 feet, to provide sufficient clearance. Between New York and Philadelphia alone, 11 bridges were raised, one of them carrying a canal.

Some of the most difficult work was that required to provide sufficient clearances in tunnels. Although the tunnels had been built with space for catenary, track in the Hudson and East River tunnels at New York had to be lowered 2 to 8 inches because of the use of higher rail sections and a gradual increase of ballast depth during normal track resurfacing. In addition to lowering the track by the removal of ballast, the insulator assemblies supporting the catenary had to be recessed into the tunnel arch. The work could be done only between 2 a.m. and 5 a.m. because of traffic density in the New York tunnels.

It was necessary to completely replace a 754-foot tunnel at 32nd Street in Philadelphia. This intricate operation took 144 days. Traffic was maintained on one of the two tracks. In addition to providing two new double-track tunnels at Baltimore, the existing double-track tunnels were single-tracked to afford clearance for the overhead system.

Still another major item of work that had to be completed before electrification was the construction of an underground duct system in which communication, signal control, and secondary power lines could be placed for electrical shielding from the overhead distribution system.

Novel methods were developed to permit the installation of the overhead system with minimum disruption of traffic. Concrete pole footings and guy-wire anchors were placed from special concrete trains, which carried supplies of cement, aggregate, and water together with the necessary equipment for mixing and placing the concrete. Floodlights enabled the trains to operate around-the-clock, and heating equipment for the concrete permitted the work to continue through the winter. Five concrete trains were in operation at the height of construction activity.

The steel poles were placed by specially built steam cranes. Designed to operate within limited clearances, the cranes could work from one track without disrupting movements on the adjacent track. The overhead catenary system itself was placed from wire trains. These trains carried tower cars with outrigger platforms on each side which permitted the installation of catenary over a track adjacent to the wire train without taking that track out of service.

By mid-1934, when work on the electrification program reached its peak, the Pennsylvania reported that 76 work trains and 12,000 men were working directly on the project and estimated that at least as many more men were engaged in the manufacture of equipment and supplies for the work. All told, the extension of the Pennsylvania's electrification to Washington represented some 45 million man-hours of labor. At the depth of the depression such a project was indeed welcome.

The electrification was placed in operation in stages as the work was completed. The original New York terminal third-rail electrification between Sunnyside Yard and Manhattan Transfer was converted to A.C. operation in January 1932,

O1-CLASS No. 7852 (right) was built at Pennsylvania's Juniata Shops in Altoona, Pa., in 1930 for light passenger service. It was equipped with GE electrical components. Class P5a No. 4755 (below) was produced by General Electric in 1932 for heavy-duty passenger service.—*Right, Pennsylvania Railroad; below, General Electric.*

and M.U.-train local service to New Brunswick, N. J., began later the same year. Electric operation of through trains between New York and Wilmington was started in January 1933. Passenger trains began running all the way to Washington behind electric power in February 1935, and electric freight operation to Potomac Yard began the following June.

THE electrification of the heavily trafficked New York-Washington line necessitated an extensive development program for new electric motive power. Much had been learned already from the DD1's built for the 1910 New York terminal electrification, the experimental FF1 of 1917, and the L5 "Universal" units of the 1920's. None of these, however, was an adequate answer to the Pennsylvania's needs, and the railroad's motive-power men set out to design an entirely new series of freight and passenger units.

The principal influence on the design of the new locomotives was the development of high-horsepower A.C. motors sufficiently compact to fit between driving wheels. Previous Pennsylvania designs employed large motors and side-rod drive, an arrangement the railroad never found fully satisfactory, although it was the only way to apply sufficient horsepower to each driving axle to develop the full tractive effort that the Pennsylvania's high axle loadings permitted. The new motors, developed in the late 1920's to meet the Pennsylvania's requirements, permitted the application of more than 1000 h.p. to each driving axle in a twin-motor, between-the-drivers arrangement.

The Pennsylvania's motive-power department developed standard designs for three types of box-cab electric locomotives. Maximum interchangeability of parts and components between the three classes, regardless of which manufacturer built them, was planned. This family of standardized locomotive designs comprised the O1, a 2-B-2 for light, high-speed passenger work; the P5, a 2-C-2 for heavy passenger service; and the L6, a 1-D-1 freight locomotive.

The O1 and the P5 employed the same twin-motor, geared quill drive arrangement, with traction motors rated at a continuous output of 625 h.p., giving 1250 h.p. per driving axle. The L6 design employed a single motor of the same type applied to each axle through a nose-suspended, geared drive. The passenger designs were geared for a maximum speed of 90 mph, and the freight design for a maximum of 54 mph. All three classes were mounted on roller bearings throughout.

EACH of the three classes was initially represented by experimental units. The first of the stand-ardized units to enter service were eight O1 locomotives built at the Pennsylvania's Altoona shops during 1930 and 1931. Fitted with electrical equipment supplied by GE, Westinghouse, and American Brown Boveri, the experimental units varied slightly in their performance characteristics. Total weight of each unit was 150 tons, of which half was carried on the 72-inch driving wheels. Starting tractive effort rating for a single O1 was 33,500 pounds, and the continuous horsepower rating varied from 2000 h.p. to 2500 h.p., depending on the type of motors installed.

The O1's carbody contained the main transformers, blowers for transformer and traction-motor ventilation, control equipment and other auxiliaries, an oil-fired train-heating boiler, and operating cabs at each end. M.U. controls permitted operation in multiple with other O1 or P5 units.

Two experimental P5 units built by the Altoona shops in 1931 were essentially lengthened O1's with an additional driving axle. Weighing almost 188 tons, the P5's were 62 feet 8 inches long. Continuous rating of the P5 was 3750 h.p., with a short-time maximum rating of 5600 h.p.

The L6 class was represented by two locomotives completed at Altoona in 1932. Although the continuous rating with only four traction motors was no more than that of the O1, the L6, with its greater weight on drivers, developed a starting tractive effort of 55,000 pounds.

Only one of the three experimental electric classes was successful enough to warrant quantity production. The O1 proved to be too light to assume a versatile role in passenger service, and testing revealed some tracking problems. Although the eight units remained in service for many years, the design was never repeated.

The L6 freighters came closer to quantity production. A third, heavier L6a unit was built in 1934 by the Lima Locomotive Works, with Westinghouse electrical equipment, as the prototype of a 60-unit order. At the last moment the Pennsylvania had second thoughts and canceled the order. Although another 29 locomotives were completed by Lima, their electrical equipment never was installed and the units never entered service. Part of the reason for the cancellation of the order may have been the limited power of the L6 and Pennsy's reservations about the crew safety of the box-cab design after a P5 crew was killed in a January 1934 grade-crossing accident on the New York Division. Far more significant, though, was an unforeseen series of events in the development of the railroad's principal electric passenger locomotive.

Of the three designs, the P5 gave the most promising results. On the basis of favorable experience

DISPLACED from high-speed passenger service by the great GG1, Pennsy's entire 92-unit P5a fleet was regeared for freight service between 1935 and 1940. No. 4724 led a northbound freight through Loudon Park, Md., in May 1937.—*Charles B. Chaney, collection of the Smithsonian Institution.*

PENNSYLVANIA'S successful P5a's were workhorses. P5a No. 4701 pauses at Manhattan Transfer, N. J., on a through train whose consist included another PRR workhorse—the P70 coach.—*Pennsylvania Railroad.*

THE only electric locomotives ever built by Lima Locomotive Works were Pennsy's L6a-class 1-D-1 freighters. Of the 30 that were built, only one received electrical equipment and entered service. The remaining 29 were stored at Altoona for several years and then were scrapped without once having turned a wheel in revenue service. —*Linn H. Westcott.*

(ABOVE) In 1935 a streamlined P5a led a Washington-bound express across the Fort Meade branch of the Washington, Baltimore & Annapolis Electric Railroad at Odenton, Md.—*James P. Schuman*.

(RIGHT) P5a No. 4752 sweeps through Halethorpe, Md., in 1936 with a consist of sleepers, diner, coaches, and baggage car.—*Charles B. Chaney, collection of the Smithsonian Institution*.

with the two prototypes, the Pennsylvania placed orders for 90 additional P5a's that were intended to be the basic passenger motors for the electrified main lines. The 90-unit fleet was built between 1932 and 1935 by Baldwin-Westinghouse, General Electric, and the railroad's Altoona shops. Only minor changes from the prototype were made in the production units. After the fatal 1934 grade-crossing accident, the cab design of the last 28 units was changed to a streamlined center-cab arrangement that afforded greater collision protection to the engine crew. Except for the stream-lining and a substantial increase in engine weight, the modified P5a's were identical to the original box-cab design.

When through passenger trains began operating with electric power in 1933, they were exclusively in the charge of the powerful, 90-mph P5a's. However, the P5a's showed some serious shortcomings in the demanding service to which the Pennsylvania assigned them. The locomotives were powerful enough to maintain fast schedules with trains of eight to ten cars, but could not make schedules with heavier trains without double-heading. The tracking qualities of the P5a's, although better than those of the O1, were not entirely satisfactory, and the Pennsylvania was obliged to defer a planned post-electrification speedup of its passenger schedules.

Worse yet, cracks began to develop in the driving

axles. The Pennsylvania temporarily lowered the passenger-train speed limit to 70 mph and sought a solution to the problem. Redesigned, heavier axles soon remedied this trouble on the locomotives, but the tracking problems remained.

The Pennsylvania set up a special high-speed

THE stubby Class B1 six-wheelers were the Pennsy's standard electric switcher. A total of 28 B1's were built at Altoona from 1926 to 1934. No. 3921 was photographed at Sunnyside Yard, N.Y., in 1956.—*Don Wood*.

322

SHORTLY after entering service, P5a 4775 hurried a Washington-New York train along multiple-track main line in April 1935. The 28 streamlined P5a's were mechanically identical to the earlier box-cab units.—*Pennsylvania Railroad.*

test track near Claymont, Del., in 1933 in an effort to solve the P5a's tracking problems. Special impact-recording ties were installed in a section of track, and locomotive-mounted recording equipment measured the lateral forces against axles and wheel flanges. Data from the test program led to changes in the equalization of the P5a's trucks, which improved the tracking qualities of the locomotive to a satisfactory level.

More important to the future of Pennsylvania Railroad electrification than a remedy for the troubles of the P5a was a continuation of the Claymont testing program aimed at developing an electric locomotive with better riding qualities. From the results of the Claymont tests would emerge the design for North America's greatest electric locomotive.

Supplementing the P5a tests were tests of a New Haven Class EP-3a locomotive, No. 0354. Built by General Electric in 1931, the EP-3a was the New Haven's latest electric motive power. It represented an approach to electric locomotive design substantially different from the Pennsylvania's O1, P5, and L6.

While the O1 and the P5 were characterized by the concentration of maximum weight and horsepower on a minimum number of driving axles, a typical Pennsylvania practice, the New Haven locomotive spread an equivalent weight and horsepower over many more axles. The P5a, for ex-

ample, applied 1250 h.p. and almost 77,000 pounds to each of its three driving axles, while the New Haven EP-3a applied only 573 h.p. and less than 46,000 pounds to each of six driving axles.

A further difference in the EP-3a design was the use of an articulated frame, in contrast to the rigid frame of the Pennsylvania designs. The New Haven locomotive used the 2-C+C-2 wheel arrangement that was first employed by General Electric in 1929 for locomotives built for the Cleveland Union Terminal.

The New Haven locomotive, regeared by the Pennsylvania's Wilmington shops for a 120-mph maximum speed, displayed markedly superior tracking qualities on the Claymont test track and was much easier on the track structure than even the modified P5a.

Impressed with the performance of the New Haven locomotive, the Pennsylvania ordered a prototype Class GG1 locomotive which would employ the same 2-C+C-2 wheel arrangement. Running gear was constructed by Baldwin Locomotive Works, while General Electric supplied the electrical equipment. At the same time, the railroad ordered a 2-D-2 Class R1 locomotive from Baldwin-Westinghouse. Comparable in performance characteristics, the GG1 and the R1 were to be operated in a series of comparative tests.

Delivered in September 1934, prototype GG1 No. 4899 was an impressive machine. Supported by two

GG1 PROTOTYPE 2-C+C-2 No. 4899 (above) and Class R1 2-D-2 No. 4800 (left) represented rival electric-locomotive design theories. The two locomotives were matched in test runs on Pennsy's test track near Claymont, Del., in 1934. No. 4800 hit 120 mph, but the articulated GG1 ran just as fast and proved easier on the track. The two units exchanged numbers after the GG1 emerged from the tests as the victor. —Both photos, collection of H. L. Broadbelt.

cast steel frames, hinged at the center like a Mallet steam locomotive, the GG1 measured 79 feet 6 inches between coupler faces and weighed more than 230 tons. A dozen A.C. traction motors provided a continuous rating of 4620 h.p. at a maximum speed of 100 mph, and the locomotive was capable of a short-term output of 8500 h.p. Twin traction motors drove each pair of 57-inch driving wheels through a geared quill drive of the type employed in the New Haven's EP-3a. Roller bearings were provided throughout.

A streamlined body with a box-shaped center section and a long-hooded steeple-cab arrangement at each end afforded much greater collision protection for engine crews than did the railroad's earlier box-cab designs. The transformer and the train-heating boiler were housed in the center section along with the two operating cabs, and a variety of

control and auxiliary equipment was contained in both the center section and the hoods at each end. Current-collection pantographs were mounted on the hoods at each end.

The 201-ton R1, delivered at the same time, was essentially an elongated version of the P5a with one more driving axle. Each axle was powered by the same twin-motor, geared quill drive arrangement of the 625 h.p. traction motors used on the P5a, although axle loadings were considerably lighter. The R1's streamlined body design was similar to that of the GG1.

The two prototypes underwent a long series of tests at the Claymont test track during 1934. Both locomotives proved to be superb performers, but the articulated GG1 was greatly superior to the rigid-framed R1 in tracking ability, and lateral forces on the rails were much lower with the GG1.

TECHNICIANS examine GG1 prototype No. 4899 prior to a test run at
Claymont. Visible in the track structure
ahead of the locomotive are some of the
special steel ties equipped with impact-
recording devices.—*Collection of Frederick Westing.*

LATE in 1934 GG1 prototype No. 4800 (nee 4899) at Philadelphia's venerable Broad Street Station prepares to take a Clocker
to New York City.—*General Electric.*

GG1 4800 leaves Baltimore tunnels on the opening day of New
York-Washington electrification, January 28, 1935.—*Collection
of Charles B. Chaney, from the Smithsonian Institution.*

THE 4800 strikes a classic pose at Zoo interlocking in Philadelphia with one of the K4s Pacifics
it would displace from the New York-Washington main line.—*Pennsylvania Railroad.*

In test runs with passenger trains the GG1 reached 115 mph; in other tests the GG1 and a trailing test car accelerated from a stop to 100 mph in 64.5 seconds.

The Pennsylvania Railroad had found a locomotive with the performance to fulfill the potential of its great electrification program.

There was little in Pennsylvania's GG1 design that was entirely new. The 2-C+C-2 wheel arrangement already had been used in both the New Haven's 1931 EP-3a design and the 1929 CUT units. Series commutator motors of the same general type employed in the GG1 had been used previously by the Pennsy in both locomotive and M.U.-car designs. The GG1's twin-motor geared quill drive was similar to that employed in the New Haven's EP-3a's as well as in other New Haven electric locomotives dating as far back as 1910. Rather than marking any radical advances in either its electrical equipment or its mechanical design, the GG1 represented the refinement of previously proven technology and its incorporation into a well-balanced design for a locomotive.

Following the successful testing of the prototype, orders were placed for an additional 57 GG1's, all of which were completed by August 1935. Both General Electric and Westinghouse supplied electrical equipment, and running gear and superstructures were built by Baldwin, General Electric, and the railroad's Altoona shops; but all the GG1's were essentially identical.

Relatively few mechanical or electrical changes were made between the prototype GG1 and the

INDUSTRIAL DESIGNER Raymond Loewy transformed the riveted awkwardness of the first GG1 into a classic form as evidenced by the head-on view of GG1 4856 (above) and other GG1 views on the facing page. (Above right) Workmen at GE's Erie shops welded steel sheathing onto the structural frame of a GG1 cab. (Center right) At Pennsy's Altoona shops a GG1 cab was lowered onto the articulated running gear. (Right) GG1 4824 was built by Baldwin, equipped by Westinghouse, and assembled at Altoona. Orders for the first 57 production units were divided among General Electric, Baldwin, Westinghouse, and PRR's Juniata Shops in Altoona.—*Above and center right, Pennsylvania Railroad; above right, General Electric; right, collection of H. L. Broadbelt.*

DURING the late 1930's, R1 No. 4899 leads a passenger train out of Sunnyside Yard. Although defeated by the GG1 in the 1934 tests at Claymont, the one-of-a-kind R1 ran in passenger service for more than 20 years.—*C. E. Pearce Jr.*

THE GG1-powered *Judiciary* is readied at Washington for a 227-mile run over The Standard Railroad of the World to New York City around 1935.—*H. W. Pontin.*

A NORTHBOUND GG1 and its 10-car train race through Lanham, Md., in the summer of 1935, the first year of New York-Washington electric operation.—*General Electric.*

A PINSTRIPED GG1 rumbles across the Passaic River lift-bridge and approaches the high-level platforms of Newark (N. J.) station with a Philadelphia-bound Clocker sometime during the late 1940's.—*J. A. McLellan.*

A SEEMINGLY endless string of P70 coaches is hurtled through Wynnewood, Pa., by shiny GG1 4829 in the 1930's. The 4829 had mechanical and electrical equipment built by Baldwin and Westinghouse, and was assembled in Pennsylvania's Altoona shops.—*Pennsylvania Railroad*.

THE Delaware River basin served by Pennsylvania's New York-Washington route represents one of America's greatest industrial concentrations. Typical of the railroad activity in this region in earlier days of electrification is this view near Wilmington of twin GG1's rolling tonnage past a freight yard and a pair of waiting P5a's.—*H. W. Adams*.

MORE than a dozen GG1-powered football specials line up near the gates of Philadelphia's Municipal Stadium in the late 1940's to load homeward-bound fans from the annual Army-Navy football game.—*Collection of Electric Railroaders' Association.*

A STREAMLINED P5a assisted a Class L1 2-8-2 at Whiteland, Pa., on the grade west of Paoli in November 1947. The operation of special passenger trains to the Army-Navy football game that weekend meant reassignment of GG1's and brought steam out under wire.—*Charles A. Brown.*

production models. The production units were equipped with liquid-cooled main transformers instead of the prototype's air-cooled transformer. The 90-mph gearing of the production units gave them a somewhat higher tractive effort than the 100-mph prototype. The appearance of the production units was greatly improved by industrial stylist Raymond Loewy, whose principal design contribution was an arc-welded body in place of the awkward riveted body of the prototype.

In service, the GG1's enormous power was able to keep passenger trains of more than 20 cars on time under the most demanding of schedules, and the advent of the giant electrics on the New York-Washington line permitted the Pennsylvania to greatly increase train speeds. The time of the premier *Congressional Limited* was cut from 4 hours 15 minutes to 3 hours 35 minutes, an overall speed of more than a mile-a-minute despite six intermediate stops. Other schedules were similarly reduced. Running times of the New York-Philadelphia "Clockers," for example, which already had been reduced when the first electrics began operating, were cut again when the GG1's entered service. Some trains made the 90-mile run, with three intermediate stops, in as little as 94 minutes. When the occasion required, the big electrics proved equally capable in freight service.

The GG1's replaced many of the P5a's in passenger service, and the railroad began regearing the box-cab units for freight service in 1935. At about the same time the railroad canceled its order for the L6 freight locomotives. As subsequent GG1 orders entered service, all 92 P5a's were regeared for freight service. They worked well as freight locomotives, and some of them remained in service as late as 1965.

Despite its success with the GG1, the Pennsylvania developed still another prototype a few years later. Completed early in 1938 by the Pennsylvania's Altoona shops and equipped with Westinghouse electrical equipment, the 2-B+B-2 DD2 incorporated features from several previous Pennsy electric designs. Like the L5's of the 1920's, the DD2 was intended to be a universal passenger/freight locomotive. With freight gearing its top speed was 70 mph; proposed passenger gearing was for a 100-mph maximum speed. Like the O1, P5, and R1, the DD2 employed two 625 h.p. motors geared to each of its four driving axles and carried an extremely high loading on each driving axle. An articulated frame similar to that of the GG1 gave the DD2 tracking qualities that were superior to those of the earlier rigid-frame locomotives, and the DD2's arc-welded body was patterned after that of the GG1.

Although it was never tried out with passenger

A SEPTEMBER sunrise in 1954 gilds the sides of a New York-bound passenger train crossing the 3269-foot, double-track bridge over the Susquehanna River between Havre de Grace and Perryville, Md. The bridge is a landmark on PRR's New York-Washington route.—*James P. Gallagher.*

LEANING hard into a curve, a GG1 rolled the Pennsy's premier *Broadway Limited* eastward through Gap, Pa., on July 1, 1957. Directly behind the R.P.O. car was a Santa Fe transcontinental Pullman.—*Fred W. Schneider III.*

gearing, the prototype DD2 performed well in freight service and remained in operation for almost 25 years. The design was not successful enough to repeat, however, and the GG1 remained the Pennsylvania's premier electric locomotive.

More GG1's were delivered beginning in late 1937, and after the final order was delivered in 1943, the GG1 fleet numbered 139 units. All of these later GG1's were somewhat heavier than the original group, and all were fitted with 100-mph gearing. A noticeable external difference in the GG1's built in 1937 and later was the provision of drop couplers and cast steel pilots in place of the flat steel pilots and fixed couplers of the original units.

EARLY in 1937 the Pennsylvania's board of directors authorized a further extension of the railroad's electrification westward to Harrisburg at a cost of nearly 50 million dollars. In addition to the electrification of the east-west Main Line between Paoli and Harrisburg, the work included the Trenton Cutoff which carried heavy east-west freight traffic around Philadelphia; the low-grade freight line between Parkesburg, Pa., Columbia, Pa., and

Enola Yard, near Harrisburg; and the route along the Susquehanna River between Columbia and Perryville, which provided a water-level freight route between the west and points in Maryland and the South. Also included in the project was the freight line from Monmouth Junction to Perth Amboy, N. J.

The Pennsylvania's engineers, by now thoroughly experienced in electrification work, carried out the Harrisburg electrification in short order. Only a year after the work had been formally authorized, passenger trains began operating behind electric power all the way to Harrisburg. Electric operation of the freight lines began three months later.

Electric traction permitted substantial improvements in the Pennsylvania's freight service just as it did for passenger service. Average freight running time between Enola Yard and the New York terminals was reduced by 2 hours. Electrification north of Potomac Yard permitted a reduction in New York-Florida freight schedules sufficient to provide third-morning instead of fourth-morning delivery.

Electrification of its heavy eastern freight traffic

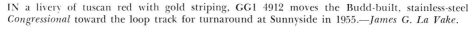

IN a livery of tuscan red with gold striping, GG1 4912 moves the Budd-built, stainless-steel *Congressional* toward the loop track for turnaround at Sunnyside in 1955.—*James G. La Vake.*

helped the Pennsylvania achieve some notable improvements in its overall operating efficiency. From 1934 to 1939, during which time freight operation was electrified both on the New York-Washington line and westward to Harrisburg, the railroad experienced a system-wide increase of almost 16 per cent in its average freight-train tonnage and a 6.5 per cent increase in average freight-train speed. Gross ton-miles per freight-train hour, an even more important index of operating efficiency, increased by 21.6 per cent.

The timing of the Pennsylvania's electrification turned out to be extremely fortunate. Little more than a year after the railroad completed the electrification to Harrisburg, Europe was at war. As America first armed the Allied nations and then joined them, the American railroad system accommodated a growing volume of freight and passenger traffic. From 1939 to 1944 the Pennsylvania's freight tonnage more than doubled, and its passenger traffic quadrupled.

This immense traffic growth was greatest in the industrial East, where the now-electrified main lines of the Pennsylvania Railroad constituted rail traffic arteries of unparalleled importance. Freight traffic hauled behind electric power reached a record level of 18 million gross ton-miles in 1944. The greatest traffic increase of all experienced by Pennsy electrification was in the passenger volume on the New York-Washington line. Before World War II the greatest single day's traffic had been 68,000 passengers, on the day of President Franklin D. Roosevelt's second inaugural in 1937. To accommodate this passenger volume the Pennsylvania had found it prudent to suspend freight traffic for 12 hours. By contrast, on the peak day during World War II — Christmas Eve 1943 — almost 179,000 passengers rode the line, and freight trains ran as usual.

Credit for the Pennsylvania's success in keeping its eastern lines fluid under the wartime traffic burden belonged to the magnificent GG1 fleet. The GG1's great power permitted it to accept substantial increases in passenger-train tonnages while still maintaining fast schedules, and the indefatigable electrics readily absorbed a phenomenal increase in their average daily mileage. If the GG1 was the greatest locomotive of American electrification, World War II was its finest hour.

IN the years following the end of World War II the Pennsylvania resumed its electric-locomotive development program. Among the important technological developments of the war years were improved mercury-arc rectifiers. The rectifier had important possibilities in railroad electrification, since it would permit combining the power-dis-

EASTBOUND on Pennsylvania's low-gradient freight line between the Susquehanna River and Atglen, Pa., a pair of P5a box-cabs speeds tonnage across a high fill west of Smithville, Pa., in July 1957.—*John J. Bowman Jr.*

SOON to be replaced by growing ranks of E44's (as well as by the workhorse, untiring GG1's), two P5a's move a freight train south over the PRR's Columbia & Port Deposit line at Safe Harbor, Pa., in January 1962. The upper trackage is the railroad's Atglen & Susquehanna branch.—*Fred W. Schneider III.*

tribution efficiencies of A.C. with the many advantages of the D.C. traction motor.

As early as 1913 Westinghouse, the Pennsylvania, and the New Haven had co-operated in testing an M.U. car which was equipped with a mercury-vapor rectifier to convert single-phase A.C. power to 600-volt D.C. Although the car operated more than 20,000 miles in revenue service on the New Haven's New Canaan branch, the rectifiers then available were unable to withstand the rigors of railroad service. For another three decades the only fully satisfactory A.C.-to-D.C. conversion system for railroad use was the motor-generator locomotive.

At the end of World War II, however, the availability of improved ignitron mercury-arc rectifiers renewed interest in the idea. In July 1949 the Pennsylvania equipped a standard MP54 M.U. car with ignitron-rectifier tubes and two 230 h.p. D.C. traction motors. The results of this experiment would have a profound effect on railroad electrification not only on the Pennsylvania Railroad but throughout the world.

In 1951, to prepare for eventual replacement of its P5a freight locomotives, the Pennsylvania ordered several prototype locomotives. The General Electric Company supplied three two-unit locomotives that employed the same type of A.C. commutator motors used in the P5 and the GG1. Both the B-B wheel arrangement and the body design were based on contemporary diesel-electric practice. The two-unit E2b-class locomotives could produce 5000 h.p. continuous output and a starting tractive effort of 122,750 pounds.

A pair of two-unit locomotives supplied by Westinghouse, however, represented a complete break with past practice. They employed ignitron rectifiers to supply D.C. power to the traction motors. Each two-unit locomotive developed a continuous output of 6000 h.p. and a maximum starting tractive effort of 189,000 pounds. Except for the trucks, the two locomotives were identical. The two Class E3b units had a B-B-B wheel arrangement, and the two E3c's, C-C.

Both experimental designs worked well but the ignitron-rectifier design was particularly successful. Although the replacement of the aging P5a fleet was to be postponed for almost another decade, the Westinghouse prototypes had clearly established the future of rectifier motive power on the Pennsylvania Railroad.

Through most of the 1950's the P5a's continued to roll freight tonnage under Pennsy catenary while the railroad concentrated its resources on the replacement of steam power with diesels. Then, impressed with the economies of dieselization, the Pennsylvania took further time to weigh the econ-

omies of continuing to operate its eastern electrification against those of dieselization. Three independent studies were initiated early in 1958. The results, to quote a company statement of 1959, "unequivocally proclaimed the superiority of the electrification."

In 1959 the Pennsylvania announced a long-term lease contract with General Electric for a fleet of 66 Class E44 rectifier freight locomotives costing 32 million dollars. Essentially an upgraded version of the rectifier locomotives GE had supplied to the Virginian Railway a few years earlier, the 193-ton E44 employed a C-C wheel arrangement and in configuration resembled a diesel road-switcher.

Power was supplied through a main transformer and a bank of 12 ignitron mercury-arc rectifiers, which delivered low-voltage D.C. to six GE Model 752 traction motors identical to those in use on thousands of diesel-electric locomotives. Unlike earlier Pennsy electrics, except for the 1951 experimentals, the E44 design used the nose-suspended motor-mounting arrangement that was standard diesel-electric practice, and included provision for dynamic braking. Continuous rating of the E44 was 4400 h.p., and its maximum starting tractive effort was 89,000 pounds. Its speed limit was 70 mph.

Deliveries of the E44 began in late 1960 and continued into 1963. Even before the last E44's were delivered, a further advance in electrical technology led to an improvement in the design. The ignitron rectifiers had presented some problems with the firing circuits and the water-cooled temperature-regulating apparatus. The thirty-seventh E44 was delivered with an air-cooled silicon-diode rectifier which eliminated these difficulties and provided a substantially increased power output.

So successful was the silicon-rectifier E44 unit that the last five locomotives in the order were similarly equipped and rated at 5000 h.p. Subsequently the railroad converted the ignitron-equipped E44's to silicon-rectifier E44a's.

The E44's were extraordinarily successful. The 66 units had been intended to replace all 92 of the P5a's. In practice, the first E44's actually proved capable of more than half again as much work per unit-month as a P5a. In heavy ore and coal drag service even the original unmodified E44's were able to handle 20 per cent more tonnage than either the P5a or a GG1. Availability, even during the break-in period, averaged almost 92 per cent. During the E44's first year of service, maintenance

BACK-TO-BACK General Electric E44's raced through Thorndale, Pa., in 1965 with an eastbound coal train. PRR's Class E44's, descendants of Virginian's rectifier units of 1956-1957, made their appearance in 1960.—*Richard Steinheimer.*

WESTINGHOUSE built a pair of two-unit rectifier locomotives for the Pennsylvania in 1951. Each unit of set 4995/4996 (above) had a B-B-B wheel arrangement; the units of set 4997/4998 (right), accelerating through Severn, Md., in June 1954, rode on C-C trucks.—*Above, Westinghouse Electric; right, H. N. Proctor.*

A PAIR of Jersey Arrow cars leave the Hudson River tubes in May 1969 on a fast New York-Trenton schedule. The State of New Jersey financed purchase of the 100-mph M.U. cars, delivered by St. Louis Car Company in 1968, for operation by Penn Central on accelerated schedules between the nation's largest city and the New Jersey state capital.—*Fred W. Schneider III.*

costs were only a third of those for the P5a's, and only 25 per cent of those for diesel-electric power in the same service.

Meanwhile the Pennsylvania began to replace its original M.U. cars. In 1958 the railroad purchased six prototype rectifier M.U. cars from the Budd Company. A version of the Budd *Pioneer III* lightweight passenger car, the Class MP85 M.U.'s were 85-foot, air-conditioned, stainless-steel cars seating 125 passengers. Four ignitron-rectifier tubes on each car supplied power to four D.C. series-wound traction motors. The combination of light weight and a 380 h.p. continuous rating gave the cars a 1.3-mph-per-second acceleration rate and a 90-mph maximum speed. In 1961 the ignitron tubes were replaced with a silicon-rectifier package.

In 1963, 38 new Budd Silverliner M.U.'s were leased to the Pennsy by the City of Philadelphia's Passenger Service Improvement Corporation. The cars generally were similar to the MP85 prototypes,

except that an increase in continuous power output to 550 h.p. for each car permitted a 2-mph-per-second acceleration rate. Another 20 cars of the same type were placed in service during 1967.

Another group of modern cars was added to the Pennsylvania M.U. roster in 1968, when the St. Louis Car Company delivered an order of 35 high-speed Jersey Arrow cars purchased by the State of New Jersey for Trenton-New York services. Generally similar in overall mechanical and electrical design to the Philadelphia Silverliner cars, the Arrows were capable of a 2.2-mph-per-second acceleration rate and a 100-mph maximum speed. A major departure from previous Pennsy M.U.-car design was the provision of sliding center doors for use at high-level platforms in addition to conventional vestibule doors and steps. Late in 1973 the General Electric Company began delivery of 200 similar cars financed jointly by the State of New Jersey and the Southeastern Pennsylvania Transportation Authority. These cars would be assigned to Philadelphia and New Jersey commuter services by Pennsy successor Penn Central.

All the while the Pennsylvania was concentrating most of its motive-power development efforts on replacing its electric freight locomotives and M.U. cars, the incomparable GG1 remained the bulwark of the railroad's under-catenary fleet. For nearly three decades the 139-unit GG1 fleet reigned supreme in electric-zone through passenger

services and ran up a sizable mileage in the freight pool as well. As late as 1968, 100-mph-geared GG1's powered the *Afternoon Congressional* on North America's fastest passenger schedules.

During the postwar years, GG1's figured in two spectacular mishaps. On the morning of January 15, 1953, five days before the inauguration of President Dwight D. Eisenhower, GG1 No. 4876 was heading the overnight Boston-Washington *Federal* on the last lap of its run to the capital. Approaching Washington the train's engineer made a routine brake application, only to find that the brakes on his train were not holding. Unable to stop, the train raced through the terminal yard and into Washington Union Station. Moving at an estimated 35 mph, the GG1 and its train plunged through the station-master's office and a newsstand and out onto the concourse floor, which collapsed, dropping the GG1 and the first two coaches into the basement baggage room. The passenger cars were retrieved with relative ease, but the GG1 had to be cut into pieces before it could be removed from the station. Although 87 persons were injured, there were no fatalities, and No. 4876 returned to service 10 months later after being rebuilt at Pennsylvania's Altoona shops.

Another kind of mishap sidelined almost the entire GG1 fleet in February 1958. Despite a record of more than 20 years of exceptional reliability under all sorts of weather conditions, the GG1's proved vulnerable to an unusual combination of extremely cold weather and some peculiarities of the locomotive's design. Exceptionally fine snowflakes penetrated the French-linen air filters on the GG1's, melting and shorting out the traction motors. The fine snow, which formed only at low levels, where the GG1's air intakes were located, caused little trouble for the P5a's and the diesels, which had air intakes at a higher level, but almost the entire GG1 fleet was disabled. Diesels borrowed from elsewhere on the Pennsy and P5a's diverted from their normal freight duties kept passenger traffic moving until the GG1's could be repaired. Modified air-intake systems and a new type of epoxy-resin motor insulation finally cured the problem, and the GG1's have operated since then without snow troubles.

On a much smaller scale, a similar problem briefly disabled the Pennsy electrification near Port Deposit, Md., in July 1947, when swarms of mayflies brought three freight trains to a halt on the Harrisburg-Perryville freight line along the Susquehanna River. An investigation revealed that the flies had been drawn into the traction motors of the locomotives and short-circuited them.

Although the great GG1 continued to dominate the Pennsylvania (and later Penn Central) electrification into the 1970's, replacement of the locomotive had been under consideration for much of the previous two decades. Soon after the New Haven's rectifier passenger electrics entered service in 1955, for example, the Pennsylvania borrowed one for testing on the New York-Washington main line.

While interest in a GG1 replacement continued, the exceptional performance of the Budd Silverliners inspired new thoughts for the future of the railroad's passenger service in electric territory. Soon after the first rectifier M.U. cars were delivered in 1958, the railroad ran some 100-mph tests on the New York-Washington line to compare the M.U.'s with a GG1-hauled standard consist. Both the Budd M.U.'s and the GG1 turned in notable performances, substantially bettering the line's fastest regular schedules.

In addition to meeting the performance standards required for a high-speed service, multiple-unit equipment also promised several advantages over conventional locomotive-drawn equipment. The elimination of a heavy locomotive greatly reduced the stresses of high-speed operation on the track structure. With power on every car, the performance characteristics of an M.U. train were constant, regardless of the length of the train. The availability of traction motors throughout an M.U. train also permitted dynamic braking on each car, an important advantage in high-speed service.

During the early 1960's there was increasing interest in the development of extremely fast train service between New York and Washington. Passage of the High Speed Ground Transportation Research and Development Act in 1965 led to a joint Pennsylvania Railroad-U. S. Government project that would bring the concept of high-speed M.U. trains to reality. The 55-million-dollar project would be financed largely by the railroad. Some 22 million dollars would pay for new rolling stock while the remainder would be used to upgrade the railroad's fixed plant to accommodate the contemplated high speeds. The ultimate goal of the project was 150-mph operation.

A WASHINGTON-BOUND *Metroliner* slams through Metuchen, N. J., on April 30, 1969, less than four months after the deluxe, high-speed M.U.'s made their debut on Penn Central's New York-Washington corridor.—*Don Wood.*

The first phase of the project was the upgrading of 21.9 miles of track between Trenton and New Brunswick, N. J., for high-speed tests with four special Budd Silverliner test cars. Testing started in late 1966 and culminated on May 24, 1967, when the four-car test train achieved 156 mph with an invited group of more than 200 newsmen and Government and railroad officials on board.

Even before the test program had been completed, the Pennsylvania had developed specifications for a fleet of Metroliner multiple-unit cars

AMTRAK'S nonstop (except for Capital Beltway, Md.) Washington-New York *Metroliner Morning Executive*, train 120, flashes through Monmouth Junction, N. J., in January 1972.—*Tom Nelligan.*

SPEEDING at 120 mph, this *Metroliner* is about to overtake the *Spirit of St. Louis*—from which this photo was taken—moving at nearly 80 mph.—*A. M. Rung.*

ONLY a few miles out of Washington, Penn Central train 102, the 8:30 a.m. *Metroliner* to New York, cruises through Landover, Md., at the 100 mph mark on a misty morning in February 1971. Penn Central advertised its high-speed New York-Washington service as the "ground shuttle;" Amtrak takeover of the operation was less than three months away.—*William D. Middleton.*

A FISH-EYE lens was used to scoop in this view of a *Metroliner* engineer at the controls of his high-speed charge. Among the advanced features in the compact cab are automatic speed-maintaining equipment, cab signals, wheel-slip control, dynamic braking, and an electronic speedometer with digital readout.—*The Washington Post.*

capable of 160-mph operation, and an order for 50 cars had been placed with the Budd Company by mid-1966. Another 11 identical cars were ordered by the Southeastern Pennsylvania Transportation Authority for a high-speed service in the Philadelphia-Harrisburg corridor.

Weighing 84 tons each, the 85-foot stainless-steel cars seated anywhere from 34 in parlor cars to 80 passengers in a straight coach version. Silicon-diode rectifiers supplied D.C. power to four 300-h.p. traction motors on each car. Dynamic braking was effective at speeds above 30 mph, while electropneumatic braking took over at lower speeds. Special features included automatic, solid-state acceleration, deceleration, and speed controls; cab signals; electronic speedometers; electrically controlled doors; and two-way radio.

Although an early test train hit 164 mph, the debut of the Metroliners was hardly a resounding success. The start-up of regular service was delayed again and again as the railroad and its suppliers struggled to overcome electrical and mechanical problems. A single *Metroliner* round trip finally began operating in January 1969, and additional trips gradually were added as the trains' problems were brought under control. Penn Central, which had inherited the project from the Pennsylvania in the previous year's merger with New York Central, was soon running three daily round trips, one of them a non-stop trip covering the 226-mile run in 2 hours 30 minutes, fully 50 minutes faster than the best schedule ever run with the GG1.

Even if neither the speed nor the nine-round-trips-daily frequency objectives of the *Metroliner* program were achieved in the first few years of operation, the service could still be considered a qualified success. Within a year the trains were operating six daily round trips, and on-time performance was at least 80 per cent, despite continuing technical troubles. By their second anniversary the trains had carried more than 2 million passengers and were holding down schedules that called for start-to-stop average speeds in excess of 95 mph. The new National Railroad Passenger Corporation (Amtrak) took over the *Metroliner* service on May 1, 1971, and by May 1972 Amtrak was operating 14 daily *Metroliner* round trips and the trains were achieving better than 90 per cent on-time performance. Most important of all, a long-term downward trend in rail passenger travel in the New York-Washington corridor had been reversed.

In the end, however, the trains never did meet their performance and reliability goals, and Amtrak soon shifted to a more conventional locomotive-hauled approach for another generation of high-speed trains. An initial attempt with a high-speed version of General Electric's E60 locomotive failed

to fill the bill, and before the end of the decade Amtrak was testing two high-speed electric locomotives leased from Sweden and France. By January 1980 GM's Electro-Motive Division had begun deliveries of a fleet of new 6000-h.p. AEM7 high-speed electrics that were based upon technology developed by Sweden's ASEA. Metroliner equipment was gradually withdrawn from New York-Washington service as AEM7's and Amfleet cars took over the schedules.

If the Metroliner equipment itself ultimately proved a failure, the trains had demonstrated that high-speed operation on the existing New York-Washington corridor was feasible and that it could attract new passenger traffic. The Metroliners had laid the foundation for newer generations of high-speed equipment and an eventual reconstruction of the entire Northeast Corridor from Washington to Boston into a modern high-speed railroad.

By the early 1970's the Pennsylvania's successor, Penn Central, had begun to plan both a conversion of the existing electrification to a 25,000-volt, 60-cycle power supply that could be fed directly from the commercial grid and extensions to the A.C. catenary. In northern New Jersey, electrification was proposed for the busy New York & Long Branch commuter line, jointly owned with Central of New

(ABOVE LEFT) Four new rectifier M.U. cars of *Pioneer III* design rolled into Overbrook, Pa., on an afternoon run to Paoli in July 1958. The Budd-built cars, Pennsy Class MP85, replaced aging MP54's.—*Aaron G. Fryer.*

(ABOVE) Outbound from Suburban Station, green PC MP54's and—almost hidden beyond—a train of Silverliners advance across the Schuylkill River as they enter Philadelphia's 30th Street Station in 1970.—*Fred W. Schneider III.*

Jersey. A much more ambitious extension of electric operation was proposed for the railroad's freight service. Following the merger with the New York Central, rerouted freight bound to and from New England had placed a heavy traffic burden on the former NYC West Shore line, and the railroad's engineers began studies of an electrification up the west bank of the Hudson River to Selkirk Yard at Albany, N. Y.

While the Long Branch electrification later went ahead as a publicly funded project, plans for any other extensions to the electrification died with the 1970 bankruptcy of the ill-starred Penn Central.

Penn Central finally emerged from bankruptcy in 1976 as a major component of the Consolidated Rail Corporation, organized by the federal government to take over Penn Central and other bankrupt eastern carriers. Conrail, too, considered major expansion of electrification in a 1979 study of an extension of catenary over both the 276 miles of main line west of Harrisburg to Conway Yard, near Pittsburgh, and a new route between Philadelphia and northern New Jersey over former

Reading and Central of New Jersey lines. Despite a projected favorable rate of return from the expanded electrification, Conrail was still a money-losing railroad, ill prepared to raise the enormous capital investment required. Again, nothing happened. Indeed, within two years Conrail had ended all electric freight operation on the existing electrification.

Despite the ending of electric freight operation, the Pennsylvania Railroad's bold venture under catenary stands as one of the most significant chapters in the history of North American railroad electrification. Its enormous capacity to move heavy traffic at high speed had kept the Pennsylvania's vital eastern lines fluid under the unprecedented freight and passenger volume of World War II. In more recent times the New York-Washington catenary has powered the fastest passenger trains ever operated in North America, and it has provided the foundation for a new era of even higher speed trains that would begin operating with the new century.

What William Wallace Atterbury set in motion in 1928 has turned out very well indeed.

(RIGHT) The Department of Transportation's Silverliner test train stands at Princeton Junction on May 24, 1967. The tests, during which the train reached 145 mph, were part of a government-financed program during 1966-1967 that eventually led to a new level of high-speed passenger service on Pennsy's New York-Washington corridor.—*Don Wood.*

(ABOVE LEFT) A two-car shuttle train of MP54's waits for mainline connections at Princeton Junction, N. J., in the autumn of 1965 before clattering down the 2.7-mile branch to Princeton, N. J.—*Richard Steinheimer.*

(LEFT) Passengers board PC's Princeton shuttle at Princeton Junction in May 1969. In Princeton the train is known as the "PJ&B" (Princeton Junction & Back).—*Fred W. Schneider III.*

(LEFT) Owl-eyed MP54's stand at Princeton's handsome stone station before departing on their 5-minute jaunt to Princeton Junction to meet mainline trains to New York and Philadelphia.—*Jim Shaughnessy.*

(RIGHT) The classic lines of PRR's MP54's are revealed in this high-angle view at Elizabeth, N. J. The cars resembled shortened mainline coaches; indeed, the first batch of MP54's were originally built for steam-hauled suburban operation. Pennsy owned more than 500 MP54's and the sturdy old cars transported commuters for over 50 years.—*Paul Carleton.*

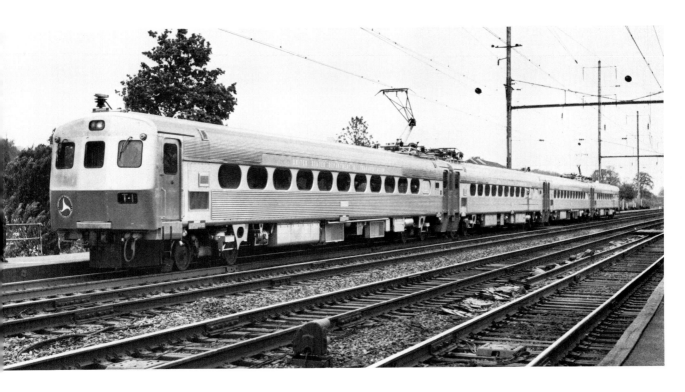

SOUTHBOUND MP54's emerge from the massive Passaic River liftbridge at Newark, N. J., and are about to enter Pennsylvania's Newark Station.—*Collection of Donald Duke.*

A PHILADELPHIA-BOUND two-car train of *Pioneer III* M.U.'s pauses in the heat of a July evening at Overbrook in 1958.—*Aaron G. Fryer.*

AFTER Great Northern dieselized its electric operations in 1956, the road sold its eight Class Y-1 motor-generator units to the Pennsy where they became Class FF2's. FF2 No. 7 emerged from Altoona shops in 1957 after modification and repainting.—*Pennsylvania Railroad.*

THE FF2's were used primarily for helper service. FF2 No. 6 shoved hard against the caboose (or cabin car, to use PRR terminology) of eastbound symbol freight NY-8 at Downington, Pa., on the long grade between Thorndale and Paoli on February 1, 1958.—*Don Wood.*

EXCEPT for the memorable snowstorm of February 1958, which crippled nearly the entire GG1 fleet, Pennsy's electrification has withstood the severest of weather conditions through the years. (Left) In the wake of the infamous February 1958 storm, a lone P5a escorted a freight through Overbrook on its way into Philadelphia. (Below) During the height of a March 1958 storm, a GG1 plowed through wet, sticky snow at Overbrook with express train 604, the *Susquehannock*, bound from Williamsport to Philadelphia. (Below right) As the storm subsided, sturdy MP54's delivered commuters as usual. (Right) Two P5a's braved the elements during a heavy snowstorm in March 1956 at Overbrook with an eastbound train of mixed merchandise.—*All photos, Aaron G. Fryer.*

TWO E33 rectifier units in their fourth paint scheme (Virginian, Norfolk & Western, New Haven, and now Penn Central) wind along the Susquehanna River.—*Fred W. Schneider III.*

THE headlight of E44 No. 4463 on westbound symbol freight P-85 pierces the evening shadows near Lancaster, Pa., in June 1969.—*Fred W. Schneider III.*

PENN CENTRAL E44's cant into a curve at Wayne, Pa., in March 1970 as they speed westbound tonnage toward Harrisburg.—*Fred W. Schneider III.*

A DRAMATIC view of E44's at Enola (Pa.) yard in 1965 was photographed from the cab of an adjacent freight as the two trains departed side by side.—*Richard Steinheimer.*

THREE Pennsy E44's—13,200 h.p. worth of power—thread through crossovers beneath complex overhead at Howard Street in Baltimore in March 1966.—*Herbert H. Harwood Jr.*

HEAD brakeman arrives at his locomotives in Enola yard in 1965.—*Richard Steinheimer.*

IN a setting unlike what one might associate with the industrialized East, two E44's race eastbound freight over Pequea Creek at Martic Forge, Pa., in May 1969. The line is Penn Central's low-gradient Atglen & Susquehanna branch between Atglen and Creswell, Pa.—*Fred W. Schneider III.*

LONG-HOOD-FORWARD Penn Central E44's, still clad in PRR paint, scatter the dust at Wildcat Tunnel on PC's Columbia & Port Deposit line in July 1969.—*Herbert H. Harwood, Jr.*

THE fireman aboard PC E33 rectifier unit 4602 waves at boaters on Fishing Creek in September 1970. The train is northbound along the Susquehanna River.—*Fred W. Schneider III.*

(ABOVE) GG1's rest at Ivy City engine terminal at Washington in June 1960 after a day of racing *Keystones, Congressionals,* and other Pennsy flagships between New York and Washington.—*Jim Shaughnessy.*

(ABOVE CENTER) Framed by the platform railings of the train's cabin car, the GG1's of PRR's Chicago-bound piggyback freight TT-1 run around the train at Kearny Meadows (N. J.) yard on a rainy February evening in 1960.—*Don Wood.*

HEADING for the East River tunnels and Penn Station, GG1 4931 pulls the consist of Southern Railway's *Southern Crescent* out of Sunnyside Yard in June 1970.—*Fred W. Schneider III.*

(ABOVE RIGHT) The Pennsylvania's long-lived but glamour-less Class B1 switchers worked in the railroad's electrified yards. No. 5685 shunted passenger cars in Sunnyside Yard one April night in 1960.—*Jim Shaughnessy.*

(BELOW) The main maintenance base for the Pennsylvania's electric locomotive fleet was at Wilmington. GG1's in various stages of overhaul and disassembly stood in the main shop bay in 1960.—*Don Wood.*

MEN at work on their railroad: (Above) Engineer E. A. Branyan signals a warning to unwary motorists that his fast-moving GG1 bound for Harrisburg with merchandise will not tolerate an entanglement. (Above right) In the time-honored tradition of railroading, the engineer of a slightly weathered GG1 compares watches with his train's conductor at Penn Station prior to departure with a string of varnish.—*Above left, Richard Steinheimer; above, Pennsylvania Railroad.*

(BELOW) Tri-level auto-rack cars, loaded with new Chevrolets at Baltimore, hurtle through Trenton, N. J., behind a grimy pair of "G's" in 1967. Paired GG1's are the normal power assignment for freight runs.—*J. C. Smith Jr.*

A FISHERMAN pauses briefly to acknowledge the passing of a GG1 with a Washington-New York express as it glides onto the bridge across an inlet of Chesapeake Bay north of Edgewood, Md., in April 1969.—*Fred W. Schneider III.*

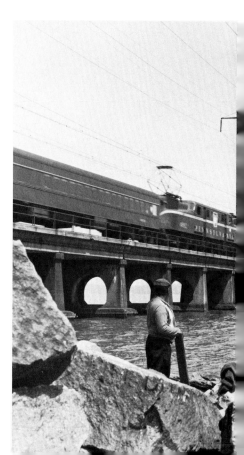

BOSTON-BOUND train 172, the *Senator* from Washington, is about to be swallowed by one of the twin tubes that carry the Penn Central main line under the Hudson River and into Manhattan, in May 1969.—*Fred W. Schneider III.*

(BELOW RIGHT) GG1 4873 kicks up the flakes of an Easter Sunday snowstorm in 1970 as it rolls a container train through Lancaster. Penn Central container trains were a holdover from New York Central management.—*Fred W. Schneider III.*

WIDE-STRIPED GG1 4923 gracefully sweeps around the curve north of 30th Street Station, Philadelphia, with the **PRR-RF&P-ACL** *West Coast Champion* bound for Florida.—*J. C. Smith Jr.*

WITH the U.S. Capitol in the background, two GG1's, one lettered for **PRR** and the other for PC, roll toward Potomac Yard, Va., with symbol freight MD-117 in 1970.—*Fred W. Schneider III.*

AS it departs the nation's capital, GG1 4919 makes easy work of accelerating the *Representative* through the throat of Washington Union Station in 1967.—*William D. Middleton.*

358

AMTRAK'S refurbished *Broadway Limited* zips through Metropark (Iselin), N.J., on its maiden westbound run on May 2, 1972. Although still owned by the Penn Central, GG1 902 (formerly PC No. 4902) has traded its somber PC paint scheme for Amtrak red, blue, and platinum mist. Amtrak's red-nosed G's became known to many fans as "W. C. Fields GG1's."—*Don Wood.*

AMISH-SETTLED eastern Pennsylvania provides a contrast to Manhattan skyscrapers—the more stereotyped setting for GG1's—as No. 4911 thunders eastbound across Water Works Bridge near Lancaster in 1970.—*Peter Rickershauser.*

GG1'S 4882 and 4887 roll westbound TH-3 along the Susquehanna River in October 1969. The auto-racks were picked up at the Chrysler plant in Newark, Del.; PC will forward them to the N&W at Hagerstown, Md.—*Victor Hand.*

PENN CENTRAL'S Northeast Corridor means traffic density: Photographed from the cab of a freight train, Amtrak's southbound *Washingtonian* crosses from track 3 to 4; in the distance a Clocker races east to New York while a freight approaches on track 4.—*Victor Hand*.

A YARD LIGHT shines with a moonlike glow in the misty atmosphere of a November evening in 1965 as GG1 No. 4869 and E44 No. 4434 are serviced at Pennsy's Enola yard near Harrisburg.—*Richard Steinheimer.*

PENNSYLVANIA No. 23, the *Manhattan Limited* to Chicago whizzes through the gloom of a November afternoon in 196 on its way to Harrisburg. Photographer Steinheimer capture the action from the cab of an E44.—*Richard Steinheimer.*

PERHAPS the most unusual North American electrification was the 22,000-volt, 25-cycle, single-phase A.C. system installed on Henry Ford's Detroit, Toledo & Ironton in 1925. Although electric operation lasted less than five years, the DT&I pioneered the motor-generator locomotive concept with this remarkable 5000 h.p. Ford-Westinghouse machine, which was the railroad's only electric motive power.—*Ford Motor Company, collection of Donald Duke.*

12. Mine haul and miscellaneous

ELECTRIC TRACTION sometimes was used by steam roads for light branchline electrifications. The equipment and standards paralleled those used for street and interurban electric railways.

Already noted among electrifications of this type were the Burlington & Mount Holly electrification of the Pennsylvania Railroad in 1895, and the branchline electrifications of the New Haven Railroad in Massachusetts, Rhode Island, and Connecticut from 1895 to 1907, all of which provided electric traction experience to railroads that subsequently developed two of the most important mainline electrifications in North America.

Not as well known as the Pennsylvania and New

Haven branchline electrifications was a 1900 electrification by the Boston & Albany Railroad of its mile-long branch line between Riverside and Newton Lower Falls, Mass. The line was operated by a single motorized passenger car and used low-voltage D.C. overhead trolley wire and trolley-pole current collection. Power was purchased from a nearby street railway.

A similar branchline electrification was installed in 1904 by the Philadelphia & Reading Railway on a 7-mile branch between Cape May Point and Sewells Point, N. J. A 20-ton steeple-cab locomotive, typical of those built for interurban railway service, handled both freight and passenger traffic on the line.

In 1906 the Pennsylvania Railroad electrified its

KNOWN to local residents as the "ping-pong," this oversized trolley car shuttled back and forth on the Boston & Albany's mile-long branch from Newton Lower Falls, Mass., to Riverside, where connections were made with Boston trains. —*Collection of Norton D. Clark.*

(RIGHT) Fitted with such trolley-car accouterments as motors, trolley poles, headlights, and bell, the Pennsylvania Railroad's elderly wooden combine No. 4503 plied the 600-volt D.C. electrification of the Cumberland Valley branch between Dillsburg and Mechanicsburg, Pa., for 22 years. The crew posed for a final photograph on the last day of electric operation, December 28, 1928. —*Collection of Richard H. Steinmetz Sr.*

READING No. 1, built by Baldwin-Westinghouse in 1904, powered freight and passenger trains on the Reading's 7-mile branch between Cape May Point and Sewells Point, N. J.—*Collection of H. L. Broadbelt.*

SIX heavy wooden M.U. cars such as No. 3100 were built by St. Louis Car Company for the Erie's 1907 single-phase electrification between Rochester and Mount Morris, N. Y.—*Collection of Electric Railroaders' Association.*

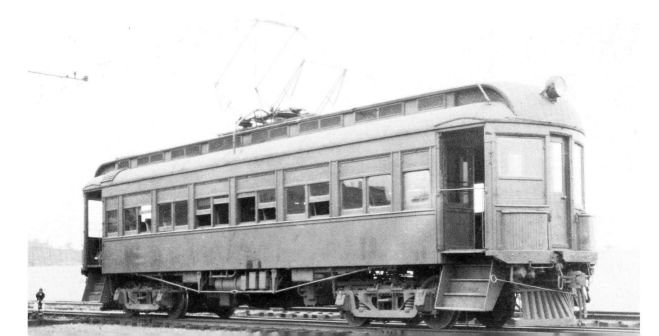

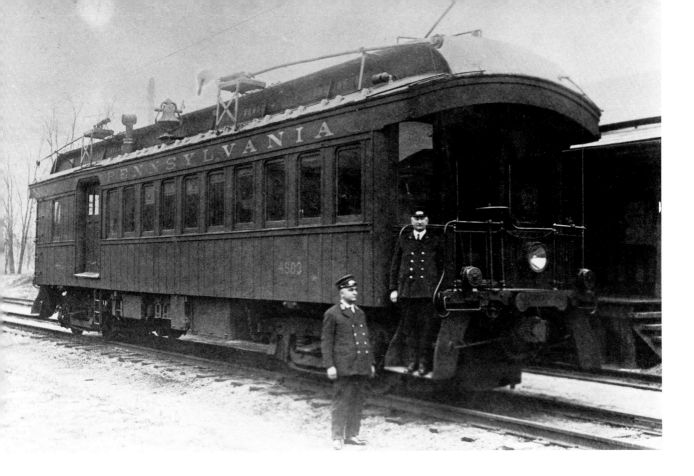

8-mile Cumberland Valley branch between Dillsburg and Mechanicsburg, Pa. Two wooden combines, equipped with motors, trolley poles, and controls, provided passenger service on the line.

A more extensive and technologically significant project was launched by the Erie Railroad in 1907 when it electrified 34 miles of its Rochester Division between Rochester and Mt. Morris, N. Y. Unlike other steam roads, which electrified branch lines with low-voltage systems during this period, the Erie adopted an 11,000-volt, 25-cycle, single-phase A.C. system. It was the first single-phase A.C. operation on any steam railroad in North America, preceding by several months the opening of New Haven's electrification from Woodlawn, N. Y., to Stamford, Conn.

Most steam road electrifications of the time generated their own power, but the Erie drew its power over 60,000-volt transmission lines from the hydroelectric plant of the Ontario Power Company at Niagara Falls. A 2250-kilowatt substation at Avon, N. Y., converted the power supply to the

ERIE'S 34-mile electrification connected at Avon, N. Y., 19 miles south of Rochester, with one of Erie's New York-Buffalo lines.—*Library of Congress.*

trolley-wire voltage. A simple-catenary overhead distribution system was supported by brackets from wooden poles spaced 120 feet apart.

For passenger service six wooden motor cars were supplied by the St. Louis Car Company. The cars were 51 feet 4 inches long and weighed 48 tons. Each car was equipped with a 200-kilowatt transformer and four Westinghouse 132-A single-phase electric motors rated at 100 h.p. each, providing sufficient power to haul trailer cars. An electropneumatic multiple-unit control system permitted the operation of two or more motor cars in a train. Current collection was by means of a spring-raised pantograph. The American Car & Foundry Company supplied two additional cars of similar design in 1913.

Electric operation on the branch was confined to interurban passenger service, while through passenger and freight trains continued to operate with steam locomotives. The electrification, which opened to regular service in May 1907, was an immediate success. The savings afforded by the electric equipment enabled the Erie to increase the frequency of its local service. Passenger revenues soon increased by 50 per cent over those of the previous steam-powered service.

Several steam road electrifications were almost indistinguishable from interurban railway operations. Notable among these were electrifications of the New York Central's West Shore Railroad between Syracuse and Utica, N. Y., in 1907, and the Southern Pacific's subsidiary Portland, Eugene & Eastern between Portland and Corvallis, Ore., completed in 1917.

The 49-mile West Shore electrification, operated by the subsidiary Oneida Railway, used an under-running 600-volt D.C. third-rail system identical to that installed by parent New York Central in New York City. Local passenger service was operated with interurban equipment, which left the electrified steam road tracks and used streetcar lines to reach downtown stations in Syracuse and Utica. Through passenger and freight service continued to operate with steam power.

The SP's Oregon system utilized a 1500-volt D.C. power-distribution system and heavy, high-speed steel cars representative of the best interurban railway practice. Service was provided over two routes between Portland and Whiteson, Ore., and south of Whiteson on a single route to Corvallis.

Some interurban railways developed from steam-operated short lines. The Waterloo, Cedar Falls & Northern and the Fort Dodge, Des Moines & Southern, two of the most important Iowa interurbans, began operation as steam railroads. A portion of Illinois' Rock Island Southern Railway was originally a steam road, as was a part of Canada's

Montreal & Southern Counties Railway, a subsidiary of the Grand Trunk Railway.

Electrification sometimes was attractive to small terminal and switching lines operating in congested urban areas, where the railroads were susceptible to complaints about the smoke and dirt of steam operation.

Two electrifications of this type already mentioned were the Buffalo & Lockport and the Hoboken Shore Road, both of which commenced electric operation before the turn of the century. Another early electric switching line was the Bush Terminal Railroad, which began electric operation in 1904 on its system serving docks and warehouses in South Brooklyn, N. Y. These and other small terminal lines typically employed light steeple-cab locomotives similar to those used by interurban railways.

One of the largest electric switching lines in America was the Niagara Junction Railway at Niagara Falls, N. Y., which operated an industrial switching network of 44 track-miles. Built during the 1890's by the Niagara Falls Power Company, the Niagara Junction supplied switching services to in-

THE Niagara Junction Railway was a busy switching line at Niagara Falls, N. Y. Seven steeple-cab switchers built by GE in 1952 constituted the NJ's most recent electric motive power. Three views depict the unglamorous but dependable machines going about their daily switching chores. Electric operation ended in 1979 after the line was absorbed into Conrail. Three of the durable electrics went on to new switching duties in New York's Grand Central Terminal.—*Left, Jim Shaughnessy; above and right, Fred W. Schneider III.*

dustries that had developed in the Falls area to use the utility company's hydroelectric power. Initially the railway was operated with steam power. In 1913, when growing traffic necessitated an increase in motive power capacity, the power company elected to scrap its steam locomotives and electrify. A low-voltage D.C. catenary system was adopted. Power, of course, came from the parent company's Niagara Falls hydroelectric plant. Locomotives were of the double-truck steeple-cab variety, equipped with pantographs. The line was absorbed into Conrail and electric operation ended in 1979.

In 1922 the Montreal Harbor Commission electrified its 45-track-mile switching network serving the Montreal (Que.) docks. Smoke abatement in the congested harbor area was the primary reason for the electrification. The harbor commissioners chose the same 2400-volt D.C. system that had been adopted a decade earlier by the Canadian Northern Railway for its Montreal terminal and tunnel electrification. A fleet of nine 100-ton B+B box-cab locomotives, built in 1924 and 1926 by the English Electric Company, were similar in performance characteristics to the CN's GE-built electric locomotives. Indeed, when the harbor electrification was discontinued 20 years later, the British-built electrics went to work on the CN electrification after only minor modification.

Electric traction was as well suited for mining operations as it was for switching lines. As far back

REPRESENTATIVE of dozens of mining electrifications is this view of Mesaba-Cliffs Mining Company steeple-cab locomotive No. 206 spotting dump cars at the Hill-Trumble Mine iron-ore loading pocket near Marble, Minn., in 1970. The off-center trolley wire is necessary to avoid interference with loading operations.—*Franklin A. King.*

NINETY cars of copper ore stretch out on the Kennecott Copper Corporation main line near Salt Lake City, Utah, in April 1956. The 16-mile, 3000-volt D.C. line moves the mining company's ore from the open pit at Bingham Canyon to concentrators at Arthur and Magna and the smelter at Garfield. GE built the big steeple-cabs in 1947.—*Richard Steinheimer.*

COPPER ore is loaded into hopper cars (left) at Kennecott's open-pit mine at Santa Rita, N.M. (Above) A train starts out of the world's largest open-pit copper mine at Bingham Canyon, Utah, behind a GE steeple-cab in April 1956. Portable supports for the trolley wire permit relocation as the pit is enlarged.—*Left, Kennecott Copper Corporation; right, Richard Steinheimer.*

THE only electric locomotive of Henry Ford's Detroit, Toledo & Ironton was a 5000 h.p., 372-ton 2 (D+D) machine. Westinghouse manufactured No. 501's electrical equipment, and the locomotive itself was built in Ford's River Rouge automobile plant. The arched concrete catenary supports remain in place today, more than four decades after the catenary came down. *—Ford Motor Company, collection of Robert J. Wayner.*

as the late 1880's small electric locomotives were used for underground mining operations. As larger and more powerful locomotives were developed early in the 20th century, electric power became equally popular for heavier above-ground mining work.

Typically, above-ground mining applications of electric power were relatively small operations, employing the standardized steeple-cab locomotives manufactured by both General Electric and Baldwin-Westinghouse. Several, however, were electrifications of mainline proportions.

The Kennecott Copper Corporation, which had heavy-duty electrifications at its mines in New Mexico and Utah, was probably the largest operator of electrified mining trackage. In 1940 Kennecott replaced steam with 50 miles of 750-volt D.C. electrification in and around the Chino Mines Division open-pit mine at Santa Rita, N. Mex. A more extensive electrification was developed by Kennecott's Utah Copper Division, near Salt Lake City. Installed from the late 1920's onward, the 750-volt D.C. catenary within the huge Bingham Canyon open-pit mine eventually hung over more than 100 miles of track. Kennecott's Utah electrification was extended in 1948, when a 16-mile line-haul electric railroad was constructed to replace the company's subsidiary Bingham & Garfield steam railroad. The new line was powered at 3000 volts D.C. Electric locomotives weighing 150 tons hauled copper ore from the mine to concentrators at Magna and Arthur and concentrates to the Garfield smelter.

Although most of Kennecott's New Mexico electrification was discontinued in the early 1960's, electric power continued to operate on the Utah lines until the end of 1982.

AN ELECTRIFICATION unlike any other in North America was undertaken by Henry Ford's Detroit, Toledo & Ironton Railroad in 1925.

The DT&I originated at Detroit and extended 365 miles southward across Ohio to Ironton, on the Ohio River. Ford acquired the DT&I in 1920 to serve his Detroit-area automobile plants, and over the next few years he made several improvements to the railroad. In 1923 plans were announced for the electrification of 16 miles of DT&I double track between Ford's River Rouge auto plant and the

THE heart of the Ford-Westinghouse DT&I locomotive was the motor-generator set (above), which consisted of a 1500-kilowatt D.C. generator driven by a 2100 h.p. A.C. synchronous motor. A motor-generator set was installed in one section of each of the locomotive's two units. (Right) The other section of each unit, one of which is shown under construction in Ford's River Rouge plant, contained a transformer, the control apparatus, an air compressor, and a blower. Around the perimeter of the frame were batteries for starting the motor-generator and for operating auxiliary equipment.*—Both photos, collection of the Pennsylvania Railway Museum Assn.*

STRAW-HATTED Ford, Westinghouse, and DT&I officials posed proudly with a special train pulled by a single unit of the motor-generator locomotive. The two identical units, 501A and 501B, could be operated independently.—*Collection of the Pennsylvania Railway Museum Assn.*

railroad's yard at Flat Rock, Mich. Electric operation to Toledo and even to the Ohio River also was contemplated.

"As usual," noted *Railway Age,* "Mr. Ford has not been restricted by past practice or tendencies in the choice of electrical system and of type of motive power units for his road." Both the electrification system and the motive power for the DT&I were unlike anything seen previously in North American electrification.

DT&I's overhead system was energized at 22,000 volts, double the customary voltage for single-phase A.C. systems. Even the supporting structure for the catenary was different. Instead of using wood or steel poles, Ford's engineers spanned the DT&I tracks with gracefully curved concrete arches. Power was supplied from the River Rouge steam-powered generating plant, which was greatly enlarged to carry the railroad load.

The DT&I's experimental locomotive, completed in 1925, was a remarkable machine. Ford Motor Company engineers developed the mechanical design for the locomotive, which was fabricated in the River Rouge plant. Electrical equipment was built to Ford specifications by the Westinghouse Electric & Manufacturing Company.

Only two units, normally operated together, were built. Each unit consisted of two articulated sections, each mounted on an eight-wheel truck. The two trucks were connected through a universal ball-type hinge, while the two box-cab sections were joined by means of a flexible canvas diaphragm.

Although previous single-phase locomotives had used either single-phase A.C. traction motors or a phase converter to produce power for three-phase

A.C. traction motors, the Ford design introduced the motor-generator concept to convert single-phase power to direct current for use in low-voltage D.C. traction motors. The lead section of each locomotive unit contained a 2000-kilowatt transformer, which reduced the voltage from 22,000 volts to 1250 volts, and auxiliary equipment. The rear section carried a motor-generator set with a 25-cycle, 750-rpm synchronous motor that drove a 600-volt D.C. generator. The section also housed miscellaneous auxiliaries and switch gear. A 225 h.p. traction motor was mounted on each axle of the locomotive. A quill drive provided a flexible connection between the axle-hung motors and driving pinions.

Operating cabs were at both ends of each unit. Both multiple-unit control and regenerative braking were provided. The complete two-unit locomotive was 117 feet long and weighed 372 tons. Maximum starting tractive effort was 250,000 pounds, and maximum power output was 5000 h.p. Top speed was 43 mph.

The unique electric locomotive operated successfully, but Henry Ford's grand plan for DT&I electrification never materialized. No other locomotives were built, and the electric system never grew beyond the original 16-mile section. After an anti-trust action compelled Ford to give up control of his railroad in 1929, electric operation ended, and the novel locomotive was scrapped the following year. The unusual concrete arches that supported the DT&I catenary were too costly to remove and remain today as a reminder of Henry Ford's venture in railroad electrification.

At least one feature pioneered by the Ford railroad, the motor-generator for converting A.C. to

D.C., warranted further use. Locomotives built for Great Northern's single-phase Cascade Tunnel electrification in the late 1920's used the motor-generator exclusively. Several motor-generator units also were built for the New Haven during the same period, and in the late 1940's both the Great Northern and the Virginian acquired new motor-generator units which were among the largest electric locomotives ever built.

PUBLIC CLAMOR for railroad smoke abatement influenced several major railroad electrifications in urban areas. In New York City, smoke-abatement legislation hastened the terminal electrifications of the New York Central and the New Haven railroads. Similarly, the Illinois Central's Chicago suburban electrification was forced by a smoke-abatement ordinance. But these electrifications of extremely heavy commuter traffic were introduced for economic as well as ecological reasons.

Probably the only American electrification installed solely for purposes of smoke abatement was one opened in 1930 as part of a construction project for a new union passenger terminal in Cleveland, Ohio. The Cleveland Union Terminal electrification was unlike electrifications in other metropolitan areas in that it was confined to through passenger trains and terminal switching.

The Cleveland Union Terminal resulted from years of planning for a centrally located union station in Cleveland to replace several older stations on the lakefront and elsewhere. In 1912 Cleveland's celebrated real-estate and railroad financiers, the brothers Oris Paxton and Mantis James Van Sweringen, acquired an interest in property on Cleveland's Public Square as a potential site for such a terminal. By 1920 the New York Central and Nickel Plate railroads had reached agreement on the joint project. Engineering work started in 1922, and excavation began the following year.

The central structure of the new terminal was the 708-foot Terminal Tower, at the time of its completion second in height only to New York's Woolworth Building. In addition to a through passenger terminal, the structure included office space and provision for a rapid-transit terminal. A hotel, a department store, and three 18-story office buildings were also part of the project. Construction work was required to provide access routes to the new terminal for New York Central and Nickel Plate trains.

The project took seven years and required the demolition of 2200 buildings on the 104-acre terminal site. Foundations for the Terminal Tower were sunk as deep as 239 feet to reach bedrock.

An integral part of the project was the installa-

LIKE a great beacon, the illuminated 708-foot tower of Cleveland's Union Terminal stands above a network of steel catenary bridges in a nighttime view dating from March 1953. One of CUT's 2-C+C-2 electric locomotives waits to depart with a westbound train.—*Richard J. Cook.*

375

WE'RE at Linndale, Ohio, 6 miles west of Cleveland Union Terminal in September 1953. CUT electric No. 219 has just turned over New York Central train 407, the *Cleveland-St. Louis Special*, to No. 5271, one of the celebrated J-1a Hudsons.—*Herbert H. Harwood Jr.*

MOMENTS after its 4 p.m. departure from Cleveland's skyscraper Union Terminal, visible to the right of the locomotive, New York Central train 73, the Cleveland-Chicago *Prairie State*, rolls across the Cuyahoga River viaduct on an August afternoon in 1950. CUT motor No. 214 provides the power for the train.—*Richard J. Cook.*

tion of the 3000-volt D.C. electrification system which went into service when the new terminal opened on June 28, 1930. New York Central trains were electrically operated for 17 miles between Collinwood on the east side of Cleveland and Linndale on the west. Nickel Plate trains were powered by the electric motors over a 5-mile run from East 40th Street through the terminal to West 38th Street.

Three-phase power was supplied by the Cleveland Electric Illuminating Company at 11,000 volts. A 9000-kilowatt substation, located 3½ miles west of the terminal, and a 6000-kilowatt station, 7½ miles to the east, converted the power to 3000-volt D.C. for the contact wire. A compound-catenary overhead distribution system was supported by built-up steel bridges.

General Electric and Alco built the fleet of 22 CUT electric locomotives which were delivered in 1929 and 1930. The 80-foot, 204-ton, box-cab locomotives were the first to use the articulated 2-C+C-2 wheel arrangement, which subsequently was adopted by the New Haven Railroad for a series of high-speed passenger and freight electric motors, and by the Pennsylvania Railroad for its incomparable GG1.

Six D.C. traction motors, one geared to each driving axle through a nose-suspended mounting,

376

THE first of 22 Alco-GE motors for Cleveland Union Terminal was No. 1050, completed in the summer of 1929. The design of the cab reflected the influence of New York Central, CUT's principal owner, but the 2-C+C-2 wheel arrangement was the first of its kind. —*General Electric.*

(LEFT) On the last lap of a journey that also began behind electric power, New York Central train 51, the New York-to-Cleveland *Empire State Express*, heads out of East Cleveland behind motor No. 208 in June 1951. —*Herbert H. Harwood Jr.*

MOTOR No. 216 waits on track 15 in Cleveland Union Terminal for the 12:30 a.m. departure of combined NYC trains 89, the Cleveland-Chicago *Forest City*, and 5, a nameless Buffalo-Chicago overnight.—*Richard J. Cook.*

provided an hourly rating of 2900 h.p. and a starting tractive effort of 90,000 pounds. Maximum speed was 70 mph. Power collection was by means of pantographs. The double-ended units had M.U. control.

The CUT electrification gave a good account of itself from the beginning, but post-World War II dieselization, which eliminated the steam locomotive smoke problem, brought an end to electric operation in 1953. Except for one locomotive destroyed in a 1952 fire, the entire Alco-GE fleet was rewired for 600-volt, third-rail operation on New York Central's New York terminal electrification, where some remained in service until 1974.

BOX-CAB No. 1012 of the Mexican Railway (Ferrocarril Mexicano), built by General Electric in 1929, rolls a westbound freight through semi-tropical surroundings on the outskirts of Fortín de las Flores in the state of Veracruz. Ahead lie some of the sharpest curves and steepest grades to be found on any North American main line.—*Stan Kistler.*

13. Traction in Latin America

RAILROAD electrification was no more common in Latin America than it was in the United States and Canada. Of the more than two dozen countries south of the U. S. border with railroad systems, only three — Mexico, Brazil, and Chile — had significant mainline electrifications.

Unlike the remainder of the world, where the material and technology of railroad electrification largely came from European — and later, Japanese — sources, Latin America generally employed American practice and equipment. The high-voltage D.C. electrification system championed so vigorously in North America by the General Electric Company enjoyed widespread success in Latin America. Over 80 per cent of Latin America's more than 3000 miles of electrified trackage was operated with 1500-, 2400-, or 3000-volt D.C. catenary.

Mexico

MEXICO'S only mainline electrification was constructed during the 1920's by the Mexican Railway (FCM) on a portion of its Veracruz-Mexico City line that included some of the severest operating conditions in North America. From sea level at Veracruz, the Mexicano's 264-mile main line reached a maximum elevation of 8320 feet. By far the most difficult section of line, and that selected for the Mexicano's initial electrification, was the Maltrata Incline, a spectacularly scenic climb between Orizaba and Esperanza in the shadow of the 18,000-foot Orizaba Peak.

Within the 29.5-mile length of the Incline, the rails climbed 4025 feet through almost continuous curvature. Curves as sharp as 16.5 degrees were encountered frequently. Compensated for the severe curvature, the steepest grades on the line were equivalent to 5.25 per cent, and the overall ruling grade was 4.7 per cent.

Prior to electrification, traffic over the Incline was hauled by English-built double-ended 0-6-0+ 0-6-0 Fairlie steam locomotives. The Mexicano's largest 155-ton oil-fired Fairlies, which carried their entire weight on drivers, could pull 300 tons up the Incline. To meet schedule speeds, two locomotives were assigned to the line's normal eight-car passenger trains and still the 30-mile run took 2 hours 50 minutes. With two locomotives 360-ton freight trains took 4 hours to climb the Incline.

With its Fairlie steam power the Mexicano moved 14 trains with an aggregate weight of 4648 tons up the Maltrata grade on a record-breaking day in October 1921. But an increasing traffic density threatened to exceed the capacity of the operation. Both the use of larger, Mallet steam locomotives and the laying of a second track — the latter at an estimated cost of 5 million dollars — were considered, but electrification was the Mexicano's choice.

Studies made by General Electric in 1921 indicated that electrification of the Incline could postpone the need for double-tracking, and that the operating economies of electric operation would pay off its estimated 2- to 2.5-million-dollar

ALONGSIDE the Mexicano's curving, climbing rails from Orizaba to Esperanza, the scenery changes in the space of 30 miles from lush tropical vegetation to barren high desert. This view from the observation platform encompasses track, roadbed, catenary, steep mountainsides, and the valley where the train had been an hour earlier. Mexicano used to advertise the route as "the rail trip of a thousand wonders." —*Stan Kistler.*

BITING into the steep grade, motor No. 1011 leads a pair of Nacionales de Mexico F9's across Metlac Viaduct with the Veracruz-Mexico City day train in 1961. Once privately owned, the Mexicano became part of NdeM in 1960. —*Jim Shaughnessy.*

380

WESTBOUND toward the 4.7 per cent grade of the Maltrata Incline, motor 1002 rolls past an orange grove near Fortín de las Flores with a freight in February 1960.—*Stan Kistler.*

A TUG-OF-WAR was always good press. Mexicano No. 1002 took on a New York Central 2-8-2 at GE's Erie test track in 1924—and won, naturally.—*Courtesy of Railroad Magazine.*

cost in five or six years. Contracts for the work were awarded the following year, and electric operation began in 1924.

The Mexicano adopted the 3000-volt D.C. system that had been used successfully on the Milwaukee Road's electrification. Power was purchased from the Puebla Tramway, Light & Power Company's Tuxpango hydroelectric plant near Orizaba and converted to 3000 volts D.C. at a 6000-kilowatt substation at Maltrata. A simple-catenary overhead distribution system was supported by concrete poles or steel poles fabricated from old rails.

Initial motive power for the Mexicano electrification comprised 10 Alco-GE locomotives designed for freight and passenger service. Each 53-foot box-cab unit weighed 154 tons and was mounted on three articulated four-wheel trucks similar to those employed on earlier GE locomotives for the B&O, the Detroit River Tunnel Company, the BA&P, and the Milwaukee. Six GE-278-A motors, one driving each axle through twin cushion-type gears, gave the locomotives an hourly rating of 2736 h.p. and a maximum starting tractive effort of 92,700 pounds. Top speed was 40 mph. The locomotives were equipped with multiple-unit control and regenerative braking.

The first locomotive was delivered in the summer of 1924, and operation of the Orizaba-Esperanza grade was gradually converted to electric operation as additional units were delivered. Operation was completely electrified by the end of the year.

MOTOR 1002 appears again, this time coupled to a second box-cab at the head of an eastbound freight at Esperanza, waiting for the westbound passenger train to clear. Cafe-observation car *Huamantla* was a fixture on the Mexicano day train in the early 1960's. —*Jim Shaughnessy.*

BOX-CAB No. 1011 stands at Córdoba with a freight train in 1961. The Mexicano's electrics bore a strong resemblance to Milwaukee Road's GE-built box-cabs. In the late 1960's several of the electrics appeared in NdeM's diesel livery of red, Pullman green, and yellow.—*Victor Hand.*

STEAM and electric power work side by side at Orizaba in 1960. No. 216 is a comparatively youthful 2-8-0 built by Baldwin in 1946. Motor 1006, more than 20 years older than the Consolidation, would outlive the steamer by a number of years.—*Stan Kistler.*

MEXICO'S only other electrification was the Potosí Mining Company Railway, a short 30-inch-gauge line from Hacienda Robinson, near the city of Chihuahua, to Santo Domingo. A pair of 600-volt D.C. box-cabs built by GE in 1924 head a string of ore cars in this 1968 view.—*Donald Duke.*

Operating results of the Mexicano electrification were even better than anticipated. Because of their greater speed, capacity, and availability, the electric locomotives displaced the 23 steam locomotives previously used on the grade. The electric units were available for service 90 per cent of the time while steam power averaged only 30 per cent availability. A single electric could handle passenger trains that formerly had required two steam engines, although the electric weighed no more than one Fairlie. The average running time up the 30-mile grade was reduced by an hour to only 1 hour 50 minutes. Two steam engines had been limited to a 360-ton freight train, but two electrics were allowed 660 tons. They cut over an hour and a half from the 4-hour average running time with steam.

Electric power also reduced running times for downgrade operation. Fuel and water stops no longer were required, and regenerative braking eliminated the need for stops to cool wheels and brake shoes.

An analysis comparing traffic handled on the grade with steam locomotives in 1921 and with electric power in 1928 showed that the electrics were hauling 36 per cent greater tonnage with 40 per cent fewer train hours. Average tonnage per

A PAIR of Mexicano motors with an eastbound freight train wait in a siding between Orizaba and Córdoba for the Vera-cruz-Mexico City passenger train.—*Victor Hand.*

TWO generations of German-built electrics met at Coyolar, Costa Rica, on April 7, 1962, on the Pacific Electric Railway's 3-foot 6-inch gauge, 15,000-volt electrification. No. 25, built by AEG of Berlin in 1929, held the main with an eastbound train, while No. 21, a red-and-blue B-B unit built by Henschel in the mid-1950's, enters the siding.—*Frank Barry.*

EXPOSED air-cooling pipes, A1A trucks with roller-skate-size idler wheels, and sandboxes mounted on the trucks made the dark-green AEG units somewhat less than sleekly handsome.—*L. T. Haug.*

MORE awesome in appearance than in performance, FEalP's AEG motors could pull only 185 tons on the steep climb from Puntarenas up Costa Rica's western escarpment.—*Frank Barry.*

train had increased 50 per cent, and the average running time over the line had decreased 36 per cent. Operating and maintenance costs had been reduced by one half, despite the substantial increase in tonnage handled. It was estimated that the annual savings achieved by electrification approximated 26 per cent of the cost of the installation. This was a handsome pay-off on the Mexicano's 2.4-million-dollar investment.

The railway extended its catenary eastward toward Veracruz shortly after the initial section began electric operation. A 16-mile extension opened between Orizaba and Córdoba in 1926, and an 18-mile stretch from Córdoba to Paso del Macho was added in 1928. A 3000-kilowatt substation, supplied from the same Tuxpango hydroelectric plant, was constructed at Potrero, a few miles east of Córdoba, and two additional Alco-GE electric locomotives, identical to the first 10, were acquired in 1929.

The National Railways of Mexico absorbed the FCM in 1960. For many years the electrics continued to operate, but their role gradually was diminished by diesels. By 1974, all the electrics were out of service and the wire was removed from certain segments.

Yet even as the pantographs came down from the ex-FCM catenary, Mexican railroaders began studying plans for a new double-track railroad across the narrow Isthmus of Tehuantepec that would provide a 175-mile freight traffic "land bridge" bypassing the Panama Canal between the Gulf of Mexico and the Pacific Ocean. Electrification, supplied from a nearby hydroelectric plant, would power the new line.

Costa Rica

OPERATING the hemisphere's only 15,000-volt, 20-cycle, single-phase A.C. system with German-built motive power, Costa Rica's Pacific Electric Railway (FEalP) was unique among North and Central American electrifications. The 72-mile, 3-foot 6-inch gauge, former steam line was electrified between the Pacific port of Puntarenas and the Costa Rican capital of San Jose in 1929. The line's original locomotives, built by AEG of Berlin, were unorthodox box-cab units with an A1A+A1A wheel arrangement. These were supplemented during the 1950's by more conventional B-B box-cab units built by Henschel of Germany.

The FEalP was merged with Costa Rica's Atlantic Railway as the Ferrocarriles de Costa Rica (FECOSA) in 1977, and still newer electric power came to the line in 1982 as part of a 66-mile electrification of FECOSA's principal banana route between the Rio Frio and Puerto Limón on the Atlantic coast. The European 50-cycle Group installed the 25,000-volt, 60-cycle electrification, and France's Alsthom supplied a dozen new dual voltage locomotives that operated on both the new electrification and the former FEalP installation. Faced with mounting losses, the entire FECOSA system shut down in 1995.

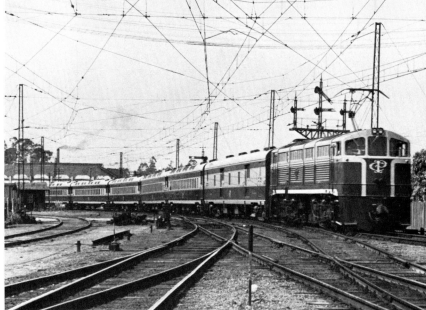

BRAZIL's Paulista Railway received a group of 5200 h.p. C-C box-cabs from GE of Brazil in 1967. (Above left) One of the units rumbles through Bras station in São Paulo on the Santos Jundiaí Railway with freight bound for the port city of Santos. (Above) A passenger train rolls through Rio Claro on Paulista's own broad-gauge track. (Left) At Luz Station in São Paulo a GE motor backs down onto a Paulista train bound for Bauru, more than 200 miles to the northwest in the rich coffee country of the state of São Paulo.—*Left and above left, Sergio Martire; above, General Electric of Brazil, from Sergio Martire.*

Brazil

BRAZIL was pre-eminent in Latin American electrification, accounting for nearly two-thirds of all steam railroad electrification in Central and South America. Brazilian railroads were handicapped by the lack of adequate supplies of coal and oil, and the wood fuel that was used almost universally was inefficient and costly. Electrification, which would permit the use of Brazil's abundant hydroelectric power resources, offered significant operating economies.

The first Brazilian road to electrify was the privately owned Paulista Railway, which operated an extensive system of both meter-gauge and 5-foot 3-inch-gauge lines into the rich coffee-producing region northwest of São Paulo in São Paulo State. Studies conducted in 1920 indicated that electrification might save the Paulista up to 85 per cent of its wood-fuel costs and as much as 65 per

cent of the overall operating costs. The Paulista decided to electrify its principal 5-foot 3-inch-gauge main line with a 3000-volt D.C. system.

Contracts for electrification of 27 miles between Jundiaí and Campinas were awarded to General Electric in 1920. Traffic in this initial electric zone was among the Paulista's heaviest, averaging 54 trains daily. Maximum grade in the zone was 1.8 per cent.

Power was supplied to the electrification by an 88,000-volt transmission line from the São Paulo Light & Power Company's Parnaíba hydroelectric plant. Three 1500-kilowatt motor-generator sets installed in a substation at Louveira supplied 3000-volt D.C. to the overhead catenary of the initial electric zone.

A dozen locomotives built by GE for the electrification were similar in mechanical and electrical details to the locomotives GE had supplied

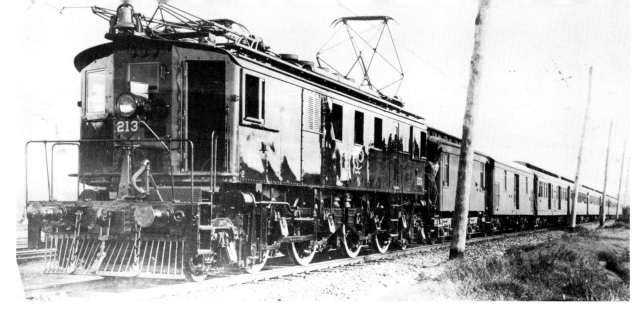

IN 1921 the Paulista Railway received two Baldwin-Westinghouse box-cab locomotives which resembled in their design and 1-B+B-1 wheel arrangement the same builder's earlier power for the New Haven and Boston & Maine electrifications. (Above) European-style buffers and screw couplings are the only noticeable departures from North American practice. (Right) The Pennsy suburban coaches barely visible in the background reveal that the location of the heavily retouched builder's photo is the East Pittsburgh works of the Westinghouse Company.—*Both photos, collection of H. L. Broadbelt.*

for the Butte, Anaconda & Pacific, the Canadian Northern, and the Milwaukee Road. Eight of the units, designed for freight service, were 100-ton B+B box-cab locomotives. Four passenger units were similar in design except for the provision of four-wheel guiding trucks at each end. In both designs, tractive forces were carried directly through the truck frames and the articulated joint, rather than through the carbody.

Each locomotive was powered by four 420 h.p. motors, one geared to each driving axle. Because of the additional space available in the broad-gauge trucks, the motors employed a self-ventilating feature instead of the customary separate blowers and ducts for cooling. Both designs had multiple-unit control and were equipped for regenerative braking. Maximum starting tractive effort for the freight units was 60,000 pounds, and their maximum safe speed was 28 mph. Passenger units were rated at 48,000 pounds starting tractive effort, and were allowed a maximum speed of 53 mph. The locomotives were equipped with vacuum braking systems and screw-and-buffer-type couplings to conform to the Paulista's European equipment.

Four more locomotives were supplied at the same time by Baldwin-Westinghouse. Two were

142-ton 1-B+B-1 passenger units, and the other two were 117-ton C+C freight locomotives.

Electric operation started in 1921, and the line was converted entirely by the following year. The estimated savings of electrification were substantiated by the operating results, and the Paulista rapidly extended its catenary northward from Campinas. By 1928 the railway was operating over 200 miles of broad-gauge main line between Jundiaí and Rincão with electric traction. In subsequent years the Paulista continued to expand its 3000-volt D.C. electrification, until more than 300 route-miles and 450 track-miles were under catenary.

GE continued to dominate the Paulista's electric motive-power roster. Notable among later locomotive purchases were 16 90-mph passenger units built in 1939 and 1947. They had a 2-C+C-2 wheel arrangement and a streamlined cab similar to GE's 1938 locomotives for the New Haven Railroad. Together with the Milwaukee Road and the Chicago South Shore & South Bend, the Paulista shared in the disposition of GE's celebrated 20 Little Joe locomotives built during 1948 and 1949 for the Soviet Union. Five of the 2-D+D-2 units, converted from Russian 5-foot gauge to the Paulista's 5-foot 3-inch

IN 1939 the Paulista purchased four GE passenger locomotives that were similar in styling and wheel arrangement to the New Haven's EP-4 and EF-3 2-C+C-2 locomotives.—*General Electric.*

ONLY the buffers, the vegetation, and the Companhia Paulista herald place the photograph of No. 380 in Brazil and not somewhere in Connecticut on the New Haven.—*General Electric.*

SAO PAULO is a long way from the Soviet Union—and a long way from South Bend, Ind., and Deer Lodge, Mont. Cold War tensions caused the cancellation of a Russian order for 20 5500 h.p. 2-D+D-2 locomotives, the "Little Joes." General Electric sold 3 to the South Shore, 12 to the Milwaukee Road, and the remaining 5 to the Paulista.—*Raymond DeGroote Jr.*

388

DURING the 1940's the Central of
Brazil bought 15 2-C+C-2 locomotives,
near-duplicates of those built for the
Paulista, from General Electric. Red-
and-yellow No. 2102 rolls northward
through São Paulo with a freight on
June 1, 1974.—*J. Parker Lamb.*

AN English Electric-built C-C locomotive lettered for **RFFSA** (Brazilian
Federal Railroad System) and the San-
tos-Jundiaí Railway pulls a merchandise train through São Paulo on June 1.
1974.—*J. Parker Lamb.*

FESTOONED with deadheads, a British-built (Metropolitan-Vickers) M.U. train of the Central
of Brazil curves past Maracaná Stadium on the outskirts of Rio de Janeiro.—*Brian Fawcett.*

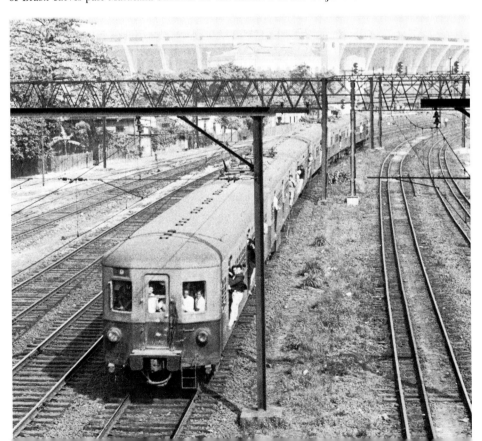

PLAIN-JANE in appearance but powerful (nearly 2000 h.p.) were 20 1-C+C-1 box-cabs built by GE for Brazil's meter-gauge Sorocabana Railroad in 1943.—*General Electric.*

gauge, were sold to the Brazilian line in 1951. More recent Paulista electric power has included C-C units built by General Electric of Brazil.

A SECOND major Brazilian broad-gauge electrification, also at 3000 volts D.C., was begun during the 1930's by the Central Railway of Brazil. Contracts were awarded during 1932 for a 15-million-dollar electrification project that included several of the railway's heavily traveled suburban lines radiating from Rio de Janeiro's Dom Pedro II station, as well as 90 miles of main line. Included in the project were two new hydroelectric plants to supply power.

Suburban operation out of Rio began in 1937.

Later extensions of electrification included the railway's São Paulo suburban services, and Central of Brazil eventually had 267 route-miles of electrified line. By 1950 the Central's suburban M.U.'s were hauling 190 million passengers annually. In addition to a substantial fleet of M.U.'s for suburban service, the Central's electric motive-power roster included a number of locomotives for through passenger and freight service. Some of the railway's earliest electric locomotives were light units built in the Central's own shops. During the 1940's General Electric delivered 15 streamlined 2-C+C-2 freight and passenger locomotives that were almost identical to those built for the neighboring Paulista Railway.

GENERAL ELECTRIC built an additional group of 1-C+C-1 locomotives for the Sorocabana in 1948. One of them, wearing blue-and-gray livery and lettered for the Paulista, brings a freight into São Paulo.—*J. Parker Lamb.*

ENGLAND meets the U.S. in Brazil as an English Electric C-C motor tows a GE 2-C+C-2 and a short freight into São Paulo from Jundiaí on 5-foot 3-inch gauge trackage.—*J. Parker Lamb.*

SOROCABANA'S latest electrics carry the builder's plate of General Electric of Brazil's Campinas works. A pair of the meter-gauge B-B locomotives stand on the plant's test track, displaying their green-and-white paint scheme.—*General Electric of Brazil, from Sergio Martire.*

A THIRD major broad-gauge electrification was started during the late 1940's by the Santos Jundiaí Railway, formerly the British-owned São Paulo Railway. Connecting with the Paulista Railway at Jundiaí, the Santos Jundiaí provided a broad-gauge connection to São Paulo and the port city of Santos for Paulista traffic. Following completion of an initial 54 route-miles of 3000-volt D.C. catenary, through electric operation over the two railroads began in 1952.

BRAZIL'S longest electrification was constructed by the meter-gauge Sorocabana Railroad, owned by the State of São Paulo. The 3000-volt D.C. system eventually encompassed more than 500 track-miles. An initial 87-mile section of electrified double track was opened between São Paulo and Santo Antonio in 1944. General Electric built 20 box-cab motors for the Sorocabana that were among the most powerful narrow-gauge electric locomotives ever built. Weighing 145 tons, the 1-C+C-1 units developed a continuous output of 1980 h.p. Twenty-six identical units were added several years later as the Sorocabana pushed its 3000-volt catenary westward toward the railway's terminus at Presidente Epitacio.

Two other Brazilian meter-gauge railways also installed 3000-volt D.C. electrifications. The Paraná-Santa Catarina Railway in the state of Paraná, southwest of São Paulo, installed about 50 miles of catenary, and the Leste Brasileiro Railway

TWO Sorocabana B-B motors work back-to-back to bring a freight into São Paulo on June 8, 1974.—*J. Parker Lamb.*

FIFTEEN Baldwin-Westinghouse 115-ton C+C freight locomotives were included in the Chilean State Railways' initial electric motive-power order. One of the units was photographed at Baldwin Locomotive Works before installation of electrical equipment.—*Collection of H. L. Broadbelt.*

electrified more than 100 miles of its line out of Salvador, Baía. Two other meter-gauge lines, the Campos do Jordão in São Paulo and the Centro Oeste near Rio de Janeiro, installed a total of some 350 miles of 1500-volt D.C. electrification.

Chile

SECOND only to Brazil in Latin American electrification was Chile, where electric operation, almost all of it high-voltage D.C., reached a total of well over 700 track-miles. As in Brazil, the availability of hydroelectric power contributed to Chilean interest in electric traction.

Chile's first electrified railroad was constructed in 1916 by the Bethlehem Chile Iron Mines Company as part of a mining project at Tofo, 300 miles north of Valparaíso on the Pacific Coast. As part of the development of the mines, Bethlehem constructed a standard-gauge electric railroad to haul iron ore to the nearby port of Cruz Grande. Although scarcely 2 miles from the port, the Tofo mines were 2200 feet above sea level, requiring 15 miles of railroad to cover the distance between the two points. Even at that, all but a mile of the railroad was laid at a uniform 3 per cent grade.

Contracts for the railroad's electrical equipment were awarded to the General Electric Company, and the technical features of the installation were almost identical to those of the Butte, Anaconda & Pacific. An overhead catenary system was energized with 2400-volt D.C. power supplied from the mining company's own steam power plant. Except for

their considerably greater size and output, the three 120-ton, 1370 h.p., B+B box-cab locomotives built for the line by GE were patterned after the BA&P locomotives in general arrangement and technical features.

CHILE'S largest electrification was opened in 1923 on the Chilean State Railways' 5-foot 6-inch-gauge system. Included in the initial electrification were the railway's 116-mile main line between the port of Valparaíso and Santiago, the capital, and a 28-mile branch to Los Andes. Within this electric zone the railway encountered some of its most severe operating conditions. In the mountains between Valparaíso and Santiago were 2.25 per cent grades and 10-degree curves. The capacity of the single-track line with steam power was rapidly being approached, and electrification offered an alternative to double-tracking the line.

In common with most of the Brazilian railroads that electrified, the Chilean State Railways adopted the popular 3000-volt D.C. system. Unlike almost every other contract for high-voltage D.C. electrification of the same period, however, the 7-million-dollar contract for the Chilean installation was landed by Westinghouse rather than GE.

Power was supplied to the railway from hydroelectric plants of the Chilean Electric Company at Maitenes and Florida, on the Maipo River, and from a steam plant at Mapocho. High-voltage transmission lines distributed power to five railway-owned substations, each of which was

AN EXPRESS from the port of Valparaíso rolls into the tall, arched trainshed of Mapocho Station, Santiago, behind a Chilean State Railways 1-C+C-1, one of six such 130-ton, 2460 h.p. locomotives built by Baldwin-Westinghouse in 1923.—*Ewing Galloway.*

equipped with two 2000-kilowatt motor-generator sets to produce 3000-volt D.C. for the contact wire. Power was distributed through a conventional overhead catenary system supported by steel and concrete poles.

Included in the electrification contract were 39 Baldwin-Westinghouse electric locomotives. Six were 130-ton 1-C+C-1 express passenger locomotives rated at 2250 h.p. and capable of a 62.5-mph maximum speed, and 11 were 80-ton, 1500 h.p., 56-mph B+B local passenger locomotives. Freight service was operated with 15 C+C road freight locomotives weighing 115 tons and rated at 1680 h.p. Seven B-B steeple-cab locomotives were purchased for switching service. The express passenger and

freight locomotives were equipped for regenerative braking.

The fleet of 39 electric locomotives displaced 110 steam locomotives. Whereas two steam locomotives required 40 minutes to take a 300-ton passenger train up the severe 12-mile Tabon grade, a single electric unit took the same train up in only 21 minutes. Freight-train tonnages were increased from 350 to 700 tons, and express passenger-train running times between Valparaíso and Santiago were cut by 50 minutes. During the first few years of electric operation annual savings of more than $840,000 in fuel costs were reported by the railway.

A later extension of the Chilean State's broad-gauge electrification southward from Santiago to

A FULL 50 years after it was delivered to the Chilean State Railways, Baldwin-Westinghouse unit No. 2107 was still hard at work in the yards at Santiago on March 20, 1972. Eleven of these 80-ton, B+B box-cab units were supplied for passenger-train duties.—*Ron Ziel.*

Chillán during the 1950's added 250 miles of 3000-volt D.C. catenary to the system. More recent extensions of Chilean electrification have pushed the catenary southward from Chillán to San Rosendo, and southwestward to the port city of Concepción. The original fleet of electric motive power was supplemented during the 1930's by similar Baldwin-Westinghouse units. During the late 1940's General Electric supplied a dozen new electric locomotives that included four near-duplicates of the New Haven-inspired streamlined 2-C+C-2 units built by GE during the same period for the Paulista and the Central of Brazil. Other modern electric power was supplied by Italian builders.

SEVERAL YEARS after the electrification of the Chilean State Railways, the meter gauge Transandine Railway installed a 3000-volt D.C. electrification on the Chilean portion of its extraordinarily difficult crossing of the Andes Mountains into Argentina. Rising to an altitude of 10,471 feet, the railway incorporated an Abt rack system on its main ascent, which included grades of 8 per cent. The 95-ton Swiss-built adhesion-and-rack locomotives employed on the 44-mile electrification were, understandably, equipped for regenerative braking.

The Tocopilla-El Toco Railroad, which extended inland from the Pacific port of Tocopilla, north of Antofagasta, to several nitrate mines, electrified 26 miles of its 3-foot 6-inch-gauge line in 1927 with a 1500-volt D.C. system. Two subsidiary 3-foot 6-inch-gauge mining railways at María Elena and Pedro de Valdivia comprising more than 150 miles of track also were electrified, but with 550-volt D.C. systems.

In 1926 another standard-gauge mining railroad in the same area, operated by the Chile Exploration Company at Chuquicamata, installed a third-rail and overhead 600-volt D.C. system that eventually covered more than 100 miles of track.

Argentina, Bolivia, Venezuela, and Cuba

ELSEWHERE in Latin America, electrification was scattered. At Buenos Aires, Argentina, extensive suburban electrifications were carried out by three railways beginning in 1916. Now operated by the Mitre, Sarmiento, and Urquiza railways of the Argentine Railways system, the three lines eventually completed 600- or 800-volt D.C. overhead and third-rail electrifications of more than 200 miles of track. Services were operated largely with multiple-unit equipment.

Bolivia boasted Latin America's first electrification. Opened in 1905 by the meter-gauge Guaqui-La Paz Railway, the 6-mile 600-volt D.C. system helped the railway overcome grades of 6.5 per cent entering La Paz.

In Venezuela the La Guaira & Caracas Railway completed a 23-mile 1600-volt D.C. installation between its two terminal cities in 1928.

The only other Latin American country to electrify was Cuba, where a 650-volt D.C. electrification of the United Railways of Havana, now almost entirely vanished, reached a total of 168 miles of track between 1907 and 1914. Both freight and passenger services were operated.

IN recent years European builders have supplied much of the Chilean State Railways' new electric motive power. Streamlined B-B locomotive No. 3021, shown on a passenger train at Santiago's Central Station in 1972, came from Italian builders.—*Ron Ziel.*

GENERAL ELECTRIC built eight 77-ton B-B road-switchers for the Chilean State Railways in 1949. The locomotives operated from the 3000-volt catenary in road service, but in switching service operated on 1500 volts produced by a motor-generator driven by the 3000-volt current from the catenary. The lower voltage provided better control at switching speeds.—*General Electric.*

THE Chile Exploration Company purchased three standard-gauge B-B units from GE in 1943 for use in its copper mines near Chuquicamata. The 80-ton locomotives drew 600-volt D.C. power by means of pantographs, third-rail shoes, and a 3000-foot extension cable. —*General Electric.*

A new era for North American railroad electrification began in the first year of the new century as Amtrak's *Acela Express* high-speed trains began operating at speeds up to 150 mph in the Boston-New York-Washington Northeast Corridor. Headed by power car No. 2005, one of the swift trains raced southward through Metuchen, N. J., during pre-inaugural testing in April 2000.—*Joseph M. Calisi.*

14. What future for electrification?

ONE of the earliest forerunners of the modern rectifier locomotive was this experimental rig shown at GE's Schenectady test track in 1912. The mercury-arc rectifiers on the flat car converted 10,000-volt A.C. to 1200-volt D.C. for box-cab No. 18.—*Industrial Photo Service.*

FOR most of the first half of the twentieth century the United States led the world in railroad electrification. By the time the last extension of the Pennsylvania's great electrification reached Harrisburg in 1938, the U. S. had some 2400 route-miles and more than 6300 track-miles operating under electric power, far more than any other country and more than 20 per cent of the world total.

In almost every instance U. S. electrification was a huge success. Running times were reduced. Tonnage capacities were increased. Electric locomotives delivered transportation at much lower fuel costs. Electric locomotive maintenance costs were a fraction of those for steam power, their availability was two or three times greater, and their effective service lives promised to be twice as long as those of steam locomotives. In many cases the savings resulting from electric operation were sufficient to repay the cost of electrification in as little as five years.

During these golden years of lengthening catenary and third rail, the wonders of railroad electrification were recounted frequently in the popular press, which predicted a coming age of nearly universal electric transportation. Representative of the popular enthusiasm for the subject was the title — somewhat premature as it turned out — of a 1915 *Scientific American* recap of developments in railroad electrification: "The Passing of the Steam Locomotive."

Articles in the railway trade press by such tireless electrification advocates as Westinghouse's F. H. Shepard and GE's W. D. Bearce and A. H. Armstrong, if more restrained and scholarly, were no less enthusiastic. Endless charts, tables, and graphs led always to the same conclusion: Electrification, at least of the principal trunk lines, was the way to a new era of efficiency and prosperity in railroading.

Typical was a 1920 *Railway Age* article by GE's Armstrong, whose thesis was clearly revealed by his title, "A Comparison of Electric and Steam Motive Power — From Which It Would Appear That the Steam Locomotive Has About Outlived Its Usefulness."

Yet despite all the enthusiasm, despite the seemingly unassailable arguments for electrification, despite the many successes, railroad electrification in North America failed to achieve the wide application that was so confidently predicted.

For every electrification project that became a reality, there was another that didn't. The roll call of the electrifications that existed only on paper can lead to fascinating speculation in what-might-have-been.

In 1909, for example, the Southern Pacific engaged Frank J. Sprague to study a 140-mile electrification of the railroad's crossing of the rugged Sierra Nevada. During the same period similar electrification studies were completed for SP's Siskiyou and Tehachapi lines. In all three cases, however, SP elected to stay with steam.

The Denver & Rio Grande Railroad came close to electrification. In late 1912 D&RG's directors announced a decision to install 115 miles of D.C. catenary over Soldier Summit between Salt Lake City and Helper, Utah, and another 88 miles over Colorado's Tennessee Pass. "We feel confident that the first electrically operated trunk line in this part of the mountain West will be the Rio Grande," said D&RG vice-president E. L. Brown of the 6-million-dollar project, "and that its trains will be in daily

AN artist's rendering contemplated what New York Central mainline electric power of the 1940's might have looked like. Specifications for the 5000-h.p., 2-C+C-2 locomotive called for an acceleration rate of 0 to 100 mph in less than six minutes with a 15-car passenger train. *From "A Practical Evaluation of Railroad Motive Power," by Paul W. Kiefer, Simmons-Boardman, 1948.*

TWO of the Pennsylvania's experimental mercury-arc rectifier locomotives, Nos. 4997 and 4998, accelerated through Thorndale, Pa., with eastbound tonnage in May 1952. Their success was followed by orders for similarly equipped GE units for New Haven and Virginian during the next few years, and by PRR's own order for 66 rectifier units in 1960.—*John E. Pickett.*

GENERAL ELECTRIC built six of these experimental E2b class locomotives for the Pennsylvania in 1951. They were based upon GE's ideas for a "standard" electric locomotive, and employed A.C. commutator motors rather than the newer technology of rectifiers and D.C. traction motors. Several of the units were demonstrated on the Great Northern and New Haven A.C. electrifications before going into PRR service. Demonstrators Nos. 5025 and 5026 were ready to leave the New Haven's Cedar Hill Yard at New Haven, Conn., with a train in the spring of 1952.—*Author's Collection.*

movement with this power by July 1, 1913." At the last moment, however, the railroad turned away from electrification, and steam continued to reign on the Rio Grande main line in the Wasatch and Sawatch ranges.

A year later the Santa Fe was studying electrification of its 23-mile Raton Pass grade between Trinidad, Colo., and Raton, N. Mex., which comprised both the steepest main line grades and the highest elevation on the AT&SF system. The Santa Fe, too, stayed with steam, and wires never went up on Raton Pass.

In 1923 the Santa Fe was again looking at electrification, this time for a proposed 25-million-dollar line between San Francisco and Los Angeles via Bakersfield. After the announcement of surveys for the project, little more was ever heard of either the new line or Santa Fe electrification.

Electrification of suburban services to alleviate the smoke nuisance of high-density service in congested urban areas was a particularly popular idea with the general public. The railroads serving New York and Philadelphia had almost entirely electrified their commuter services by the early 1930's, but elsewhere commuter electrification made little headway.

In 1910 the Massachusetts Legislature required the railroads serving Boston — the Boston & Maine, the Boston & Albany, and the New Haven, all of which operated extensive commuter services — to undertake electrification studies. The three railroads subsequently reported that about 590 track-miles of electrification would be required at a total cost of more than 40 million dollars. No one had that kind of money to offer and, except for those people riding the modest 1928 electrification of the Boston, Revere Beach & Lynn, Boston commuters continued to ride behind steam.

At Chicago, too, terminal electrification received considerable attention. As early as 1908, a special Mayor's committee considered the subject and recommended immediate electrification. Other studies followed, notable among them one completed in 1915 by a special committee of the Chicago Association of Commerce. It outlined a Chicago terminal electrification that would have comprised more than 3400 track-miles and would have cost almost 188 million dollars. Needless to say, no one had that kind of money either. Except for the Illinois Central's suburban electrification of the 1920's, Chicago's commuter railroads, too, stayed with steam.

399

(Left)
NEW HAVEN led the way with the first North American production order for mercury-arc rectifier locomotives. GE delivered ten of these 4000-h.p., EP-5 class units in 1955. Incorporating many of the practices and components of diesel-electric locomotives, they were fitted with the same GE 752 traction motors used in diesel-electric units. Waiting on the New Haven ready track in 1960, No. 375 is seen in the dramatic red, white, and black livery introduced a few years earlier by the New Haven's new Patrick McGinnis administration.—*Jim Shaughnessy.*

(Below)
THE New Haven's venture in rectifier motive power was followed almost immediately by a Virginian order for a dozen ignitron-rectifier units that were completed by GE during 1956-1957. Rated at 3300 h.p., the Virginian EL-C's employed the same road-switcher configuration that had proved so popular for diesel-electric power.—*General Electric.*

TWO Virginian EL-C's headed a westbound train of empty coal hoppers at Merrimac, Va., in March 1958. The big electrics ultimately had four owners. Rendered surplus by abandonment of the former Virginian electrification several years after its 1959 merger with Norfolk & Western, all but one of the EL-C's were sold to the New Haven, becoming Penn Central units following the New Haven's 1968 inclusion in the Penn Central merger.—*Herbert H. Harwood Jr.*

THE Pennsylvania replaced its entire roster of older electric freight units during 1960-1963 with a fleet of 66 of these GE-built Class E44 rectifier units that were essentially an upgraded version of the builder's earlier Virginian electrics.—*General Electric.*

THE highly productive E44's proved an extremely successful replacement for the Pennsylvania's older electrics. A pair of the big electrics led by No. 4448 headed a southbound freight through Metuchen, N. J., in the fall of 1969.—*J. C. Smith Jr.*

401

BY this time under Penn Central ownership, a train of the New Haven's rectifier M.U. cars of 1954 sped across the West River on the west side of New Haven, Conn., on its way into Grand Central from New Haven in 1970.—*William D. Middleton.*

Erie, the only major New York commuter railroad that didn't electrify, once planned to string catenary over its New Jersey and New York suburban lines. Cars bought during the late 1920's for the Erie's steam services were designed for conversion to electric operation, complete with windows for future motormen in each end.

Another eastern road that looked at electrification but never put up catenary was the Lehigh Valley, which in 1929 was reported to be making estimates for electrification of 75 miles of its double-track main line over the mountains between Mauch Chunk and Wilkes-Barre, Pa.

Of all the railroads that courted electrification but never reached the altar, none was a more constant suitor than Canadian Pacific. In 1894 *The Railway Age and Northwestern Railroader* reported that CP was investigating the feasibility of operating one of its mountain divisions with electric locomotives, utilizing hydroelectric power. Considering the state of electrification technology at the time, CP evidently

concluded — and wisely — that railroad electrification was not yet ready to take on the Rockies.

In 1910 Canadian Pacific again looked at electrification, this time for terminal operations on 2.2 miles of line with a steep grade against westbound traffic from Montreal's Windsor Station to Westmount. A detailed study for a 1200-volt D.C. electrification was made, but the project was canceled at the last moment.

Three years later another CP electrification scheme, this time in the Selkirk Mountains of British Columbia, came so close to reality that it was reported by the trade press to be actually under construction. Comprising 30 miles of the Rossland Subdivision between Rossland and Castlegar, the project included grades as severe as 4 per cent. A 2400-volt D.C. system was planned. In 1914 a similar electrification was planned for CP's proposed new 5-mile Connaught Tunnel at Rogers Pass near Glacier, also in the Selkirk Mountains. Once again, CP stopped short of construction, and neither of the high-voltage D.C. installations went in.

Facing page

(Top) NEW HAVEN also pioneered the use of rectifier M.U. cars with a fleet of 100 cars built in 1954 for the railroad's New York commuter services by Pullman Standard's Worcester (Mass.) plant. A train of seven of the new cars is seen under the distinctive triangular catenary of the New Haven's original electrification section between Woodlawn, N. Y., and Stamford, Conn.—*Penn Central Company.*

(Middle) IN 1958 the Pennsylvania acquired six new MP85 ignitron-rectifier M.U. cars based upon the Budd Company's Pioneer III stainless-steel car design that served as prototypes for a fleet of Silverliner M.U.'s that ultimately numbered in the hundreds. Two of those original cars were westbound to Paoli on the PRR Main Line at Radnor, Pa., in April 1964.—*William D. Middleton.*

(Bottom) CAPABLE of 85-mph speeds, the Pennsylvania's Silverliner M.U.'s proved capable of holding down fast intercity runs as well as commuter service. A westbound Silverliner train, by this time operating under Penn Central colors, raced westbound from Philadelphia to Harrisburg at Bird-in-Hand, Pa., during a December 1969 snow storm.—*Fred W. Schneider III.*

GENERAL MOTORS DIESEL, LTD. illustrated the ease with which a diesel builder could produce a straight electric locomotive when it built five motor-generator units for a new Iron Ore Company of Canada commercial frequency, single-phase electrification of its Carol Mining Division Railway at Labrador City, Labrador, in 1963. The 1200-h.p. units were essentially an all-electric version of GM's standard diesel-electric switcher. Operating under automatic control, one of them pulled a 19-car string of ore hoppers from the loading pocket to the crusher in 1969.—*Iron Ore Company of Canada.*

BASED upon electrification technology licensed from Sweden's ASEA, GM's Electro-Motive Division ventured into the electric traction market in 1975 with two prototype units for anticipated U. S. electrification. The carbody of a GM6C prototype was lowered onto its six-wheel trucks at Electro-Motive's McCook, Ill., plant early in 1975.—*Electro-Motive Division, General Motors.*

THE design of Electro-Motive's GM6C prototype No. 1975 clearly reflected a high degree of conformance to diesel-electric practice and the use of standard diesel-electric components. Rated at 6000 h.p., the unit was capable of a short-time starting tractive effort of over 125,000 pounds. After extensive engineering and field tests, the prototype was placed in revenue service on Penn Central.—*Electro-Motive Division, General Motors.*

A second Electro-Motive prototype, introduced in 1976, was the 10,000-h.p. GM10BH, which employed a B-B-B wheel arrangement and was capable of a short-time starting tractive effort of almost 140,000 pounds. Assigned the road number 4976, the big electric was eastbound with a fast trailer train, crossing over from Conrail's Royalton Branch to the Amtrak main line at Roy interlocking in Middletown, Pa., in 1980.—*Dan Cupper.*

In 1923, a decade later, a CP Rocky Mountain electrification once more was reported near reality. The railway surveyed hydroelectric power sites on the Columbia River, and it was confidently reported by *Electric Railway Journal* that work would begin the following year. In 1924 CP president E. W. Beatty told the press that "serious thought" was being given to the proposal, and then talk of Canadian Pacific electrification faded away once again.

Several of the railroads that did electrify had plans for further electrification that were never fulfilled. The New Haven, of course, was ready to extend its single-phase catenary all the way to Boston when the financial reverses of 1913 ended the catenary at New Haven; and the Pennsylvania, which completed the greatest of all North American electrifications, was never able to accomplish its much-discussed extension of catenary across the Alleghenies to Pittsburgh.

Electrification of the west end of New York Central's subsidiary Boston & Albany was recommended by the Central's engineers in 1923, when the railroad was completing major improvements in the Albany (N. Y.) area. Included in the pro-

GENERAL ELECTRIC'S E50 rectifier locomotives for Ohio's coal-hauling Muskingum Electric anticipated a new era of standardized electric locomotives, with trucks, traction motors, and other components identical to those of diesels. Within the E50's road switcher carbody a bank of sophisticated silicon-diode rectifiers converted commercial frequency A.C. power to low-voltage D.C. for the traction motors of the 204-ton, 5000-h.p. unit.—*General Electric.*

posed 3000-volt D.C. electrification were 100 miles of B&A main line through the Berkshires between Albany and Springfield, Mass., and the Hudson River Connecting Railroad then under construction westward from a junction with the B&A near Niverville, N. Y., across a new Hudson River bridge at Castleton to the Central's new Selkirk Yard south

ELECTRIFIED with a 25,000-volt, 60-cycle, single-phase A.C. system, the 78-mile Black Mesa & Lake Powell coal-hauling line in Arizona was widely viewed as a prototype for future western electrification when it opened in 1973. Two of the line's big GE E60 units pulled a coal train at Page, Ariz., in 1974.—*Donald Duke.*

of Albany. Selkirk Yard, the largest yard in the world at the time of its completion, and other yards in the Castleton-Ravena area also would have been electrified.

Electrification of the New York Central westward to Buffalo or Cleveland was a recurring proposal. In 1930, for example, *The Business Week* reported that NYC had completed detailed plans for a 150-million-dollar New York-to-Buffalo electrification. Nothing came of either the B&A or the mainline proposals, however, and the Central's use of electric traction remained confined to Grand Central and the New York commuter zone, the Detroit River tunnel, and Cleveland Union Terminal.

In 1930 the Baltimore & Ohio, which had started it all with the 1895 Baltimore tunnel electrification, was rumored to be ready to acquire control of the Reading-Jersey Central route between New York and Philadelphia and then electrify the line all the way between New York and Washington, paralleling the rival Pennsylvania's electrified track. This project, too, failed to materialize.

In the West, extension of Great Northern's Cascade Tunnel electrification westward to Seattle was studied on several occasions. A GN electrification proposal of 1913 would have put wire over a planned 530-mile line extending westward from New Rockford, N. Dak., to Lewistown, Mont. Neither the new line nor the electrification ever went in.

406

DEVELOPED for the Black Mesa & Lake Powell electrification, GE's E60 rectifier locomotive design was later adopted for Amtrak Northeast Corridor service, Mexican National Railways electrification, and the Deseret Western coal line electrification in Utah and Colorado. The big units weighed 210 tons and had a one-hour rating of 5600 h.p.—*Donald Duke.*

GENERAL ELECTRIC came up with a smaller rectifier locomotive for the Texas Utility Company's coal line electrification in 1976. GE built seven of these 4000-h.p. E25B thyristor-controlled rectifier units for the northeast Texas operation.—*General Electric.*

NEW MEXICO'S Navajo Mine Railroad acquired two GE E60CP units at bargain basement prices for the 1984 electrification of its 14-mile coal line. Originally built for Amtrak, they had subsequently hauled trains for NJ Transit before going west to the New Mexico line. One of them headed a train at the Navajo Mine coal loadout in May 1987. The line's unusually high catenary provided ample clearance during coal loading operations.—*Warren J. Kiefer.*

407

A fourth electrified western coal road opened in 1984 when the Deseret Western Railway began operating its 35-mile mine-to-power-plant line in northern Utah and Colorado. E60C units WFU1 and WFU2, the line's total motive power roster, headed a train downgrade in Holum Pass near the Deserado Mine in Colorado in 1985.—*Warren J. Kiefer.*

During the 1920's and early 1930's, when electrification was making some of its greatest gains in North America, several intriguing proposals for large-scale electrification were put forth.

In a 1920 article for the *General Electric Review,* GE's W. B. Potter considered the idea of complete

railroad electrification throughout what he called the "Super-Power Zone" of the northeastern U. S., extending from Washington to Boston and inland as far as Harrisburg and Albany. Looking ahead to the soon-realized concept of an interconnected power generation and distribution system, Potter

GENERAL MOTORS CANADA built seven of these GF6C C-C electrics for the British Columbia Railway's Tumbler Ridge coal line. Rated at 6000 h.p., the units employed thyristor-controlled rectifier technology from Sweden's ASEA.—*Warren J. Kiefer.*

AMBITIOUS plans for National Railways of Mexico (FNM) electrification ran into trouble, and opening of an initial 153-mile section between Mexico City and Queretaro was delayed for more than a decade. Soon after some electric operation finally began, E60C No. EA034, another E60C, and diesels headed a southbound freight north of Mexico City in April 1994.—*J. W. Swanberg.*

AFTER only a few years of operation, FNM ended electric operation and put its fleet of E60C electrics up for sale. U. S. coal road electrifications were the beneficiaries. Texas Utility Company acquired three of the big E60C electrics for its northeast Texas lines, two more went to the Deseret Western, and six of them replaced the Black Mesa & Lake Powell's original E60's. Still in its original colors, former FNM unit EA031 headed a Deseret Western coal train ready to depart from the Deserado Mine coal loadout near Rangeley, Colo., for the generating plant at Bonanza, Utah, in 1999.—*Warren J. Kiefer.*

(Top) PLAGUED by technical problems, the high-speed Metroliner equipment developed by the Pennsylvania was never able to fully meet its performance objectives, but the speedy trains proved there was a market for high-speed rail in the Northeast Corridor and paved the way for a continuing development of high-speed service in the corridor. Penn Central's northbound Washington-New York *Metroliner* 106 leaned into a Bowie, Md., curve at high speed in February 1971.—*William D. Middleton.*

(Middle) A fleet of 26 6000-h.p., 120-mph E60CP and E60CH units built by GE during 1974-1975 was intended to power Amtrak's Northeast Corridor high-speed services. Tracking problems, however, limited the units to a 90-mph maximum speed. Amtrak sold some, limited the remainder to slower corridor trains, and began a new search for its next generation of high-speed motive power. E60CP No. 968, a head-end power version, raced past the Landover (Md.) substation with northbound train 176, the Washington-Boston *Senator,* in October 1979.—*William D. Middleton.*

(Bottom) BASED upon successful trials with the Swedish-built Rc4 unit leased from the Swedish National Railways, the 5800-h.p., 125-mph AEM7 proved to be the Northeast Corridor high-speed locomotive that Amtrak was looking for. AEM7 No. 900, the first delivered of a fleet that grew to a total of 52, rolled through the Wilmington, Del., station with the Electro-Motive dynamometer car and a test train in January 1980.—*William D. Middleton.*

UNDETERRED by heavy snow, AEM7 No. 902 accelerated out of New Haven, Conn., with southbound Boston-Washington train 173, the *Yankee Clipper,* in March 1992.—*J. W. Swanberg.*

envisioned the region's 30,000 track-miles under catenary. He estimated that 6 billion kilowatt-hours annually from the regional power grid would transport 170 billion gross ton-miles at a net fuel savings of 14 million tons of coal.

In 1923 a grandiose 76-million-dollar scheme was put forth by promoters for the Staley System of electrified railway, an entirely new 1307-mile line extending from southern Colorado through New Mexico and Arizona to Mexico and California. The principal traffic for the line would have been coal from southern Colorado, which would move to eastern U. S. markets through a new deepwater port on the Gulf of California. Through regenerative braking, the promoters claimed, coal trains descending to tidewater from coal fields at altitudes of 6000 feet or more would return more than enough power to the catenary to haul the empties back to the mines. The Interstate Commerce Commission, however, thought the company's estimates of revenues were too high and of expenses too low. An ICC certificate of public convenience and necessity was denied, and the project was soon forgotten.

THE powerful AEM7's proved easily capable of 125-mph maximum speeds, and could produce a maximum starting tractive effort of 51,500 pounds. Headed by AEM7 No. 913, Amtrak's northbound Washington-Boston train 178, the *Merchants Limited,* was a few miles west of Baltimore in August 1989.—*William D. Middleton.*

Probably the most comprehensive and specific proposal for large-scale U. S. electrification was advanced in a 1936 report on railroad electrification by the Federal Power Commission. The FPC study, part of a broad survey of the power industry and its potential markets, suggested that electrification of an additional 12,000 miles of track on 20 U. S. railroads was economically feasible.

The FPC study and all the other proposals proved to be no more than idle speculation. Scarcely two years after the expansive FPC report rolled off the presses in Washington the Pennsylvania Railroad completed the last major extension of its catenary into Harrisburg, Pa. With that, railroad electrification in North America came to a halt. U. S. electrification had peaked out with scarcely 6300 track-miles — about 2 per cent of the U. S. total — under electric operation.

What went wrong? Why had electrification failed to achieve its potential?

A persistent problem throughout the electrification era was the failure to standardize systems and equipment. Except for Great Northern's lone attempt at a three-phase system and DT&I's unique 22,000-volt experiment, A.C. advocates had at least settled on the 11,000-volt, 25-cycle, single-phase system as a standard. D.C. advocates, however, offered low-voltage third rail systems at 600 volts and high-voltage catenary systems at 1200, 1500, 2400, and 3000 volts.

DISPLACED from the Northeast Corridor's *Metroliner* schedules by AEM7/Amfleet equipment, a number of the Metroliner cars were reassigned to Amtrak's Philadelphia-Harrisburg schedules. A three-car Metroliner train operated as eastbound Harrisburg-Philadelphia train 616 at Mount Joy, Pa., in April 1984. Heat- and dust-sensitive equipment had been relocated to rooftop pods in an attempt to improve reliability of the equipment.— *William D. Middleton.*

AMTRAK sent the celebrated GG1 locomotive out in style. GG1 No. 4935 was refinished in its original Pennsylvania Railroad colors and striping for its last several years of operation. On October 27, 1979, the handsome electric raced past the Landover (Md.) interlocking and substation, southbound to Washington and running "on time" with *Metroliner* 105 from New York.— *William D. Middleton.*

THE GG1's very last run for Amtrak came on April 26, 1980, when No. 4935 headed train 41, the westbound *Broadway Limited*, from New York to Harrisburg. Late in the afternoon the big electric swept around the curve at Gap, Pa., with the town's famous clock tower in the background.—*Fred W. Schneider III.*

THE most visible element of the New York Metropolitan Transportation Authority's rehabilitation and modernization of the Long Island Rail Road was a fleet of 770 advanced M-1 Metropolitan M.U. cars built by Budd and General Electric during 1968-1972. A train of new M-1's was en route from Babylon to Penn Station, New York, west of Lynbrook, N. Y., in May 1970.—*William D. Middleton.*

Even where there was agreement on current and voltage, there were wide variations in power distribution systems and electric motive power. Third rails came in both overrunning and underrunning varieties, and their dimensions varied widely from one railroad to another. Similarly, there were wide variations in the design and construction of overhead distribution systems. Although there was some limited standardization of apparatus, electric motive power generally was custom-designed for each railroad just as steam power was. Thus the interchangeability and the economies of standardization were lost.

The seriousness of the standardization problem was recognized as early as 1910 by electrification pioneer George Westinghouse. Looking ahead to the future merging of expanding electric zones, Westinghouse urged the adoption of a standard voltage and frequency, the establishment of uniform standards for the location of conductors, and uniformity of control equipment.

In an address to a joint meeting of American and British mechanical engineering societies Westinghouse said: "I can only repeat, and earnestly recommend to the serious consideration of railway engineers and those in authority the pressing need of determining the system which admits of the largest extension of railway electrification and of a prompt selection of those standards of electrification which will render possible a complete interchange of traffic in order to save expense in the future and to avoid difficulties and delays certain to arise unless some common understanding is arrived at very shortly."

Westinghouse's advice went largely unheeded, and many roads, confused by the inability of the experts to agree on the relative merits of rival systems and designs, simply held back from electrification.

Despite all the fervor with which it had been carried on, the battle between the various electrification systems ultimately proved to have been a contest over trifles. Regardless of which system was chosen,

INBOUND from Port Washington to New York as late afternoon train 465, a train of M-1's rounded a sharp curve on single-track between Port Washington and Plandome in May 1970.—*William D. Middleton.*

THE former New York Central third-rail lines north of New York had passed from Penn Central hands to Conrail just a few months before this long Hudson Division express made up of GE-built M-1's headed north through Hastings-on-Hudson in July 1976.—*Harre W. Demoro.*

INBOUND from North Brewster, N. Y., to Grand Central, a train of Metro North M-1's approached Brewster station in September 1996. The train operated over the railroad's newest stretch of third rail, completed between North White Plains and North Brewster in 1984. —*William D. Middleton.*

415

the differences in the results of electrification turned out to be insignificant. The simple truth of the matter was that *any* well-designed electrification produced enormous improvements in operations.

A far greater problem for most railroads was the cost of electrification. Typically, total costs ranged upward from $50,000 a route-mile to several times that amount, even in 1920 dollars. In addition to the costly distribution systems themselves, entirely new motive-power fleets had to be acquired. Transmission lines and substations had to be installed and sometimes, particularly during the early years, the lack of adequate commercial power supplies obliged the railroads to build their own generating plants.

Despite the costs, electrification progressed at a brisk pace throughout the 1920's, when railroad traffic levels were high and earnings were good. The depression soon dried up the capital required for electrification, and even the mighty Pennsylvania was able to complete its massive electrification only on the strength of RFC and PWA loans.

By the time the depression was over and traffic began to pick up, World War II intervened — only temporarily it was thought — to bring the continuing expansion of U. S. electrification to a halt.

While the war delayed any additional electrification, it helped to accelerate some technological developments that promised to make it more attractive than ever before.

By far the most important of these was the development of practical rectifiers for railroad motive power, an advance that resolved several long-standing problems. For a half century the industry had debated the relative merits of single-phase A.C. vs. D.C. for railroad electrification. High-voltage, single-phase A.C. provided substantial efficiencies in power distribution, while low-voltage D.C. series traction motors offered the best control and performance characteristics. The rectifier, which permitted the efficient conversion of A.C. to D.C. power on a car or locomotive, made it possible to combine the best of both systems. Previously, too, the large single-phase motors used for A.C. electrification had required the use of low-frequency power. With the use of rectifiers, the catenary could be energized with 60-cycle current directly from the commercial power grid, eliminating the costly substations, conversion equipment, and separate transmission lines that had previously been required for A.C. electrification.

Rectifiers had been around for a long time. General Electric had experimented with a mercury-arc rectifier power supply for electric locomotives as early as 1912, while the following year Westinghouse, together with the Pennsylvania and the New Haven, had outfitted a New Haven M.U. car with an experimental mercury-vapor rectifier. The technology proved too fragile for railroad use, but by

NEW YORK'S MTA and the Connecticut Department of Transportation supplied the former New Haven commuter lines with a fleet of M-2 Cosmopolitan M.U.'s equipped for both third-rail D.C. and overhead catenary A.C. operation. The system passed through Penn Central and Conrail ownership before becoming part of Metro-North Railroad on January 1, 1983. A train of Metro-North M-2's, operating as late morning shopper's special train 6525 from New Haven to Grand Central, sped through Rye, N. Y., under the distinctive triangular catenary of the original New Haven electrification in December 1991.—*J. W. Swanberg.*

the end of World War II a considerably advanced technology was available, and a 1949 Pennsylvania trial with ignitron mercury-arc rectifiers on an M.U. car proved highly satisfactory.

Still another handicap to widespread electrification had been the anticipated unbalanced power loads that would have resulted from powering large single-phase railroad electrifications from the three-phase commercial power system. The growth of the electric power market after World War II, however, minimized this potential problem, and by 1960 the threat of unbalanced railroad power demands ceased to be a major deterrent to electrification.

416

Even dieselization, the principal rival to electrification, brought developments that were seen as helpful to electric power as well. Since they were, after all, simply electric locomotives that carried their own power plant with them, diesel-electrics incorporated a number of components that were common to straight electric power as well. Thus, the mass production techniques that the diesel-electric builders applied to locomotives for the first time produced rugged, efficient, low-cost traction motors, trucks, drive systems, controls, and other components that were equally applicable to straight electric locomotives.

Diesels could help in another way, too. In the pre-diesel era the full economic advantages of electrification could be realized only through the complete replacement of steam power and its costly servicing and maintenance facilities. To do this, electrification had to include yard tracks, branches, and other lightly used trackage at great additional cost. But by operating such secondary trackage with diesel-electric power, which required no expensive duplicate servicing facilities, it became possible to confine electrification to the main running tracks.

With all of these new advantages, together with the new technologies that were now available, there was much talk of renewed electrification in the years immediately after World War II. Surveying the potential market for electrification shortly after the war, Earl Bill, manager of General Electric's railroad rolling stock division, identified electrification projects totaling some 1200 route-miles that were then under consideration. Most were additions to existing electrifications, including an extension of Pennsylvania catenary from Harrisburg to Pittsburgh, the New Haven's long-deferred New Haven-Boston electrification, extension of Great Northern's Cascade electrification into Seattle, and — the longest of all — a New York Central electrification from Harmon, N. Y., to Buffalo. An entirely new electrification under discussion would have put the Denver & Rio Grande Western under catenary through the Rockies.

In the Pacific Northwest there was talk of low power rates from federal hydroelectric power plants and government investment to supply power at the trolley wire on as many as 8000 miles of line. Similarly, the Tennessee Valley Authority was looking at railroad electrification as a new market for its power generation plants.

"Currently there is enough interest in electrification so that should the projects materialize into actualities the electric locomotive manufacturers would be unable to handle the business," commented Bill.

INBOUND to the old Lackawanna Terminal in Hoboken from NJ Transit's Morris & Essex Lines, a train of Jersey Arrow III M.U.'s passed stored trains waiting for the afternoon rush hour just outside the terminal platforms in May 1995.—*William D. Middleton.*

BOUND for Penn Station, New York, from Trenton, N. J., in May 1995, a long train of NJ Transit Jersey Arrow III's hurried through Harrison, N. J., on Amtrak's Northeast Corridor. Just behind the train is the massive steelwork of the complex Passaic River drawbridges.—*William D. Middleton.*

OUTBOUND from New York's Penn Station, an evening rush hour NJ Transit train emerged from the Passaic River drawbridge to enter Penn Station, Newark, in May 1995. The train of Jersey Arrow III M.U.'s was en route to Trenton over Amtrak's Northeast Corridor.—*William D. Middleton.*

AN interesting contrast to the multiple track and intense traffic of the Northeast Corridor is the single-car NJ Transit train that shuttles over single track to link Princeton, N. J., with the corridor trains at Princeton Junction. Jersey Arrow III car No. 1316 was just beginning a shuttle trip from the junction in May 1995.—*William D. Middleton.*

While there was no immediate action toward any of these new electrifications, there were some interesting applications of many of the new technologies on existing electrifications. Both of the principal suppliers of electric motive power, General Electric and Westinghouse, soon came forth with new experimental units for the Pennsylvania that were seen as prototypes for the anticipated new electrification market.

During 1951 General Electric delivered six E2b class units based upon ideas its engineers had developed for a "standard" locomotive for new U. S. electrification. The car body design and B-B wheel arrangement closely resembled contemporary diesel-electric practice. Instead of employing the new rectifier technology, with D.C. traction motors, GE used A.C. commutator motors similar to those employed on earlier Pennsylvania electrics.

Based upon the Pennsylvania's encouraging results from its 1949 ignitron-rectifier tests, the same technology was selected for a pair of experimental two-unit locomotives delivered by Baldwin-Lima-Hamilton and Westinghouse during 1951 and 1952.

Both experimental designs worked well, but the Westinghouse ignitron-rectifier design was particularly successful. While the Pennsylvania itself delayed the replacement of its aging electric freight locomotive fleet for almost another decade, other roads soon adopted the new electric locomotive technology.

Despite the Westinghouse success with its experimental ignitron-rectifier locomotives for the Penn-

sylvania, General Electric came up with all of the orders. The first production model rectifier locomotives to operate in the U. S. were the ten 4000-h.p. FP-5 electrics completed by GE for the New Haven in 1955. The Virginian followed suit a few years later with its order for a dozen 3300-h.p. EL-C GE ignitron-rectifier units. And in 1960 GE began deliveries of the 66 4400-h.p. E44 class ignitron-rectifier units for the Pennsylvania that would represent one of the builder's last big orders for electric motive power.

Rectifier technology was equally applicable to M.U. cars. The New Haven had been the first road to try rectifier M.U.'s on more than an experimental basis with its 1954 order for 100 ignitron-rectifier cars for its New York suburban services. The Pennsylvania acquired its first rectifier-equipped M.U. cars in 1958, and over the next decade large fleets of similar equipment were ordered for both Pennsylvania and Reading commuter services at Philadelphia, and for the Pennsylvania's New Jersey services. Rectifier M.U. cars proved so successful in regular service that the Pennsylvania adopted exceptionally powerful M.U. cars instead of locomotive-drawn trains for its Northeast Corridor high-speed Metroliner program of the late 1960's.

Despite the prodigious performance of this advanced electric motive power, U. S. electrification languished. Not a single one of the new electrifications that had seemed so likely at war's end ever went ahead, while elsewhere in the world the new

419

INBOUND from Paoli, Pa., on SEPTA's R5 Line, eastbound train 546 loaded passengers at Wayne, Pa., on the former PRR main line in October 1988. The two-car Silverliner IV train would pass through downtown Philadelphia in SEPTA's Center City Commuter Tunnel to continue outbound on the former Reading line to Doylestown, Pa.—*William D. Middleton.*

rectifier-based, industrial frequency technology had contributed to an enormous growth in electrification. By the early 1970's the U. S., which had once led the world in electric operation, had declined to 17th place behind even Czechoslovakia, Austria, Norway, and Brazil. The Soviet Union, which now led the world with almost 22,500 electrified route-miles, had almost 20 times the U. S. electric mileage.

What had impeded this new era of U. S. electrification?

A simple answer to that question was: the diesel-electric.

But there was more to it than that, for the failure of electrification was linked as well to such considerations as the availability of capital, the prospective availability and cost of electric power, and the willingness of railroad managers to commit to such a costly, long-term, and — ultimately — uncertain investment.

The diesel-electric locomotive, of course, was the primary force that frustrated electrification. When

SEPTA Regional Rail trains met in the new Market East station on the authority's Center City Commuter Tunnel in December 1985. The tunnel linked the former Pennsylvania and Reading commuter rail systems into an integrated regional system.—*William D. Middleton.*

the Pennsylvania undertook what proved to be the last major electrification in the 1930's, diesel motive power was still very much an unproven experiment. But by the time the war was over there was little doubt about what the diesel-electric could do.

The war had left the railroads with some hard choices to make. With plants and equipment worn out by the demands of wartime traffic, they were faced with large and costly renewal and replacement requirements. At the same time, the capital available to meet these needs was limited.

Under these conditions, dieselization was an attractive investment. From a strictly operational point of view, electrification had a significant advantage over either steam or diesel-electric power in both performance characteristics and operating costs. But the diesel, itself a self-contained form of electrification, afforded many of these same operating efficiencies at a significantly lower capital cost. Some data developed by GE's Earl Bill from a 1946 study of New York Central motive power modernization between Harmon and Buffalo is revealing.

The Central's study, which compared capital and operating costs for electric, diesel-electric, and modern steam power, projected annual operating and fixed charge savings of more than 2.9 million dollars for electric power over those for steam. Comparable savings for diesel-electric operation were slightly less than 1.8 million dollars. Although this would seem to give a clear advantage to electrification, the picture changed when a return on investment was considered. A Harmon-Buffalo conversion

to modern steam power would have cost the Central an estimated 80.5 million dollars, while dieselization would have cost 104.5 million dollars and electrification 135 million dollars. At these estimated costs the Central's return on the excess cost of electrification over modern steam power would have been 5.39 per cent, while the return would have risen to 7.5 per cent for the excess cost of dieselization over steam power. When the relative investments required for electrification and dieselization were compared, the return on the excess first cost of electrification was only 3.75 per cent.

With numbers like this and investment capital in short supply, the New York Central began a conversion to diesel-electric motive power. For other roads considering electrification, the results were more or less the same, and none of the expansive electrification projects being talked about at war's end ever moved beyond the drawing board.

Not only had railroad electrification ceased to grow, it began to decline as well. Here, too, the diesel-electric was often the culprit.

One decided advantage of the diesel-electric over steam power was its ability to run through over long distances without changes of power. Electrifications that had been installed primarily for smoke abatement in long tunnels impeded the efficiencies of run-through operation, while diesel exhaust proved to be manageable through improved tunnel ventilation systems. The Boston & Maine ended electric operation through the long Hoosac Tunnel as early as 1946; and before the end of the 1950's, the B&O's

ON a warm July morning in 1995 an Outbound R1 Line train for the Philadelphia International Airport pulled away from the platforms at SEPTA's handsome new University City station, completed earlier that year.—*William D. Middleton.*

THE completion of a SEPTA Regional Rail extension to the Philadelphia International Airport in 1984 made Philadelphia the first American city with commuter rail airport access, providing 30-minute service throughout the day that was linked to the entire regional rail system. A single-car R1 line train arrived at the airport in 1987.—*Fred W. Schneider III.*

Howard Street Tunnel at Baltimore, Michigan Central's Detroit River Tunnel, GN's Cascade Tunnel, and CN's St. Clair River Tunnel had all been dieselized. Urban smoke abatement had been the only reason for the Cleveland Union Terminal electrification, and it was gone by 1953.

The merger movement that began to rearrange the U. S. railroad industry in the 1950's took more electrification off the map. Following the merger of the Virginian with Norfolk & Western in 1959, the N&W substantially revised the flow of heavy coal traffic to take advantage of the best grades on the merged system. This left the former Virginian electrification with only a largely one-way eastbound traffic over its eastern end. This handicapped the utilization of both electric and diesel-electric motive power, and N&W shut down the electrification in 1962.

The Pennsylvania's extensive freight service electrification survived intact into the Penn Central merger of 1968, but the subsequent PC bankruptcy and the government-sponsored formation of Conrail in 1976 brought substantial changes to the flow of freight that had once moved over the Pennsy electrification. The Northeast Corridor — the former Pennsylvania main line — had been conveyed to Amtrak, and Conrail shifted much of the freight to non-electrified former Reading and Lehigh Valley lines, while much of the traffic west of Philadelphia that had once moved over the Pennsylvania's electrified low-grade line was shifted to former Reading track. With these changes electric operation was no longer economic, and Conrail ended electric freight operation in 1981.

A few electrifications disappeared for still other reasons. When the installation of a new ore concentrator at Butte, Mont., dramatically reduced ore traffic over the Butte, Anaconda & Pacific, the railroad shifted what traffic remained to diesels and shut off the power in 1967. After 50 years of operation, the motive power and power system on the Milwaukee Road's Pacific Extension electrifications in Montana, Idaho, and Washington were largely worn out. Run-through diesels took over an increasing share of the traffic, and the catenary was de-energized on the last segment in 1974.

Even as many of these older electrifications were fading away, there was once again renewed consideration of the promise of electric operation for American railroads. The new rectifier equipment, the feasibility of commercial-frequency electrification, and the concept of standardized, mass-produced electric motive power inspired by diesel-electric practice all promised to reduce materially the initial investment cost that had so long thwarted widespread electrification.

ILLINOIS CENTRAL'S electrified Chicago suburban services were modernized with an entirely new fleet of bi-level gallery M.U. cars delivered in 1971 and 1978. Wearing the colors of Metra Electric, which took over the system in 1988, a southbound four-car train of the big bi-levels rumbled up out of the IC's Randolph Street suburban station in the Chicago Loop in April 1998.—*William D. Middleton.*

MARYLAND RAIL COMMUTER SERVICE adopted locomotive-drawn, push-pull equipment for its electrified Penn Line service in Amtrak's Northeast Corridor. One of MARC's five AEM7 electrics raced through West Baltimore with a Washington-Baltimore train in August 1989.—*William D. Middleton.*

Public utility companies were showing an increasing interest in railroad electrification as a desirable new load for their power systems. Indeed, there was much discussion of an arrangement under which the utility companies would build, maintain, and operate the entire power supply and distribution system, including the overhead catenary, with electric power being metered "at the wire" for use in the railroad's locomotives.

Along with the technological developments, there were other factors contributing to the resurgence of interest in electrification. One was a steady growth in traffic on some of the principal railroad routes. In some cases mergers tended to concentrate tonnage on the best routes, but more often the increases were owed to a steady, long-term growth in railroad freight traffic. In the decade from 1962 to 1972, U. S. rail freight tonnage increased by 31 per cent to a record level of 778,137 million ton-miles annually. The growth rate was even greater in the South and the West, where the freight tonnage increases over the 10-year period were 55 and 44 per cent respectively.

In the West, the combination of traffic growth and the relatively limited number of principal routes was producing a growing amount of main-line mileage with the traffic density to support electrification.

Also contributing to the interest in electrification were the motive-power requirements of the freight train speedup of the 1960's. To meet the "mile-a-minute" freight schedules that became commonplace, the railroads had to double or triple their

customary horsepower-to-train-weight ratios. Although high-horsepower diesel-electrics were equal to the task, it was only at greatly increased costs for motive-power ownership, maintenance, and fuel. Electric locomotives, with their capability for continuous high-horsepower output at much lower maintenance and fuel costs, offered an attractive alternative to diesel-electric power.

Reflecting the growing interest in electrification from the early 1960's onward were several significant developments.

In 1965 a special task force of the Edison Electric Institute, a utility industry association, studied electrification of the New York Central main line between Harmon, N. Y., and Cleveland as a basis for investigating the technical and economic feasibility of electrification of high-traffic-density railroad operations. Its report, published in 1970, concluded that there were no serious technical obstacles to commercial-frequency electric operation and recommended electrification of high-density corridors as both advantageous to the railroads and a desirable new market for utility companies. About 22,000 track-miles of U. S. railroads, the report estimated, supported a traffic density sufficient to warrant electrification, representing a potential power market for 18 to 20 billion kilowatt-hours annually.

This new interest in electrification took on a new urgency with the advent of the energy crisis of the early 1970's and the run-up in diesel fuel prices that came with it. By 1980 the price of diesel fuel had increased to almost eight times what it had been a decade earlier.

The Southern Pacific began studying electrification of its Sunset Route between Colton, Calif., and El Paso, Texas, in the late 1960's. By the early 1970's, Canadian Pacific was considering an 850-mile electrification across the Rocky Mountains to help support an enormous increase in export coal traffic. Union Pacific began electrification studies of its main line from North Platte, Nebr., to Salt Lake City and Pocatello, Ida., in the early 1970's. Both CP and UP went so far as to erect test sections of overhead catenary, while CP leased a Swedish State Railways electric locomotive for testing in Norway under winter conditions similar to those in Canada.

Burlington Northern began electrification studies for several principal lines in 1973, with the 856-mile route between Laurel, Mont., and Lincoln, Nebr., a principal candidate because of growing traffic in low-sulfur coal. The Santa Fe, which had studied electrification at the end of World War II and again in 1960, launched still another study in 1972, this time for its entire Chicago-Los Angeles main line. Illinois Central Gulf studied an electrification of its Chicago-New Orleans main line and several of its principal branches. Together with the Tennessee Valley Authority, the Southern Railway began a study of electrification of its Cincinnati-Chattanooga main line, later extended all the way to Atlanta. In 1971, even in bankruptcy, Penn Central was study-ing an extension of its former PRR electrification up the west shore of the Hudson River to Selkirk Yard at Albany, N. Y. By the end of the decade, only a few years before it shut down its existing electrification, successor Conrail was studying a Harrisburg-Pittsburgh electrification over the Alleghenies that the Pennsylvania had considered many times before. Still other roads that at least considered the idea of electrification included Missouri Pacific; Duluth, Missabe & Iron Range; Bessemer & Lake Erie; Canadian National; Denver & Rio Grande Western; Quebec, North Shore & Labrador; and C&O/B&O.

All of these new studies were based upon a new concept of high-voltage, commercial frequency A.C. electrification. The principal motive power suppliers saw it as a major new market. "We're committed to electrification," said a GE spokesman, "the apparent economic benefits make it inevitable." Even diesel builder Electro-Motive hedged its bet and acquired licenses for electrification technology from Swedish manufacturer ASEA. In 1975 and 1976 EMD put experimental 6000 and 10,000 h.p. prototypes for a new line of electric freight power into service on Penn Central.

Several new mining railroads were seen as prototypes for this new vision of railroad electrification. The first was a 15-mile coal line completed by the American Electric Power Company in 1968 at its

ORIGINALLY an electric interurban railway, the Chicago South Shore & South Bend has long since evolved into a modern electrified commuter railroad. Modernization at the hands of the Northwest Indiana Commuter Transportation District, which now owns the railroad, included a fleet of 58 modern stainless-steel M.U. cars. Eight of the new cars are seen here at Roosevelt Road in April 1998, arriving at Chicago over Metra Electric's former IC Suburban electrification as westbound train 12 from South Bend.—*William D. Middleton.*

REHABILITATION and modernization of the former Canadian National suburban electrification at Montreal during 1993-1995 included a new 25,000-volt, 60-cycle, single-phase A.C. electrification and a fleet of 58 stainless-steel M.U. cars built by Canada's Bombardier. Inbound to Central Station from Roxboro/Pierrefonds as train 912, a train of the new cars made a station stop at Canora in September 1996.—*William D. Middleton.*

Muskingum Mine in southeastern Ohio. The line was electrified with a 25,000 volt, 60-cycle, single-phase A.C. system, and operated with a pair of 5000-h.p. E50-type rectifier locomotives supplied by General Electric. An advanced version of the E33 and E44 units previously supplied to the Virginian and the Pennsylvania, the E50's employed the same road switcher configuration and C-C wheel arrangement. An oil-filled main transformer delivered A.C. power to a group of thyristor-controlled silicon-diode rectifiers, which supplied variable voltage D.C. through a smoothing reactor to six of the same GE-752 low-voltage D.C. series traction motors already proven in hundreds of the builder's diesel-electric units. The units were capable of a starting tractive effort of 122,400 pounds.

In 1973 trains began running over another brand-new electrified coal road, the 78-mile Black Mesa & Lake Powell in Arizona. The first of its kind in the world, the BM&LP was electrified with a 50,000-volt, 60-cycle, single-phase system that was seen as the prototype for western electrification. The higher voltage permitted the railroad to operate from a single substation at the Navajo generating plant, while three or four substations would have been needed for a 25,000-volt system. General Electric supplied the line with three huge E60C thyristor-controlled C-C rectifier locomotives that were a continuation of the technology incorporated in the earlier Muskingum units. Although similar to the

Ohio units in overall dimensions, size, and their C-C wheel arrangement, the E60's employed a single-end, box-cab configuration. The units were capable of an hourly rating of 5600 h.p. and a maximum speed of 72 mph; and a three-unit E60 combination proved capable of pulling 10,000-ton unit trains over the Arizona coal line.

In 1976 the Texas Utilities Co. began operating 19-mile and 13-mile lignite lines in northeast Texas that were powered with a 25,000-volt, 60-cycle, single-phase system. General Electric supplied seven 4000-h.p. E25B thyristor-controlled rectifier locomotives for the two lines.

In 1983 two former Amtrak E60CP units began hauling trains on another new 25,000-volt, 60-cycle, single-phase coal line, the 14-mile Navajo Mine Railroad in New Mexico. Two more 50,000-volt, 60-cycle, single-phase electrifications followed in 1984. Both, like the earlier projects, were specialized coal lines. The 35-mile Deseret Western in northern Utah and Colorado hauled coal from mine head to generating plant, while the British Columbia Railway electrified its entire 81-mile Tumbler Ridge branch to handle an export coal movement. GE built two E60 units for the Deseret Western, while General Motors Canada supplied seven GF6C C-C electric locomotives to BC Rail for the Tumbler Ridge line. The 6000-h.p. units employed an ASEA thyristor-controlled rectifier technology.

426

DEVELOPMENT of a new generation of Amtrak high-speed trains included demonstration of two successful European designs in the Northeast Corridor. First to enter revenue service was this six-car Swedish State Railways X2000 high-speed tilting train built by ABB Traction and adapted for corridor operation.—*ABB Traction.*

OPERATING southbound at high speed as New York-Washington *Metroliner* 117, the X2000 demonstrator met MARC's diesel-powered northbound Washington-Baltimore train 422 south of Odenton, Md., in September 1993.—*William D. Middleton.*

But for those who saw these new lines as leading the way to a new era of railroad electrification, there was little but disappointment. For despite all of the interest and all of the studies, there was to be only a single new main line electrification project to follow, and it was a failure. Early in the 1980's the National Railways of Mexico (FNM) decided to install a 25,000-volt, 60-cycle, single-phase A.C. electrification on its new 153-mile double track line that would replace the existing route between Mexico City and Querétaro, with plans for a later extension of electric operation over other major FNM routes. A fleet of 39 big 6000-h.p. E60C rectifier locomotives supplied by GE in 1982 lay idle for more than a decade awaiting completion of the electrification. The installation finally began limited operation in 1994, but the break up and privatization of the Mexican system that followed a few years later radically altered the motive power situation, and the electrification was abandoned and the locomotives put up for sale.

What happened this time?

After a decade of sharply rising diesel fuel prices, the petroleum-based energy crisis of the 1970's had largely abated by the early 1980's, and diesel prices even began to come down. At the same time, the diesel-electric locomotive continued to present what Electro-Motive Division General Manager B. B. Brownell so aptly termed "a moving target" in a 1971 interview with *Modern Railroads*. A steadily advancing technology was producing new generations of diesel-electric motive power of formidable performance characteristics and increasing fuel efficiency. Over the 40-year period from 1955 to 1995, for example, diesel-electric fuel efficiency as measured by revenue ton-miles per gallon had more than doubled, from 184 to 375 ton-miles per gallon. Those trends have only continued as still newer generations of A.C. propulsion, high adhesion, 6000-h.p. diesel-electric units take to the rails. The diesel-electric was — and is — a tough competitor.

The enormous capital cost and the risks associated with electrification projects, too, were still strong deterrents. Even if the projected return on investment looked good — as it usually did — there was still plenty to worry about. Could the electrification be completed on time and at the projected cost? Would electric power be available at stable rates? Change any of these parameters and electrification might not produce the anticipated benefits. There were other things to worry about as well. Would the utilities have the generating capacity that was needed to take on the railroad load? If new power plants were needed, could the utilities bring them on line in time?

Once again widespread electrification had been frustrated, this time by the continuing gains in diesel-electric productivity and efficiency, together with all of the risks and uncertainties that accompanied expensive electrification projects.

While the freight railroads had once again turned away from electric operation, there were much more encouraging prospects for electric traction in a resurgent North American passenger rail industry.

Amtrak's Washington-New York-Boston Northeast Corridor represented close to a quarter of the national system's total annual passenger-miles and its best opportunity for financial viability, and the railroad had continued the Northeast Corridor high-speed train program that it inherited from Penn Central in 1971. The modest improvements initiated in the corridor by the Pennsylvania for high-speed service ultimately grew into the massive, federally funded Northeast Corridor Improvement Program, which rebuilt fixed plant all the way from Washington to Boston by the time the 2.5-billion-dollar program was substantially complete by the mid-1980's. Track reconstruction, highway grade separation, electrification improvements, and new train control and signaling allowed Amtrak to operate at speeds up to a maximum of 125 mph.

Disappointed in the Metroliner program, Amtrak shifted to a locomotive-hauled strategy for its high-speed trains. In 1972 the railroad ordered 26 General Electric units that were a 120-mph high-speed version of the 6000-h.p. E60 units supplied to the Black Mesa & Lake Powell. The fleet was divided between seven E60CP units equipped with steam generators and 19 E60CH units equipped with head-end power alternators. While the E60's had been seen as an eventual replacement for the aging GG1 fleet, tracking problems at high speed eventually led to a 90-mph speed limit for the big electrics, and Amtrak resumed its search for a new high-speed electric locomotive.

In July 1976, Amtrak began Northeast Corridor trials with a leased Swedish State Railways 6000-h.p. Rc4 unit, followed the next year by a leased French National Railways 7725-h.p. Alsthom-Atlantique unit. The French-built locomotive was sent home after only 90 days of test operation, but the little Swedish B-B unit proved a solid success. By the end of 1977 Amtrak had placed an order for the first eight of an AEM7 fleet that reached a total of 52 locomotives by 1987. Built under license from ASEA by GM's Electro-Motive Division, the AEM7 was a 5800-h.p., 125-mph, U. S. version of the lightweight, high-speed, four-axle thyristor locomotives that ASEA had been supplying by the hundreds to the Swedish State Railways and other European systems since 1965.

The fast AEM7's quickly displaced both the Metroliner M.U.'s and Amtrak's GG1 fleet in Northeast Corridor high-speed service. The Metroliners

A GERMAN FEDERAL RAILWAY'S InterCityExpress (ICE) high-speed train followed the X2000 into Northeast Corridor demonstration service in 1993. The fast trainset was eastbound at Middletown, Pa., on a demonstration run over the Philadelphia-Harrisburg Main Line in July 1993.—*Dan Cupper.*

were gradually withdrawn from New York-Washington schedules, with some continuing in Philadelphia-Harrisburg service, while the GG1's made their last runs on Amtrak in 1980. With the sturdy Swedish electrics in operation, 120 mph and 125 mph high-speed operation became commonplace in the New York-Washington corridor.

Even before government support of intercity passenger service began with the formation of Amtrak in 1971, there was a growing move toward public support for the nation's increasingly troubled and deteriorating commuter rail services.

The major state-supported rehabilitation and modernization of New York's Long Island Rail Road was only the first in a series of similar commuter railroad transformations under public ownership and operation.

Similar Metropolitan Transportation Authority modernization programs were carried out for the former New York Central and New Haven commuter lines north of New York City, which successively passed through Penn Central and Conrail ownership before becoming — in 1983 — the publicly owned MTA Metro-North Railroad. Former New Haven lines in Connecticut came under state ownership, but were operated by Metro-North. Even before the transition to public ownership, MTA and the State of Connecticut had begun to finance new rolling stock for the commuter lines. In 1972 the former NYC lines got 128 GE-Budd high performance M-1 M.U. cars that were essentially identical to the Long Island's M-1 cars, while the following year the MTA and the Connecticut Department of Transportation jointly financed a fleet of 144 similar General Electric Cosmopolitan high performance rectifier M.U. cars that were equipped for A.C. op-

eration on the former New Haven lines. Subsequent orders brought the M-1 and M-2 fleet to a total of 420 cars. Another 142 Budd M-3 cars for Metro-North's third rail lines were added in 1984, while in 1988 the former New Haven A.C. lines got 54 M-4 rectifier cars built by Japan's Tokyu Car Corporation and arranged in a semi-permanently coupled motor-trailer-motor "triplex" arrangement. Another 36 similar M-6 A.C. cars in a triplex arrangement were supplied by Morrison Knudsen in 1994.

Together with new rolling stock, public ownership brought major rehabilitation and modernization of the deteriorated Metro-North commuter lines, and — in 1984 — a 28-mile extension of its Harlem Division third rail northward from North White Plains to Brewster.

Similar public support transformed electrified commuter rail services in northern New Jersey, which ultimately came under public ownership and operation with the formation of New Jersey Transit Rail Operations in 1983. The first New Jersey investment in commuter rail services was a fleet of 25 100-mph, stainless-steel Jersey Arrow I M.U. cars ordered from the St. Louis Car Company in 1968 for Penn Central service between New York and Trenton. Subsequent orders for similar M.U. cars from General Electric included 70 Arrow II cars delivered during 1974-1975 and 230 Arrow III cars delivered during 1977-1978. This additional equipment was sufficient to replace all older M.U. rolling stock operating in former PRR commuter services, as well as enough to completely re-equip electrified lines on the former Lackawanna's Morris & Essex Division.

More recently, NJ Transit has begun a shift to locomotive-drawn equipment for its electrified services. GG1's employed on the former New York & Long Branch were first displaced by surplus E60 units acquired from Amtrak. Beginning in 1990 these were in turn replaced by a fleet of 7000-h.p. ABB Traction ALP44 electrics that had reached a total of 32 units by 1996. Reflecting a planned transition to more locomotive-drawn services on its electrified system, NJ Transit had on order for 2002-2003 delivery a fleet of 20 7350-h.p. Adtranz electrics that would be capable of moving a 10-car train of 10 bi-level commuter cars at 110 mph.

Public support had also provided major improvement and expansion of northern New Jersey's electrified commuter rail system. During 1981-1983 the former Lackawanna's aging 3000-volt D.C. Morris & Essex electrification was completely rebuilt and converted to a 25,000-volt, 60-cycle system compatible with a planned future conversion of the Northeast Corridor. Electric operation over NJ Transit's North Jersey Coast Line, the former New York & Long Branch, was extended some 5 miles from South Amboy to Matawan in 1982, and another 16 miles beyond Matawan to Long Branch in 1988.

During the 1990's NJ Transit completed major projects that helped to better integrate the former Pennsylvania and Lackawanna electrifications. In 1991 trains began operating over a newly established Waterfront Connection link between the former Lackawanna Terminal at Hoboken and the former PRR Penn Station in Newark. In 1997 NJ Transit completed its Kearney Connection, near Newark, which linked the former Lackawanna lines with the Northeast Corridor, permitting for the first time direct service to Pennsylvania Station in midtown Manhattan from the Morris & Essex lines. The New Jersey agency also funded signaling improvements that would increase Northeast Corridor capacity between Newark and Penn Station and began a major expansion of its facilities within Penn Station to help accommodate the steadily growing commuter traffic.

At Philadelphia, public support of electric commuter services on the Pennsylvania and Reading railroads began in 1958 with a city-supported subsidy program for the two systems. The regional Southeastern Pennsylvania Transportation Authority (SEPTA), created in 1963 to take over local transit services, became the owner and operator of the former PRR and Reading commuter lines in 1983.

New equipment for the Philadelphia services was first provided in 1963, when the City of Philadelphia purchased 55 new Budd Silverliner II M.U.'s for the two railroads. Another 20 publicly funded Silverliner III cars were delivered from the St. Louis Car Company in 1967, while General Electric delivered 232 Silverliner IV M.U.'s between 1973 and 1976. More recently, SEPTA, too, has added elec-

tric locomotive-drawn trains to its commuter fleet with the delivery of seven AEM7 electrics from Electro-Motive in 1987, together with non-powered coaches for push-pull train service. Another similar ALP44 was received from ABB Traction in 1995.

In addition to new equipment, SEPTA has completed major rehabilitation and improvement projects for its Philadelphia commuter rail system. In addition to the Center City Commuter Rail Connection that tied the former PRR and Reading systems together into an integrated regional system, SEPTA in 1984 completed an extension of the regional rail system to the Philadelphia International Airport. Still another extension of regional rail service came in 1997, when service on SEPTA's Philadelphia-Wilmington (Del.) line was extended 12 miles south to Newark, Del., over Amtrak's Northeast Corridor.

Still another convert to electric locomotive-drawn commuter services was the Maryland Rail Commuter Service (MARC), which replaced leased M.U. cars in its Northeast Corridor service between Baltimore and Washington in 1986 with push-pull trains powered by a new fleet of four AEM7 electrics from Electro-Motive. Another six electrics were on order for 2001 delivery as an add-on to Amtrak's contract for High Horsepower Locomotives.

At Chicago, public support enabled the Illinois Central to complete the modernization of its electrified suburban service. Financed by the Chicago South Suburban Mass Transit District and delivered by Canada's Bombardier in 1978, 30 new double-deck M.U. cars, identical to the 130 cars acquired in 1971, permitted the retirement of the last of IC's original M.U. fleet. More recently, in 1987, ownership of the former IC service passed to Metra, the commuter rail subsidiary of the Chicago area's Regional Transportation Authority.

Similar public support from Metra and the Northern Indiana Commuter Transportation District permitted the rehabilitation and re-equipment of the Chicago South Shore & South Bend with a fleet of new stainless-steel M.U. cars built by Japan's Nippon Sharyo that had reached a total of 68 cars with the delivery of the most recent order in 2000.

Canada's only electric commuter rail service, the Canadian National's Deux Montagnes line at Montreal, underwent a similar rehabilitation and modernization with public support, but it came much later. Under a 278-million-dollar (Canadian) program carried out by the Société de transport de la Communauté urbaine de Montréal (STCUM) during 1993-1995, the line was completely rebuilt and the electrification converted from 2400-volt D.C. to a modern 25,000-volt, 60-cycle, single-phase A.C. system. Canada's Bombardier supplied a new fleet of 58 modern stainless-steel M.U. cars for the rebuilt line.

As the new century began, a new era of high-speed electrified rail travel was at hand for North-

IN addition to *Acela Express* trainsets, Amtrak's high-speed train contract with Bombardier/GEC Alsthom included 15 new High Horsepower Locomotives rated at 8000 h.p. and capable of a 150-mph maximum speed. One of the first HHL's completed is seen here on the test track at the Federal Railroad Administration's Pueblo, Colo., Transportation Technology Center in 1999.—*William C. Vantuono.*

east Corridor travelers as the first major expansion of U. S. catenary in more than 60 years went into service. Begun a decade earlier, Amtrak's Northeast High Speed Rail Improvement Project included 1.3 billion dollars in major reconstruction and improvements to track, structures, and signaling, and the installation of 25,000-volt, 60-cycle, single-phase A.C. catenary over 156 route-miles between New Haven, Conn., and Boston, completing an electrification the New Haven had planned more than 90 years before. The railroad's goals for the program included the attainment of a three-hour Boston-New York service with new high-speed trains, with a 150-mph maximum operating speed.

Initial federal funding for the program was appropriated in 1990, and construction was in progress by 1994. Track was upgraded with concrete ties and continuous welded rail, while 227 curves were modified or realigned for higher speeds. New high-speed interlockings were installed at five locations, almost 150 bridges and overhead structures were modified to provide adequate catenary clearance, and 57 open deck bridges were rebuilt with ballasted decks. Three drawbridges were scheduled for replacement, while the historic 165-year-old Canton Viaduct in Massachusetts was modified and reinforced to accommodate the high-speed trains. A new microprocessor-controlled, bi-directional signaling system was installed, and the entire route was brought under the control of Amtrak's Centralized Electrification and Traffic Control (CETC) system.

Installation of the electrification itself began in 1996. A modern, weight-tensioned simple catenary system was installed in spans of up to 230 feet on straight track, supported by brackets from steel masts in double-track sections and portals in multi-track sections. Power from public utility companies was fed to the system at 115,000 volts through substations at Branford and New London, Conn.; Warwick, R. I.; and Roxbury, Mass., each equipped

with two main power transformers which stepped the power down to 50,000 volts to feed the overhead contact system. Autotransformers in paralleling stations anywhere from 5 to 7½ miles apart in turn converted the 50,000-volt supply to the 25,000-volt contact wire voltage.

In 1993 Amtrak began a series of demonstrations with European high-speed equipment. First, an X2000 high-speed tilting train leased from Sweden's ABB Traction was placed in revenue Metroliner service between New York and Washington, where the train easily met demanding 2-hour 40-minute *Express Metroliner* schedules and proved highly popular with passengers. Later in the year a leased German Federal Railways InterCityExpress (ICE) trainset made up of two locomotives and six cars entered similar Metroliner service and acquitted itself equally well, achieving speeds of up to 140 mph in revenue service.

Amtrak's experience with the two European trains helped the railroad to complete specifications for a new fleet of high-speed trains, and a request for proposals went out to three pre-qualified supplier teams in October 1994. A contract award worth nearly a billion dollars finally went to a Bombardier/GEC Alsthom team early in 1996 for a fleet of 20 high-speed trainsets, 15 new high horsepower electric locomotives, and maintenance facilities for the trains and locomotives at Boston, New York, and Washington that would be operated by the suppliers.

Incorporating some technical features from the French TGV high-speed trains, each of the 664-foot 2¾ inch, 552.9-ton, eight-car trainsets, which Amtrak named the *Acela Express*, seated a total of 304 passengers. Microprocessor-controlled power cars at each end generating a combined 12,500 h.p. were capable of attaining a 165-mph maximum speed. The six 87-foot 5-inch passenger cars in each train included one first class car, four business class cars,

SOUTHBOUND from Boston during pre-inaugural testing, an Acela Express high-speed train emerged from the south portal of New York's landmark Hell Gate Bridge over the East River on the bright fall morning of November 2, 2000. The first regularly scheduled service with the new trains began operating between Boston and Washington on December 11, 2000.—*Joseph M. Calisi.*

and one café car. To permit higher speeds in curves without passenger discomfort the passenger cars, but not the power cars, were fitted with an active tilting mechanism with a maximum tilt capability of 6.5 degrees, although tilt would be limited to 4.2 degrees in service. Interiors featured seating in a 1-2 arrangement for first class, and a 2-2 arrangement elsewhere. Plush reclining seats were provided with footrests and adjustable head cushions. Each seat had electrical outlets and large tray tables to accommodate laptop computers, adjustable high- and low-intensity lighting, and headsets for two-channel audio programming. Luggage storage included both enclosed overhead bins and large compartments for oversized bags. Other features of the trains included a number of conference tables throughout the train and public telephones. Meal and beverage service was provided in a pub-like setting in the café car, with at-seat attendant service in first class.

The 15 High Horsepower Locomotives (HHL) that were part of the project were double-end, 8000-h.p. units capable of a 150-mph maximum speed with longer trains than could be handled by an AEM7.

In addition to replacing its *Metroliner* service with the *Acela Express* trainsets, Amtrak was introducing an *Acela Regional* service to be operated with the new HHL's, and an *Acela Commuter* service that would be powered by 30 of Amtrak's existing AEM7 fleet, which were being overhauled and retrofitted with A.C. traction equipment.

By 1999 both an *Acela Express* trainset and an HHL were in test operation on the Association of American Railroads' Transportation Technology Center test track at Pueblo, Colo., and extensive test operation on the Northeast Corridor followed. Technical problems identified during tests delayed a planned late 1999 start-up for high-speed operation, but a limited start to all-electric high-speed service began in January 2000, when two Boston-Washington *Acela Regional* trains began operating under the new catenary between Boston and New Haven. The first two *Acela Express* trainsets entered revenue service December 11, 2000, with the balance of the 20-train order following as additional equipment was readied for regular service. A new age of high-speed electric railroading had finally arrived in North America.

The interest in high-speed electrified passenger railroading was not confined to the Northeast Corridor. During the 1990's expansive new high-speed train projects were being advanced in Florida, Texas, and California. While both the Florida and Texas projects fell short, California's High Speed Rail Authority was developing plans for a 700-mile system that would operate at speeds of 200 mph or more to link San Francisco and Sacramento with Los Angeles and San Diego.

While proposals for new high-speed rail systems offered long range prospects for railroad electrification elsewhere in North America, more likely early prospects for new electrification were to be found in the burgeoning commuter or regional passenger rail market. At Boston, for example, future electrification of some of the Massachusetts Bay Transportation Authority's fast-growing commuter service appeared likely. Electric operation would be required for a proposed North-South Rail Link tunnel in Boston that would link MBTA commuter lines north and south of Boston into a unified system, while an electrification of MBTA's Boston-Providence service could utilize Amtrak's new Northeast Corridor electrification. Similarly, Amtrak's new Northeast Corridor electrification would permit easy conversion of the Connecticut Department of Transportation's Shore Line East commuter service between New Haven and New London to electric operation.

At New York, major improvements and expansion were in prospect for the region's electrified commuter rail systems. As the new century began, engineering was underway for the LIRR's East Side

432

Access Project, which will provide the railroad a second entry into Manhattan via the Metropolitan Transportation Authority's 63rd Street tunnel under the East River to Grand Central Terminal. Completion of the 3.2-billion-dollar project by 2009 was planned. Metro-North Railroad was completing a Penn Station Access Study that was considering measures to improve access to Manhattan's West Side from the area north of New York City that included new services into Penn Station over the Hell Gate Bridge and Amtrak's West Side Manhattan line along the east bank of the Hudson. The MTA's Lower Manhattan Access Study was considering major commuter rail extensions from both Grand Central and Penn Station to Lower Manhattan and Flatbush Terminal in Brooklyn. Together with the MTA and NJ Transit, the Port Authority of New York and New Jersey was completing an Access to the Region's Core Study that proposed the construction of additional Hudson River tunnels into Penn Station, as well as a tunnel between Penn Station and Grand Central that would permit a linking of all three of the region's commuter rail systems.

At Philadelphia, major expansion of SEPTA's electrified regional rail service was forecast by studies in progress for a projected Schuylkill Valley Metro, a 62-mile extension of electric service to Reading, Pa., in the right-of-way of the former Reading main line.

An entirely new commuter electrification was in prospect at San Francisco, where the Peninsula Corridor Joint Powers Board was well-advanced in studies of a proposed 25,000-volt, 60-cycle, single-phase A.C. electrification that would expand capacity and improve performance of its fast-growing 80-mile Caltrain commuter rail system extending from downtown San Francisco to San Jose and Gilroy.

Aside from prospects for passenger rail electrification, what was the likelihood of widespread North American freight railroad electrification as the new century began?

In the short term, at least, the prospects did not seem very promising. Diesel fuel prices remained relatively stable, while locomotive manufacturers continued to make the improvements that had long made the diesel-electric locomotive a "moving target" in terms of capacity, performance, and efficiency. And in an era in which the North American railroad industry was rapidly consolidating into a handful of major carriers of transcontinental scope, available capital was being devoted to the improvements required to effectively integrate merged systems.

But a more extended view of the industry based upon long-term trends suggests that widespread electrification could indeed become an imperative in the decades ahead. Based upon both continuing growth in the U. S. economy and a reinvigorated rail freight industry, annual freight ton-miles have been growing steadily for almost four decades. From an all-time record level of over 737-billion ton-miles in wartime 1944, rail freight had been in more or less continuous decline for almost 20 years, bottoming out at just over 563-billion ton-miles in 1961. A deregulated, resurgent railroad industry has been steadily gaining tonnage ever since. Growing by as much as 4 per cent a year, freight ton-miles were back up to the peak level of World War II by 1966. By the end of the century annual freight traffic had exceeded 1400 billion ton-miles, almost double the peak of wartime 1944.

As the industry continued to consolidate through mergers, more and more traffic was being concentrated on a limited number of key routes. Second main tracks that had been taken up in an earlier era of retrenchment were being replaced. Lines that had never had it were getting double track. In one extreme case, the Union Pacific in 1999 completed triple-tracking of a 108-mile segment of its Overland Route between North Platte and Gibbon, Nebr., where traffic had reached a daily average of 140 trains.

Increasingly, too, the railroads were carrying a different *kind* of freight traffic. The high value, high priority intermodal traffic that represented a fast growing segment of the market demanded near passenger train speeds. Manufacturing and distribution based upon just-in-time delivery concepts required fast and on-time freight delivery.

All of these were trends that could make electrification an increasingly attractive alternative for key segments of the North American railroad network. For despite all of the gains in the capabilities of diesel-electric motive power, electric traction still offered a superior ability to increase capacity, improve overall train speeds and operating performance, and reduce operating costs.

Thus one could hazard the prediction that one day — perhaps not very far off — new electrification may well become almost an imperative for a growing North American railroad industry. But if and when that day comes, will the railroads have the will and the resources to carry it out? Or will it take government support, as it did to get — finally — New Haven catenary into Boston in 2000, or as it had where electrification has flourished almost everywhere else in the world?

As they had been for so many years, the future prospects for North American railroad electrification remained uncertain. But as railroad electrification began its second century one thing *was* clear: The story wasn't yet over.

The technology of electrification

Direct-current systems

Practical direct-current electrical systems preceded the development of alternating-current systems by several years. By the time the first steam railroad electrifications were carried out in the 1890's, D.C. electrification was already well established in both street railway and rapid-transit applications. The D.C. series motor was relatively light in weight, inexpensive, and trouble-free, and its performance characteristics were well suited to railway service. Generators, switchgear, distribution systems, and the other appurtenances of direct-current electrification were equally simple and rugged.

From the time of the first experimental electrifications through the first few years of this century, low-voltage D.C. systems of the type employed in street railway and rapid-transit service, typically energized at 550 to 650 volts, were used for steam road electrifications. Indeed, the experimental branchline electrifications of the New Haven and Pennsylvania railroads differed little in their electrical equipment and rolling stock from street and interurban railways.

Low-voltage D.C. systems had some serious disadvantages, however. Because of the low voltage employed, large current flows were required for heavy railroad service. To avoid excessive voltage drops, heavy feeder cables were necessary and substations had to be close together. On the New York Central's early D.C. electrification out of New York's Grand Central Terminal, for example, substations were spaced an average of less than 6 miles apart. As traffic increased, the railroad found it necessary to install more substations at intermediate locations, reducing the average substation spacing to 3½ miles. Except for a few light branchline or switching electrifications, the large current demands of low-voltage D.C. operation precluded the use of overhead wire. Instead, third-rail systems, with their safety and clearance problems, were required to provide sufficient current-carrying capacity.

Although low-voltage D.C. systems were successful in relatively short suburban and terminal electrifications, their disadvantages in supplying power over long distances made them unsuitable for long-haul mainline electrification. No long electrifications were ever attempted with low-voltage D.C. in North America.

The disadvantages of low-voltage D.C. systems were largely overcome by the development of high-voltage direct-current systems during the first decade of the century. High-voltage D.C. equipment was developed around 1906 by the General Electric Company, which aggressively marketed the system as an alternative to the single-phase A.C. system advocated by the Westinghouse Company.

The earliest high-voltage D.C. installations were on interurban railways, where a potential of either 1200 or 1500 volts was typically used. Except for Southern Pacific's 1200-volt East Bay suburban electrification and Illinois Central's 1500-volt Chicago suburban electrification, 2400-volt and 3000-volt D.C. systems were used by steam railroads. The 2400-volt system was developed by GE for its 1913 electrification of the Butte, Anaconda & Pacific, and the 3000-volt system a few years later for the Milwaukee Road installation. Following the completion of these two installations, the high-voltage D.C. system (2400 or 3000 volts) became one of the most popular and was used throughout the world.

High-voltage D.C. systems enjoyed almost all of the advantages of 600-volt D.C. systems. Except for heavier insulation, the series motors and other apparatus were almost identical to those used for 600-volt operation. Because of the higher potential, control equipment was somewhat more complex and expensive than that for 600-volt operation.

The great advantage of high-voltage D.C. was that the increased voltage reduced the amount of current required to transmit a given amount of electrical energy. A locomotive operating at 3000 volts, for example, draws only one-fifth of the current required by a locomotive of equal power operating at 600 volts. Thus power transmission lines and catenary systems could be made of lighter wire. The increased voltage facilitated current transmission over long distances, reducing the number of substations needed. On the Milwaukee Road's 3000-volt D.C. electrification, for example, the average spacing of substations was 32 miles.

Alternating-current systems

The development during the 1880's of the transformer, which permitted the voltage of alternating current to be stepped up or down, rapidly established A.C. as the superior system for power generation and distribution. A.C. power could be stepped up to high voltages for transmission, affording economies in conductors and efficiencies in transmission that were unattainable with direct-current systems.

The earliest A.C. electrifications, carried out in Europe around the turn of the century, used three-phase power. The induction motors used in such electrifications were rugged, simple, and efficient machines that produced high power and constant, uniform torque. The three-phase system also provided high efficiency in power distribution and permitted regenerative braking without special control equipment.

Three-phase electrification had disadvantages, however, which prevented it from gaining wide popularity. Probably the most serious of these was the complicated power distribution system. Typically the running rails were used as the conductor for one phase and two overhead wires for the other two. Since the two wires had to be insulated from each other, three-phase overhead systems were complex and costly, particularly at turnouts and crossings. The insulation problems limited the voltages that could be used with three-phase systems.

Although three-phase proponents liked to consider it an advantage, the constant speed of the induction motor was another handicap to the three-phase system. Except for a few special situations, railroad men regarded constant-speed operation as a disadvantage. The only three-phase installation in America was Great Northern's first Cascade Tunnel electrification in 1909, which operated at 6600 volts, 25 cycles. Although the system worked well, it was displaced by a conventional single-phase system less than 20 years later when GN extended its electric territory as part of the new Cascade Tunnel project.

Single-phase A.C. systems, which required only a single overhead contact wire, were more adaptable to railroad requirements. High contact-wire voltages were possible, permitting great economies in conductor size and transmission efficiencies. Transformers in the locomotives stepped the contact-wire voltage down for the motors.

Most of the disadvantages of single-phase A.C. were in the single-phase commutator motors normally used, which tended to be more complex, heavier, and more expensive than D.C. series motors of equal capacity. Because of the commutator motor's operating characteristics, a relatively low frequency was required (25 cycles was used in North America), necessitating costly frequency-conversion equipment wherever 60-cycle commercial power supplies were used. Complicated control systems were necessary for regenerative braking.

In a few electrifications the power distribution advantages of single-phase A.C. were combined with the performance characteristics of three-phase electrification by means of phase-splitting equipment in the locomotive. In several other electrifications motor-generator equipment in the locomotive was used to combine single-phase distribution with D.C. traction motors. In recent years rectifiers have been used for the same purpose.

3300-volt and 6600-volt systems were widely used on interurban railways, but 11,000-volt, 25-cycle A.C. was almost universally used in North American single-phase electrifications. The only major exceptions were the 22,000-volt, 25-cycle Detroit, Toledo & Ironton installation and the 3300-volt, 25-cycle St. Clair Tunnel electrification.

The development of rectifiers for locomotives over the past 50 years has led to commercial frequency (50 or 60 cycles), single-phase electrification. Since low-frequency power for commutator motors is not required, power can be supplied directly from commercial electric systems, eliminating the need for intermediate frequency conversion equipment. Potentials of both 25,000 and 50,000 volts are employed. Widely used elsewhere in the world, commercial frequency electrification has been adopted in North America for several new electrified coal roads in the U. S. and Canada; new installations in Mexico and Costa Rica; conversions of the former New Haven and Lackawanna electrifications at New York and the former Canadian National suburban electrification at Montreal; and Amtrak's Northeast Corridor high-speed installation between New Haven and Boston.

Power supply

Most of the early mainline electrifications were obliged to rely on their own generating plants for electric power because public utilities could not provide sufficient power. A few of the earliest branchline electrifications, including the Pennsylvania's Burlington & Mt. Holly installation of 1895, and the New Haven's 1895 Nantasket Beach and 1902 Providence, Warren & Bristol systems, included power plants in which D.C. was generated at the distribution system voltage. The Baltimore & Ohio's 1895 Baltimore tunnel electrification alone among mainline electrifications operated a direct-current generating plant.

Although D.C. power generation directly at the distribution system voltage worked well for lightly traveled branch lines and for short hauls such as B&O's 3½-mile installation, it was unsuitable for transmission of large amounts of power over any distance. By the turn of the century the superiority of alternating-current equipment for power generation and distribution was so well established that it was used thereafter for every railroad electrification system of any consequence. Railroad-owned plants installed early in the century typi-

cally generated three-phase, 25-cycle power at voltages ranging from 3300 volts in the Grand Trunk Railway's Port Huron (Mich.) power plant to 13,200 volts in the Southern Pacific's Fruitvale (Calif.) plant. Because of its popularity for single-phase A.C. systems, 11,000 volts was by far the most common generation voltage.

Except for several early D.C. plants which used reciprocating steam engines to drive the generators, steam turbines were almost universally used to generate power in the railroad-owned plants. The only railroad-owned hydroelectric plant was the Great Northern's plant on the Wenatchee River near Leavenworth, Wash., although commercial hydroelectric power was used to supply several electrifications in whole or in part, notably those of the Butte, Anaconda & Pacific, the Milwaukee, the Great Northern, and the Pennsylvania.

Although railroad-owned power plants were constructed as late as 1925, when the Virginian completed its Narrows (Va.) plant, most new electrifications after 1910 purchased power from public utility companies, which by then had developed sufficient capacity for heavy railroad loads. One of the earliest installations to use commercial power was the Erie's 1907 branchline electrification between Rochester and Mt. Morris, N. Y., which was supplied from Niagara Falls.

As public-utility power supplies became more abundant, many early electrifications were converted to commercial supplies; in several cases the railroad-owned plants were sold to public utility companies. Among the few electrifications which relied on railroad-generated power throughout their existence were those of the Norfolk & Western and the Virginian.

In a few cases power was transmitted at the generating voltage, but usually transformers were used to step up the voltage for greater efficiency. Transmission voltages varied, from 11,000 volts to 132,000 volts.

Substations or converter stations were required to convert transmission-line power to the proper distribution current and voltage.

Direct-current substations were equipped with transformers to step down the transmission-line A.C. voltage and some type of A.C.-to-

435

D.C. conversion equipment. The earlier installations were equipped with rotating conversion equipment. The simplest type of conversion equipment was the motor-generator set, which consisted of a synchronous or induction A.C. motor and a D.C. generator mounted on a common shaft. The synchronous or rotary converter, which essentially incorporated the armatures of the motor and the generator into a single unit, was another common type of rotating conversion equipment.

Later, mercury-arc rectifiers provided a more efficient means of converting A.C. to D.C. The mercury-arc rectifier is based on the principle that a mercury electrode in contact with mercury vapor will conduct current in only one direction. Thus bidirectional A.C. can be converted to unidirectional D.C. Although the principle was discovered in 1902 by Dr. Peter Cooper Hewitt, more than two decades elapsed before high-capacity rectifiers were used for railroad power supply. The first major rectifier installation was made during the 1920's on Illinois Central's 1500-volt D.C. Chicago suburban electrification. The original IC substation installation included mercury-arc rectifiers with a capacity of 9000 kilowatts, in addition to 33,000 kilowatts supplied from conventional rotary converters. Thereafter, rectifiers became increasingly popular for D.C. power supply. The entire substation capacity of 37,000 kilowatts for the Lackawanna's 1930 electrification was supplied by mercury-arc rectifiers.

A common feature in the substations of early D.C. electrifications was a large bank of storage batteries, which served the purposes of leveling off peak-period demands on power plants and providing an emergency power supply. The batteries in the substations of the original New York Central electrification were capable of operating the railroad for an hour in the event of power failure.

A.C. substations were much simpler than those for D.C. On the short-distance tunnel electrifications of the Grand Trunk and the Boston & Maine, power was generated and transmitted at the proper distribution voltage and frequency, and there was no need for substations at all, but only for the necessary switchgear and circuit-protection equipment. On A.C.

electrifications that extended over greater distances, transformers were provided at intervals to step down the transmission voltages to the contact-wire potential.

Where the power for A.C. electrifications was generated at the required 25-cycle frequency, step-down transformers, together with switchgear and protection equipment, constituted the principal substation equipment. Later, however, almost all utility companies adopted the 60-cycle frequency as standard, and frequency-converter equipment became necessary wherever commercial power supplies were used. These were essentially motor-generator sets which employed three-phase, 60-cycle synchronous motors to drive single-phase, 25-cycle generators. Some of those installed for the Pennsylvania's mainline electrification project were quite large, producing, for example, as much as 30,000 kilowatts from a single machine.

For modern commercial-frequency electrification, only transformers are required to step up or step down the transmission voltages.

Current distribution

Third Rail: A third-rail distribution system almost always was used to provide adequate capacity and contact surface for the heavy current demands of low-voltage D.C. mainline electrification. Typically the third rail was a high-conductivity steel rail mounted alongside the track and slightly higher than the running rail. Dimensions varied from one system to another, but generally the third rail was 26 to 30 inches horizontally from the inner face of the running rail, with the contact surface 2¾ inches to 3½ inches above the surface of the running rail.

The most common third-rail installation was the overrunning type, in which the contact surface was the top of the rail. An alternate type was the Sprague-Wilgus underrunning third rail, developed by

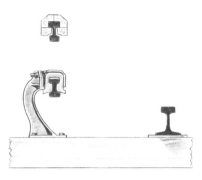

UNDERRUNNING THIRD RAIL.

Frank J. Sprague and William J. Wilgus for New York Central's Grand Central Terminal electrification. The contact surface was at the bottom, affording considerably greater protection from sleeting and accidental contact.

Third rails usually were mounted on long ties spaced about every fourth or fifth tie. Overrunning third rails normally were supported by a porcelain insulator, while the underrunning type required a more complicated cast-iron bracket which held the rail from above in a porcelain insulator. California's North Shore Railroad used blocks of California redwood mounted on every fifth tie to support the power rail. On double-track sections the line's power rail was supported by wooden pieces laid across two ties or set on posts driven into the ground.

A protective cover was usually provided for third-rail systems. Originally wood was universally used for this purpose, but in recent years several roads have developed plastic covers.

Two of the earliest third-rail installations were highly unorthodox. The B&O's 1895 Baltimore tunnel electrification was equipped with a heavy metal trough or channel section suspended above the track, and portions of the New Haven's Massachusetts and Connecticut branch-line electrifications of the late 1890's employed a center third rail. The B&O installation was converted to a conventional overrunning third rail in 1902, and the New Haven's center-third-rail electrifications were discontinued after only a few years.

Overhead: Overhead wire distribution systems were used in North America for all except low-voltage D.C. electrification. Although direct-suspension single-wire overhead systems were commonly used in street and interurban railway installations, their low current-carrying capacity and

OVERRUNNING THIRD RAIL.

the variation in contact-wire height resulting from the sag between supports made them unsuitable for heavy-duty mainline electrification. Direct-suspension overhead was employed only for a few branchline and light-traffic electrifications and Great Northern's three-phase Cascade Tunnel electrification of 1909.

With these few exceptions, all overhead distribution systems for mainline electrification employed some type of catenary, so called for the curve assumed by a suspended wire under uniform load. In its simplest form, catenary overhead consisted of a single catenary messenger wire from which a contact wire was suspended at intervals by hangers. This arrangement afforded increased current-carrying capacity and a more uniform height for the contact wire.

To provide an even more level contact wire and to impart a uniform stiffness to the overhead system, a compound-catenary system was used by the New Haven, the Pennsylvania, and some other roads for high-speed operation. The contact wire was suspended by clips from an auxiliary messenger, which in turn was suspended from the catenary messenger by the customary hangers. "Stitched" catenary is a variation of compound catenary in which the auxiliary messenger is used only in the immediate vicinity of the support points for the main messenger.

The New Haven Railroad employed some novel variations in catenary design. Between Woodlawn, N. Y., and Stamford, Conn., on the railroad's original electrification, a triangular catenary was installed. Triangular hangers suspended from a pair of messenger cables supported the contact wire. After the resulting system was found to be too stiff, a new contact wire was suspended by clips from the original contact wire. In later extensions the New Haven employed a type of compound catenary in which main messenger cables supported transverse I-beams at the quarter points of main spans. Conventional compound-catenary subspans were in turn suspended from the transverse beams.

Although shorter spans were used in a few cases, catenary spans typically varied between 150 feet and 300 feet. The usual height of the contact wire was 21 to 22 feet. At points of restricted clearance the wire was as low as 15 feet 8 inches.

BRACKET construction usually is used for single-track catenary. This DL&W installation employs compound catenary and double contact wire.—*Fred W. Schneider III.*

Steel, bronze, aluminum, and copper wire were all widely used in catenary construction.

Wooden or steel poles normally supported catenary systems. Although concrete poles were commonly used in overseas installations, they were used in the U. S. only on the Detroit, Toledo & Ironton. Rolled shapes, tubular sections, and fabricated members were all used in steel catenary structures.

On single-track lines, and sometimes on double track, catenary was carried on brackets from a single line of poles. On multiple track the catenary was often carried on steel bridges across the tracks. An alternate system for multiple track was the use of a wire "cross catenary" spanning between poles on opposite sides of the track, an arrangement which necessitated guy wires for each pole.

Most electrifications employed heavy and complex overhead distribution systems. Much simpler and lighter catenary designs are now being employed for modern electrifications. Typically these are simple catenary designs made up of a single messenger wire and a single contact wire. Temperature expansion and contraction has always been a prob-

THE Lackawanna used simple H-section bridges (above) to support catenary on the multiple-track portion of its electrification. (Left) The 1943 extension of Canadian National's Montreal electrification employed catenary bridges fabricated from steel structural shapes.—*Above, Delaware, Lackawanna & Western: William B. Barry, Jr.; left, Canadian National Railways.*

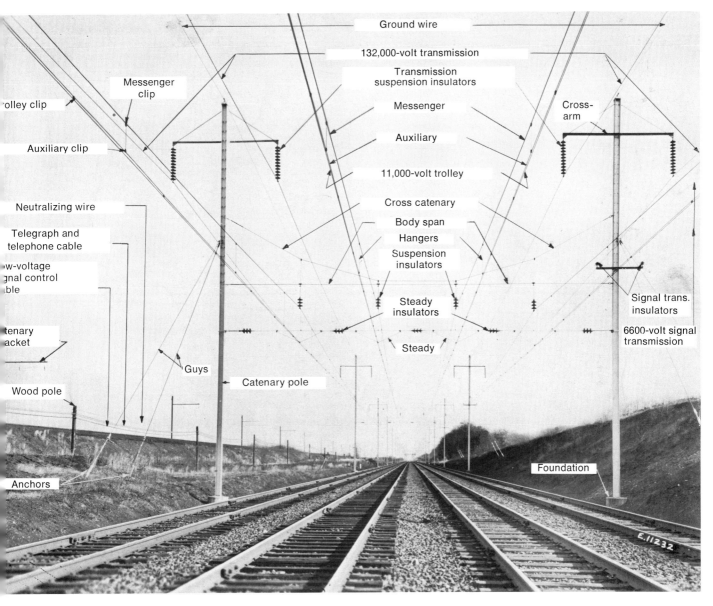

Ground wire

132,000-volt transmission

Transmission
suspension insulators

Messenger
clip

Messenger

Cross-
arm

Trolley clip

Auxiliary

Auxiliary clip

11,000-volt trolley

Cross catenary

Neutralizing wire

Body span

Telegraph and
telephone cable

Hangers

Suspension
insulators

Low-voltage
signal control
cable

Signal trans.
insulators

Steady
insulators

Catenary
bracket

6600-volt signal
transmission

Steady

Guys

Wood pole

Catenary pole

Foundation

Anchors

E.11232

A FOUR-TRACK electrified line of the Pennsylvania serves as an example of cross-catenary construction and illustrates the various components of overhead wire systems.—*Penn Central.*

lem with overhead catenary systems. In extremely cold weather contraction can cause wire breaks, while sagging of the catenary in extremely high temperatures can interfere with smooth pantograph operation at high speeds. In most modern catenary systems this is overcome by the use of a constant-tension, or weight-tensioned, system. On Amtrak's New Haven-Boston electrification, for example, this is accomplished through the use of overlapping tension sections close to a mile in length. Beyond the overlap the wire is connected with balance weight assemblies suspended from a catenary support mast to provide a constant tension on the wire regardless of the temperature.

The motive power of electrification

Electric-locomotive classification

Because of the wide variety of wheel and truck arrangements used for electric locomotives, the Whyte system of notation used to describe steam-locomotive wheel arrangements is inadequate for electric-locomotive classification. The Whyte system is based on the number of wheels in each truck or frame, and uses numerals to designate both powered and non-powered wheels. Thus, for example, a Pacific-type locomotive with its four-wheel guiding truck, six drivers, and two-wheel trailing truck is a 4-6-2.

The classification system developed for electric locomotives is based upon the number of axles. To differentiate between powered and non-powered axles, letters are used for powered axles and numerals for non-powered axles.

The number of adjacent driving axles in either a rigid frame or a truck is designated by a letter. A stands for one driving axle, B for two, C for three, and so on.

The number of adjacent idler, or non-powered, axles in a rigid frame or truck is given by a numeral.

When driving and idler axles are included in the same rigid frame or truck, the appropriate numerals and letters in proper order are used. For example, 1B designates a truck with one idler and two driving axles, and A1A designates a truck with one idler axle between two driving axles.

When trucks or motive-power units are connected by an articulated connection through which tractive force is transmitted, the connection is designated by a plus sign. The separation between swiveling trucks, or between a rigid frame and adjacent guiding or carrying trucks not connected through an articulated joint, is represented by a hyphen or minus sign. Some examples:

B-B — Locomotive with two four-wheel (two-axle) swiveling driving trucks.

C+C — Locomotive with two six-wheel (three-axle) articulated driving trucks.

2-C+C-2 — Locomotive with two articulated frames, each with three driving axles, and a four-wheel non-powered guiding truck at each end.

When two or more motive-power units with the same wheel arrangement normally are operated in mul-tiple as a single locomotive, the number of units is indicated by a numeral preceding the symbol of one unit within parentheses. For example, 3(1-D-1) denotes a three-unit locomotive with two guiding axles and four driving axles on each unit.

When two or more motive-power units of different wheel arrangements normally are operated in multiple as a single locomotive, the classifications of each unit are put in parentheses and connected by plus signs. For example, (2-B+B)+ (B+B)+(B+B-2) denotes a three-unit locomotive with 2-B+B units at each end, and a B+B unit in the center.

The same system of notation is used for classification of diesel locomotives. In European practice a distinction is made for adjacent driving axles that are individually powered. A four-wheel driving truck powered through a jackshaft and side-rod drive is represented by a B, for example, while a truck of the same wheel arrangement with each axle powered by a separate traction motor is represented by Bo.

Electric-locomotive power

The normal horsepower rating of an electric locomotive is the total of the continuous ratings of its traction motors. The continuous rating is the horsepower output which the traction motor can produce continuously without overheating. As with most electrical machinery, however, traction motors can operate above their normal capacity for short periods of time, being limited only by the effects of overheating. Consequently, electric locomotives are also given a higher hourly rating, which represents the output that can be exerted for a period of 1 hour without overheating the motors beyond safe limits. Even greater outputs are possible over shorter periods of time. The Pennsylvania Railroad's GG1's, for example, have a continuous rating of 4620 h.p. but are capable of a short-term output of 8500 h.p.

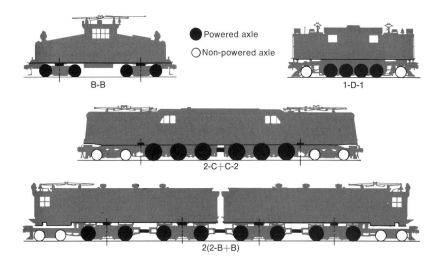

● Powered axle
○ Non-powered axle

B-B

1-D-1

2-C+C-2

2(2-B+B)

TYPICAL ELECTRIC LOCOMOTIVE WHEEL ARRANGEMENTS

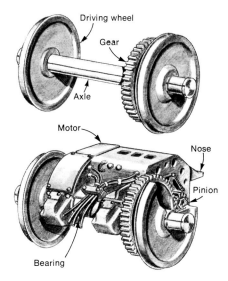

GEARED ELECTRIC MOTOR DRIVE

Drive systems

Geared drive: The earliest successful type of motor mounting was the axle-hung or nose-suspended arrangement developed by Frank J. Sprague in 1885 for street railway service. One side of the motor, which was geared directly to the axle, was suspended from the truck frame on a spring mounting, and the other was carried directly by the axle, an arrangement which minimized unsprung weight. Bearings on the axle permitted the motor to rotate about the axle, maintaining alignment between the gears on the motor shaft and the axle regardless of the movement of the axle. The Sprague design was almost universally used for street and interurban railway equipment, rapid-transit cars, and steam railroad M.U. equipment. Although a few early electric locomotives used nose-suspended motors, the design originally was not considered suitable for large locomotives. The space available between the wheels

limited the size of the motor that could be used, and the location of the motors placed the locomotive's center of gravity too low for good tracking. Later, the development of compact, lightweight motors overcame the disadvantages of the design, and nose-suspended traction motors are used almost universally in diesel-electric locomotives. Since World War II every electric locomotive built for service in North America has employed geared, nose-hung traction motors like those used in diesels.

Gearless drives: A number of early electric locomotives employed drive systems that eliminated gearing between the traction motors and the axles altogether. In all of these gearless drives the motor armature was placed on the axle in some manner. In a few cases the motor armature was pressed directly on the axle, while the motor fields were carried on the locomotive frame. New York Central's S-class motors and the Milwaukee Road's bipolar passenger locomotives employed this arrangement. Although the bipolar gearless design had the disadvantages of high unsprung weight and a low center of gravity, the two North American designs that used it enjoyed long and productive lives. Some of the original New York Central units, nearing the end of their seventh decade, are still in service.

Another type of gearless drive, used in the 1895 B&O locomotives and the New Haven's initial A.C. locomotive fleet, was the gearless quill drive. In this arrangement the traction motor armature was carried on a hollow quill surrounding the axle. Power was transmitted to the wheels through flexible spring or rubber connections. This design permitted the entire weight of the motor, including the quill and ar-

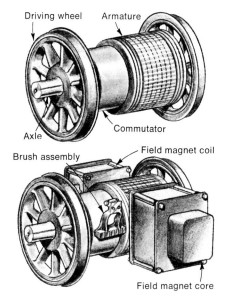

GEARLESS DRIVE

mature, to be suspended through springs from a cradle supported at the journal boxes, greatly reducing the unsprung weight. The flexible connection between the quill and the driving wheels, normally a coil-spring and cup arrangement, reduced the stresses of starting and acceleration on motors and wheels. The design still had the disadvantage of a low center of gravity, and the placement of traction motors between the driving wheels limited motor size.

Geared quill drive: One of the most widely used drives for electric locomotives was the geared quill drive, which first was used in three of the New Haven's four experimental Baldwin-Westinghouse units of 1910-1911. In this arrangement the traction motors were mounted on the locomotive frame above the running gear. They were geared to hollow quills that surrounded the axles and drove the

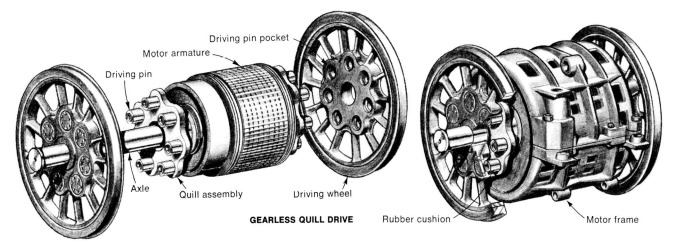

GEARLESS QUILL DRIVE

441

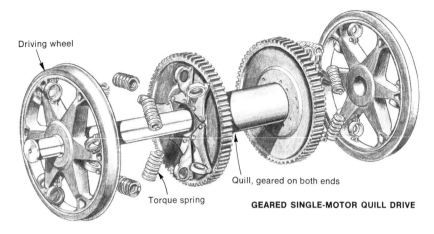

Driving wheel

Torque spring

Quill, geared on both ends

GEARED SINGLE-MOTOR QUILL DRIVE

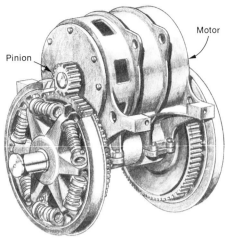

Motor

Pinion

wheels through flexible connections of the type employed in the gearless quill drive. This design retained the advantages of the gearless quill drive. Placing the traction motors above the running gear raised the center of gravity, improving tracking qualities, and provided room for larger traction motors. Intermediate gearing between the traction motors and the driving axles permitted higher motor speeds than were possible with the gearless design, allowing the same power output with smaller motors.

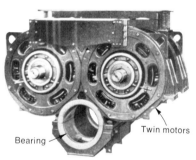

Bearing

Twin motors

Driving wheel

Gear, quill, and drive assembly

GEARED TWIN-MOTOR QUILL DRIVE

Some of the earliest geared quill drives employed a single traction motor geared to each driving axle. Because of the high torque produced by the large traction motors used in this arrangement, the motor was normally geared to the quill at both ends to avoid excessive loads on the gear teeth.

A popular variation of this design was the use of twin motors geared to each quill. Dividing the torque between two motor armatures reduced the loads on pinions and gears. First used on one of the New Haven's 1910 Baldwin-Westinghouse units, the twin-motor geared quill drive was subsequently employed on virtually every New Haven electric locomotive through the 1940's and was adopted by the Pennsylvania Railroad for its principal electric road locomotives, including the celebrated GG1.

Side-rod drive: In order to drive more than one axle from a single large traction motor, several early electric locomotives employed a side-rod drive that closely paralleled steam-locomotive running-gear design. By carrying the motor on the frame above the running gear, this arrangement made the full width of the locomotive cab available for a large motor and afforded the better tracking qualities of a high center of gravity. Each end of the armature shaft was fitted with cranks, which were connected by rods to cranks on a jackshaft. Side rods connected the jackshaft to counterbalanced driving wheels similar to those of steam locomotives. By coupling all of the driving wheels together, the side-rod design eliminated the slipping of driving wheels which sometimes occurred because of uneven weight distribution on locomotives with independently powered driving axles.

Typically the wheel arrangements of side-rod electric locomotives duplicated those of steam locomotives. For example, the most successful of all U. S. side-rod electrics, the Pennsylvania's DD1, was the electric equivalent of two 4-4-0 steam locomotives back-to-back.

Gear and side-rod drive: A variation of side-rod drive adopted by the Norfolk & Western and the Virginian for their original electric locomotives introduced intermediate gearing between single or twin traction motors and a jackshaft, which in turn powered the driving wheels through side rods. Gearing permitted the use of higher-speed motors. Typically the jackshaft was connected to the side rods through flexible couplings like those used in quill drives.

Electrical systems

D.C. locomotives: D.C. locomotives are generally far less complex electrically than A.C. machines. In low-voltage D.C. equipment, where traction motors can operate at the full line voltage, power from the third rail or contact wire is supplied directly to the motors. Motor

Motor Jackshaft Connecting rod

SIDE-ROD DRIVE

speed is regulated by resistances, field control, and grouping of motors. Typically motors are grouped in even-numbered combinations — often four — and transitioned through full series, series-parallel, and full parallel arrangements. High-voltage D.C. motive power is operated in essentially the same manner. Since the manufacture of D.C. motors for more than 1500 volts is impractical, high-voltage D.C. motive power is operated with two or more motors in series across the line voltage at all times. For control purposes each grouping of two or more motors is considered a single unit.

Single-phase A.C. locomotives: Since A.C. locomotives are operated from a high line voltage, transformers are needed to reduce the catenary voltage to the much lower

voltage required by the traction motors. In most single-phase locomotives the traction motors are permanently connected in parallel, and the traction-motor voltage, and hence speed, is varied by connecting the motors to different taps or leads on the transformer, each of which produces a different voltage. By switching progressively through taps of increasing voltage it is possible to apply power to the locomotive gradually and obtain smooth acceleration.

Three-phase A.C. locomotives: Three-phase locomotives employed induction motors which rotated at a constant speed that depended on the power-supply frequency. To bring a three-phase locomotive up to this constant speed a resistance was inserted in the secondary winding. A method of control known as

cascade connection, or concatenation, permitted three-phase locomotive operation at several different constant speeds. At least two motors connected in parallel were required for this arrangement, which made use of an induced current from the rotor of one motor to drive a second motor. Just as in the single-phase locomotive, a transformer was required to reduce the high line voltage to a lower level for the traction motors.

Three-phase locomotives had the advantages of great ruggedness and uniform torque, and they were well adapted for regenerative braking. However, the constant-speed operation was considered disadvantageous for most kinds of service other than mountain drag-freight service.

Split-phase A.C. locomotives: In

Twin motors Spring drive

GEAR AND SIDE-ROD DRIVE

443

Boiler blower motor

Air pump motor

Boiler

Sand box

No. 2 m
contro

4811

← 36" Wheels

57" Drive

← 11' 10" →

← 13' 8" →

37' 4

69' 0

79' 6

ELECTRIC LOCOMOTIVE

CUTAWAY view of Pennsylvania Railroad's GG1 passenger locomotive illustrates the placement
of equipment within the carbody and also the equipment itself. A locomotive intended for freight
service would not have a train-heating boiler; a D.C. locomotive would lack a transformer.

order to combine the advantages of
the constant-speed three-phase motor with the greater simplicity of
single-phase power distribution,
several roads employed what were
known as "split-phase" locomotives. Single-phase power from the
contact wire was converted to three-
phase power by a rotary phase converter in the locomotive. The remainder of the locomotive's
electrical equipment was identical
to that of an ordinary three-phase
unit.

Motor-generator locomotives:
The earliest successful means of
combining the advantages of
single-phase A.C. power supply
with those of D.C. traction motors
was the motor-generator locomotive, in which A.C. power from the
distribution system powered a
single-phase synchronous motor,
which in turn drove a low-voltage
D.C. generator. As in any high-voltage A.C. locomotive, a transformer
was required to reduce the line voltage to a level that could be used in
the single-phase motor. The remainder of the motor-generator locomotive's electrical equipment was
identical to that of a typical D.C.
locomotive. Although the motor-
generator concept was employed in
1907 in an interurban car of the
Paul Smith's Electric Railroad in

New York, the first locomotive to
use this concept was the 1925 experimental built for the Detroit,
Toledo & Ironton. The Great
Northern used motor-generator
locomotives exclusively on its
single-phase Cascade Mountain
electrification.

Rectifier locomotives: During the
past quarter century the development of the rectifier has provided a
superior means of converting A.C.
to D.C. In the rectifier locomotive a
transformer reduces the line voltage. Low-voltage A.C. from the
transformer is fed into rectifiers,
which supply direct current
through a smoothing reactor for
conventional D.C. traction motors.
In addition to providing greater
electrical efficiency, the rectifier locomotive, unlike almost all other
A.C. motive power, does not require a low-frequency power
supply, but can operate at the normal 60-cycle commercial frequency.

Attempts were made to develop
rectifier motive power as early as
1906, when the Paul Smith's Electric Railroad equipped its interurban car with rectifiers. The experiment was unsuccessful, and the
rectifiers soon were replaced with
the motor-generator installation
noted previously. General Electric
operated an experimental rectifier

locomotive at Schenectady in 1912,
and in 1913 Westinghouse installed
rectifiers in an M.U. car that operated experimentally for several
months on the New Haven Railroad. It was not until 1949, however, when the Pennsylvania Railroad equipped an M.U. car with
rectifiers, that rectifier motive
power could be considered
successful.

The first rectifier equipment employed mercury-arc ignitron rectifiers, which required a complex firing circuit and a cooling system. By
the early 1960's the silicon diode
rectifier had become a practical alternative to the ignitron rectifier.
Much more compact than ignitron
equipment of comparable capacity,
the silicon diode rectifier requires
neither firing circuits nor a complex liquid cooling system.

TYPICAL TRACTION MOTOR

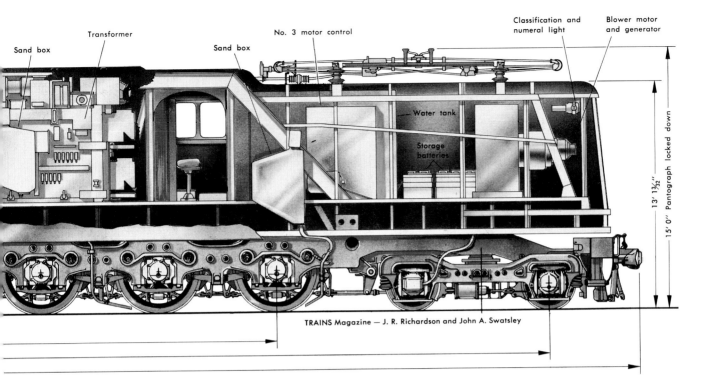

Sand box | Transformer | Sand box | No. 3 motor control | Classification and numeral light | Blower motor and generator

Water tank

Storage batteries

13' 13⁄32"

15' 0" Pantograph locked down

TRAINS Magazine — J. R. Richardson and John A. Swatsley

Traction motors

D.C. series motor: The most common type of electric railway traction motor is the D.C. series motor, so called because its armature and field are wired in series. The performance characteristics of the series motor meet the varying requirements of railroad service better than any other type of motor. As the load increases, the field strength increases automatically, and the result is an increase in torque with a decrease in speed. Conversely, the speed increases as the load decreases. Consequently, the series motor tends to adjust itself readily to the varying tractive effort required to accelerate and propel a train.

Single-phase A.C. motors: Several types of motors have been used in single-phase A.C. operation. The most commonly used type is the series-commutator motor, which is nearly identical to the D.C. series motor. Indeed, the series-commutator motors used in the New Haven's 11,000-volt, single-phase locomotives also operated on the New York Central's 660-volt D.C. electrification into Grand Central Terminal. Other common types of single-phase traction motors were the doubly fed motor and the interpole motor, which varied in the arrangement and windings of the motor fields. All types of single-phase traction motors required relatively

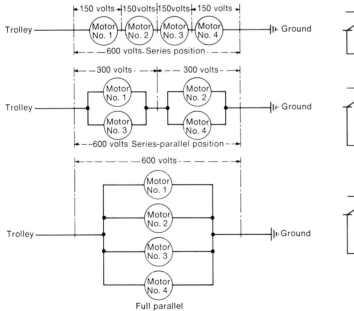

MOTOR CONNECTIONS FOR A 600-VOLT LOCOMOTIVE

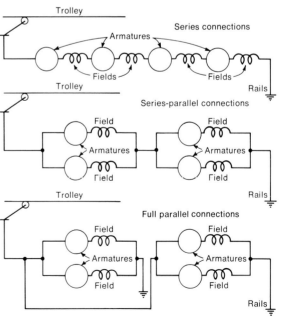

MOTOR COMBINATIONS FOR STARTING

445

low-frequency A.C. for satisfactory operation. In North America 25-cycle A.C. was used for single-phase electrification; in Europe frequencies of 15 and 16⅔ cycles were common.

Three-phase A.C. motors: The three-phase induction motor was used for the few three-phase and split-phase installations in North America. In the induction motor there is no electrical connection between the armature and the windings; instead, rotation of the armature is caused by a current induced in the armature. The speed of rotation depends on the frequency of the three-phase power supply and consequently the induction motor is essentially a constant-speed machine. As the load on an induction motor increases, the current and the torque increase while the speed of the motor remains constant. This constant-speed characteristic was considered desirable in those few cases where it was adopted for heavy mountain service. It was possible to obtain several different speeds by switching from four-pole to eight-pole operation, or by the use of cascade connection or concatenation.

Control equipment

Electric locomotives almost always have used an electropneumatic control system. A master controller located at the engineer's position is connected to low-voltage D.C. circuits, usually powered from batteries. These circuits control air-operated switches which in turn open, close, and regulate the circuits to the traction motors. Similar low-voltage control circuits and air switches permit the engineer to control pantographs, third-rail shoes, and other auxiliary apparatus. Two or more locomotives can be controlled by a single engineer by means of control-circuit jumper cables.

Braking systems

Regenerative braking: Some electric locomotives were equipped so that the energy of a train descending a grade could be absorbed by operating the traction motors as generators. In addition to providing a braking effect, regenerative braking returned substantial amounts of power to the distribution system. The Milwaukee Road, for example, attributed overall savings of 15 per cent in power consumption to the use of regenerative braking. Regen-

erative braking lessens wear on wheels and brake shoes and avoids the problems of heat buildup associated with conventional air braking in mountain operation. Regenerative braking also proved capable of controlling trains more smoothly than air braking.

D.C. series motors can readily operate as generators. To obtain control of the regenerated voltage, which has to be slightly higher than the line voltage, some form of separate field excitation is required, as are other control features. This separate excitation current usually is supplied from batteries, motor-generator sets, or axle-mounted generators.

Regeneration is accomplished in a similar manner with A.C. series-commutator motors. A separate motor-generator set can be used to supply the necessary excitation current, or one of a group of four traction motors can be operated as the excitation generator for the other three.

In three-phase and split-phase equipment, regeneration was automatically accomplished without special control equipment. The characteristics of the three-phase induction motor are such that as soon as a train was moving faster than the synchronous speed of the motors, the motors automatically began to function as generators and return power to the distribution system.

Dynamic braking: The arrangement in which regenerated power is dissipated through resistance grids rather than returned to the contact wire is referred to as dynamic braking. Because their electrical characteristics do not permit the return of power to the distribution system, rectifier locomotives are equipped for dynamic braking rather than regenerative braking. Dynamic braking, of course, is the standard arrangement for electrical braking of diesel-electric motive power.

Current-collection equipment

Third-rail shoes: A flat cast-iron sliding shoe is used for third-rail current collection. Hangers attached to the truck or locomotive frame support a horizontal shoe-beam, to which the sliding shoe and its mounting bracket are attached. The shoe-beam, which is made of wood or some other insulating material, insulates the shoe from the locomotive's running gear. On many overrunning third-

GRAVITY-TYPE OVERRUNNING
THIRD-RAIL SHOE

SLIPPER-TYPE SHOE FOR
UNDERRUNNING THIRD RAIL

rail installations for interurban or rapid-transit railways the shoe was held against the third rail by gravity, but for heavier steam railroad electrifications, springs provide positive pressure. Third-rail shoes for underrunning installations are almost identical. Upward spring pressure holds the shoe against the bottom of the third rail. Normally, the shoe itself is designed to be the weakest part of the current-collection system, so that it will break rather than the mounting bracket or shoe beam if it should strike an obstruction. Most third-rail shoe designs were stationary; the New Haven Railroad employed air-operated folding shoes that could be raised out of the way except when the locomotive or car was operating from third rail.

Overhead pantographs: The pole trolley generally used for overhead current collection on street and interurban railways was ill suited to the heavy currents of steam railroad electrification. Only the Great Northern's three-phase electrification and a few minor branchline installations used pole trolleys. Instead, a pantograph is used. It consists of a diamond-shaped framework supporting a contact shoe. It can adjust to variations in the height of the contact wire. Normally, the pantograph is raised against the contact wire by spring tension, and lowered by air pressure. The type of contact shoe depends on the current-collection requirements. In some A.C. instal-

446

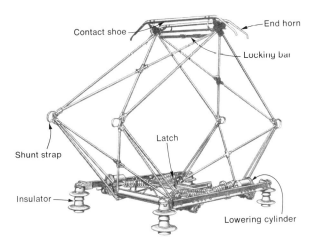

Contact shoe

End horn

Locking bar

Latch

Shunt strap

Insulator

Lowering cylinder

PANTOGRAPH

lations where currents were comparatively small, a flat steel shoe often was used. The addition of copper strips greatly increases the current-collecting capacity. In high-voltage D.C. systems, where starting currents sometimes exceed 1000 amperes, double shoes usually are used. Roller pantographs were used in some early D.C. installations. The rollers, however, were much heavier than an ordinary collection shoe, and the high rotating speed of the rollers caused bearing problems. Much more effective for heavy current was the use of graphite or carbon contact strips in the pantograph collection shoe. Regardless of the type of shoe, most pantographs are fitted with downward-curving horns at each end of the contact shoe to prevent snagging of the contact wire at crossovers.

In recent years several types of lightweight pantographs have come into use. The most common is the Faively pantograph, which has only a single arm instead of the customary diamond shape.

Other locomotive auxiliaries

Electric locomotives also require a variety of other auxiliary equipment. An air compressor, normally driven by an electric motor, supplies air for braking and control systems. Blowers force air through ducts to cool the transformers, traction motors, and other apparatus. Large banks of resistance grids are provided to regulate voltage to the traction motors in direct-current locomotives. In a few early locomotives, a water rheostat served the same purpose. Batteries are needed to power the low-voltage control circuits, and a source of low-voltage D.C., such as a motor-generator set, is required for charging the batteries. Motor-generator sets or other sources of auxiliary power also are required for heating, lighting, and ventilating systems. Oil-fired boilers normally are installed in passenger locomotives to supply steam for train heating.

Multiple-unit car equipment

The electrical systems and equipment installed on multiple-unit car equipment closely parallel those for electric locomotives. Typically M.U. cars have swivel trucks and nose-suspended traction motors. Quite often only one truck on each motor car is powered, and trailer cars are common. Recent M.U. car designs feature semi-permanently coupled pairs of cars, with shared auxiliary equipment.

The what, where, and when of electrification

THE following synopsis of railroad electrification in North America lists the name of the railroad, the location of its electrification and date constructed (subdivided where various segments were constructed in different years), route- and track-miles, purpose of electrification and character of service, power supply used, power-distribution and current-collection system, type of motive power used, and additional notes.

NEW ENGLAND

Boston & Albany

Newton Lower Falls to Riverside, Mass., 1900. 1.2 route-miles; 1.2 track-miles. General economy of operation for local passenger service. 550 volts. D.C. Trolley wire; trolley pole. Motor passenger car. Electric operation discontinued 1930.

Boston & Maine

Hoosac Tunnel Station to North Adams, Mass., 1911. 7.9 route-miles; 21.4 track-miles. Tunnel operation for heavy freight and passenger service. 11,000-volt, single-phase, 25-cycle A.C. Catenary; pantograph. Locomotives. Electric operation discontinued 1946.

Boston, Revere Beach & Lynn

Boston to Lynn and Winthrop, Mass., 1928. 13.8 route-miles; 31.0 track-miles. General economy of operation for suburban passenger service. 600 volts D.C. Catenary; trolley pole. Multiple-unit passenger cars. Railroad abandoned 1940.

New York, New Haven & Hartford— Nantasket Beach branch

Nantasket Junction to Pemberton and Braintree to Cohasset, Mass.: Nantasket Junction to Pemberton, 1895; Nantasket Junction to East Weymouth, 1896; East Weymouth to Braintree, 1898; Nantasket Junction to Cohasset, 1899. 20.3 route-miles; 41.0 track-miles. General economy and efficiency of operation for local passenger service. 600 volts D.C. Trolley wire, Nantasket Junction to Pemberton; center third rail, Braintree to Cohasset; trolley-pole and third-rail shoe. Motor passenger cars. Braintree to Cohasset electric operation discontinued 1904; remainder of electric operation discontinued 1932.

New York, New Haven & Hartford— Connecticut branches

Various branches in the Stamford, New Haven, New Britain, Hartford, and Taft, Conn., areas; Hartford to New Britain to Berlin, 1896; Manufacturers Railroad, New Haven, 1896; New Britain to

Bristol, 1898; Stamford to New Canaan, 1899; Berlin to Middletown, Meriden to Westfield, Middletown to Cromwell, Taft to Central Village, 1906. East Hartford to Vernon to Rockville to Melrose, 1907. 81 route-miles. Interurban passenger operation, freight switching (at New Haven). 600 volts D.C. Center third rail, New Britain area lines; trolley wire, all other lines; third-rail shoe or trolley pole. Motor passenger cars, locomotives (New Haven). New Britain area third-rail lines discontinued electric operation 1906; Stamford to New Canaan branch converted to 11,000 volts A.C., 1908; all other passenger lines discontinued electric operation at various dates prior to 1930 except New Haven switching line, which operated until 1948.

New York, New Haven & Hartford— Providence, Warren & Bristol branch

Providence to Warren and Bristol, R. I., and Fall River, Mass., 1901. 24.0 route-miles; 48.5 track-miles. General economy of operation for local passenger service. 650 volts D.C. Trolley wire; trolley pole. Motor passenger cars. Warren to Fall River electric operation discontinued 1932; Providence to Warren and Bristol electric operation discontinued 1938.

New York, New Haven & Hartford

New York, N. Y., to New Haven, Conn., and branches: Woodlawn to Stamford, 1907; Stamford to New Canaan, 1908; Harlem River to New Rochelle, 1912; Stamford to New Haven, 1914; New Haven to Cedar Hill Yard, 1915; South Norwalk to Danbury, 1925. 106.9 route-miles; 550.7 track-miles. Terminal and suburban operation and general economy of operation for heavy freight and passenger service, and suburban passenger service. 11,000-volt, single-phase, 25-cycle A.C. Catenary; pantograph. Locomotives and multiple-unit passenger cars. Electric operation discontinued South Norwalk to Danbury 1961; remainder of electrification operated successively by Penn Central, Conrail, and, now, Metro-North Railroad; power supply converted to 12,500-volt, 60-cycle, single-phase A.C. during 1985-1986.

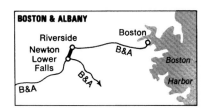

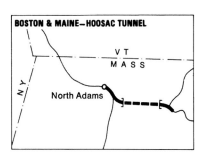

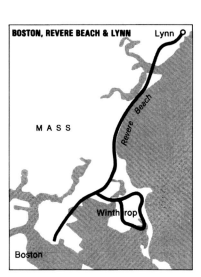

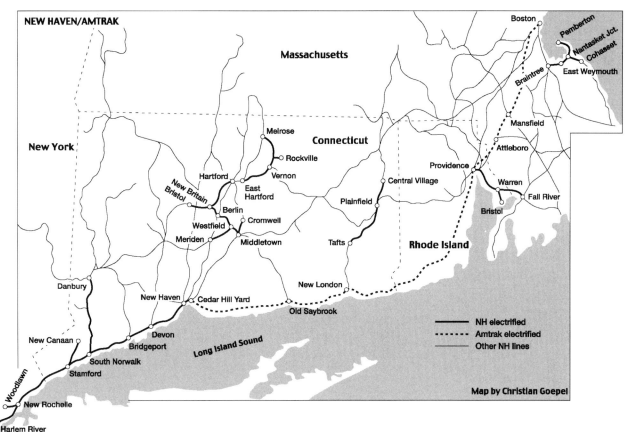

Amtrak

New Haven to Boston, 2000. 156 route-miles; 312 track-miles. General economy and efficiency of operation for high-speed passenger service. 25,000-volt, 60-cycle, single-phase A.C. Catenary; pantograph. Locomotives.

EASTERN

Baltimore & Ohio

Baltimore, Md., 1895. 3.6 route-miles; 9.6 track-miles. Tunnel and terminal operation for heavy freight and passenger service. 650 volts D.C. Over-head conductor, 1895-1902; third rail, 1902-1952; pantograph and sliding shuttle, 1895-1902; overrunning third-rail shoe, 1902-1952. Locomotives. Electric operation discontinued 1952.

Baltimore & Ohio — Staten Island Rapid Transit

St. George, Staten Island, to Arlington, South Beach, and Tottenville, N. Y., 1925. 21.6 route-miles; 50.0 track-miles. General economy and efficiency of operation and anticipated tunnel operation for suburban passenger service. 650 volts D.C. Overrunning third rail; third-rail shoe. Multiple-unit passenger cars. Electric operation of South Beach and Arlington lines discontinued 1953; St. George-Tottenville line purchased from B&O by Metropolitan Transportation Authority 1971.

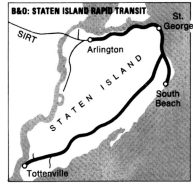

Delaware, Lackawanna & Western

Hoboken to Newark, Summit, and Dover, N. J., and branches, 1930-1931. 70.0 route-miles; 133.0 track-miles. General economy and efficiency of operation

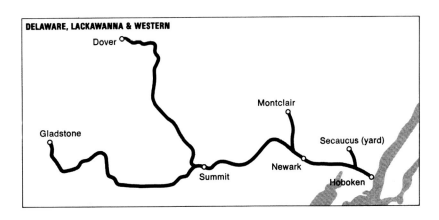

for suburban passenger service and freight switching service. 3000 volts D.C. Catenary; pantograph. Multiple-unit passenger cars, tri-power locomotives. Freight electrification to Secaucus Yard discontinued 1946; DL&W merged with Erie in 1960 to form Erie Lackawanna Railroad; EL became part of Conrail in 1976; New Jersey Transit took over the former DL&W electrified lines in 1983; electrification converted to 25,000-volt, 60-cycle, single-phase A.C. in 1984.

Erie

Rochester to Mt. Morris, N. Y., 1907. 34.0 route-miles; 38.0 track-miles. General economy and efficiency of operation for interurban passenger service. 11,000-volt, single-phase, 25-cycle A.C. Catenary; pantograph. Multiple-unit passenger cars. Electric operation discontinued 1934.

Hudson & Manhattan

New York, N. Y., to Hoboken, Jersey City, Harrison, and Newark, N. J.: New York to Hoboken, 1908; New York to Jersey City, 1909; Jersey City to Newark, 1911. 13.8 route-miles; 43.1 track-miles. General economy and efficiency of operation for intercity rapid-transit passenger service. 600 volts D.C. Overrunning third rail; third rail shoe. Multiple-unit passenger cars. Service from Hudson Terminal to Newark operated jointly with Pennsylvania 1911-1967, operating on PRR tracks from tunnel portals in Jersey City to Newark; trackage between Journal Square and Harrison was shared with PRR; the Port Authority of New York and New Jersey assumed operation of H&M in 1962 through subsidiary Port Authority Trans-Hudson Corporation (PATH).

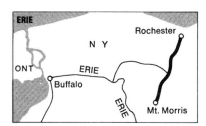

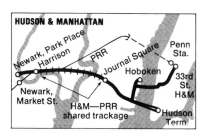

Long Island

Sunnyside, Queens, and Brooklyn to Whitestone Landing, Port Washington, Huntington, Ronkonkoma, Hempstead, Babylon, Long Beach, and Rockaway, N. Y., and branches: Flatbush Avenue, Brooklyn, to Rockaway Park, Jamaica, Belmont Park, and Valley Stream, 1905; Queens to Hempstead, 1908; Long Island City to Jamaica, Valley Stream to Long Beach, Rego Park to Ozone Park, 1910; Winfield Junction to Whitestone Landing, 1912; Whitestone Junction to Port Washington, 1913; Jamaica to Babylon, 1925; Valley Stream to Mineola, 1926; Floral Park to Creedmoor and Garden City to Salisbury Plains, 1929; Mineola to Huntington, 1970; Hicksville to Ronkonkoma, 1988. 126.5 route-miles, 317.5 track-miles. Smoke abatement, general economy and efficiency of

operation for suburban passenger service. 650 volts D.C. Overrunning third rail; third-rail shoe. Locomotives and multiple-unit passenger cars. Whitestone Landing branch discontinued 1932; West Hempstead to Garden City abandoned 1948; Garden City to Mineola and Garden City to Salisbury Plains electrifications discontinued 1948; Creedmoor branch electrification discontinued 1950; Jamaica Bay line to Far Rockaway Beach sold to New York City Transit System in 1952, operation by LIRR ended 1953; LIRR sold in 1966 to Metropolitan Transportation Authority; a new electrified line to Grand Central Terminal via the 63rd Street East River tunnel in planning for 2009 completion, 2000.

Long Island

Bay Ridge to Fresh Pond Junction, N. Y., 1927. 11.9 route-miles; 82.7 track-miles. Through freight operation with NYNH&H and car-float terminal switching. 11,000-volt, single-phase, 25-cycle A.C. Catenary; pantograph. Locomotives. Through freight service operated by NYNH&H; Bay Ridge line sold to PRR 1966; electric operation discontinued 1969.

New York Central & Hudson River

New York, N. Y., to Brewster and Croton, N. Y., and branches: Grand Central Terminal to North White Plains and Croton, 1906-1913. Port Morris branch and Getty Square (Yonkers) branch, 1926; West Side freight line, 1931; North White Plains to Brewster (by Metro-North Railroad), 1984. 97.8 route-miles; 423.0 track-miles. Terminal and suburban operation for heavy freight and passenger, and suburban passenger service. 660 volts D.C. Underrunning third rail;

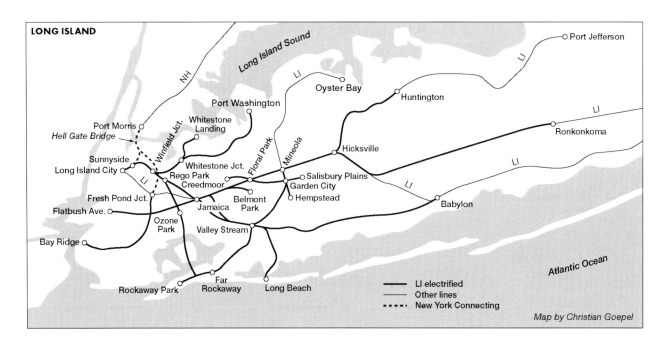

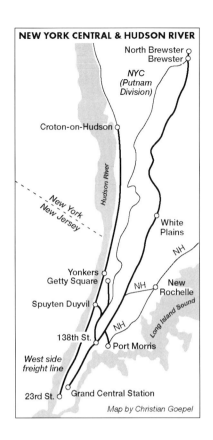

NEW YORK CENTRAL & HUDSON RIVER

North Brewster
Brewster

*NYC
(Putnam
Division)*

Croton-on-Hudson

Hudson River

*New York
New Jersey*

White
Plains

NH

Yonkers
Getty Square

NH

New
Rochelle

Spuyten Duyvil

NH

Long Island Sound

138th St.
Port Morris

*West side
freight line*

23rd St.
Grand Central Station

Map by Christian Goepel

third-rail shoe. Locomotives and multiple-unit passenger cars. Electric operation discontinued on Getty Square branch 1943, on Port Morris branch 1965, on West Side freight line 1959; NYC merged into Penn Central 1968 and became part of Conrail 1976; New York suburban lines taken over by Metro-North Railroad 1983.

New York Connecting

Port Morris to Fresh Pond Junction and Sunnyside Yard, N. Y.: Port Morris to Sunnyside Yard, 1918; Sunnyside Yard to Fresh Pond Junction, 1927. 9.0 route-miles; 25.8 track-miles. Terminal operation and general economy of operation for heavy freight and passenger service. 11,000-volt, single-phase, 25-cycle A.C. Catenary; pantograph. No motive power. Operated by NYNH&H; electric operation discontinued Sunnyside Junction to Fresh Pond Junction 1969; remainder of electrification became part of Penn Central in 1969; acquired by Amtrak as part of the Northeast Corridor 1976.

New York, New Haven & Hartford — New York, Westchester & Boston

Harlem River to Port Chester and White Plains, N. Y.; Harlem River to White Plains, 1912; New Rochelle to Port Chester, 1921-1929. 25.9 route-miles; 73.0 track-miles. General economy of operation for suburban passenger and local freight service. 11,000-volt, single-phase, 25-cycle A.C. Catenary; pantograph. Multiple-unit passenger cars,

locomotive. Operation discontinued 1937; entire railway dismantled during 1940 except section between E. 180th Street and Dyre Avenue, which was bought by New York City and operated as an extension of the IRT subway.

Niagara Junction

Niagara Falls, N. Y., 1913. 11.0 route-miles; 44.0 track-miles (including 21 miles of sidings owned by industrial plants). General economy of operation for freight switching service. 660 volts D.C. Catenary; pantograph. Locomotives. Originally owned and controlled by Niagara Falls Power Co.; purchased jointly by New York Central, Erie, and the Lehigh Valley in 1948; became part of Conrail 1976; electric operation discontinued 1979.

Pennsylvania — Burlington & Mount Holly Traction

Burlington to Mount Holly, N. J., 1895. 7.2 route-miles. Experimental operation for local passenger service. 500 volts D.C. Trolley wire; trolley pole. Motor passenger cars. Electric operation discontinued 1901.

Pennsylvania — West Jersey and Seashore

Camden to Millville and Atlantic City, N. J., 1906. 75.0 route-miles; 150.4 track-miles. General economy and efficiency of operation for passenger service. 650 volts D.C. Overrunning third rail and trolley wire; third-rail shoe and trolley pole. Multiple-unit passenger cars. WJ&S became part of Pennsylvania-Reading Seashore Lines in 1933; Newfield-Atlantic City electrification discontinued 1931; Camden-Millville electrification discontinued 1949.

Pennsylvania — Cumberland Valley branch

Dillsburg to Mechanicsburg, Pa., 1906. 7.7 route-miles. Experimental operation, general economy of operation for local passenger service. 600 volts D.C. Trolley wire; trolley pole. Motor passenger cars. Electric operation discontinued 1928.

Pennsylvania — New York terminal

New York City to Manhattan Transfer, N. J., 1910. 13.4 route-miles; 110.1 track-miles. Tunnel and terminal operation for suburban and through passenger service. 675 volts D.C. Overrunning third rail; third-rail shoe. Locomotives and multiple-unit passenger cars. Third rail removed between Manhattan Transfer and west portals of Hudson River tunnels following installation of A.C. electrification in 1932, and A.C. locomotives substituted for D.C. units for most operations; became part of Penn Central in 1968 merger; acquired by Amtrak as part of Northeast Corridor 1976; remainder of third-rail system still used by Amtrak for work trains and LIRR operations into Penn Station.

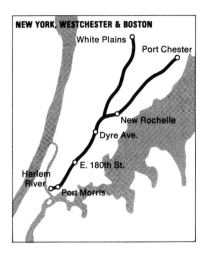

NEW YORK, WESTCHESTER & BOSTON

White Plains
Port Chester
New Rochelle
Dyre Ave.
E. 180th St.
Harlem River
Port Morris

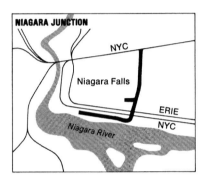

NIAGARA JUNCTION

NYC
Niagara Falls
ERIE
NYC
Niagara River

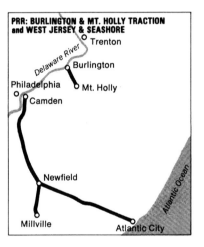

PRR: BURLINGTON & MT. HOLLY TRACTION and WEST JERSEY & SEASHORE

Delaware River
Trenton
Burlington
Philadelphia
Mt. Holly
Camden
Newfield
Atlantic Ocean
Millville
Atlantic City

Pennsylvania

New York, N. Y., to Washington, D. C.; Trenton, N. J., Philadelphia, Pa., and Perryville, Md., to Harrisburg, Pa.; and various branches and secondary lines. Philadelphia to Paoli, Pa., 1915; Philadelphia to Chestnut Hill, Pa., 1918; Allen Lane to Whitemarsh, Pa., 1924; Philadelphia to West Chester, Pa., and Wilmington, Del., 1928; Philadelphia to Norristown, Pa., and Trenton, N. J., 1930; New York City to New Brunswick, N. J., 1931; New Brunswick to Trenton, 1933; Wilmington to Washington, D. C., and Alexandria, Va., 1935; Paoli and Trenton to Harrisburg and Enola, Pa.,

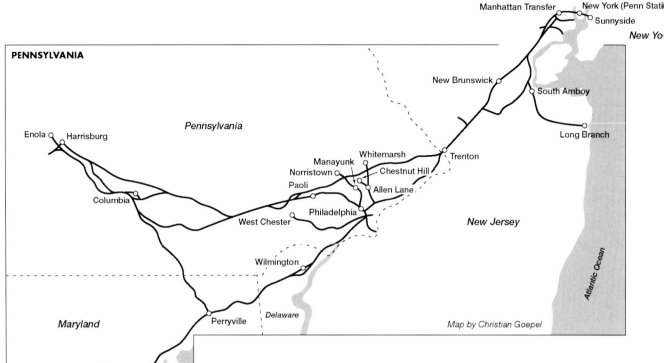

Pennsylvania

Enola Harrisburg

New Jersey

Manhattan Transfer   New York (Penn Stati
Sunnyside
New Yo

New Brunswick
South Amboy

Trenton

Long Branch

Whitemarsh
Manayunk   Chestnut Hill
Norristown
Paoli   Allen Lane
Columbia
Philadelphia
West Chester

Wilmington

Atlantic Ocean

Perryville   *Delaware*

Maryland

Baltimore

Map by Christian Goepel

Virginia
Washington
Alexandria

and Columbia, Pa., to Perryville, Md., 1938; Philadelphia to Philadelphia International Airport completed by Southeastern Pennsylvania Transportation Authority, 1984; South Amboy to Long Branch completed by NJ Transit, 1982, 1988. 656 route miles; 2150 track-miles. Increased capacity; general economy and efficiency of operation for heavy freight, passenger, and suburban passenger service. 11,000-volt, single-phase, 25-cycle A.C., Catenary; pantograph. Locomotives and multiple-unit passenger cars. Electrification discontinued

between Manayunk and Norristown, Pa., 1960, and between North Philadelphia and Camden, N. J., 1966; Pennsylvania merged with New York Central in 1968 to form the Penn Central Transportation Company; Northeast Corridor, including Philadelphia-Harrisburg line, acquired by Amtrak, 1976; Penn Central merged into Conrail, 1976; Conrail ended electric freight operation in 1981 and electrification discontinued between Perryville and Royalton, Pa., and on the Trenton-Enola Low-Grade freight line and other former PRR freight trackage.

Reading

Philadelphia, Pa., to Norristown, Chestnut Hill, Doylestown, Hatboro, Warminster, and Fox Chase, Pa., and West Trenton, N. J.; Philadelphia to Doylestown, Hatboro, and West Trenton, 1931;

Philadelphia to Norristown and Chestnut Hill, 1933; Philadelphia to Fox Chase, 1966; Hatboro to Warminster, 1973; Philadelphia Center City Commuter Tunnel completed by Southeastern Pennsylvania Transportation Authority (SEPTA), 1984. 93.2 route-miles; 196.0 track-miles. General economy and efficiency of operation for suburban passenger service. 11,000-volt, single-phase, 25-cycle A.C. Catenary; pantograph. Multiple-unit passenger cars. Reading was merged into Conrail, 1976; commuter rail system acquired by SEPTA, 1983.

POCAHONTAS

Norfolk & Western

Iaeger to Bluefield, W. Va., and branches: Bluefield to Vivian, 1915;

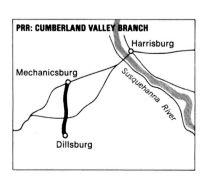

PRR: CUMBERLAND VALLEY BRANCH
Harrisburg
Mechanicsburg
Susquehanna River
Dillsburg

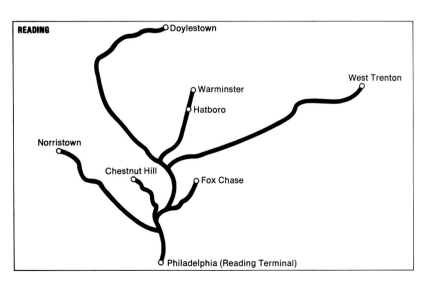

READING
Doylestown
West Trenton
Warminster
Hatboro
Norristown
Chestnut Hill
Fox Chase
Philadelphia (Reading Terminal)

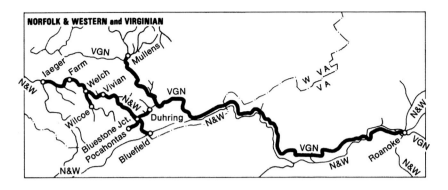

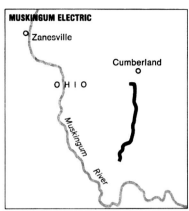

Bluestone Junction to Duhring and Pocahontas, 1915-1916; Vivian to Farm and Welch to Wilcoe, 1918-1923; Farm to Iaeger, 1923-1924. 55.9 route-miles; 208.7 track-miles. Grade and tunnel operation for heavy freight and passenger service. 11,000-volt, single-phase, 25-cycle A.C. Catenary; pantograph. Locomotives. Electric operation discontinued 1950 following completion of a major line relocation on Elkhorn grade; see also Virginian Railway for details of electrification operated by N&W following merger with VGN in 1959.

Virginian

Mullens, W. Va., to Roanoke, Va. 1925. 134.5 route-miles; 229.0 track-miles. Grade and tunnel operation for heavy freight service. 11,000-volt, single-phase, 25-cycle A.C. Catenary; pantograph. Locomotives. VGN merged into N&W 1959; ex-VGN electrification discontinued 1962.

MIDWESTERN

Cleveland Union Terminal

Collinwood to Linndale, Cleveland, Ohio, 1930. 17.0 route-miles; 56.0 track-miles. Smoke abatement, passenger service. 3000 volts D.C. Catenary; pantograph. Locomotives. Electric operation discontinued 1953.

Detroit, Toledo & Ironton

Fordton to Flat Rock, Mich., 1926. 16.0 route-miles; 50.0 track-miles. Smoke abatement, general economy of operation for heavy freight service and switching. 22,000-volt, single-phase, 25-

cycle A.C. Catenary; pantograph. Locomotives. Electric operation discontinued 1930.

Illinois Central

Chicago to South Chicago, Blue Island, and Richton, Ill., 1926; Richton to University Park, 1977. 39.6 route-miles; 159.9 track-miles. Smoke abatement, general economy and efficiency of operation for suburban passenger service and freight switching. 1500 volts D.C. Catenary; pantograph. Multiple-unit passenger cars, switching locomotives. Electric switching operations discontinued 1941; acquired by Northeastern Illinois Regional Commuter Railroad Corporation as Metra Electric, 1987.

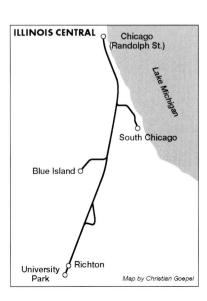

Map by Christian Goepel

Muskingum Electric

Muskingum Mine, Ohio, 1968. 15.0 route-miles; 15.0 track-miles. General economy and efficiency of operation for coal hauling, demonstration of modern electrification. 25,000-volt, single-phase, 60-cycle A.C. Catenary; pantograph. Locomotives. Automated operation.

New York Central System — Michigan Central Railroad

Detroit River Tunnel between Detroit, Mich., and Windsor, Ont., 1910. 4.5 route-miles; 28.6 track-miles. Tunnel operation for heavy freight and passenger service. 650 volts D.C. Underrunning third rail; third-rail shoe. Locomotives. Electrification constructed by Detroit River Tunnel Company, a subsidiary of Michigan Central Railroad; electric operation discontinued 1953.

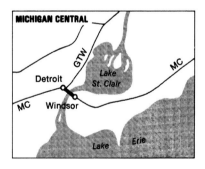

WESTERN

Black Mesa & Lake Powell

Black Mesa Mine to Navajo Generating Station, Ariz., 1973. 78.0 route-miles. Environmental considerations, general

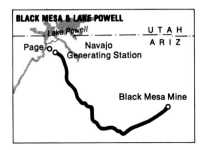

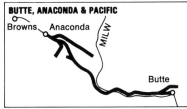

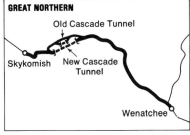

economy and efficiency of operation for coal hauling. 50,000-volt, single-phase, 60-cycle A.C. Catenary; pantograph. Locomotives. Automated operation.

Butte, Anaconda & Pacific

Butte to Anaconda, Mont., 1913. 37.4 route-miles; 121.8 track-miles. General economy of operation for heavy freight and passenger service. 2400 volts D.C. Catenary; pantograph. Locomotives. Electric operation discontinued 1967.

Chicago, Milwaukee, St. Paul & Pacific

Harlowton, Mont., to Avery, Ida.; Othello to Tacoma and Seattle, Wash.; Great Falls yard, Mont.: Great Falls yard, 1915; Harlowton to Avery, 1915-1916; Othello to Tacoma, 1919-1920; Black River Junction to Seattle, 1927. 663.4 route-miles; 892.1 track-miles. General economy of operation for heavy freight and passenger service. 1500 volts D.C. (Great Falls yard), 3000 volts D.C. (all other lines). Catenary; trolley pole (Great Falls yard); pantograph. Electric operation in Great Falls yard (6.9 track-miles) discontinued 1937; Othello to Tacoma and Seattle electrified train operation ended 1972; Harlowton to Avery eletrification discontinued 1974.

Deseret Western Railroad

New line from the Deserado Mine in Colorado to the Bonanza generating plant near Bonanza, Utah, 1984. 35.0 route-miles. General economy of operation for heavy haul coal service. 50,000-volt, single-phase, 60-cycle A.C. Catenary; pantograph. Locomotives.

Great Northern

Cascade Tunnel, Wash., 1909. 4.0 route-miles; 6.0 track-miles. Tunnel operation for heavy freight and passenger service. 6600-volt, three-phase, 25-cycle A.C. Double trolley wire; trolley poles. Locomotives. Three-phase electrification replaced in 1927 by an 11,000-volt, single-phase, 25-cycle A.C. system.

Great Northern

Skykomish to Wenatchee, Wash., 1927-1929. 72.9 route-miles; 93.2 track-

miles. Tunnel operation and general economy of operation for heavy freight and passenger service. 11,000-volt, single-phase, 25-cycle A.C. Catenary; pantograph. Locomotives. Installed through old Cascade Tunnel on extended route in 1927; new Cascade Tunnel opened and electrified in 1929; electric operation discontinued 1956.

Navajo Mine Railroad

New line serving the Navajo generating station in Utah, 1983. 14.0 route-miles. General economy of operation for heavy haul coal service. 25,000-volt, single-phase, 60-cycle A.C. Catenary; pantograph. Locomotives.

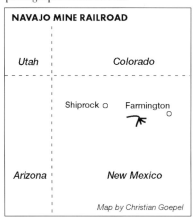

Northwestern Pacific

Sausalito to San Anselmo and San Rafael, Calif., and branches: Sausalito to San Anselmo and Almonte to Mill Valley, 1903; Baltimore Park to San Rafael and San Anselmo, 1904; San Anselmo to Manor, 1908. 20.6 route-miles; 41.6 track-miles. General economy and efficiency of operation for suburban passenger service. 600 volts D.C. Overrunning third rail; third-rail shoe. Multiple-unit passenger cars. Original electrification constructed by North Shore Railroad,

which became part of Northwestern Pacific in 1907; electrification, suburban passenger operation, and the Sausalito-San Francisco ferry discontinued in 1941.

Southern Pacific

Oakland to Alameda and Berkeley, Calif., 1911. 49.6 route-miles; 118.0 track-miles (track- and route-miles do not include Bay Bridge trackage used by Interurban Electric Railway, 1939-1941). General economy and efficiency of operation for suburban passenger service. 1200 volts D.C. Catenary; pantograph. Multiple-unit passenger cars. Operation of SP's East Bay electric lines assumed by subsidiary Interurban Electric Railway Co. in 1938; operation through to San Francisco's East Bay Terminal via the San Francisco-Oakland Bay Bridge commenced early in 1939; IER ended operation in 1941, with portions of some lines continuing in operation by the Key System.

Texas Utilities Company

Two new lines serving the Monticello generating station near Mt. Pleasant, Texas, and the Martin Lake station near Henderson, Texas, 1976. 19.0 route-miles and 13.0 route-miles. General economy of operation for heavy haul coal service. 25,000-volt, single-phase, 60-cycle A.C. Catenary; pantograph. Locomotives.

CANADA

British Columbia Railway

Tumbler Ridge branch between Wakely and Quinette, British Columbia, 1984. 81.0 route-miles. Tunnel operation

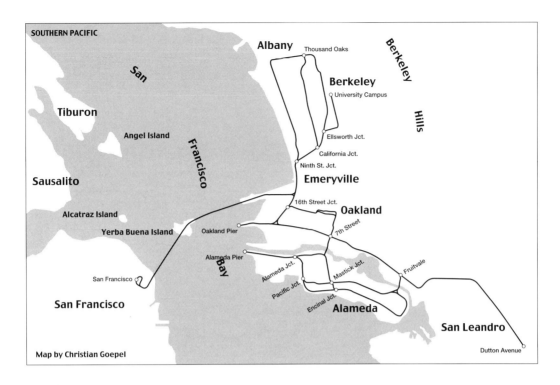

Map by Christian Goepel

BRITISH COLUMBIA RAILWAY

Fort St. John
Chetwynd
Dawson Creek
Mackenzie
Kennedy
Tumbler Ridge
Wakely
Quinette
Fort St. James
O'Dell
Alberta
CN
Prince George
British Columbia
CN
Quesnel

Map by Christian Goepel

and general economy of operation for heavy haul coal service. 50,000-volt, single-phase, 60-cycle A.C. Catenary; pantograph. Locomotives.

Canadian National

St. Clair Tunnel between Port Huron, Mich., and Sarnia, Ont., 1908. 4.2 route-miles; 12.2 track-miles. Tunnel operation for heavy freight and passenger service. 3300-volt, single-phase, 25-cycle A.C. Catenary; pantograph. Locomotives. Original electrification constructed by St. Clair Tunnel Co., a subsidiary of Grand Trunk Railway; GTR became part of

CANADIAN NATIONAL—ST. CLAIR TUNNEL

Lake Huron
GTW
Port Huron
Sarnia
GTW
Detroit
MC
Lake St. Clair
MC
Lake Erie

Canadian National in 1923; electric operation discontinued in 1958.

Canadian National

Montreal to Deux Montagnes, Cartierville, and Montreal Nord, Que.: Montreal to Lazard (later Val Royal) and Cartierville, 1918; Lazard to St. Eustache (later Deux Montagnes), 1925; Central Station across Victoria Bridge to Turcot Yard, 1943; Eastern Junction to Montreal Nord, 1946. 27.0 route-miles; 46.0 track-miles. Tunnel operation and general economy of operation for suburban passenger service and through passenger train operation in tunnel and terminal. 2400 volts D.C. Catenary; pantograph. Locomotives and multiple-unit passenger cars. Original electrification constructed by Canadian Northern Railway, which became part of Canadian National in 1919; electric motive power was used for all mainline trains and some switching at CN's Montreal Central Station following its completion in 1943; except for tunnel traffic and limited switching, electric operation of through trains was discontinued following CN dieselization in 1958; electric operation between Eastern Junction and Montreal Nord discontinued 1969; Val Royal-Cartierville branch abandoned 1988; operation taken over by Sociéte de transport de la Commu-

CANADIAN NATIONAL—MONTREAL

Montreal Nord
Deux-Montagnes
Cartierville
Eastern Jct.
Turcot Yard
Val Royal
Central Station
Montreal
St. Lawrence River

nauté urbaine de Montréal (STCUM), 1982; electrification replaced with a 25,000-volt, single-phase, 60-cycle A.C. system, 1995.

Iron Ore Company of Canada

Labrador City, Newfoundland, 1963. 7.5 route-miles; 15.0 track-miles. Mine tunnels, general economy and efficiency of operation for heavy mine-haul work. 2300-volt, single-phase, 60-cycle A.C. Catenary; pantograph. Locomotives. Automatic, crewless operation.

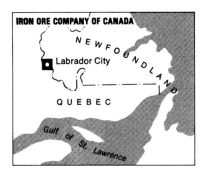

Montreal Harbor Commission

Montreal (Que.) Harbor, 1922. 19.0 route-miles; 63.0 track-miles. Smoke abatement, general economy and efficiency of operation for freight switching. 2400 volts D.C. Catenary; pantograph. Locomotives. Electric operation discontinued 1942.

MEXICO

Mexican National Railways (FNM)

Mexico City to Queretaro, 1994. 136.0 route-miles. Capacity and general economy and efficiency of operation for freight traffic. 25,000-volt, single-phase, 60-cycle A.C. Catenary; pantograph. Locomotives. System only operated on a limited basis; operation discontinued about 1996.

Mexican Railway (FCM)

Esperanza, Puebla, to Paso del Macho, Veracruz: Esperanza to Orizaba, 1924; Orizaba to Cordoba, 1926; Cordoba to Paso del Macho, 1928. 64.0 route-miles; 74.8 track-miles. General economy and efficiency of operation for through freight and passenger service. 3000 volts D.C. Catenary; pantograph. Locomotives. FCM merged into National Railways of Mexico (NdeM) in 1960; electrification inoperative in 1974.

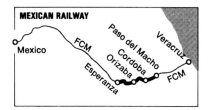

Potosí Mining Company Railway

El Potosí Mine to Morse Smelter, Chihuahua, 1925. 14.9 route-miles; 19.2 track-miles. General economy and efficiency of operation for freight service. 600 volts D.C. Trolley wire; pantograph. Locomotives. Two-foot six-inch gauge; presently named Minerales Nacionales de Mexico.

COSTA RICA

Ferrocarriles de Costa Rica (FECOSA)

Rio Frio area to Puerto Limón, 1982. 66.0 route-miles. General economy of operation. 25,000-volt, single-phase, 60-cycle A.C. Catenary; pantograph. Locomotives. Three-foot six-inch gauge. Operation suspended 1995.

Pacific Electric Railway (FEaIP)

Puntarenas to San Jose, Costa Rica, 1929. 79.0 route-miles; 93.0 track-miles. General economy and efficiency of operation for freight and passenger service. 15,000-volt, single-phase, 20-cycle A.C. Catenary; pantograph. Locomotives. Three-foot six-inch gauge. Merged with the Atlantic railway 1977 as Ferrocarriles de Costa Rica (FECOSA). Operation suspended 1995.

Bibliography

The principal reference sources utilized in the preparation of this book are summarized below. In addition to sources of a general nature, significant references for each principal North American electrification are listed by railroad companies.

General References

Books and Pamphlets

Barriger, John W. *The Prospects for Railway Electrification in the United States.* High Speed Ground Transportation Journal, 1972.

Buck, A. Morris. *The Electric Railway.* New York: McGraw-Hill Book Co., 1915.

Burch, Edward P. *Electric Traction for Railway Trains.* New York: McGraw-Hill Book Co., 1911.

Bureau of the Census, Central Electric Light & Power Stations & Street & Electric Railways, 1912. Washington, D. C., 1912.

Central Electric Light & Power Stations & Street & Electric Railways. Washington, D. C.: Bureau of the Census, 1912.

The Electric Railway Number of Cassier's Magazine of August 1899. London: The Light Railway Transport League, 1960 (reprint).

Electrification of Steam Railways. New York: National Electric Light Association, 1933.

Garin, P. V., W. R. O'Neil, and G. B. Adams. *The Future of Railroad Electrification in the United States.* Paper presented at the XII Pan American Railway Congress, 1968.

Harris, Ken. *World Electric Locomotives.* New York: Jane's Publishing, Inc., 1981.

Haut, F. J. G. *A History of the Electric Locomotive, Volume II: Railcars and the Industrial Locomotive.* New York: A. S. Barnes & Co., 1981.

———. *The Pictorial History of Electric Locomotives.* South Brunswick, N. Y.: A. S. Barnes & Co., 1970.

MacLeod, D. R. *Silicon Rectifier Electric Locomotives in the United States.* Paper presented at the XI Pan American Railway Congress, 1963.

Manson, Arthur J. *Railroad Electrification and the Electric Locomotive.* New York: Simmons-Boardman Publishing Co., 1923.

Railroad Electrification (3 volumes). New York: Edison Electric Institute, 1970.

Ransome-Wallis, P. *World Railway Locomotives.* London: Hutchinson & Company, 1959.

Sprague, Frank J. "Electric Traction in Space of Three Dimensions." *The Journal of the Maryland Academy of Sciences,* December 1931 and July 1932.

———. *The Growth of Electric Railways.* American Electric Railway Association, 1916.

Steam Road Electrifications. Mansfield, Ohio: The Ohio Brass Co., March 1917.

Street and Electric Railways, 1907. Special Reports, Department of Commerce and Labor, Bureau of the Census. Washington, D. C.: Government Printing Office, 1910.

The Use of Electric Power in Transportation. Washington, D. C.: Federal Power Commission, 1936.

Wayner, Robert J. *Electric Locomotive Rosters.* New York: Wayner Publications, 1965.

Periodicals

Among the best sources of information concerning the technical details of the individual electrifications, as well as electrification developments in general, are the several railroad and electric railway trade periodicals.

Although devoted largely to developments in the street and interurban electric railway industries, the electric railway trade periodicals *Electric Railway Journal* and *Electric Traction,* as well as their variously named predecessor journals, usually reported developments in steam railroad electrification in great detail, and good accounts of almost every major electrification can be found in the issues dating from the period of their construction. The *General Electric Review,* published by the General Electric Company, included many excellent articles about that company's many railroad electrifications.

The railroad trade press generally did equally well in reporting steam railroad electrification. *Railway Age* and the predecessor *Railway Age Gazette* provide detailed coverage throughout the history of North American electrification. In more recent years *Modern Railroads* also joined this field.

The leading railway enthusiast journals have also provided significant coverage of electrification. Chief among them have been *Railroad,* published by Popular Publications at New York until 1976, and *Trains,* published by Kalmbach Publishing Company at Milwaukee or, later, Waukesha, Wisconsin. Of particular interest is the July 1970 (30, no. 9) "all-electric" issue of *Trains.* Although primarily devoted to street, metro, and interurban railways, *Headlights,* published at New York by the Electric Railroader's Association, and the periodic Bulletins of the Central Electric Railfans' Association at Chicago have included numerous railroad electrification references.

Some of the most significant articles in these and other periodicals are summarized below or are listed among sources for the individual railroad electrifications.

General References

Curran, Arthur. "Steam's Triumph Over 'Juice.'" *Railroad Man's Magazine* (September 1911): 615–619. (This is an interesting debunking of electrification by a pro-steam writer.)

"Electrification: New Interest in an Old Idea." *Railway Age* 180, no. 15 (August 13, 1979): 24–26.

Friedlander, Gordon D. "Electrification Returns to the Railroads." *Electrical World* 195, no. 11 (December 1982): 65–76.

———. "Railroad Electrification: Past, Present, and Future (3 parts)." *IEEE Spectrum* 5, no. 7 (July 1968): 50–65; 5, no. 8 (August 1968): 56–66; and 5, no. 9 (September 1968): 77–90.

Lang, A. Scheffer. "Electrification: A Dissenting View." *Railway Age* 182, no. 1 (January 12, 1981): 36–37.

Malone, Frank. "Mainline Electrification: Who Will Be the First?" *Railway Age* 182, no. 11 (June 8, 1981): 34–37, 44–46.

Martin, Thomas M. C. "We Should Have Electrified 15 Years Ago!" *Trains* 22, no. 6 (April 1962): 18–23.

Middleton, William D. "Electrification: Is It Going to Happen?" *Railway Age* 176, no. 5 (March 10, 1975): 28–29, 32–34, 37.

———. "Railroad Electrification and Energy Conservation." *Traffic Quarterly* 32, no. 3 (July 1978): 383–397.

Neuberger, Richard L. "Water Power vs. Oil." *Railroad* 41, no. 1 (October 1947): 48–59.

"Notable Progress in Heavy Electric Traction." *Electric Railway Journal* 73, no. 2 (January 12, 1929): 67–70.

Sennhauser, George J. "Why We Don't Electrify." *Trains* 23, no. 2 (December 1962): 40–44.

Shepard, F. H. "Electric Locomotive Drives." *Electric Railway Journal* 47, no. 24 (June 10, 1916): 1085–1089.

Weiss, Willard. "U. S. Dawdles While the Rest of the World Turns On." *Railway Age* 177, no. 4 (February 23, 1976): 28–31, 34–35.

"Why Is There Renewed Interest in U. S. Electrification?" *Railway Age* 174, no. 12 (June 25, 1973): 28–29, 32–33, 36.

Withington, Sidney. "Railroad Electrification of 4,500 Miles." *Electric Railway Journal* 75, no. 10 (September 15, 1931): 537–541.

Withun, William L. "Risk and the Real Cost of Electrification." *Railroad History* 181 (Autumn 1999): 80–91.

The Individual Railroad Electrifications

UNITED STATES

ATCHISON, TOPEKA & SANTA FE RY.

Abbey, Wallace W. "Why the Santa Fe Isn't Under Wires." *Railroad History* 181 (Autumn 1999): 92–102.

Ripley, Joseph P. "Electrification of Heavy Mountain Grades." *Railway Age Gazette* 56, no. 7 (February 13, 1914): 313–316.

BALTIMORE & OHIO RR

"The Baltimore & Ohio Railroad Tunnel at Baltimore." *Scientific American Supplement* 1023 (August 10, 1895): 16346–16348.

Book of the Royal Blue, published monthly by the B&O Passenger Department, contained several articles on the Baltimore tunnel electrification:

"The Electric Service of the B&O Railroad at Baltimore." Vol. 4, no. 3 (December 1900).

"Getting Work out of Electricity." Vol. 1, no. 4 (January 1898): 18–20.

"The Largest Electric Motor in the World." Vol. 6, no. 12 (September 1903).

"Monstrous Electrical Motors." Vol. 6, no. 9 (June 1903): 10–11.

Young, W. D. "The Electrical Third Rail System in use on the Baltimore & Ohio Railroad." Vol. 5, no. 10 (July 1902): 1–6.

Duke, Donald. "America's First Main Line Electrification." Pp. 86–109 in *American Railroad Journal—1966*. San Marino, Calif.: Golden West Books, 1966.

"Operation on the Baltimore & Ohio Electrification." *Electric Railway Journal* 47, no. 24 (June 10, 1916): 1074–1079.

Sagle, L. W. "Baltimore Belt Line." *Trains* 3, no. 6 (April 1943): 8–19.

BALTIMORE & OHIO RR,
STATEN ISLAND RAPID TRANSIT RY.

Bogart, Stephen. "Little-known railroad." *Trains* 11, no. 4 (February 1951): 20–26.

Krampf, Melvin. "Island Electric." *Railroad* 49, no. 2 (July 1949): 10–27.

Staten Island Rapid Transit. Brooklyn: Silver Leaf Rapid Transit, 1965.

BLACK MESA & LAKE POWELL RR

"BM&LP: First 50-kv Electrification." *Railway Age* 175, no. 5 (March 11, 1974): 9–10.

Pfister, Jack. "Electrification of the Black Mesa & Lake Powell Railroad." Paper presented at Third International Electric Vehicle Symposium, Railroad Electrification Session, Washington, D. C., February 19–21, 1974.

Shedd, Tom. "Hot Line to the Future." *Modern Railroads* 29, no. 4 (April 1974): 74–75.

Wahmann, Russell. "The World's Quietest Railroad." *Railroad* 94, no. 5 (September 1973): 28–32.

BOSTON & MAINE RR

Cramer, F. M. "Hoosac Tunnel." *Trains* 2, no. 4 (February 1942): 28–37.

"Electrification of the Hoosac Tunnel." *Electric Railway Journal* 38, no. 1 (July 1, 1911): 6–12.

BOSTON, REVERE BEACH & LYNN RR

"'Narrow Gauge' Electrified for Economy." *Electric Railway Journal* 72, no. 23 (December 8, 1928): 991–997.

BUTTE, ANACONDA & PACIFIC RY.

Cox, J. B. "Electrical Operation on the B., A. & P. Ry." *Electric Railway Journal* 44, no. 19 (November 7, 1914): 1050–1051.

———. "The Electrical Operation of the Butte, Anaconda & Pacific Railway." Bulletin GEA-312. (Reprint from *General Electric Review*, November 1925.) Schenectady, N. Y.: General Electric Co., 1915.

Electrification of the Butte, Anaconda & Pacific Ry. Bulletin GEA-828. Schenectady, N. Y.: General Electric Co., 1928.

Rogers, Gordon W. "Where Electrification First Made Good." *Trains* 23, no. 9 (July 1963): 16–28.

Sims, Donald. "Copper Hauler." *Railroad* 63, no. 2 (March 1954): 80–99.

CHICAGO, MILWAUKEE, ST. PAUL & PACIFIC RR

Armstrong, A. H. "Comparative Cost of Steam and Electric Operation." Bulletin GEA-33. (Reprint from *General Electric Review*, April 1925.) Schenectady, N. Y.: General Electric Co., 1925.

———."Electric Operation on the St. Paul." *Electric Railway Journal* 47, no. 25 (June 17, 1916): 1130–1133.

———. *The Future of Our Railways*. Schenectady, N. Y.: General Electric Co., 1920.

Bearce, W. D. "Electrification Economies on the Chicago, Milwaukee & St. Paul Railway." Bulletin GEA-33. (Reprint from *General Electric Review,* April 1925.) Schenectady, N. Y.: General Electric Co., 1925.

Beeuwkes, R. "Notes on the C. M. & St. Paul Electrification." *Railway Age* 68, no. 25 (June 18, 1920): 1923–1925.

Bowers, Edwin H. "Milwaukee Electrification." *Trains* 1, no. 9 (July 1941): 4–11.

Brain, Insley J., Jr. *The Milwaukee Road Electrification*. San Mateo, Calif.: Bay Area Electric Railroad Association and *The Western Railroader,* 1961.

"The Chicago, Milwaukee & St. Paul Electrification." *Electric Railway Journal* 44, no. 21 (November 21, 1914): 1153–1155.

Dellinger, E. S. "Trail of the Olympian, Part II." *Railroad* 52, no. 2 (July 1950): 36–55.

Derleth, August. *The Milwaukee Road*. New York: Creative Age Press, 1948.

Dietrich, Donald C. "The Story of Milwaukee Road Electrification." *Railroad* 87, no. 2 (June 1970): 18–27.

The Electric Divisions of the Chicago, Milwaukee & St. Paul Railway. Bulletin GEA-150. Schenectady, N. Y.: General Electric Co., October 1925.

"Electric Passenger Locomotives for the St. Paul." *Railway Age* 68, no. 3 (January 16, 1920): 233–236.

Goodnow, C. A. "Some Practical Results Obtained by Electrification on the Chicago, Milwaukee & St. Paul Railway." *General Electric Review* (November 1916): 910–966.

"Operating Plans for the Electrified Division of the C., M. & St. P." *Electric Railway Journal* 44, no. 25 (December 19, 1914): 1341–1342.

Solomon, Richard J. "Juice Jacks Over the Rockies." *Headlights* 23, no. 10 (October 1961): 3–5.

"The St. Paul Electric Passenger Locomotives." *Railway Age* 68, no. 13 (March 26, 1920): 1051–1056.

"Those Russian Locomotives." *Headlights* 29, no. 6 (June 1967): 4–9.

CLEVELAND UNION TERMINAL CO.

"Cleveland Terminal Electrification Plans." *Electric Railway Journal* 72, no. 7 (August 18, 1928): 287–288.

Cook, Richard J. "Skyscraper Station." *Railroad* 55, no. 1 (June 1951): 18–33.

DELAWARE, LACKAWANNA & WESTERN RR

"Lackawanna Electrification Plans Completed." *Electric Railway Journal* 73, no. 17 (August 1929): 769–771.

Meyers, Stephen. "Lackawanna." *Headlights* 11, no. 1 (January 1949): 1–3.

"Scheduled Speed Increased by Electrification." *Electric Railway Journal* 74, no. 12 (November 1930): 683–684.

DESERET WESTERN RY.

Kiefer, Warren J. "Uintah II: The Deseret Western Railway." *National Railway Bulletin* 51, no. 1 (1986): 4–13.

Malone, Frank. "DWR: One of a Kind." *Railway Age* 185, no. 3 (March 1984): 63–64.

DETROIT, TOLEDO & IRONTON RR

Allison, Fred, H. L. Maher, and L. J. Hibbard. "Electric Locomotives for the Detroit & Ironton." *Railway Age* 77, no. 16 (October 18, 1924): 685–686.

"D. T. & I. Electric Locomotive Completed." *Railway Age* 79, no. 9 (August 29, 1925): 389–392.

"D. T. & I. Overhead Contact System." *Railway Age* 79, no. 25 (December 19, 1925): 1156–1159.

"D. T. & I. to Electrify." *Railway Age* 75, no. 3 (July 21, 1923): 125.

"Ford Motor-Generator Locomotive on Test." *Electric Railway Journal* 66, no. 10 (September 5, 1925): 352–355.

"Henry Ford's Railroad Experiment." *Railroad* 24, no. 2 (July 1938): 9–28.

Trostel, Scott D. *The Detroit, Toledo and Ironton Railroad: Henry Ford's Railroad*. Fletcher, Ohio: Can-Tech Publishing, 1988.

ERIE RR

Gordon, William Reed. *Erie Railroad—Rochester Division*. Rochester, N. Y.: W. R. Gordon, 1965.

Smith, W. N. "Single-Phase Electric Traction on the Rochester Division of the Erie R. R." *Engineering News* 58, no. 16 (October 17, 1907): 397–404.

GREAT NORTHERN RY.

"Electric Colossus of Rails Now Hauling Great Northern Trains." *Electric Railway Journal* 70, no. 2 (July 9, 1927): 53–57.

The Electrification of the Cascade Tunnel of the Great Northern Railway Company. Bulletin No. 4755. Schenectady, N. Y.: General Electric Co., June 1910.

"Great Northern Electrification Extended." *Electric Railway Journal* 73, no. 3 (January 19, 1929): 110–113.

"The Great Northern Railway Extends Electrification." Bulletin GED-129. Reprint from *General Electric Review* 30, no. 10 (October 1927): 472–484.

Hutchinson, Gary T. "The Electric System of the Great Northern Railway at Cascade Tunnel." *Electric Railway Journal* 34, no. 20 (November 20, 1909): 1052–1061.

McLaughlin, D. W. "Cascade Passage—2: The Reason for America's Longest Tunnel." *Trains* 22, no. 2 (December 1961): 22–33.

White, Victor H. "Through Cascade Tunnel." *Trains* 1, no. 8 (June 1941): 4–9.

HUDSON & MANHATTAN RR

Cudahy, Brian J. *Rails Under the Mighty Hudson*. Brattleboro, Vt.: The Stephen Greene Press, 1975.

Fitzherbert, Anthony. *"The Public Be Pleased," William G. McAdoo and the Hudson Tubes*. Supplement to *Headlights*. New York: Electric Railroaders' Association, June 1964.

"Hudson & Manhattan." *Railroad* 44, no. 2 (November 1947): 105–112.

"Hudson & Manhattan Railroad." *Electric Railroads* 27. New York: Electric Railroaders' Association, August 1959.

ILLINOIS CENTRAL RR

Corliss, Carlton J. *Main Line of Mid-America*. New York: Creative Age Press, 1950.

Downs, Lawrence A. "The Electrification of the Illinois Central." Address delivered to the Fifty-first Convention of the National Electric Light Association, 1928.

Ingles, J. David. "Lowdown on the Highliners." *Trains* 33, no. 4 (February 1972): 42–47.

Kalmbach, A. C. "Easy Come, Easy Go." *Trains* 3, no. 12 (October 1943): 3–15.

Middleton, William D. "1,000,000,000 Commuters." *Trains* 17, no. 2 (December 1956): 16–25.

"A Study of Illinois Central Suburban Operations." *Railway Age* 132, no. 17 (April 28, 1952): 39–45.

Long Island Rail Road

"Long Island Railroad Electrification Work." *Electric Railway Journal* 34, no. 22 (December 4, 1909): 1161–1162.

Middleton, William D. "Deciding the Future of the 5:15." *Trains* 31, no. 4 (February 1971): 40–46.

———. "Long Island: Back from Looneyville?" *Trains* 31, no. 3 (January 1971): 20–26.

———. "Long Island Comes Back." *Trains* 18, no. 2 (December 1957): 14–32.

Thompson, Harry C. "Everything Happens to the Long Island." *Railroad* 49, no. 3 (August 1949): 10–21.

Ziel, Ron, and George Foster. *Steel Rails to the Sunrise*. New York: Duell, Sloan and Pearce, 1965.

Muskingum Electric RR

"New Ohio coal line: Prototype for U. S. electrification?" *Railway Locomotives and Cars,* November 1967.

"Prototype 25 kV Railway to Serve Muskingum Mine." Bulletin GEA-8852. (Reprinted from *Railway Gazette,* January 17, 1969.) Erie, Pa.: General Electric, Transportation Systems Division, 1969.

National Railroad Passenger Corporation (Amtrak)

Howell, Richard P. "Upgrading the Northeast's Rail Corridor." *The Military Engineer* 458 (November–December, 1978): 396–401.

Kardos, Thomas L. "High Speed Wires Go Through to Boston." *Railway Gazette International* 149, no. 12 (December 1993): 845, 847–848.

Middleton, William D. "Northeast Corridor Speed-up Forging Ahead." *Railway Gazette International* 152, no. 11 (November 1996): 721, 723–724, 726.

Stangl, Peter E. "High-speed Rail Comes to the Northeast Corridor." *Railway Gazette International* 152, no. 11 (November 1996): 726–728.

Vantuono, William C. "Amtrak's vision: Today, the Northeast. Tomorrow, America." *Railway Age* 200, no. 4 (April 1999): 56–58, 60, 62.

———. "High Speed Rail: Finally on a Fast Track." *Railway Age* 199, no. 4 (April 1998): 41–42, 46.

New York Central System

Burpo, Robert S. "A Brief History of the Electric Locomotives on the New York Central Railroad." *Railroad History* 106 (1962): 19–23.

"Comparative Tests of Steam and Electric Locomotives." *Scientific American Supplement* 1544 (August 5, 1905): 24734.

"Construction and Characteristics of Electric Locomotives for the New York Central & Hudson River R. R." *Engineering News* 52, no. 20 (November 17, 1904): 450–453.

"Electric Equipment and Reconstruction of the New York Terminal Lines and Grand Central Station, New York Central & Hudson River R. R." *Engineering News* 54, no. 20 (November 16, 1905): 499–509.

Electrification of the Detroit Tunnel Lines of the Michigan Central Railroad. Bulletin GEA-504. Schenectady, N. Y.: General Electric Co., August 1926.

"Electrification of the New York Central Terminal In and Near New York City." *The Railway Age* 41, no. 4 (January 26, 1906): 126–154.

"The Electrification of the New York Central's Terminal Lines." *Scientific American Supplement* 1562 (December 9, 1905): 25022–25031.

Kiefer, P. W. *A Practical Evaluation of Railroad Motive Power.* New York: Simmons-Boardman, 1948.

Krampf, Melvin. "Commuting on the New York Central." *Railroad* 56, no. 3 (December 1951): 14–33.

The New York Central Electrification. Bulletin GEA-902. Schenectady, N. Y.: General Electric Co., January 1929.

Pinkepank, Jerry A. "A Tale of Two Tunnels." *Trains* 24, no. 11 (September 1964): 36–44; and 24, no. 12 (October 1964): 40–47.

———. "Can NYC Live Happily Ever After with Its 34,000 Commuters?" *Trains* 25, no. 9 (July 1965): 20–27.

———. "If Central Says YES . . ." *Trains* 25, no. 10 (August 1965): 48–55.

Reich, Sy. "Electrics Into Grand Central." *Railroad* 20, no. 1 (December 1958): 34–35.

Wilgus, William J. "The Electrification of the Suburban Zone of the New York Central and Hudson River Railroad in the Vicinity of New York City." *Transactions* 61 (December 1908): 73–155. American Society of Civil Engineers.

New York Connecting RR

"Bay Ridge Electrification Completed." *Electric Railway Journal* 72, no. 22 (December 1, 1928): 948–951.

"The New York Connecting Railroad." *The Railroad Gazette* 41, no. 26 (December 28, 1906): 570–572.

New York, New Haven & Hartford RR

Craib, Rod. "The Striped Beasts." *Trains* 17, no. 5 (March 1967): 18–24.

Craton, Forman H. "Hell Gate + Hurricane = Locomotive Test." *Trains* 31, no. 5 (March 1971): 46–49.

"Electric Locomotives of the New York, New Haven & Hartford Railroad." *Street Railway Journal* 30, no. 8 (August 24, 1907): 278–285.

"Electric Traction on the New York, New Haven & Hartford R. R." *Engineering News* 37, no. 20 (May 20, 1897): 318–319.

"Golden Anniversary of Electrification." *Along the Way* (May 1945): 1–9, 22. New York, New Haven & Hartford Railroad Co.

Lamme, B. G. "Alternating-Current Electric Systems for Heavy Railway Service." *Street Railway Journal* 27, no. 12 (March 24, 1906): 450–462.

McHenry, E. H. "Heavy Electric Traction on the New York, New Haven & Hartford Railroad." *Street Railway Journal* 30, no. 7 (August 17, 1907): 242–254.

Murray, W. S. "The Log of the New Haven Electrification." *Electric Railway Journal* 32, no. 29 (December 19, 1908): 1598–1606.

New York, New Haven & Hartford Railroad Electrification.
Special Publication 1698. East Pittsburgh, Pa.:
Westinghouse Electric & Manufacturing Co., June
1924.

Palmer, Howard S. *New England in National Leadership—
1895—The First Steam Railroad Electrification!* New York:
Newcomen Society, 1945.

Pinkepank, Jerry A. "Why NH re-electrified." *Trains* 24,
no. 10 (August 1964): 20–26.

Reich, Sy. "New Haven Electrification." *Railroad* 70, no.
1 (December 1958): 30–35; 70, no. 2 (February 1959):
30–33; 70, no. 3 (April 1959): 48–54; 70, no. 4 (June
1959): 48–51.

"Single-Phase Electric Equipment for the New York Terminal Division of the New York, New Haven & Hartford R. R." *Engineering News* 55, no. 12 (March 22,
1906): 342–344.

Swanberg, J. W. *New Haven Power: 1838–1968.* Medina,
Ohio: Alvin F. Staufer, 1988.

Weller, John L. *The New Haven Railroad—Its Rise and Fall.*
New York: Hastings House, 1969.

Withington, Sidney. *The New Haven Railroad as a Pioneer
in Railroad Electrification.* Reprint from Proceedings of
the New York Railroad Club, March 1931.

NEW YORK, WESTCHESTER & BOSTON RR

Arcara, Roger. *Westchester's Forgotten Railway.* New York:
1962.

Groh, Karl. "New York, Westchester & Boston Railway."
Electric Railroads 31. New York: Electric Railroader's
Association, April 1962.

Harwood, Herbert H., Jr. "Grass Grows on the Westchester." *Trains* 11, no. 12 (October 1951): 42–47.

NIAGARA JUNCTION RY.

Kramer, Ken. "Niagara Junction Railway: The Eccentric
Electric." *The Bulletin* 38, no. 2 (1973): 33–39, 54. National Railway Historical Society.

"Where a River Means Commerce and Industry."
Headlights 34, no. 11–12 (November–December
1972): 10–11.

NORFOLK & WESTERN RY.

Comstock, Henry B. "Geared for Tonnage." *Railroad* 36,
no. 4 (September 1944): 8–43.

"A Decade of the N. & W. Electrification." *Electric Railway
Journal* 62, no. 6 (August 11, 1923): 203–208.

Dobson, J. V. "Motors and Phase Converters on the N. &
W. Locomotives." *Electric Railway Journal* 47, no. 14
(April 1, 1916): 644–645.

"4,000-Hp. Electric Locomotives for N. & W." *Electric
Railway Journal* 60, no. 27 (December 30, 1922): 1012–
1015.

Grubb, Eric A. "Coal supports the Norfolk & Western."
Trains 8, no. 1 (November 1947): 12–23.

Norfolk & Western Electrification from the Railroad Viewpoint.
Reprint No. 56. East Pittsburgh, Pa.: Westinghouse
Electric & Manufacturing Co., July 1917.

"Single-Phase-Polyphase Motors for the Norfolk & Western." *Electric Railway Journal* 42, no. 8 (August 23,
1913): 298–299.

"The Norfolk & Western Electrification." *Electric Railway
Journal* 45, no. 23 (June 5, 1915): 1058–1069.

NORTHWESTERN PACIFIC RR

Demoro, Harre W. *Electric Railway Pioneer.* Interurbans
Special 84, Glendale, Calif.: Interurban Press, 1983.

Sievers, Walt. "Electric Interurban Service of Marin
County." *The Western Railroader* 17, no. 10 (August
1954): 3–16.

PENNSYLVANIA RR

Alexander, Edwin P. *The Pennsylvania Railroad: A Pictorial
History.* New York: Bonanza Books, 1967.

Bezilla, Michael. *Electric Traction on the Pennsylvania Railroad, 1895–1968.* University Park, Pa.: The Pennsylvania State University Press, 1980.

Burgess, George H., and Miles C. Kennedy. *Centennial
History of The Pennsylvania Railroad Company.* Philadelphia: Pennsylvania Railroad Co., 1949.

Clodfelter, Frank. "Pennsy's Steel Thunderbolts." *Railroad* 44, no. 3 (December 1947): 52–57.

Colvin, Fred H. *The Pennsylvania Railroad's New Electric
Locomotives.* Reprint from *American Machinist,* June 19
and July 3, 1935.

Dimmler, Henry F. "Pennsy's New Juice Jacks." *Trains* 14,
no. 4 (February 1954): 15–21.

"Electric Locomotives for the Pennsylvania." *Railway Age
Gazette* 50, no. 9 (March 3, 1911): 439.

Electrification of Steam Railways. Report of the Railway Electrification Committee 247. New York: National Electric Light Association, March 1933.

Gibbs, George. "Construction and Operating Details of
Philadelphia Electrification." *Electric Railway Journal*
46, no. 5 (January 29, 1916): 203–205.

———. "Station Construction, Road, Track, Yard Equipment, Electric Traction, and Locomotives." *Transactions
of the American Society of Civil Engineers* 69 (October
1910): 226–383.

Grimshaw, F. G. "Operation of the P. R. R. Philadelphia-
Paoli Electrification." *Electric Railway Journal* 47, no.
15 (April 8, 1916): 681–684.

Grubb, Eric A. "A Ride in the Cab of a GG1." *Trains* 7, no.
12 (October 1947): 16–20.

Horine, J. W., and D. R. MacLeod. *Rectifier Type Locomotives for the Pennsylvania Railroad.* Conference Paper No.
CP 62-269, American Institute of Electrical Engineers,
1962.

———, and H. S. Ogden. *The Pennsylvania Railroad Class
GG-1 Electric Locomotives.* Transactions Paper No. 60-
48, American Institute of Electrical Engineers, 1960.

Houser, F. N. "Meet the Metroliners." *Railway Age* 163,
no. 21 (December 4, 1967): 22–27, 51–53.

Kalmbach, A. C. "Epoch of Electrification." *Trains* 6, no.
6 (April 1946): 40–47.

Middleton, William D. *Manhattan Gateway.* Waukesha,
Wis.: Kalmbach Books, 1996.

Morgan, David P. "Enter the E-44's." *Trains* 21, no. 4 (February 1961): 22–23.

Osborne, W. R. "Greatest Show on Earth." *Trains* 2, no. 3
(January 1942): 8–25.

"Pennsylvania Electrification Links Philadelphia and New
York City," and other articles. *Railway Age* 94, no. 8
(February 25, 1933): 268–302.

*The Pennsylvania Railroad Electrification: New York–Wash-
ington.* Bulletin GEA-2091. Schenectady, N. Y.: General Electric Co., ca. 1935.

"Pennsylvania Railroad Speeds Electrification Program." *Electric Railway Journal* 75, no. 3 (March 1931): 125–127.

"Pennsylvania Railroad To Be Electrified from New York to Wilmington." *Electric Railway Journal* 72, no. 18: 806–808.

Pennypacker, Bert. "PRR vs. Car, Plane, Bus." *Trains* 28, no. 1 (November 1967): 18–28.

———. "36 Years of High-Speed Pennsy Electrics." *Railroad* 80, no. 2 (December 1966): 22–26.

"Philadelphia-Paoli Electrification." *Electric Railway Journal* 46, no. 20 (November 13, 1915): 981–989.

Reich, Sy. "Roll Call of Pennsy Electrics." *Railroad* 73, no. 6 (October 1962): 28–33.

Rohde, William L. "Sunnyside Yard." *Railroad* 45, no. 4 (September 1944): 10–25.

Staufer, Alvin F. *Pennsy Power.* Medina, Ohio: Alvin F. Staufer, 1962.

———. *Pennsy Power II.* Medina, Ohio: Alvin F. Staufer, 1968.

"Under Pennsy Wires." *Railroad* 31, no. 2 (January 1942): 51–60.

Westing, Frederick. "GG1." *Trains* 24, no. 5 (March 1964): 20–36.

———. "The Locomotive That Made Penn Station Possible." *Trains* 16, no. 12 (October 1956): 28–38.

———. "What's new under Pennsy pantographs." *Trains* 18, no. 8 (June 1958): 45–49.

Penn Central Co.

Kelley, W. E. *Historical Summary, Performance and Future of Penn Central Company Railroad Electrification (Formerly Pennsylvania Railroad Company).* Paper, Philadelphia: Penn Central Co., 1968.

Moxie, J. E., and B. J. Krings. "Propulsion Control for Passenger Trains Provides High-Speed Service." *Westinghouse ENGINEER* (September 1970): 144–149.

Reading Co.

"Bluebirds for Philadelphia." *Headlights* 27, no. 2 (February 1965): 6–9.

Pennypacker, Bert. "How *Flexible* Is Railroad Commuter Service?" *Trains* 23, no. 12 (October 1963): 20–16.

Wright, G. I. "Reading Company's Philadelphia Suburban Electrification Making Rapid Progress." *Electric Railway Journal* 74, no. 4 (April 1930): 212–215.

———. "Cars for Reading Electrification Embody Advanced Design." *Electric Railway Journal* 75, no. 5 (May 1931): 253–255.

Southern Pacific Co.

Babcock, Allen H. "Mountain Railway Electrification." *Railway Age Gazette* 55, no. 11 (September 12, 1913): 447–449.

"The Big Red Cars." *The Western Railroader* 19, no. 7 (May 1956): 3–15.

Coppin, C. C., R. T. Kulvicki, and P. V. Garin. *Feasibility of Electrification for a Western Trunk Line Railroad.* Conference Paper No. 70 CP 674—PWR, The Institute of Electrical and Electronic Engineers, 1970.

"East Bay Electric Service of the Southern Pacific Railroad." *Electric Railway Journal* 61, no. 15 (April 14, 1923): 633–637.

Ford, Robert S. *Red Trains in the East Bay.* Interurbans Special 65, Glendale, Calif.: Interurbans Publications, 1977.

"Southern Pacific Electrification at Oakland, Cal.—Rolling Stock and Repair Shops." *Electric Railway Journal* 37, no. 24 (June 17, 1911): 1048–1053.

Texas Utilities Co.

Ellsworth, Kenneth. "Electrification: Two New Texas Coal Lines Are Coming in Under Wire." *Railway Age* 176, no. 24 (December 29, 1975): 22–23.

Virginian Ry.

Johnson, F. L. *Electrification of the Virginian Railway from a Transportation Standpoint.* Appendix I to 1927–1928 report of the Electrification of Steam Railroads Committee. New York: National Electric Light Association, November 15, 1928.

McBride, H. A. "Coal carrier." *Trains* 10, no. 3 (January 1950): 20–26.

Reid, H. *The Virginian Railway.* Milwaukee: Kalmbach Publishing Co., 1961.

"6800 Horsepower Virginian Electrics." *Railroad* 45, no. 4 (May 1948): 70–73.

The Virginian Railway Electrification. Special Publication 1733. East Pittsburgh, Pa.: Westinghouse Electric & Manufacturing Co., May 1925.

West Jersey & Seashore RR

The Electrification of the West Jersey and Seashore Railroad. Bulletin 4501B. Schenectady, N. Y.: General Electric Co., 1909.

CANADA

British Columbia Ry.

Bridge, Peter. "Tumbler Ridge Coal Keeps Moving." *Railway Gazette International* 142, no. 10 (October 1986): 739, 741, 743.

"Tumbler Ridge Turns On." *Railway Age* 185, no. 2 (February 1984): 52–53.

Canadian National Rys.

Clegg, Anthony. *The Mount Royal Tunnel.* Montreal: Trains and Trolleys Book Club, 1963.

Davidson, W. A. B. "New Montreal Terminal." *Trains* 4, no. 1 (November 1943): 30–35.

"The Iron Link: Port Huron-Sarnia Railway Tunnel." *Michigan History* 54, no. 1 (Spring 1970): 62–72.

Lancaster, W. C. "Canadian Northern Electrification at Montreal." *Railway Age Gazette* 62, no. 19 (May 11, 1917): 999–1003.

———. "Rolling Stock for Montreal Tunnel and Terminal." *Electric Railway Journal* 44, no. 7 (August 15, 1914): 295–299.

Pinkepank, Jerry A. "A Tale of Two Tunnels." *Trains* 24, no. 11 (September 1964): 36–44; and 24, no. 12 (October 1964): 40–47.

"Single-Phase Electric Traction Equipment of the St. Clair Tunnel, Grand Trunk Ry." *Engineering News* 55, no. 3 (January 18, 1906): 59–62.

COSTA RICA

Costa Rica Rys. (FECOSA)

Middleton, William D. "Coast to Coast by Narrow Gauge." *Trains* 46, no. 11 (September 1986): 42–48.

PACIFIC ELECTRIC RY. (FEALP)

Swinney, Thomas C. "Costa Rica's Pacific Electric Railway." *Headlights* 22, no. 8 (August 1960): 1–2.

MEXICO

MEXICAN RY. (FCM)

Bearce, W. D. "Ten Electric Locomotives Do Work of 23 Steam Engines." Bulletin GED-16. (Reprint from *AERA*, July 1925.) Schenectady, N. Y.: General Electric Co., 1925.

DeGolyer, Everett L., Jr., and Stan Kistler. "Mexicano!" *Trains* 21, no. 7 (May 1961): 15–25.

"Electrification of the Mexican Railway." Bulletin X-701. Reprint from *General Electric Review* 26, no. 3 (March 1923): 184–185.

The Electrification of the Mexican Railway. Bulletin GEA-851. Schenectady, N. Y.: General Electric Co., February 1928.

The Electrification of the Mexican Railway. Bulletin GED-337. Schenectady, N. Y.: General Electric Co., January 1930.

Index

William D. Middleton has been active as a transportation and engineering historian and journalist for more than fifty years. Among his 16 books are a number of titles concerned with the history of electric railways and rail transit in North America, including *The Time of the Trolley* and *The Interurban Era*. Other recent titles are *Landmarks on the Iron Road, "Yet there isn't a train I wouldn't take,"* and *The Bridge at Québec,* all published by Indiana University Press.

Middleton is a 1950 civil engineering graduate from Rensselaer Polytechnic Institute and is a registered Professional Engineer in Virginia and Wisconsin. His professional career has also included work as a structural engineer and a bridge designer. He retired from the U. S. Navy's Civil Engineer Corps as a commander in 1979, and then served until 1993 on the general faculty and as the chief facilities officer at the University of Virginia. He remains active as a consultant in higher education facilities management.